Praise for Alan Cooper's *About 1*

D0520862

"Alan Cooper is a software god. With Visual Basic, he designed one of the key tools for designing new software. Now he's sharing his wisdom about how to make that software useable. This is a landmark book."
—**Stewart Alsop, Editor in Chief, *InfoWorld***

"*About Face* defines a new interface design vocabulary that speaks to programmers in their own terms. We have come a long way from the time when there were just modal (bad) and modeless (good) interfaces, and this book reflects that progress."
—**Charles Simonyi, Chief Architect, Microsoft Corp.**

"Alan Cooper's mind harbors a deep, compelling model of software-human interaction, which he presents clearly and applies systematically to real-world design problems in *About Face*. This book is fast-paced, irreverent, and no-nonsense. I would recommend it to any software development executive or designer."
—**John Chisholm, President, Decisive Technology Corp., & Columnist, *UNIX Review***

About Face

The Essentials of User Interface Design

Alan Cooper

A Division of IDG Books Worldwide, Inc.

Foster City, CA • Chicago, IL • Indianapolis, IN • Braintree, MA • Southlake, TX

About Face: The Essentials of User Interface Design
Published by
IDG Books Worldwide, Inc.
An International Data Group Company
919 East Hillsdale Boulevard, Suite 400
Foster City, CA 94404

Library of Congress Catalog Card No.: 95-75055
ISBN 1-56884-322-4
Printed in the United States of America
First Printing, August, 1995
10 9 8 7 6 5 4 3 2
Distributed in the United States by IDG Books Worldwide, Inc.

Published in the United States

Welcome to the world of IDG Books Worldwide.

IDG Books Worldwide, Inc., is a subsidiary of International Data Group, the world's largest publisher of computer-related information and the leading global provider of information services on information technology. IDG was founded more than 25 years ago and now employs more than 7,700 people worldwide. IDG publishes more than 250 computer publications in 67 countries (see listing below). More than 70 million people read one or more IDG publications each month.

Launched in 1990, IDG Books Worldwide is today the #1 publisher of best-selling computer books in the United States. We are proud to have received 8 awards from the Computer Press Association in recognition of editorial excellence and three from Computer Currents' First Annual Readers' Choice Awards, and our best-selling ...*For Dummies*® series has more than 19 million copies in print with translations in 28 languages. IDG Books Worldwide, through a joint venture with IDG's Hi-Tech Beijing, became the first U.S. publisher to publish a computer book in the People's Republic of China. In record time, IDG Books Worldwide has become the first choice for millions of readers around the world who want to learn how to better manage their businesses.

Our mission is simple: Every one of our books is designed to bring extra value and skill-building instructions to the reader. Our books are written by experts who understand and care about our readers. The knowledge base of our editorial staff comes from years of experience in publishing, education, and journalism — experience which we use to produce books for the '90s. In short, we care about books, so we attract the best people. We devote special attention to details such as audience, interior design, use of icons, and illustrations. And because we use an efficient process of authoring, editing, and desktop publishing our books electronically, we can spend more time ensuring superior content and spend less time on the technicalities of making books.

You can count on our commitment to deliver high-quality books at competitive prices on topics you want to read about. At IDG Books Worldwide, we continue in the IDG tradition of delivering quality for more than 25 years. You'll find no better book on a subject than one from IDG Books Worldwide.

John J. Kilcullen

John Kilcullen
President and CEO
IDG Books Worldwide, Inc.

IDG Books Worldwide, Inc., is a subsidiary of International Data Group, the world's largest publisher of computer-related information and the leading global provider of information services on information technology. International Data Group publishes over 250 computer publications in 67 countries. Seventy million people read one or more International Data Group publications each month. International Data Group's publications include: **ARGENTINA:** Computerworld Argentina, GamePro, Infoworld, PC World Argentina; **AUSTRALIA:** Australian Macworld, Client/Server Journal, Computer Living, Computerworld, Digital News, Network World, PC World, Publishing Essentials, Reseller; **AUSTRIA:** Computerwelt, PC TEST; **BELARUS:** PC World Belarus; **BELGIUM:** Data News; **BRAZIL:** Annuário de Informática, Computerworld Brazil, Connections, Super Game Power, Macworld, PC World Brazil, Publish Brazil, SUPERGAME; **BULGARIA:** Computerworld Bulgaria, Networkworld/Bulgaria, PC & MacWorld Bulgaria; **CANADA:** CIO Canada, ComputerWorld Canada, InfoCanada, Network World Canada, Reseller World; **CHILE:** Computerworld Chile, GamePro, PC World Chile; **COLUMBIA:** Computerworld Colombia, GamePro, PC World Colombia; **COSTA RICA:** PC World Costa Rica/Nicaragua; **THE CZECH AND SLOVAK REPUBLICS:** Computerworld Czechoslovakia, Elektronika Czechoslovakia, PC World Czechoslovakia; **DENMARK:** Communications World, Computerworld Danmark, Macworld Danmark, PC World Danmark, PC World Danmark Supplements, TECH World; **DOMINICAN REPUBLIC:** PC World Republica Dominicana; **ECUADOR:** PC World Ecuador, GamePro; **EGYPT:** Computerworld Middle East, PC World Middle East; **EL SALVADOR:** PC World Centro America; **FINLAND:** MikroPC, Tietoverkko, Tietoviikko; **FRANCE:** Distributique, Golden, Info PC, Le Guide du Monde Informatique, Le Monde Informatique, Reseaux & Telecoms; **GERMANY:** Computer Business, Computerwoche, Computerwoche Extra, Computerwoche Focus, Electronic Entertainment, GamePro, I/M Information Management, Macwelt, PC Welt; **GREECE:** GamePro, Macworld & Publish; **GUATEMALA:** PC World Centro America; **HONDURAS:** PC World Centro America; **HONG KONG:** Computerworld Hong Kong, PCWorld Hong Kong, Publish in Asia; **HUNGARY:** ABCD CD-ROM, Computerworld Szamitastechnika, PC & Mac World Hungary, PC-X Magazine; **INDIA:** Computerworld India, PC World India, Publish in Asia; **INDONESIA:** InfoKomputer PC World, Komputek Computerworld, Publish in Asia; **IRELAND:** ComputerScope, PC Live!; **ISRAEL:** PC World 32 BIT, People & Computers; **ITALY:** Computerworld Italia, Computerworld Italia Special Editions, Lotus Italia, Macworld Italia, Networking Italia, PC Shopping, PC World Italia, PC World/Walt Disney; **JAPAN:** Macworld Japan, Nikkei Personal Computing, SunWorld Japan, Windows World Japan; **KENYA:** East African Computer News; **KOREA:** Hi-Tech Information/Computerworld, Macworld Korea, PC World Korea; **MACEDONIA:** PC World Macedonia; **MALAYSIA:** Computerworld Malaysia, PC World Malaysia, Publish in Asia; **MEXICO:** Computerworld Mexico, GamePro, Macworld, PC World Mexico; **MYANMAR:** PC World Myanmar; **NETHERLANDS:** Computable, Computer! Totaal, LAN Magazine, Macworld, Net Magazine; **NEW ZEALAND:** Computer Buyer, Computerworld New Zealand, MTB, Network World, PC World New Zealand; **NICARAGUA:** PC World Costa Rica/Nicaragua; **NIGERIA:** PC World Africa; **NORWAY:** Computerworld Norge, Computerworld Privat, CW Rapport Klient/Tjener, CW Rapport Nettverk & Telecom, CW Rapport Offentlig Sektor, IDG's KURSGUIDE, Macworld Norge, Multimedia World, PC World Ekspress, PC World Nettverk, PC World Norge, PC World's Produktguide, Windows Spesial; **PAKISTAN:** Computerworld Pakistan, PC World Pakistan; **PANAMA:** GamePro, PC World Panama; **PARAGUAY:** PC World Paraguay; **P. R. OF CHINA:** China Computerworld, China Infoworld, Computer & Communication, Electronic Product World, Electronics Today, Game Camp, PC World China, Popular Computer Week, Software World, Telecom Product World; **PERU:** Computerworld Peru, GamePro, PC World Profesional Peru, PC World Peru; **POLAND:** Computerworld Poland, Computerworld Special Report, Macworld, Networld, PC World Komputer; **PHILIPPINES:** Computerworld Philippines, PC Digest, Publish in Asia; **PORTUGAL:** Cerebro/PC World, Correio Informático/Computerworld, Mac•In/PC•In Portugal; **PUERTO RICO:** PC World Puerto Rico; **ROMANIA:** Computerworld Romania, PC World Romania, Telecom Romania; **RUSSIA:** Computerworld Rossiya, Network World Russia, PC World Russia; **SINGAPORE:** Computerworld Singapore, PC World Singapore, Publish in Asia; **SLOVENIA:** MONITOR; **SOUTH AFRICA:** Computing S.A., Network World S.A., Software World; **SPAIN:** Computerworld España, COMUNICACIONES WORLD, Dealer World, Macworld España, PC World España; **SWEDEN:** CAP&Design, Computer Sweden, Corporate Computing, MacWorld, Maxi Data, MikroDatorn, Nätverk & Kommunikation, PC/Aktiv, PC World, Windows World; **SWITZERLAND:** Computerworld Schweiz, Macworld Schweiz, PCtip; **TAIWAN:** Computerworld Taiwan, Macworld Taiwan, PC World Taiwan, Publish Taiwan, Windows World; **THAILAND:** Thai Computerworld, Publish in Asia; **TURKEY:** Computerworld Monitör, MACWORLD Turkiye, PC WORLD Turkiye; **UKRAINE:** Computerworld Kiev, Computers & Software Magazine, PC World Ukraine; **UNITED KINGDOM:** Acorn User, Amiga Action, Amiga Computing, Amiga, Appletalk, CD Powerplay, CD-ROM Now, Computing, Connexion, GamePro, Lotus Magazine, Macaction, Macworld, Open Computing, Parents and Computers, PC Home, PC Works, The WEB; **UNITED STATES:** Cable in the Classroom, CD Review, CIO Magazine, Computerworld, Computerworld Client/Server Journal, Digital Video Magazine, DOS World, Electronic, InfoWorld, I-Way, Macworld, Maximize, MULTIMEDIA WORLD, Network World, PC World, PUBLISH, SWATPro Magazine, Video Event, WebMaster; **URUGUAY:** PC World Uruguay; **VENEZUELA:** Computerworld Venezuela, GamePro, PC World Venezuela; and **VIETNAM:** PC World Vietnam.　　　　10/17/95b

For More Information

For general information on IDG Books Worldwide's books in the U.S., please call our Consumer Customer Service department at 800-762-2974. For reseller information, including discounts and premium sales, please call our Reseller Customer Service department at 800-434-3422.

For information on where to purchase IDG Books Worldwide's books outside the U.S., contact IDG Books Worldwide at 415-655-3021 or fax 415-655-3295.

For information on translations, contact Marc Jeffrey Mikulich, Director, Foreign & Subsidiary Rights, at IDG Books Worldwide, 415-655-3018 or fax 415-655-3295.

For sales inquiries and special prices for bulk quantities, write to the address above or call IDG Books Worldwide at 415-655-3200.

For information on using IDG Books Worldwide's books in the classroom, or ordering examination copies, contact the Education Office at 800-434-2086 or fax 817-251-8174.

For authorization to photocopy items for corporate, personal, or educational use, please contact Copyright Clearance Center, 222 Rosewood Drive, Danvers, MA 01923, or fax 508-750-4470.

About Face: The Essentials of User Interface Design is distributed in Canada by Macmillan of Canada, a Division of Canada Publishing Corporation; by Computer and Technical Books in Miami, Florida, for South America and the Caribbean; by Longman Singapore in Singapore, Malaysia, Thailand, and Korea; by Toppan Co. Ltd. in Japan; by Asia Computerworld in Hong Kong; by Woodslane Pty. Ltd. in Australia and New Zealand; and by Transword Publishers Ltd. in the U.K. and Europe.

About the Author

Alan Cooper, the "Father of Visual Basic," is an award-winning user interface consultant and software designer. His company, Cooper Software, Inc, has worked with a broad range of clients to improve their products and help them create exciting and successful new software products. His experiences in implementing his unique approach to creating better software through goal-directed design led him to write this book.

Since 1976, Alan Cooper has designed and developed software, including *SuperProject* (Computer Associates), *MicroPhone II for Windows* (Software Ventures), and the visual programming interface for *Visual Basic* (Microsoft). In 1976, he founded Structured Systems Group, which Freiberger and Swaine, in their book *Fire in the Valley*, credited with producing "perhaps the first serious business software for a microcomputer."

Bill Gates presented Cooper with a *Windows Pioneer* award at the Windows World conference in 1994. This rare and coveted award recognized how Cooper's part in the invention of Visual Basic contributed to the success of Microsoft Windows.

Alan Cooper is a director of both the Association for Software Design and the Software Entrepreneur's Forum. He founded SEF's Windows SIG, the largest Windows developer group in the world. He is also a frequent, opinionated and engaging industry speaker and writer on the topics of user interface and conceptual software design.

Credits

**Senior Vice President
and Group Publisher**
Brenda McLaughlin

Publishing Director
John Osborn

Senior Acquisitions Manager
Amorette Pedersen

Managing Editor
Kim Field

Editorial Director
Anne Marie Walker

Editorial Assistant
Dan Hilldale

Production Director
Beth Jenkins

Production Assistant
Jacalyn L. Pennywell

**Supervisor of
Project Coordination**
Cindy L. Phipps

Supervisor of Page Layout
Kathie S. Schnorr

Supervisor of Graphics and Design
Shelley Lea

Reprint Coordination
Tony Augsburger
Theresa Sánchez-Baker
Todd Klemme

Blueline Coordinator
Patricia R. Reynolds

Project Editor
Elizabeth Rogalin

Manuscript Editor
Karen Goeller

Technical Reviewer
Neil J. Rubenking

Graphics Coordination
Gina Scott
Angela F. Hunckler

Media/Archive Coordination
Leslie Popplewell
Melissa Stauffer
Jason Marcuson

Production Page Layout
Benchmark Productions, Inc.
Elizabeth Cárdenas-Nelson

Proofreaders
Dwight Ramsey
Carl Saff

Indexer
Liz Cunningham

Book & Cover Design
Donald Maurer, Benchmark
  Productions, Inc.
TonBo Design

To Sue,
for your love and patience
while I was submerged

Acknowledgments

Those who have tackled big writing projects know that there are few other tasks that require such a single-minded, non-stop outpouring of effort. Although this is my first book, I've written big software programs before, so I am well-acquainted with the immense demands a project of this scope makes. My friend Gary Kratkin says a big solo writing project is like having a hungry and bad-tempered monster chained up in your basement: You can go out and have fun, but eventually you must return home and feed the hungry beast. There are many people who have helped me feed this beast over the past year who deserve my sincere thanks for their patience, their contributions, or both.

Without a doubt, the people who sacrificed the most have been my family. My lovely wife (and business partner), Sue, has supported me and reassured me and read all of my drafts throughout the monster-feeding process. Thank you for lighting up my life. My two sons, Scott and Marty, missed many nights and weekends with me when I was locked in my office writing instead of playing with them. Thank you, and I love you both beyond measure.

Three of my colleagues at Cooper Software made material contributions to the quality and content of this book. Wayne Greenwood, a talented software designer, carefully read all of the chapters and made many invaluable contributions to the manuscript. In many cases, he was the first person to vet my terms and theories. He also helped with most of the illustrations. Geetha Reddy, another skilled interface designer, read many of the drafts and politely pointed out my successes and failures. Alice Blair's comments were also very useful in straightening out some dodgy prose.

Several people read an early draft of the book and provided worthwhile comments and guidance that had a major effect on the eventual shape of the manuscript. I would like to deeply thank Deborah Kurata (good luck on your own book), Mike Nelson (your moderating voice culled some too-hot flames), Diana Nelson (your insights were valuable throughout) and Frank Cohen (for your unique viewpoint).

Several other people read chapters, sent email, contributed ideas or generally helped to shovel monster food. Thank you Carl Quinn, Andrew McCarthy, Geoff Faraghan, Peter Rosberg, Janell Bandy, Liz Cunningham, Nanci Kavanagh, Andrew Singer, Mike Geary, Fran Finnegan, John Zicker, Steven List, Cynthia Lewis, Geoff Nicholls, Jeff Prosise, David Rygmyr, Paul Yao, Jim Fawcette, Gregg Irwin, Ted Young, Constance J. Petersen, Rowan Hutchinson, Harmon Rogers, Dan Barclay, J. D. Evans, Jr., Joe McGinn, Cam Marshall, Mark Pruett, Dick Grier, David K. Headley, and my best friend David Carlick for the "March of Paradigms."

At Programmers Press, several individuals made enormous contributions to the quality of the book. Both Chris Williams and Trudy Neuhaus were the first to see the potential of this book. Anne Marie Walker stepped into this project at the eleventh hour and injected a much-needed dose of enthusiasm and energy. Amy Pedersen offered consistent support with the care and feeding of captive monsters. I owe a huge debt of thanks to my skilled editor Karen Goeller and my technical editor Neil J. Rubenking. Their comments and queries contributed materially to the final quality of the book. They both kept me from putting my foot in my mouth many times. Any mistakes that slipped by them are my responsibility. I'd also like to thank Bill Gladstone and Matt Wagner at Waterside, and John Kilcullen at IDG Books for helping to pull *About Face* out of the ordinary mass of technical books.

The publisher would like to give special thanks to Patrick McGovern, without whom this book would not have been possible.

Table of Contents

Foreword

1876 saw the construction of many bridges, and the completion of the Brooklyn Bridge. One out of every four of those new bridges, however, failed. It is hard for us now to imagine how the outcome of so basic a construction project could be so unpredictable. It would be an extraordinary event for a bridge built today to fail. But every aspect of our understanding of the world begins with ignorance and uncertainty.

For nearly a half a century, a new field of construction, that of information technology, has been emerging. Using the most insubstantial materials, electromagnetic fields and electrons, and software — the abstract description of pure processes — we can build structures for our minds to inhabit and create fabulous tools that extend our mental reach. But this field is still very much in its infancy, and in our ignorance, many of the things we have built thus far fail.

A bridge that is too narrow for the traffic it must bear will be useless, regardless of how structurally sound it is. Likewise, our inability to clearly understand and express the purpose of a particular tool or structure, or to shape something that fits the mind that must use it, can make even the most elaborate construction efforts worthless.

Although there have already been significant efforts to understand and improve the structural integrity, the engineering, of software, thus far only modest attention has been paid to improving its *design*, the process whereby it is given form.

This book represents one of the first attempts to address this problem. As such, it constitutes an important contribution to the nascent literature on software design, especially as it is expressed in a way that is useful to the practicing designer rather than the theoretician.

You may not agree with everything presented in this book, but thoughtful software designers will undoubtedly find the issues raised to be relevant and stimulating. Unlike a number of books from the human-computer-interaction (HCI) community, it addresses issues like functionality that go beyond mere interface design.

In all likelihood, Alan Cooper will always be known principally for his role in the development of Visual Basic, but I think this book may be his greater contribution to our field. For now, it stands virtually alone on the software design bookshelf.

Andrew Singer
June, 1995

Biography of Andrew Singer

Andrew Singer is best known for his work on programming environments and work-group tools at Think Technologies, a company he co-founded in 1982, and whose product development efforts he led until its acquisition by Symantec in 1987.

He chairs the board of the Association for Software Design, a non-profit professional society he organized in 1992 with Mitchell Kapor.

Interval Research Corporation
1801 Page Mill Road
Palo Alto, CA 94304
<singer@interval.com>

Introduction

This book is intended to provide you with effective and practical tools for designing user interfaces. These tools come in two distinct varieties: tactical and strategic. Tactical tools are hints and tips about using and creating user interface idioms, like dialog boxes and push buttons. Strategic tools are ways to think about user interface idioms—in other words, the ways in which the user and the idiom interact.

Although books are available that deal with either strategic or tactical tools, my goal has been to create a book that weaves the two together. I want to give you a cornucopia of insights about user interface design as a whole. While helping you design more attractive and effective dialog boxes, this book will simultaneously help you understand how the user comprehends and interacts with your software.

I believe that integrating the tactical and the strategic approaches is the key to designing effective software interfaces. For example, there is no such thing as an objectively good dialog box—the quality depends on the situation: who the user is and what his background and goals are.

1

Merely applying a set of tactical dictums will make user interface creation easier, but it won't make the end result better. Just thinking beautiful thoughts about how users "should" interact with your system won't improve the software, either. What will work is maintaining a strategic sensitivity for how users interact with specific software. This will enable you to correctly choose the appropriate tactics to apply in a particular situation.

The first three parts of this book stress strategy, but you'll find tactics interwoven throughout.

There are two steps to user interface design: the synthesis of a solution, and the testing of the validity of that solution. The latter is a discipline widely known as usability, while the former is referred to simply as user interface design. There is a significant and growing body of *usability* literature, but there is very little in print about user interface design synthesis—the invention of user interfaces from direct analysis of the tasks, the technology and the user's goals. Accordingly, I will focus exclusively on the design of user interface solutions and ignore the processes of testing those solutions. However, this is not a slur on usability: You will always achieve the best results by combining the two disciplines in a harmonious relationship.

Who should read this book

I wish I could say this book is for user interface designers and let it go at that. Most user interfaces are still designed by programmers, an increasing number of whom are growing uneasy as they glimpse the gulf between the skill set needed for software construction and the skill set needed for software design. Documentation writers, trainers and technical support people increasingly share this same worry. It is for this growing community of design-aware developers that this book is written.

Eighty years ago, the automobile industry came to understand that a well-engineered car is less appealing and less successful than a car that is both well-designed and well-engineered. Until the software industry comes to the same conclusion, the burden of quality design will fall largely on conscientious software engineers.

To the industry's credit, a small but growing cadre of software and user interface designers is beginning to make its presence felt. It is finally possible for software developers to hire people trained in the art of software design, both in the cauldron of industry and in forward-thinking universities. Eventually, we will see a bifurcation in the industry: Designers will design the software and engineers will build it. This is currently considered a luxury by those development shops that haven't realized the fiscal and marketing advantages that come with professional software design.

Why I wrote this book

Since 1976 I have been creating successful software for personal computers. In the early days of the industry, I invented, designed, coded, documented, marketed, sold, supported and revised retail products including accounting, word processing, spreadsheet, project management and visual programming languages. During the 1980s, I was an independent software author—much like a freelance inventor. I identified problems and created innovative software solutions for them. Then, working alone or with a small team, I completed them for sale to a software publisher who brought them to market. For all these years, I designed my software without reflecting much on the process. More recently, I have offered my services as a software design consultant, helping other companies to design new products and improve their existing ones.

When I became a consultant, I discovered that I had to articulate to my clients the reasons *why* a certain design solution was better. I knew the answer, but I had no words with which to say it. In response to my own needs, I began to formulate the axioms, ideas and terms that are in this book. Many of my clients and people I have spoken with have requested that I record my thinking in a book; *About Face* is the result.

My twenty years of software design and development have taught me that the task of user interface design is fundamentally different from software engineering. Most of the writing available on user interface design approaches it from an engineering or a user-testing point of view. There is little on the shelves that addresses the creation of user interface design directly from the statement of the problem. The tools of the engineer are excellent ones, but not for interface design, which isn't an engineering problem and can't be well-defined in those terms.

This book is based on my personal experiences, not on studies of published works in the area of human-computer interaction, usability, cognitive psychology or ergonomics. All of the opinions, terms, axioms, tips and conclusions contained in this book derive from my own observations. Where I have knowingly adopted the thinking of others, I have said so in the text. Where my thinking may seem to echo the work of others without credit, it is because we have independently arrived at similar views and I am ignorant of their work. It does not represent a desire to appropriate their vision or to negate their efforts.

A taxonomy of software design

Webster defines taxonomy like this:

> **Tax·on·o·my** \tak-'sän-e-mee\ *n* 1 : the study of the general principles of scientific classification: CLASSIFICATION; *specif* : orderly classification of plants and animals according to their presumed natural relationships

Biologists, anthropologists and natural scientists of all stripes use a taxonomy as their primary tool, both for their ease in communicating concepts and as a mental model of the purposes and relationships of things in the real world. Although a taxonomy is a more formal dialect within a broader language, all language is taxonomic. Our perceptions of the way the world works are colored and influenced by the structure and usage of our language.

Physical scientists spend extravagant amounts of time learning the terms specific to their discipline. These terms not only illuminate the specific process or object at hand, but they influence how we think about them in relationship to life. Doctors must learn the names of every bone, muscle, nerve and organ in the human body as well as terms that indicate their direction, orientation and condition, in health, trauma or illness. How else could one doctor express to another a question, a concern or a discovery? A thorough taxonomy is the cornerstone of each science, from the study of spiders to the behavior of printing presses.

The computer industry is no exception. We have a rich and complex language to describe the nuances of the field—words like "concurrency," "recursion," "hexadecimal" and "raster scan." But the completeness and effectiveness of this programming terminology is really just a sham. The language of programming is too new and evolving too fast to yet have a firm foundation. While the natural taxonomy of plants and animals was developed over hundreds of years, the computer taxonomy has grown—out of control—for less than fifty. There is certainly a small core of commonly agreed-upon terms (like RAM and ROM), but there is an ocean of words that either have no meaning—like "virtual reality," "bug-free," and "artificial intelligence"—or that have meanings so bowdlerized, so bastardized, as to be useful only for resumes and bull-sessions around the water cooler—words like "standard," "object-oriented," "macro," and "client/server."

I've heard and read countless discussions about the relative "efficiency" or "elegance" of some software artifact. But when someone speaks of an "efficient" user interface, is he referring to the code? to the gizmo-count? to the ease of programming? ease-of-learning? ease-of-use? Certainly, these are real words with real meanings that conjure up useful imagery in the minds of intelligent, technical people. But are these terms well-enough defined to base million-dollar decisions on? What would you think if your doctor said something like "Well, it seems you've got a swollen thingy on the front part of your arm. We'll have to cut it off." Cut *what* off?! The swollen thingy *or my arm*? Get that quack away from me!

All of this brings us to user interface design. Our discipline is less than half the age of the computer science field. Little of our work has been tested in the modern crucible of personal computing in which, for the first time, the majority of computer-human interaction is with non-computer-professionals.

The terms we have to work with are so weak and ill-defined that they make the computer science taxonomy seem robust by comparison. In user interface design we are dealing with so many new concepts—concepts that have no parallel in the non-digital world—that there are no terms to borrow from. We find ourselves performing functions daily that we could never imagine before we had personal computers.

The lack of consistent, specific terminology in the world of software design frustrates interface designers enormously. Without precise terminology, we are forced to speak in vague generalities and hand-waving. Without clearly differentiated terms, we accidentally group things in the wrong places, overlook significant facts and inadvertently mistake the bad for the good.

Language defines our perceptions. The words we use influence our mental picture of the world around us. To design effective software for the information age, we must have a vocabulary that accurately describes the goals we seek, the tools we use to achieve them, and the side effects of our journey. Software design will not become a real science or art or craft until we create our own taxonomy. It will not become a *successful* practice until we develop accurate ways of thinking and talking about what we do; until we develop a taxonomy.

To **neologize** means to invent words, and many of today's computer practitioners are reluctant to neologize. They imagine that having more words complicates things and makes communications more difficult. When speaking of familiar things in the familiar world, this is true, but in the mostly new world of computer-human interaction, old, ambiguous or inaccurate words hurt us more than they help. Our mental images also color our thinking.

Any discipline that wants to be practiced seriously and effectively must develop a powerful, descriptive and discriminative language. User interface design is a prime example of this imperative. Not only can we not function effectively, but our credibility to the outside world, particularly to the world of software engineering, is threatened unless we can agree on terms to describe what we do, what we care about and how to judge our relative success at achieving our goals. In this spirit, I try to continuously fill the vacuum with neologisms— words that I have created to describe common ideas, things, principles, actions or conditions that relate to our practice.

Conventions used in this book

The platform

This book is about user interface design using Microsoft Windows. The majority of today's PCs run Windows and, as a result, that is where the greatest need exists for an understanding of how to create effective, goal-directed user interfaces.

Having said that, I believe that most of the material in this book transcends platforms. It is equally applicable to all desktop platforms—Macintosh, Motif, NeXT, OS/2, and others—and the majority of it is relevant even for more divergent platforms such as kiosks, handhelds, embedded systems and more.

As I write this, Microsoft is preparing Windows 95 for release. This is the fifth major release of Windows in its decade of life, and it promises to ratchet the industry forward another much-needed notch. Because of the newness of Windows 95, some of my examples come from the older Windows 3.x. However, the principles of user interface design transcend the artifacts of any particular release or platform.

The examples

I use several programs as examples. Mostly, I've used the Microsoft Office suite of Word, Excel and PowerPoint; a little Adobe Illustrator and some

CompuServe Navigator, because these are the programs I use most. I have tried to stay with mainstream programs for most examples for two reasons. First, most readers will likely be at least slightly familiar with the examples. Second, it's important to show that the user interface design of even the most finely honed products can be significantly improved with a goal-directed approach.

Pronouns

It is my sincere desire to be non-sexist in my writing. I have wrestled with clumsy constructions like "s/he," "she/he" and "his or her" which seem like inkspots or thumbprints on the page to me—I have, therefore, abandoned them. I also tried the dreaded genderless plurals, "they," "their" and "them." In this case, the cure seemed worse than the disease to me.

The solution I finally adopted was to use feminine pronouns exclusively, and that was how the manuscript was originally drafted. Many focus groups and reviews later, my editor and publisher—both female—insisted that I return to the masculine form so as to avoid offending my readers. I want to change the world of user interface design, not rattle the world of book publishing, so I reluctantly agreed. I apologize for the male pronouns, and sincerely hope that you will read them merely as placeholders for intelligent and capable people of either sex.

Special notations

As I study software design, I find it powerful and effective to encapsulate my discoveries as axioms. These brief aphorisms encapsulate a great deal of wisdom and are easy to remember. In this book, axioms are general principles of software design and user interface design. Each one represents a guiding principle that is always true. Pose these axioms to yourself as design tests when you find yourself stuck on tough problems. All of the axioms have been highlighted in the text as shown here.

Buy low, sell high

Some aphorisms aren't as general as axioms, but they're just as useful in their specific area. When you are working with a particular design element, the design tips from that area can help to unstick your creative mind. A complete listing of all axioms and design tips can be found in the Reference Section at the back of the book.

Design Tip: Keep your powder dry

When mentioned for the first time, terms with specific meanings for the user interface design practitioner are highlighted in the text in **boldface**. Most of these terms are my own neologisms, but many of them were coined by others or are in common use. If the term is one of my own, I will introduce it by saying "I call this...." All of the design terms are mentioned in the index, with the page number where they are first mentioned indicated.

Let's design

I hope this book informs you and intrigues you, but most of all, I hope it makes you think about software design in new ways. The practice of user interface design is not only constantly changing, it is also big and varied enough to seem different to disparate observers. If you have a different opinion or just want to discuss things with me, I'd like to hear from you at alan@cooper.com.

That's enough preliminary stuff; let's design.

Part I: The Goal
Designing for Users

Technology is the engine that drives user interface design. This synergy is a two-edged sword, because even as the power of the technology frees us to perform great feats of invention, it simultaneously ties us to ways of thinking that are contrary to the natural direction of human behavior. Almost all of the problems with modern software user interface design originate from well-intentioned, intelligent and capable people focusing on the wrong things. Instead of technology and tasks, we must focus our gaze on the goals toward which users strive, even if they themselves are sometimes unaware of them.

Goal-Directed Design

This book has a simple premise: If achieving the user's goals is the basis of our user interface design, then the user will be satisfied and happy. If the user is happy, he will gladly pay us money, and then we will be successful.

Most software isn't designed. Rather, it *emerges* from the development team like a zombie emerging from a bubbling vat of Research and Development juice. When a discipline is hugging the ragged edge of technology, this might be expected, but much of today's software is comprised of mostly "D" and very little "R."

The little software that is consciously designed is usually designed from the point of view of the programmer, sometimes the marketing department, and occasionally from the user's point of view. None of these points of view reflect the user's *goals*. The programmer has a different set of imperatives, typically centering on technology and programming methodology. The marketing department is likely focused on what seems to create the loudest hubbub in the industry. And users tend to focus on their everyday tasks—contrary to what you might suspect, few users are consciously aware of their goals.

11

Software that merely enables users to perform their *tasks* will rarely be successful. If the task is to enter 5,000 names and addresses into a database, a smoothly functioning data-entry program won't satisfy the user nearly as much as an automated system that extracts the names from the invoicing system. While it is the user's job to focus on tasks, the designer's job is to look beyond the task to identify the user's goals. Therein lies the key to creating the most effective software solutions.

The well-tempered software designer must be sensitive to and aware of the users' goals amid the pressures and chaos of the software development process. This isn't as hard as you might think, as long as you know how, but it certainly isn't formulaic.

Keep in mind the old saying: "If you give a man a fish, you feed him for a day. If you teach him how to fish, you feed him for life." In this book, I'm going to teach you how to fish in these waters.

We will talk a lot about the techniques and tools of interaction, but no matter how far we stray we will always return to the user's goals. They are the bedrock upon which all good design is founded.

So, what are the user's goals? How can we identify them? How do we know that they are real? Are they the same for all users? Do they change over time?

The user's goals

The user's goals are often very different from what we might guess them to be. For example, we might think that an accounting clerk's goal is to process invoices efficiently. This is probably not true. Efficient invoice processing is more likely the goal of the company or the clerk's boss. The clerk is more likely concentrating on goals like

- ○ Not looking stupid
- ○ Not making any big mistakes
- ○ Getting an adequate amount of work done
- ○ Having fun (or at least not being too bored)

If you think about it, those are pretty common goals. Regardless of the work we do, and the tasks we must accomplish, most of us share those very basic, simple goals. Even if you have much higher aspirations, they are still more personal than work-related:

○ Be the best at what I do

○ Get onto the fast track and win that big promotion

○ Learn all there is to know about this field

○ Be a paragon of ethics, modesty and trust

Even for the sociopath, goals don't diverge from the focus on the individual:

● Learn the boss's password

● Embezzle a million dollars

● Hide my perfidy

● Discover the original recipe for Coca-Cola

However, many of the books on user interface that I've read assume that the user's goals have something to do with the program's business purpose. Software designed to achieve purely business goals will fail, but if it is designed with the personal goals of the user in mind, it will also achieve its business goals. Of course, the program must satisfy the business problem at hand, but the people who use it cannot and will not behave like invoices, database records or modules of code.

If you examine most commercially available software today, you will find user interfaces that are particularly adept at several things:

● Making the user look stupid

● Causing the user to make big mistakes

● Slowing the user so he doesn't get an adequate amount of work done

● Preventing fun and boring the user

Most of that same software is equally bad at achieving its business purposes. Invoices don't get processed all that well. Customers don't get serviced on time. Decisions don't get properly supported. I see a connection here.

This is a sad and preventable situation, but not a surprising one, because the authors of these packages are focusing on the wrong things. Most of us pay far too much attention to the technology used to implement computer solutions, which distracts us from the user. When we do focus on the user, we pay too much attention to the tasks that users engage in and not enough attention to their goals. Software can be technologically superb and perform each business task with diligence, yet still be a critical and commercial failure. To create successful, effective software, we must see that it achieves the user's goals. We can't ignore technology or tasks, but these elements are like salt on a meal: they make it palatable, but they don't nourish all by themselves.

Let me give you some examples of the results of focusing on technology and tasks instead of on the user and his goals.

Software that is rude

Software is often rude to the user. It blames the user for making mistakes that are not the user's fault, or should not be. Error message boxes like the one in Figure 1-1 pop up like weeds announcing that the user has performed yet another dunderheaded stunt. The messages then all demand that the user acknowledge their failure by saying "OK."

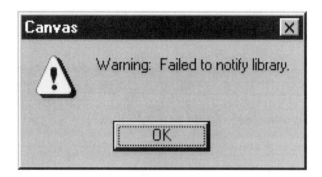

Figure 1-1

Thank you so much for sharing that pithy observation with us. Why didn't you notify the library? What did you want to notify it about? Why are you telling me? What do I care? Maybe you'd like to comment on what I'm wearing, too? And besides, what am I "OK"ing? It is *not* OK with me that this failure occurred!

Software too frequently assumes that its user is computer-literate. For example, when a user is finished editing a document, he closes it, and the program asks if he wants to save it. The technology behind this issue is not trivial—it has to do with the ability of the CPU to directly address information stored on rotating memory—but how is the novice user to know that?

Software frequently interrogates the user, peppering him with a string of terse questions that he is neither inclined nor prepared to answer: "Where did you hide that file?" "What interrupt request line is free?"

It is difficult for the user to concentrate on the task at hand when bombarded by tangential interruptions that require acknowledgment, by managing dialog boxes that forget what he did just moments ago or by forcing him to go through unnecessary steps.

Patronizing questions like "Are you sure?" and "Did you really want to delete that file or did you have some other reason for pressing the delete key?" are equally irritating.

Software that is obscure

Software is frequently obscure, hiding meaning, intentions and actions from the user. Programs often express themselves in incomprehensible jargon that cannot be fathomed by normal users ("How many stop bits?") and sometimes even by experts ("Please specify IRQ.").

Features are hidden behind a veil of menus and dialogs and windows. How can the user know that the answer lies in the help system if he can't find the help system? Even when the user finds the right dialog, he might find it populated with terse abbreviations, obscure commands and inscrutable icons.

More frequently than you might think, software demands that its users answer tough questions before telling them the effects their answers might have. For example, how can a user possibly decide between a full installation, custom installation and laptop installation if he isn't told what each of them means in terms of functionality as well as disk space?

Software with inappropriate behavior

If most 10-year-olds behaved like some of these software programs, they'd find themselves grounded for a week. Programs forget to shut doors behind themselves, leave shoes in the middle of the living room floor, and can't remember what you told them only five minutes earlier. In rapid sequence I save a document, print it, then try to close it, but the program asks me if I want to save it first! Evidently the act of printing caused the program to think I had changed it. Sorry, Mom, I didn't hear you.

Programs often require us to step out of the main flow of tasks to perform functions that should fall immediately to hand. Dangerous instructions, though, are right up front where they can be accidentally triggered and frighten unsuspecting users.

The overall appearance of many programs is an exercise in window pollution, with popups popping up all over and making navigation difficult.

Another irritant is the "settings" that programs offer for our confirmation without allowing us to change the values we disagree with. We're forced to leave the task at hand and fight our way through thickets of dialog boxes and approvals to get to where we can enter the new values.

Let's go back to our earlier list of user goals. We can reliably say that we will make the user look stupid if we let him make big mistakes, keep him from getting an adequate amount of work done or boring him. Stating this axiomatically:

Don't make the user look stupid

This is probably the most important design guideline. In the course of this book we will examine numerous ways in which existing software makes the user look stupid and explore ways to avoid that trap.

The essence of user interface design

The practice of user interface design is not formulaic. There is no such thing as a "good user interface," just as there is no such thing as a "good furniture arrangement." A furniture arrangement can only be judged within the context of its intended use. An aesthetically pleasing arrangement of sofa, endtable and lamp is bad when placed in a bathroom. By the same token, a toilet and sink in the living room would be somewhat uncomfortable and inappropriate.

The only true test of the quality of a user interface is in context: How will the software be used? Who will use it? How frequently? For how long? How important are considerations of data integrity? Learnability? Portability? The answers to these questions vary widely and are not consistent from application to application. The first task of the software designer hasn't much to do with software: it is seeking and finding answers to these and other, user-centered questions.

The source for determining whether or not a feature *should* be included in a product shouldn't rest solely on the technological underpinnings of that feature. The driving force behind the decision should not be that "we have the technical capability to do this." The primary factor should always be the goals of the user.

Let me illustrate: One of my clients sells an automated call-distribution system. The people who use their product are paid based on how many calls they handle, not by the hour. Their most important consideration is not ease of learning, but the efficiency with which calls can be routed to the answerer and the rapidity with which they can be completed. Ease of learning is important, as it affects the happiness and ultimately the turnover rate of employees, so both ease and throughput should be accommodated where possible. But there is no doubt that throughput is the dominant demand placed on the system and, if necessary, ease of learning takes the back seat. A program that walks the user through step-by-step will merely frustrate him once he's learned the ropes.

We assume that making things easier is the target. But if all we want is easy, we could stay in bed all day. A user interface designer who proclaims "Ease of learning is the most important consideration" is fooling himself. This statement *may* be true, but it may also be false depending on the goals of the user. If you test this phone-call distribution product with a dozen first-time users, you'll find ways to improve the learnability of the product. However, if you test the more-learnable version with a dozen experienced users, you'll find them impatient with the intermediate steps. You can't create good design by following rules disconnected from the goals of the user.

A more concise way to state this is to say *good design makes the user more effective*. This takes into account the universal goal of not looking stupid, along with any particular goals of business throughput or ease of use that are relevant in this situation.

The goal of all software users is to be more effective

It is up to you as a designer to determine how "effectiveness" manifests itself in the circumstances. If the software is a kiosk in a corporate lobby helping visitors find their way around, ease of use for first-time users is clearly the goal. If the software is a threat-detection and monitoring display on board an AWACS radar airplane operated by a highly trained soldier, ease of use for first-timers is a distant second consideration. The design of this is moot if the soldier cannot clearly and easily distinguish a hostile aircraft from a sky crowded with commercial and friendly aircraft. The recent incident in the Mid-East where controllers aboard an AWACS plane directed jet fighters to shoot down two friendly helicopters is evidence that their support software failed them, and that some software designer wasn't focusing on the user's goal. Whatever the software on board that plane was, it wasn't "effective."

A fresh look at features

Most software that we run on our personal computers today is feature-centric rather than goal-centric. A wildly successful program like Microsoft Word for Windows offers me hundreds of functions (I'm writing this book with it). It offers functions like paragraph formatting, field insertion, page layout view and toolbar configuration. I could easily be considered an expert user of Word, and I know how to use each of these tools in creating the many different documents needed in my writing and my business. But, none of the functions are goal-centered. If I want to write a letter, the program comes with a template for a business letter, but what if I want to write a personal letter to my Aunt Mary Lee? Rather than a canned template, I'd like to see a dialog box like the one in Figure 1-2.

With this dialog box I wouldn't have to worry about finding the right template, nor would I have to fret over the margins, typeface, clip art and other aspects of the letter. I'd just say what I had to say to Aunt Mary Lee, and the program would take care of the rest. I would tell the program my *goals*, and it would tell each little feature how to behave to achieve them.

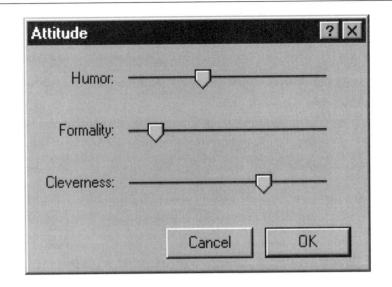

Figure 1-2

This is a "goal-directed" dialog box. It doesn't give me tools, it gives me answers: I get to select the amount of formality, humor and cleverness in the presentation of the letter I'm typing. It would govern such things as the typeface, its regularity, its style and its arrangement on the page. It would have an effect on the margins, the spacing, the colors and additional visual elements like rules and clip art. Sure, I could control each aspect individually and get the same result, but that's what programmers like to do, not what users like to do.

This example is purposefully overstated, but regardless of what all of us control-freak-programmer-types think about it, if someone created a letter-writing-specific word processor with dialog boxes like this one, it would be a big success. Goal-directed design is compelling to everyone, even those who aren't intrigued by technology.

To those who *are* intrigued by the technology, which includes most of us programmer types, we share a strong tendency to think in terms of functions and features. This is only natural, as this is how we build software: function by function. The problem is that this isn't how users want to use it. Developers are frequently frustrated by this, since it requires us to think in an unfamiliar way, but after the initial strangeness wears off, goal-directed design is a boon—it is a powerful tool for answering the most important questions that crop up during the design phase:

○ What should be the form of the program?

○ How will the user interact with the program?

○ How can the program's functions be most effectively organized?

○ How will the program introduce itself to first-time users?

○ How can the program put an understandable and controllable face on technology?

○ How can the program deal with problems?

○ How will the program help infrequent users become more expert?

○ How can the program provide sufficient depth for expert users?

We will answer these questions and more in the remainder of the book.

Software Design

When we think about complex mechanical devices, we take for granted that they have been carefully designed and engineered. Software is usually far more complex than most mechanical objects, but is rarely consciously designed.

Software isn't designed

We are just leaving what is called the **mechanical age**, an era in which the objects of value are manufactured.

We are entering an era called the **information age**, in which the objects of value are merely digital representations of things: movies, music, databases and programs.

Most manufactured objects are quite simple, and even the more complex manufactured products are immensely simpler than most digital objects, particularly programs.

A first-release software program might contain 40,000 lines of code, not including the millions of lines of supporting code in the third-party libraries and operating system needed to run it. A typical shrink-wrapped business application program, say Microsoft Excel, running on a typical desktop computer has considerably more than

1,000,000 lines of code, including many thousands of variables, conditions and comparisons—the software equivalent of moving parts. Compare this to a mechanical artifact of almost overwhelming complexity like the Navy's swing-wing supersonic F-14 fighter jet. That jet probably has about 10,000 parts, and "only" about 1,000 of them might be *moving* parts.

Most artifacts of the mechanical age are designed by professionals. Our cars are designed by trained, professional automobile designers, not by mechanical engineers. Our houses are designed by professionally trained and certified building designers—architects—not by structural engineers. Our toys and clothes and bookcases are designed by toy designers, clothes designers and industrial designers.

The process of determining what software will do and how it will communicate with the user is closely intertwined with its construction. Most software is built like crazy Mrs. Winchester's house, who thought that she'd die if she ever stopped building. Rooms and stairs and cupboards and walls are added in manic confusion as the need and opportunity presents itself during construction. Programmers, deep in their thoughts of algorithms and coding arcana, design user interfaces the way miners design the landscape with their cavernous pits and enormous tailing piles. The software design process alternates between the accidental and the non-existent.

As we move deeper into the information age, the overwhelming majority of "manufactured" artifacts will be software. Since our future will be dominated by vast amounts of software, the idea that it isn't consciously and conscientiously designed by trained professionals generates some justifiable unease.

Software creators have been policing their own profession since programming began. Some of us have been warning of the inevitability of the regulation of our industry. Possibly because of the libertarian leanings of many in the programming community, these warnings are widely ignored. Unfortunately, the consumer market won't tolerate this lack of order for very long.

The Intel Pentium bug scandal of 1995 made headlines and became rich fodder for talk-show monologues. The fact that there were equally serious bugs in the 286, 386 and 486 processors lulled Intel into a false sense of security. The difference was that the Pentium was the first CPU widely advertised on prime-time TV. Intel failed to realize that when you sell directly to consumers, they apply their own standards, which are often enormously different from those of industry insiders. The family of programmers will forgive minor bugs in a CPU chip because they know how complex it is and understand what the potential impact of the bug will be. The consumer doesn't care. He expects perfection and, in today's litigious, consumer-advocate climate, will get it.

Another story in the news lately tells of parents who purchased CD-ROM-equipped computers for their families, only to learn firsthand of the nightmarish difficulties getting them to work as advertised. Assembling bicycles on Christmas Eve was a cakewalk compared to getting *The Lion King* CD-ROM to work.

This state of affairs cannot continue for long. Either the software industry will regulate itself like doctors and architects do, or the government will regulate it like hairdressers and taxi-drivers. The choice is in the industry's hands.

Conflict of interest

There is a conflict of interest in the world of software development because the people who build it are also the people who design it. If carpenters designed houses, they would certainly be easier or more interesting to build, but not necessarily better to live in. The architect, besides being trained in the art of what works and what doesn't, is an advocate for the client, for the user. An equivalent role in the world of software has not fully developed yet, although several groups are eyeing it jealously.

Many software tools are available to describe software, but almost all of them double as programming tools. There is a real danger in using programming tools as design tools. Programming has a life of its own, and once something has been set into code, even if it's just hack code in a prototyping tool, it tends to exhibit a powerful inertia. Any code, even prototype code, tends to never be thrown away. It's as though the scaffolding is so labor-intensive that the urge to incorporate it into the finished house is irresistible. If designers give coding tools a wide berth—including prototyping tools—they will avoid the conflict of interest between the practices of design and development.

All of the designers at my company work on paper with a pencil. We also use computers, but only word processors and drawing programs. Prototyping is useful for design verification, but we are very wary of mixing the design process with the prototyping process.

The profession of software design

Thankfully, there is a growing awareness of this conflict in the software industry. More and more developers are thinking about design and viewing it as a separate discipline from programming. Many observers of digital technology sense the increasing pervasiveness of software in every aspect of our lives. They are also beginning to see the need for professional software designers, and this trend is very encouraging.

There is some confusion over the correct terminology to refer to those who design software. The term "software architect" is a good one, and it benefits from the fairly accurate analogy with building architects. However, that term has long been appropriated by the software engineers who build system internals. The term "software designer" is the one I and many others have settled on (including the Association of Software Design). Unfortunately, this term also is losing some of its value because it is widely used as a boutique term for senior programmers.

I define software design as that portion of the development process that is responsible for determining how the program will achieve the user's goals. The questions answered by this phase include

1. What the software program will do

2. What it will look like

3. How it will communicate with the user

User interface design is a subset of software design that encompasses items 2 and 3, although it is often difficult to separate them from item 1. This book focuses on user interface design, so it emphasizes interactive visual communications more than application problem solving.

Supporting software design disciplines

Members of another rapidly growing group call themselves "usability professionals." These people do not necessarily come from the ranks of programmers. Rather, they specialize in the study of how people interact with software. They primarily conduct interviews and focus groups with users, observe them using software, and then evaluate the quality of user interfaces and make recommendations. Their efforts are a great help in both weeding out bad user interfaces and in raising the awareness—inside and outside the industry—of the crisis in software design.

Another discipline, called variously "human factors engineering," "human-computer interaction" or "ergonomics," researches the behavior of people as they interact with computers and other technological artifacts. It provides significant insight into the nuances of how we relate to our technical devices.

Another growing academic specialty is cognitive psychology, popularized at the University of California (San Diego) by Donald Norman. This discipline looks at how people think and understand the world around them, particularly the technical artifacts they work with.

The Three Models

P eople in the computer industry frequently toss around the term "computer literacy." They talk about how some people have it and some don't; about how those who have it will succeed in the information age and those who lack it will fall between the social and economic cracks of the new age. But computer literacy is nothing more than a euphemism for making the user stretch to reach an information age appliance rather than having the appliance stretch to meet the user.

The manifest model

Any given machine has a method for accomplishing its purpose. A motion picture projector, for example, uses a complicated sequence of intricately moving parts to create its illusion. It shines a very bright light through a translucent, miniature image for a fraction of a second. It then blocks out the light for a split second while it moves another miniature image into place. Then it unblocks the light again for another moment. It repeats this process with a new image twenty-four times per second. The actual method of how a device works is what I call its **implementation model**.

From the movie-goer's point of view, it is easy to forget the nuance of sprocket holes and light-interrupters while watching an absorbing drama. The viewer imagines that the projector merely throws onto the big screen a picture that moves. This is what is called the user's mental model, or sometimes his conceptual model.

People don't need to know all of the details of how some complex process actually works in order to use it, so they create a mental shorthand for explaining it, one that is powerful enough to cover all instances, but that is simple and easy. For example, many people imagine that when they plug their vacuums and blenders into outlets in the wall, electricity travels up to them through little black tubes. This mental model is perfectly adequate for using all household appliances. The fact that the implementation model of household electricity involves nothing actually travelling up the cord or that there is a reversal of electrical potential 120 times per second is irrelevant to the user, although the power company needs to know these details.

In the digital world, however, the differences between a user's mental model and an actual implementation model may be stretched far apart. We ignore the fact that a cellular telephone might swap connections between a dozen different cell antennas in the course of a two-minute phone call. Knowing this doesn't help us to understand how to work our car phones. This is particularly true for computer software, where the complexity of implementation can make it nearly impossible for the user to see the connections between his action and the program's reaction. When we use the computer to digitally edit sound or display video effects like morphing, we are bereft of analogy to the mechanical world, so our mental models are necessarily different from the implementation model. Even if the connections were visible, they would remain inscrutable.

Computer software has a behavioral face it shows to the world, one made up by the programmer or designer. This posture is not necessarily an honest representation of what is really going on inside the computer, although it frequently is. This ability to *represent* the computer's functioning independent of its true actions is far more pronounced in software than in any other medium. It allows a clever designer to hide some of the more unsavory facts of how the software is really getting the job done. This disconnection between what is real and what is offered as explanation gives rise to a *third* model in the digital world, which I call the manifest model. It is the way the program represents its functioning to the user.

In the world of software, a program's manifest model can be quite divergent from the actual processing structure of the program. For example, an operating system can make a network file server look as though it were a local disk. The fact that the physical disk drive may be miles away is not made manifest by the model. This concept of the manifest model has no widespread counterpart in the mechanical world. The relationship between the three models is shown in Figure 3-1.

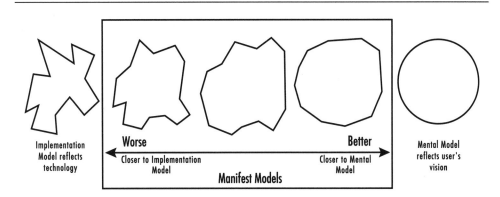

Figure 3-1

The way the engineer must build the program is usually a given. We call this the implementation model. The way the user perceives the program is usually beyond our control. He will conjure up a likely image that we call the mental model. The way the designer chooses to render the program we call the manifest model; this is the one aspect of the program that we can change significantly. If we use logic and reason to make the manifest model follow reality—the implementation model—shown on the left, we will create a bad interface. On the other hand, if we abandon logic and make the manifest model follow the user's imagination—the mental model—shown on the right, we will create a good interface.

Although software developers have absolute control over a program's manifest model, considerations of efficiency will strongly dictate their choice. Designers, on the other hand, have considerable leeway in their choice of manifest model. The closer our manifest model comes to the user's mental model, the easier he will find the program to use and to understand. Generally, offering a manifest model that closely follows the implementation model will reduce the user's ability to use and learn the program.

We tend to form mental models that are simpler than reality, so creating manifest models that are simpler than the actual implementation model can help the user achieve a better understanding. Pressing the brake pedal in your car, for example, may conjure a mental image of pushing a lever that rubs against the wheels to slow you down. The actual mechanism includes hydraulic cylinders, tubing and metal pads that squeeze on a perforated disk, but we simplify all of that in our minds, creating a more effective, albeit less accurate, mental model. In software, we imagine that a spreadsheet "scrolls" new cells into view when we click on the scrollbar. Nothing of the sort actually happens. There is no sheet of cells out there, but a tightly packed heap of cells with various pointers between them, and the program synthesizes a new image from them to display in real-time.

The ability to tailor the manifest model is a powerful lever that the software designer can use positively or negatively. If the manifest model takes the trouble to closely represent the implementation model, the user can get confused by useless facts. Conversely, if the manifest model closely follows a likely mental model, it can take much of the complexity out of a user interface.

When we interact with computer software, we tend to create anthropomorphic mental models. My program "reads" what I type in and "answers" me back with an appropriate response. It doesn't really do anything of the sort, but this mental model is still a very effective tool to manage the complexity of a system. If the software manifests this same anthropomorphic model, it will be easier for the user to relate to.

Even hard-core propeller-heads anthropomorphize computers in order to better understand them. This mental model isn't "real," but it is analogically and symbolically valid, and very practical. Programmers often curse at their recalcitrant computers, even though they know they aren't listening. We do this partly because our bodies have a mechanical structure. Our limbs, hands and fingers are levers, so we think of automobile suspension systems as arms or ankles, even though they are much more complex than that.

A mental model doesn't necessarily have to be true or accurate, but it enables the user to work effectively with the modeled process. For example, most non-technical computer users imagine that their video screen is the heart of their computer. This is only natural because the screen is what they stare at all the time and is the place where they see what the computer is doing. If you point out that the computer is actually a little chip of silicon in that big steel box sitting under their desk, they will probably shrug and ignore this pointless factoid. The fact that the CPU isn't actually in the video display doesn't help them think about how they work with their computer, even though it is a more technically accurate concept. The industry doesn't invest a lot of effort in disabusing people of this mental model because it so clearly helps and it doesn't seem to get in anybody's way.

Most software conforms to implementation models

Because software interfaces are often designed by engineers who know exactly how the software works, the result is software with a manifest model very consistent with its implementation model. This is logical and truthful, but not very effective. The user doesn't care all that much about how a program is actually implemented. Of course, he cares about any problems that arise because of the difference between the models, but the difference itself is of no particular interest. There is a real communication gap between technical people who understand implementation models and non-technical users who think purely in terms of mental models. Any time a user telephones a software company's technical support hotline, he will probably fall into that gap.

Understanding how software actually works will always help someone to use it, but this understanding usually comes at a significant cost. The manifest model allows software creators to solve the problem by simplifying the apparent way the software works. The cost is entirely internal, and the user never has to know. User interfaces that abandon implementation models to follow mental models more closely are better.

In Adobe PhotoShop the user can adjust the color balance of an illustration. A small dialog box, instead of offering a numeric setting—the implementation model—shows a series of small, sample images, each with a different color balance. The user can click on the image that best represents the desired color setting. Because the user is thinking in terms of colors, not in terms of numbers, the dialog more closely follows his mental model.

User interfaces that conform to implementation models are bad

A prime example of a user interface conforming to the implementation model instead of to the user's mental model can be found in Delrina's WinFax LITE product. Every step of the process is agonizingly wrought in discrete steps that the user must laboriously control, and none of which are necessary from the user's point of view. The interaction with the user is rendered in perfect conformance with the internal logic of the software. Every possible user action is duly represented by a separate dialog box. You can see some of this in Figure 3-2. The user is prompted for information when it is convenient for the program to receive it—not when it is natural for the user to provide it. The manifest model of the WinFax program closely follows the implementation model and ignores the user's mental model. Instead of imagining the steps the *user* might take to create and send a fax, the designer imagined what the *program* had to do. This is typical of a user interface designed by programmers.

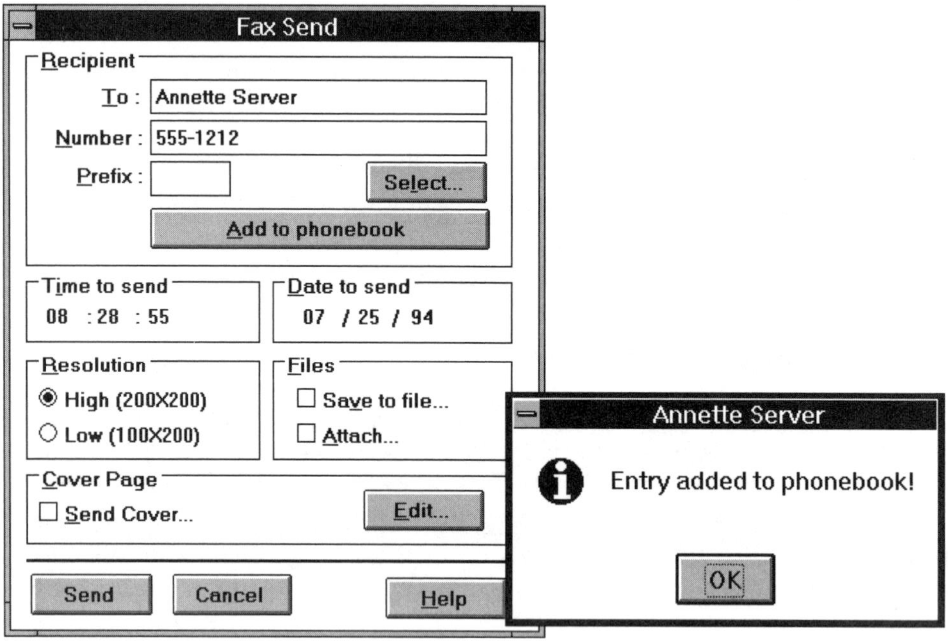

Figure 3-2

Delrina's WinFax LITE is a great study in aggravating users. Even in an application as simple as this one, they can't seem to resist adding complications. For most people on *this* planet, there are only two options: selecting an existing number or entering a new one. They have to ask for both options explicitly, and both options force a secondary dialog. Even though you can add a new number to the phonebook in place, they force a completely extraneous dialog box on you just to make sure that any ease-of-use you might be experiencing is destroyed.

When I want to send a fax, it will either be to a person whose name I haven't yet entered into the program or one I already have. The code that performs these functions is encased in separate modules inside the program, so the program encases these functions in separate dialog boxes. To either select or enter names, I have to sidestep the main program, even though selecting and entering names is the program's primary function. Similar logic in automobile design would have us manually setting the spark advance lever as we accelerated and manually flipping the brake light switch when we decelerated.

Here's a better way to manage the WinFax problem: Whenever I enter a new fax name and number, the program should automatically record it. WinFax's main window should display a list of the names of previous fax recipients, allowing me to quickly choose one from the list if I want.

Even Windows 95 misses this point. The Explorer attempts to show all of the storage devices on the computer as a unified system, but to successfully communicate that to the user, their behavior must also be unified. Instead, their behavior depends on the physical nature of the particular storage device. If you drag a file between directories on the same hard drive, the program interprets this as a MOVE, that is, the file is removed from the old directory and added to the new directory, closely following the mental model. However, if you drag a file from hard drive C to hard drive D, the action is interpreted as a COPY; that is, the file is added to the new directory but *not* removed from the old directory. This is consistent with the implementation model—the way the underlying file system actually works. When the operating system moves a file from one directory to another on the same drive, it merely relocates the file's entry in the disk's table of contents. It never actually erases and rewrites the file. But when it moves a file to another physical drive, it must physically copy the data onto the new drive. To conform to the user's mental model, it should then erase the original, even though that contradicts the implementation model. Microsoft's programmers evidently couldn't bring themselves to manifest it in any terms other than the physical ones. Actually, this behavior can be desirable, especially when copying files from a hard drive to a floppy drive, so many people aren't aware that it is just a terrifically inconsistent side effect. As computers mature and logical "volumes" represent more than just physical drives, the side effects stop being useful and become merely irritating because you have to memorize the idiosyncratic behavior.

Mathematical thinking

The interface designer must shield the user from the implementation models that the software engineer used to solve the internal problems of the software. Just because a certain tool is well-suited to attacking a problem in software construction doesn't necessarily mean that it is well-suited as a mental model for the user. In other words, just because your house is constructed of two-by-four studs and sixteen-penny nails, it doesn't mean that you should have to be skilled with a hammer to live there.

Most of the data structures and algorithms used to represent and manipulate information in software are logic tools based on mathematical models. All programmers are fluent in these models, including such things as recursion, hierarchical data structures and multi-threading. The problem arises when the user interface manifests the concepts of recursion, hierarchical data or multi-threading.

Mathematical thinking is an implementation model trap that is particularly easy for programmers to fall into. They solve programming problems by thinking mathematically, so they naturally see these mathematical models as appropriate terms for inventing user interfaces. Nothing could be further from the truth.

Design tip: Users don't understand Boolean

For example, one of the most durable and useful tools in the programmer's toolbox is Boolean algebra. It is a compact mathematical system that conveniently describes the behavior of the strictly on-or-off universe that exists inside all digital computers. There are only two main operations: AND and OR. The problem is that the English language also has an "and" and an "or," and they are usually interpreted—by non-programmers—as the exact opposite of the Boolean AND and OR. If the program expresses itself with Boolean notation, the user can be *expected* to misinterpret it.

For example, this problem crops up frequently when querying databases. If I want to extract from a file of employees those who live in Arizona along with those who live in Texas, I would say, in English, "get employees in Arizona and Texas." To say that properly in Boolean algebraic terms, I would say "get employees in Arizona OR Texas." No employee lives in two states at once, so saying "get employees in Arizona AND Texas" is nonsensical in Boolean and will always return the empty set as an answer. If you want to extract from that database all of the employees who started work between January 1st and February 28th, it seems natural to say, in English, "get employees with start dates of January and February." In Boolean, you would say "get employees with start dates of January OR February."

A database query program—or any other program, for that matter—that interacts with the user in Boolean is doomed to suffer severe user interface problems. It is unreasonable to expect users to penetrate the confusion. They are well-trained in English, so why should they have to express things in an unfamiliar language that—annoyingly—redefines key words.

Bringing mechanical age models into the information age

We are experiencing an incredible transformation from a mechanical age to an information age. The change has only begun, and the pace is accelerating rapidly. The upheaval that society underwent as a result of industrialization will be dwarfed by that associated with the information age.

It is only natural for us to drag the imagery and taxonomy of the earlier era into the new one. As the history of the Industrial Revolution shows, the fruits of new technology can often only be expressed at first with the language of an earlier technology. For example, we called railroads "iron horses," automobiles "horseless carriages," and radio "wireless." Unfortunately, this imagery and taxonomy colors our thinking more than we might admit.

Importing linguistic or mental images directly from the pre-digital world is an example of what I call **mechanical age modeling**.

We use old representations in the new environment. Sometimes, the usage is valid since the function is identical, even if the underpinning technology is different. For example, when we translate the process of typewriting with a typewriter into word processing on a computer, we are doing mechanical-age modeling of a common task. Typewriters used little metal tabs to slew the carriage rapidly over several spaces and come to rest on a particular column. The process, as a natural outgrowth of the technology, was called "tabbing" or "setting tabs." Word processors also have tabs because their function is the same: whether you are working on paper rolled around a platen or on images on a video screen, you need to rapidly slew to a particular margin offset.

Sometimes, however, the mechanical-age model can't make the cut into the digital world. We don't use reins to steer our cars, or even a tiller, although both of these older models were tried in the early days of autos. It took many years to develop an idiom that was unique to and appropriate for the car.

When technology changes dramatically, we often find that the nature of the tasks we perform generates what I call **information age models**.

These are tasks, processes or concepts that arise solely because the new technology makes them possible for the first time. With no reason to exist in the non-digital version, they were not conceived of in advance. When the telephone was first invented, for example, it was touted solely as a business tool. Its use as a personal tool wasn't conceived of until it had been in use for 40 years. Today, of course, the phone is used at least as much for personal reasons as it is for business. When your teenage son spends an hour on the phone, it is a usage model that was invisible from the older world.

New conceptual models are not exclusive to the digital world; they are part of any rapidly shifting context, and technology is our current context. Digital technology is the most rapidly shifting context humankind has witnessed so far, so new and surprising information-age models are and will be plentiful.

An interesting thing about information-age models is that we have a hard time seeing them with our mechanical-age mindset. Often, the real advantages of the software products we create remain invisible until they have a sizable population of users. For example, the real advantage of e-mail isn't that it's faster mail, but rather the flattening and democratization that it promotes in the modern business organization—the information-age advantage. The real advantage of making it possible for everybody to communicate online isn't cheaper and more-efficient communications—the mechanical-age viewpoint. Instead, it is the creation of virtual communities—the information-age advantage that was revealed only after it materialized in our grasp.

The language we bring to the new environment creates a problem because it is always derived from mechanical-age models. Forty years ago, the computer was envisioned as a big collating machine, and we applied the collation model to it. We saw it as a "unit-record" device for 80-column-wide keypunch cards. Today, when computers are ubiquitous personal productivity machines, we still find vestigial indications of that 80-column, unit-record world.

The taxonomy of the mechanical-age model tends to obscure the recognition of information-age models. The mechanical taxonomy hinders invention and goal-directed design by focusing our thinking on old-paradigm goals. For example, in the non-digital world calendars are made of paper and are usually divided up into a one-month-per-page format. This is a reasonable compromise based on the size of paper, file folders, briefcases and desk drawers.

Now that we have desktop computers, we frequently see programs with graphic representations of calendars, and they almost always show one month at a time. Why? Paper calendars showed a single month because they were limited by the size of the paper, and a month was a convenient breaking point. Computer screens are not so constrained, but they copy the mechanical-age artifact faithfully. On a computer, the calendar could easily be a continuously scrolling sequence of days, weeks or months as shown in Figure 3-4, rather than a series of discrete pages, as in Figure 3-3. Scheduling something from April 28th to May 4th would be simple if weeks were contiguous instead of broken up by the arbitrary monthly division.

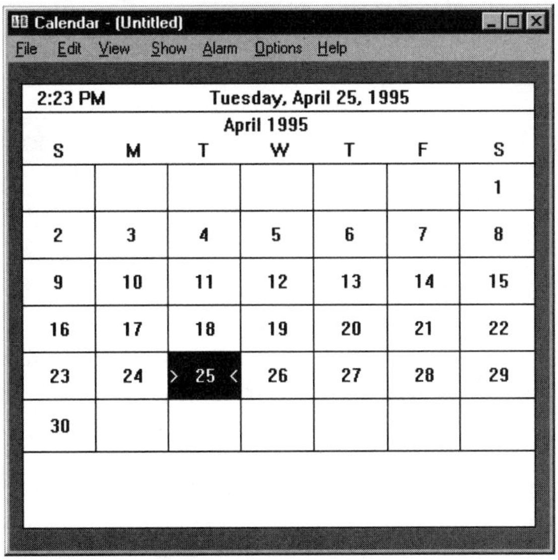

Figure 3-3

The ubiquitous calendar is so familiar that we rarely stop to apply our information-age design sensibilities to it, but that old calendar was designed for small pieces of paper, not for computer screens. The one shown here is from the Calendar in Windows 3.1. How would you redesign it? What aspects of the calendar are artifacts of its old, mechanical-age platform?

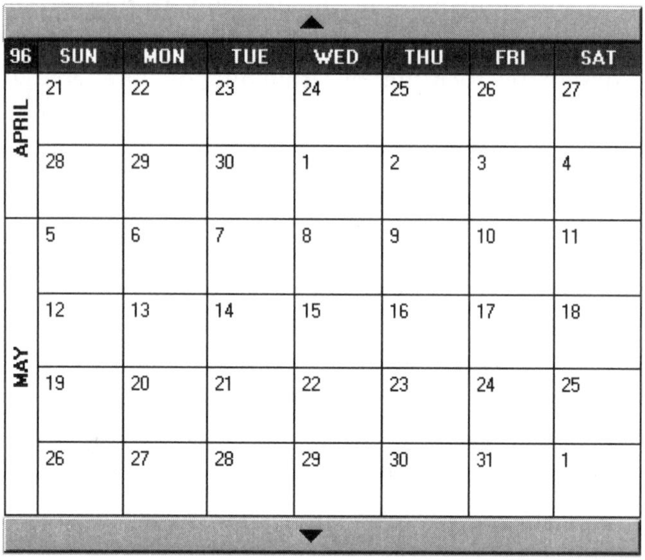

96	SUN	MON	TUE	WED	THU	FRI	SAT
APRIL	21	22	23	24	25	26	27
	28	29	30	1	2	3	4
	5	6	7	8	9	10	11
	12	13	14	15	16	17	18
MAY	19	20	21	22	23	24	25
	26	27	28	29	30	31	1

Figure 3-4

Scrolling is an idiom extremely familiar to computer users. Why not add scrolling to the calendar to create a better one? This perpetual calendar can do everything the old one can, and it also solves the mechanical-age problem of scheduling things across monthly boundaries. Why drag old limitations onto new platforms just out of habit? What other improvements can you think of?

Similarly, the grid pattern in digital calendars is almost always of a fixed size. Why couldn't the width of columns of days or the height of rows of weeks be adjustable like a spreadsheet? Certainly you'd want to adjust the sizes of your weekends to reflect their relative importance over your weekdays. Likewise, your vacation-week calendar would demand more space than a working week. The idioms are as well known as spreadsheets—that is to say, universal—but the mechanical-age models are so firmly set in our taxonomy that we rarely see software publishers deviate from the trajectory of the past. We have the tools, we just don't have the language.

The designer of the software thought of calendars as a canonical image—one that couldn't be altered from the familiar. This calendar software often exhibits interesting new information-age features, like the ability to page instantly forward and backward months or years at a time, or to add graphic representations of holidays to the little day rectangles. These same calendars rarely break the one-month-per-screen archetype, though, and it is this one thing that really holds digital calendars back. Surprisingly, most time-management software probably handles time internally—its implementation model—as a continuum, and only renders it as discrete months in its user interface—its manifest model!

Sometimes people counter that the one-month-per-page calendar is better because it is familiar and unthreatening to users. I doubt it. Most people's mental models don't break time into monthly chunks, but rather see it as a continuum of days. Nor do people find it difficult to adapt to newer, simpler manifestations of familiar systems. We adapted to electric from gas stoves without a hitch. Similarly, the transition from manual transmissions to automatics, from AM radio to FM, from conventional to microwave ovens and from vinyl records to compact discs was simple and painless.

All of those paper-style calendars on various personal information managers (PIMs) and schedulers are mute testimony to how our taxonomy—our language—influences our designs. If we depend on words from the mechanical age, we will build software from the mechanical age. Better software is based on information-age thinking.

It's worse on a computer

We encounter another big problem when we bring our familiar mechanical-age models over to the computer. Simply put, mechanical-age processes are a lot worse when computerized. Procedures are easier by hand than they are with computers. Try to type someone's address on an envelope with a computer. The only time it gets easier is if you have 500 envelopes to address.

Transliterated mechanical models are always worse on computers

Another example, a name and address list on a computer—if it is faithfully rendered like a little bound book—will be much more complex, inconvenient and difficult to use than the actual book. The name and address book, for example, stores names in alphabetical order by last name, but what if you want to find someone by his first name? The mechanical-age artifact doesn't help you: you have to scan the pages manually. So, too, does the computerized version: it can't search by first name either. The difference is that, on the computer screen, you lose many subtle visual cues offered by the paper-based book. The scrollbars and dialog boxes are harder to use, to visualize and to understand than flipping pages. They are rocks thrown at your feet.

Whenever you take a mechanical process and put it on a computer, the user of that process will suffer. The only situation where transliterated processes yield an advantage is if the sheer quantity of items to be processed is large enough to justify doing the task en masse. Early data-processing systems did this with applications like invoicing and billing. Most of our desktop computing jobs don't involve sufficiently large quantities of information for this to remain true.

But there is another, bigger problem with transliterated mechanical models. The old mechanical method will always have the strengths and weaknesses of its medium, like pen and paper. Software has a completely different set of strengths and weaknesses, yet when those old models are brought across without change, they combine the weaknesses of the old with the weaknesses of the new. In our address book example, the computer could easily search for an entry by first name, but, by storing the names in the same paradigm as the mechanical artifact, we deprive ourselves of new ways of searching. We limit ourselves to not much more than what we could do in the world of paper and ink, but this time we have to do it through dialog boxes and menus.

When designers rely on mechanical-age paradigms to guide them, they are blinded to the far greater potential of the computer to do information management tasks in a better, albeit different, way.

Visual Interface Design

The commonly accepted wisdom of the post-Macintosh era is that graphical user interfaces, or GUIs, are better than character-based user interfaces. This is generally a true statement but, while there are certainly GUI programs that dazzle us with their ease of use, the vast majority of GUI programs irritate and annoy us in spite of their graphic nature. Why is this?

Visual Software

It's not merely the graphic nature of an interface that makes it better. Using a bit-mapped system to render the lines and characters of a character-mode program doesn't change the essential nature of the program. It's very easy to create a program with a "graphical user interface" that has the same extreme difficulty-of-use as a CP/M, DOS or UNIX application.

The qualities that make a user interface good are user-centric and not technology-centric. "Graphicalness" is a technology-centric concept. There are two really important user-centric qualities: the "visualness" of the software and the program's vocabulary.

Most humans process information better visually than they do textually. Sure, we learn by reading, but we learn much more, much faster by seeing things whole and in context. In order to realize the advantages of the technology, the interaction with the user must become visual. The issue isn't the graphic nature of the program, it's the visualness of the interaction. Instead of GUI, it's a visual user interface—a VUI—that we are looking for. Software that recognizes this is called **visual interface design**. When done well, a VUI has a feeling of fluency, of moving along smoothly and effortlessly towards the user's goals without hitching or stopping on confusing little problems of comprehension.

Visual processing

The human brain is a superb pattern-processing computer. It uses this strength to make sense of the dense quantities of visual information we are bombarded with from the moment we open our eyes in the morning. The acuity of the human eye is tremendous, and if our brain couldn't impose some management system on what our eyes report, we would collapse from overload. Look out the window. See the trees, the water, the waves, the clouds, the people, the windows, the people in the windows, the guy carrying the box, the name printed on the box, the letters in the name... If we had a difficult time with visual complexity, the sheer quantity of visual information we take in when we look out the window would put us in a state of shock. But we clearly aren't bothered by this visual complexity. When we look out the window, our eyes encompass a huge scene filled with constantly changing terabytes of complex information. Our brain manages the input by unconsciously discerning patterns, and by using these patterns to manage what we are looking at. Our brains establish a system of priorities for the things we see that allow us to consciously analyze the visual input.

Text, when viewed from a distance, forms a recognizable pattern and shape that our brains categorize. This is a different act from reading, where we scan the individual words and interpret them. Even then, we use pattern-matching more than we actually sound out each syllable the way we did as children. Each word has a recognizable shape, and this is why WORDS TYPED IN ALL CAPITAL LETTERS ARE HARDER TO READ than upper/lower case—our familiar pattern-matching hints are absent in all capitals, so we must pay much closer attention to decipher what is written. This same pattern-processing talent explains why body text in books is always in a relatively standard, serif typeface like the one you are looking at now. However, if this book were printed using a sans serif font, or a font with unusual proportions, you would find it not a strain on the eyes, but a strain on the brain.

When we look at the complex scene out the window, our brain gathers big chunks of the view into manageable pieces—building, street, ocean, sky—and lets our conscious processes grapple with higher-level issues.

If, for example, we find ourselves taking a second look at one person in the crowd on the street below, it is because our subconscious pattern-matching equipment got a hit. We next study the person's face, searching for details in order to make a positive identification. We go through the identical process when we read documents. Our unconscious mind is constantly reducing visual input to patterns, and our conscious mind is constantly ordering those patterns into hierarchies. When our eye-brain-pattern system reports an "envelope," our brain-hierarchy system isolates it and examines it for our name. The pattern system detects the envelope pattern; then the conscious system disambiguates that pattern into either a letter for us or a letter for someone else.

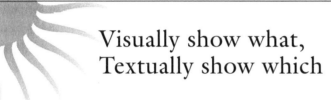

Visually show what, Textually show which

If our unconscious mind could not classify the pattern as an envelope, we would have to get our conscious mind involved in the preliminary processing. It is much faster when our unconscious mind provides the first cut because pattern-matching is so much faster and more efficient than having to think about it.

Visual patterns

If our conscious mind had to grapple with every detail of what our eyes saw, we would be overwhelmed with meaningless detail. The ability of our unconscious mind to group things into patterns based on visual cues is what allows us to process visual information so quickly and efficiently. Understanding and applying this model of how the human mind processes visual information is one of the key elements of visual interface design. The philosophy is to present the program's components on the screen as recognizable visual patterns with accompanying text as a descriptive supplement. The user can choose, on a purely pattern-matching, unconscious level, which objects to consider consciously. The accompanying text only comes into play once the user has decided it's important.

You build an effective visual interface from visual patterns. Notice that I did not say pictures or images or icons. Representational images are useful, but patterns are the engine of unconscious recognition. For the user to discern a particular icon from a screenful of similar but different icons is just as difficult as discerning a particular word from a screenful of similar but different words. Icons that must be consciously recognized or deciphered are no better—and possibly much worse—than plain text.

A visual interface is based on visual patterns

The pecking order of visual understanding always regards visual pattern-matching as superior to verbal or pictographic reading. Pattern-matching is unconscious and reading is conscious. Our visual user interface must create readily recognizable patterns. It will certainly include text, but only in a secondary role of distinguishing between objects with similar patterns.

We create patterns in very simple ways. Possibly the simplest is by creating recognizable graphic symbols and giving them value by association. As you drive down the highway, you read all of the signs you see. After a while, you begin to notice a pattern. Every time the highway you are on is identified, its number is accompanied or even enclosed by the symbol "⬡." You probably don't pay much attention to this trivial detail, and why should you? You are usually well aware of what highway you are on. Your unconscious mind filters out the ⬡ signs. Then one day you are on an unfamiliar highway and you want to know exactly which one you are on. Your conscious mind wants to know this, so your unconscious mind alerts you to the presence of each ⬡ it sees. Your conscious mind then reads the numbers on the sign to separate it from all of the other ⬡s you have seen. The ⬡ is not representational. It is not metaphoric. It is idiomatic: you learn the shape from the context in which it is used, and from then on it represents its context.

This is exactly what you do with visual interface design. You create symbols for the objects in the interface. If the program you are creating manages a restaurant, for example, you will find that tables, checks, orders, specials, and waitpersons are the fundamental elements—the building blocks—with which you must create the interface. In other words, these are the objects that the users will manipulate to achieve their goals. What you need to do is create a recognizable visual symbol for each of these primary types:

⚒ Tables

✐ Checks

◪ Orders

✦ Specials

🦅 Waitpersons

The symbols don't have to be representational, but it doesn't hurt. If you do choose a representational image, don't kid yourself about its value as a teaching tool. On the other hand, don't ignore the value of mnemonics. Each user can form his own mental cues to help him remember what the symbols represent: factories and tables both produce value; ducks and waitpersons both fly from place to place.

In order to drive home the connection between symbol and object, you must use the symbol everywhere the object is represented on the screen. Whether the object is an item in a listbox, an entire dialog box, a mention in text, or a gizmo on the toolbar, it must be accompanied by the visual symbol. You don't have to spell this out to the user: you are teaching it to his unconscious mind, and its presence alone over time is sufficient to do that. I call this a **visual fugue**.

If you have a list of waitpersons, prefix each one with the 🦅 symbol as in Figure 4-1.

The power of this technique is even greater if you have a listbox filled with heterogeneous objects. Imagine a similar listbox filled with both tables and orders as shown in Figure 4-2.

Our minds differentiate each line—each object—by its visual symbol, and once we have identified the type we are interested in, we read the text to separate it from its siblings. We don't have to read about objects we are not interested in. This type of processing is very natural to humans and we can perform it rapidly and with little effort.

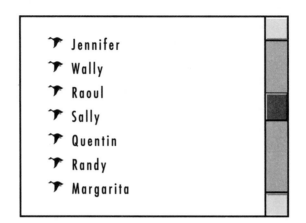

Figure 4-1

This listbox is filled with several objects of one type. You can see that unconsciously, because your mind discerns the identical symbols associated with each entry. It will probably take some additional reading to disambiguate which object is which, but without the symbols, we'd have to read them all just to know what they are and that they are all the same type. Symbols should always be associated with text in visual user interfaces.

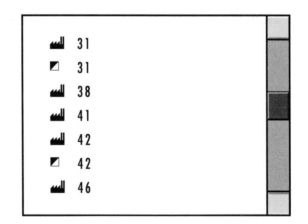

Figure 4-2

This listbox is filled with objects of two different types. Without the symbols to differentiate between tables and orders, it would be impossible to make sense of the list. We would have to label each entry with text, "Table 31," "Order 31," and so on. The symbols are much faster, letting our unconscious minds recognize the patterns before our relatively slow conscious minds even have to pay attention.

Restricting the vocabulary

When graphical user interfaces were first invented, they were so clearly superior that many observers credited their success to their graphics. This was a natural reaction, but it was only part of the story. One of the most important reasons why those first GUIs were better was that they were the first user interfaces to restrict the range of their vocabulary for communicating with the user. In particular, the input they could accept from the user went from a virtually unrestricted command line to a tightly restricted set of mouse-based actions. In a command line interface, the user can enter any combination of characters in the language—a virtually infinite number. In order for the user's entry to be correct, he needs to know exactly what the program expects. He must remember the letters and symbols with exacting precision. The sequence can be important. The capitalization can be vital.

In the GUI, the user can point to images or words on the screen with the mouse cursor. Using the buttons on the mouse, the user can click, double-click or click-and-drag. That is it. The keyboard is used for data entry, not for command entry or navigation. Instead of 26 letters, 10 digits and a couple of dozen other keys available in an infinite number of combinations in the command line interface, the user has just three basic actions to choose from. The number of atomic elements in the user's input vocabulary dropped from millions to just three, even though the range of tasks that could be performed by GUI programs wasn't restricted any more than that of command-line systems.

The more atomic elements there are in a communications vocabulary, the more time-consuming and difficult the learning process is. Vocabularies like the English language take at least ten years to learn thoroughly, and its complexity requires constant use to maintain fluency. Of course, English is a fantastically expressive language and, in the hands of an artist, can be a most compelling medium. Our users aren't artists, though, and they shouldn't have to invest that much effort in becoming effective with our software. Merely restricting the number of elements in the vocabulary reduces the expressiveness of it, so that alone is not the solution. The answer lies in the way we build our vocabularies—some parts are restricted in size, while others can be huge.

A properly formed vocabulary is shaped like an inverted pyramid. All easy-to-learn communications systems obey this pattern. It is so fundamental that I call it the canonical vocabulary. You can see a picture of it in Figure 4-3.

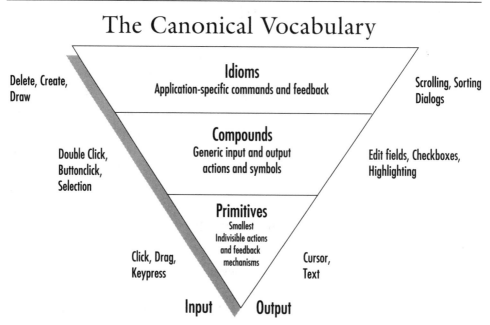

The Canonical Vocabulary

Idioms
Application-specific commands and feedback

Delete, Create, Draw

Scrolling, Sorting Dialogs

Compounds
Generic input and output actions and symbols

Double Click, Buttonclick, Selection

Edit fields, Checkboxes, Highlighting

Primitives
Smallest Indivisible actions and feedback mechanisms

Click, Drag, Keypress

Cursor, Text

Input   Output

Figure 4-3

The main reason GUIs are so much easier to use is that they were the first platform to enforce a canonical vocabulary. It has very little to do with graphics. All vocabularies follow this archetypal form.

At the lowest level is a set of primitives from which all else is constructed. Generally, the set of primitives shouldn't exceed four elements. The middle layer consists of more complex constructs built from combinations of the primitives. The upper-level idioms are compounds with the addition of domain knowledge.

The bottom segment contains what I call the **primitives**, the atomic elements of which everything in the language is comprised.

Paraphrasing Albert Einstein, this set should be as small as possible, but no smaller. In a GUI, it consists of pointing, clicking and dragging. A set of primitives of two to four items is about right. More than that leads to trouble.

The middle trapezoid contains what I call the **compounds**.

These are more complex constructs created by combining one or more of the primitives. Nothing else is added; they are built exclusively from elements below them in the pyramid. In a GUI, it contains such actions as double-clicking, click-and-dragging and manipulable objects like push-buttons and checkboxes.

The uppermost layer of the pyramid contains what I call the idioms. Idioms combine compounds with knowledge of the problem under consideration, known as domain knowledge. Domain knowledge is information related to the user's application area and not specifically to the computerized solution. The set of idioms opens the vocabulary to information about the particular problem the program is trying to address. In a GUI, it would include things like OK buttons, caption bars, listboxes and file icons.

Any language that does not follow the canonical form will be very hard to learn. Many effective communications systems outside of the computer world follow canonical vocabularies. Street signs follow a simple pattern of shapes and colors: Yellow triangles are cautionary, red octagons are imperatives and green rectangles are informative.

Our telephone system has a tiny set of primitives consisting of simple audio tones. Hearing a buzz—a dial tone—means the system is available. When the buzz alternates with silence, it means the number is busy. A warble means the phone is ringing. Silence means we have failed to enter valid numbers, or there is some other problem and we should try again.

Designing for users

Successful user interfaces are those that focus on the user's goals even if they have to ignore the technology of the implementation. Professional software designers are the primary group today acting as advocates for the user.

To create effective visual interfaces, designers must create interaction from a canonically formed vocabulary that is expressed visually. This vocabulary follows the user's mental model, even if it diverges from the physically correct model. As Frederick Brooks says, "The [designer] sits at the focus of forces which he must ultimately resolve in the user's interest."

Part II: The Form
The March of Paradigms

User interface design begins well-below the surface of our systems and applications. Imagining that we can create a good user interface for our programs after the program's internals have been constructed is like saying that a good coat of paint will turn a cave into a mansion. Software designers must fully understand why our computers work the way they do. They must make informed judgments about what to keep because it's good, and what to discard even though it is familiar. But getting intimate with the techniques of software development is a seduction that designers must resist. It is all too easy to become sympathetic to the needs of the computer, which are almost always in direct opposition to the needs of the user.

Idioms and Affordances

There is nothing in the world of software development that is quite as frightening as an empty screen. When we begin designing the user interface, we must first confront that awful whiteness, and ask ourselves: What does good software look like?

The Myth of Metaphor

Software designers often speak of "finding the right metaphor" upon which to base their interface design. They imagine that filling their interface with images of familiar objects from the real world will give their users a pipeline to easy learning. So they create an interface masquerading as an office filled with desks, file cabinets, telephones and address books, or as a pad of paper or a street of buildings. And if you, too, search for that magic metaphor, you will be in august company; some of the best and brightest designers in the interface world put metaphor selection as one of their first and most important tasks.

Searching for that magic metaphor is one of the biggest mistakes you can make in user interface design. Searching for an elusive guiding metaphor is like searching for the correct steam engine to power your airplane, or searching for a good dinosaur on which to ride to work.

Basing a user interface design on a metaphor is not only unhelpful, it can often be quite harmful. The idea that good user interface design relies on metaphors is one of the most insidious of the many myths that permeate the software community.

Metaphors offer a tiny boost in learnability to first-time users, but at a tremendous cost. By representing old technologies, most metaphors firmly nail our conceptual feet to the ground, forever limiting the power of our software. They have a host of other problems as well, including the simple facts that there aren't enough metaphors to go around, they don't scale well, and the ability of users to recognize them is questionable.

The three interface paradigms

There are three dominant paradigms in the design of user interfaces. I call these three the **technology paradigm**, the **metaphor paradigm** and the **idiomatic paradigm**. The technology paradigm is based on *understanding* how things work—a difficult proposition. The metaphor paradigm is based on *intuiting* how things work—a risky method. The idiomatic paradigm, however, is based on *learning* how to accomplish things—a natural, human process.

The field of user interface design has progressed from an orientation focused on technology, into one that focuses overmuch on metaphor. We are just now becoming aware of idiomatic design. There is ample evidence of all three paradigms in contemporary software design, even though the metaphor paradigm is the only one that has been named and described. We pay metaphors lots of lip service and, all too often, hamper the creation of really good interfaces by following their false trail.

The technology paradigm

The **technology paradigm** of user interface design is simple and incredibly widespread in the computer industry. The technology paradigm merely means that the interface is expressed in terms of its construction—of how it was built. In order to successfully use it, the user must understand how the software works. Following the technology paradigm means user interface design based exclusively on the implementation model.

There was a genre of building architecture, popular in the 1960s, called Metabolist. In Metabolist architecture, the elevator shafts, air conditioning ducts, cable runs, steel beams and other construction impedimenta are left uncovered and visible. The muscles, bones and sinews of the building are exposed—even emphasized—without any hint of modesty. The idea was that the building is a machine for living and its form should follow its implementation details. The overwhelming majority of software programs today are Metabolist in that they show us, without any hint of shame, precisely how they are built. There is one button per function, one function per module of code, and the commands and processes precisely echo the internal data structures and algorithms.

We can see how a technology program ticks merely by learning how to run it; The problem is that the reverse is also true: We *must* learn how it ticks in order to run it.

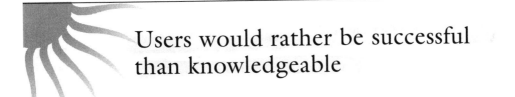

Users would rather be successful than knowledgeable

Engineers want to know how things work, so the technology paradigm is very satisfying to them (which, of course, is why so much of our software follows it). Engineers prefer to see the gears and levers and valves because it helps them understand what is going on inside the machine. That those artifacts needlessly complicate the interface seems a small price to pay. Engineers may want to understand the inner workings, but most users don't have either the time or desire. They'd much rather be successful than be knowledgeable, a state that is often hard for engineers to understand.

The metaphor paradigm

In the 1970s, the modern graphical user interface was invented at Xerox Palo Alto Research Center (PARC). It has swept the industry, but what, exactly, is it? The GUI—as defined by PARC—consisted of many things: windows, buttons, mice, icons, metaphors, pull-down menus. Some of these things are good and some are not so good, but they have all achieved a kind of holy stature in the industry by association with the empirical superiority of the ensemble.

In particular, the idea that metaphors are a firm foundation for user interface design is a very misleading proposition. It's like worshipping 5.25" floppy diskettes because so much good software once came on them.

The first commercially successful implementation of the PARC GUI was the Apple Macintosh, with its desktop, wastebasket, overlapping sheets of paper and file folders. The Mac didn't succeed because of these metaphors, however, but because it was the first computer that defined a tightly restricted vocabulary—a canonical vocabulary based on a very small set of mouse actions—for communicating with users. It also offered richer visual interaction. The metaphors were just nice paintings on the walls of a well-designed house.

Metaphors don't scale very well. A metaphor that works well for a simple process in a simple program will often fail to work well as that process grows in size or complexity. File icons were a good idea when computers had floppies or 10 MB hard disks with only a couple of hundred files, but in these days of multi-gigabyte hard disks and thousands of files, file icons can get pretty clumsy.

When we talk about metaphors in the user interface design context, we really mean visual metaphors: a picture of something used to represent that thing. Users recognize the imagery of the metaphor and, by extension, can understand the purpose of the thing. Metaphors range from the tiny images on toolbar buttons to the entire screen on some programs. They can be a tiny scissors on a button indicating "cut," or a full-size checkbook in Quicken. We understand metaphors intuitively. Webster's defines intuition like this:

> **in·tu·i·tion** \in-'tu-wi-shen\ *n* 1 : quick and ready insight 2 **a**: immediate apprehension or cognition **b**: knowledge or conviction gained by intuition **c**: the power or faculty of attaining direct knowledge or cognition without evident rational thought and inference

The dictionary highlights the magical quality of intuition, but it doesn't say *how* we intuit something. Intuition works by inference, where we see connections between disparate subjects and learn from these similarities while not being distracted by their differences. We grasp the meaning of the metaphoric controls in an interface because we mentally connect them with other processes or things we have already learned. This is an efficient way to take advantage of the awesome power of the human mind to make inferences, something that CPUs are incapable of. But this method also depends on the creaky, cantankerous, idiosyncratic human mind, which may not have the requisite language, knowledge or inferential power necessary to make the connection. Metaphors are not dependable in the way that understanding is. Sometimes the magic works, sometimes it doesn't.

Metaphors rely on associations perceived in similar ways by both the designer and the user. If the user doesn't have the same cultural background as the designer, it is easy for metaphors to fail. Even in the same or similar cultures, there can be significant misunderstandings. Does a picture of an airplane mean "send via airmail" or "make airline reservations"?

The **metaphor paradigm** relies on intuitive connections in which there is no need to understand the mechanics of the software, so it is a step forward from the technology paradigm, but its power and usefulness has been inflated to unrealistic proportions.

Recall from our definition of intuition that no rational thought is evident in the process. I think it is silly to imagine that we can base good user interface design on a kind of mental magic that thumbs its nose at thinking. In the computer industry, and particularly in the user interface design community, the word *intuitive* is often used to mean easy-to-use or easy-to-understand. I'm a big fan of easy-to-use, but it doesn't promote our craft to attribute its success to metaphysics. Nor does it help us to devalue the precise meaning of the word. There are very real reasons why people understand certain interfaces and not others.

There are certain sounds, smells and images that make us respond without any previous conscious learning. When a small child encounters an angry dog, she *instinctively* knows that bared fangs are a sign of great danger, even without any previous learning. The encoding for such recognition goes deep. Instinct is a hard-wired response that involves no conscious thought. Intuition is one step above instinct because, although it also requires no conscious thought, it is based on a web of knowledge learned consciously.

Examples of instinct in human-computer interaction include the way we are startled and made apprehensive by gross changes in the image on the screen, or react to sudden noises from the computer or the smell of smoke rising from the CPU.

Intuition is a middle ground between having consciously learned something and knowing something instinctively. If we have learned that things glowing red can burn us, we tend to classify all red-glowing things as potentially dangerous until proven otherwise. We don't necessarily know that the particular red-glowing thing is a danger, but it gives us a safe place to begin our exploration.

What we commonly refer to as intuition is actually a mental comparison between something and the things we have already learned. You instantly intuit how to work a wastebasket icon, for example, because you once learned how a real wastebasket works, thereby preparing your mind to make the connection years later. But you didn't *intuit* how to use the original wastebasket. It was just an extremely easy thing to learn. This brings us to the third paradigm, which is based on the fact that the human mind is an incredibly powerful learning machine, and that learning isn't hard for us.

The idiomatic paradigm

The idiomatic method of user interface design solves the problems of both of the previous two. I call it the idiomatic paradigm because it is based on the way we learn and use idioms, or figures of speech, like "beat around the bush" or "cool."

These idiomatic expressions are easily understood but not in the same way metaphors are. There is no "bush" and nobody is beating anything. We understand the idiom simply because we have learned it and because it is distinctive, not because we understand it or because it makes subliminal connections in our minds.

This is where the human mind is really outstanding: learning and remembering idioms very easily without relying on comparisons to known situations or an understanding of how they work. This is a necessity, because many idioms don't have any metaphoric meaning at all, and the stories behind most others were lost ages ago.

Most of the elements of a GUI interface are idioms. Windows, caption bars, close boxes, screen-splitters and drop-downs are things we learn idiomatically rather than intuit metaphorically.

We are inclined to think that learning is hard because of our conditioning from the technology paradigm. Those old interfaces were very hard to learn because you also had to understand how they worked. Most of what we know we learn *without* understanding: things like faces, social interactions, attitudes, the arrangement of rooms and furniture in our houses and offices. We don't "understand" why someone's face is composed the way it is, but we "know" his face. We recognize it because we have looked at it and automatically (and easily) memorized it.

The familiar mouse is not metaphoric of anything, but rather is learned idiomatically. There is a scene in *Star Trek IV* where Scotty returns to twentieth-century Earth and tries to speak into a mouse. It is one of the few parts of that movie that is not fiction. There is nothing about the physical appearance of the mouse that indicates its purpose or use, nor is it comparable to anything else in our experience, so learning it is not intuitive. However, learning to point at things with a mouse is incredibly easy. Someone probably spent all of three seconds showing it to you the first time, and you mastered it from that instant on. We don't know or care how mice work, and yet even small children can operate them just fine. That is idiomatic learning.

Not only can you not intuit an idiom, neither can you reason it out. Our language is filled with idioms that, if you haven't been taught them, make no sense. If I say my Uncle Joe "kicked the bucket," you know what I mean even though there is no bucket or kicking involved. You can't know this because you have thought through the various permutations of smacking pails with your feet. You can only learn this from context in something you read or by being consciously taught it. You remember this obscure connection between buckets, kicking and dying only because humans are good at remembering stuff like this.

All idioms must be learned. Good idioms only need to be learned once

The key observation about idioms is that although they must be learned, good ones only need to be learned once. It is quite easy to learn idioms like "neat" or "politically correct" or "the lights are on but nobody's home" or "in a pickle" or "inside the Beltway" or "take the red-eye" or "grunge." The human mind is capable of picking up idioms like these from a single hearing. It is similarly easy to learn idioms like check-boxes, radio buttons, push-buttons, close-boxes, pulldown menus, icons, tabs, comboboxes, keyboards, mice and pens.

Branding
Marketing professionals know this idea of taking a simple action or symbol and imbuing it with meaning. After all, synthesizing idioms is the essence of product branding, whereby a company takes a product or company name and

imbues it with a desired meaning. Tylenol is, by itself, a meaningless word, an idiom, but the McNeil company has spent millions to make you associate that word with safe, simple, trustworthy pain relief. Of course, idioms are visual, too. The golden arches of McDonalds, the three diamonds of Mitsubishi, the five interlocking rings of the Olympics, even Microsoft's flying window are non-metaphoric idioms that are instantly recognizable and imbued with common meaning. The example of idiomatic branding shown in Figure 5-1 illustrates its power.

Ironically, many of the familiar GUI elements that are often thought of as metaphoric are actually idiomatic. Artifacts like window close boxes, resizable windows, infinitely nested file folders and clicking and dragging are non-metaphoric operations—they have no parallel in the real world. They derive their strength only from their easy idiomatic learnability.

The showstoppers

If we depend on metaphors to create user interfaces, we encounter not only the minor problems already mentioned, but also two more major problems: metaphors are hard to find and they constrict our thinking.

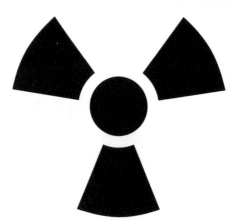

Figure 5-1

Here is a randomly chosen idiomatic symbol that has been imbued with meaning from use rather than from any inherent metaphoric value. For anyone who grew up in the '50s or '60s, this otherwise meaningless symbol has the power to cause a small shiver of fear to touch our backs. Idioms are just as powerful as metaphors. The power comes from how we use them and how we associate them, rather than from any innate imagery.

It may be easy to discover visual metaphors for physical objects like printers and documents. It can be difficult or impossible to find metaphors for processes, relationships, services and transformations—the most frequent uses of software. It can be extremely daunting to find a useful visual metaphor for buying a ticket, changing channels, purchasing an item, finding a reference, setting a format, rotating a tool or changing resolution, yet these operations are precisely the type of processes we use software to perform most frequently.

The most insidious problem with metaphors, the real showstopper, is that they tie our interfaces to mechanical age artifacts. It is easy to intuit how to use the clipboard, for example, because it is a metaphor. But if we adhere strictly to the clipboard metaphor, the facility is incredibly weak. It won't hold more than one thing, it doesn't have a memory of what it held before, it can't identify where the images came from, it can't show you thumbnails of what it holds and it doesn't save its contents from run to run. All of these actions are non-metaphoric and have to be learned. Following the metaphor gives users a momentary boost the first time they use the clipboard, but it costs them greatly after that in the arbitrary weakness of the facility.

Another really outrageous example is MagiCap, a communications interface from General Magic. It relies on metaphor for every aspect of its interface. As you can see in Figure 5-2, you metaphorically walk down a street lined with buildings representing services. You enter a building to begin a service, which is represented as a walk down a hallway that is lined with doors representing functions. This heavy reliance on metaphor means that you can intuit the basic functioning of the software, but its downside is that the metaphor restricts all navigation to a very rudimentary, linear path. You *must* go back out onto the street to go to another service. This may be normal in the physical world, but there is no reason for it in the world of software. Why not abandon this slavish devotion to metaphor and give the user services they *can't* get out on the street?

For all the limitations of metaphors, there is nothing bad about using one if it fits the situation. If I see a twenty-dollar bill lying on the sidewalk, of course I'll pick it up: I'd be a fool not to! But I'd be a bigger fool if I decided to make my living finding misplaced twenty-dollar bills. Metaphors are like that: use 'em if you find 'em, but don't bend your interface to fit some arbitrary metaphoric standard.

Figure 5-2

This is the MagiCap interface from General Magic. It is the acme of the expression of the metaphoric paradigm. Nothing in the program is done without a thorough metaphoric rationalization. I am in awe of its designers: the program is a tour de force of metaphor-finding above and beyond the call of duty. All of the interaction has been subordinated to the maintenance of these metaphors. I'm sure it was a lot of fun to design. I'll bet it is a real pain to use. Once you have learned that the substantial-looking building with the big "AT&T" on its facade is the phone company, you must forever live with going in and out of that building to call people. This most-modern, information-age software drags all of the limitations of the mechanical age into the future and forces us to live with them yet again. Is this progress?

Never bend your interface to fit a metaphor

On a design project for a library management system, we had to present a screen with multiple parts. Some gizmos were common to all of the parts, while others came and went depending on the active part. We made part of the screen look like a wire-bound notebook. The pages could flip like a notebook while the rest of the screen remained stationary. The gizmos on the flipping pages came and went while the gizmos outside of the notebook stayed still and worked globally. The notebook metaphor drew the user's attention to the difference and offered some visual help in understanding the scope of the controls. The metaphor fit naturally into the design of the overall product, so we used it.

General Magic's interface relies on what is called a **global metaphor**. This is a single, overarching metaphor that provides a framework for all of the other metaphors in the system. The desktop of the original Macintosh is also considered a global metaphor.

A hidden problem of global metaphors is the mistaken belief that other little daughter metaphors consistent with them enjoy cognitive benefits by association. The temptation is irresistible to stretch the metaphor beyond simple function recognition: That little software telephone also lets you "dial" with buttons just like those on our desktop telephones. We see software that has "address books" of phone numbers just like those in our pockets and purses. Wouldn't it be better to go beyond these confining technologies and deliver some of the real power of the computer? Why can't our communications software allow multiple connections or make connections by organization or affiliation, or just hide the use of phone numbers altogether?

It may seem clever to represent your dial-up service with a picture of a telephone sitting on a desk, but it actually imprisons you in a bad design. The original makers of the telephone would have been ecstatic if they could have created one that let you call your friends just by pointing to pictures of them. They couldn't because they were restricted by the dreary realities of electrical circuits and Bakelite moldings. On the other hand, today we have the luxury of rendering our communications interfaces in any way we please—showing pictures of our friends is completely reasonable—yet we insist on holding these concepts back with little pictures of obsolete technology.

There are two snares here, one for the user and one for the designer. Once the user depends on the metaphor for recognition, he expects consistency. This causes the snare for the designer, who will now be tempted to render the software in terms of the mechanical-age metaphor. As we saw in Part I, transliterating mechanical processes onto the computer just makes them worse than they were before.

Brenda Laurel says in her book *Computers as Theatre* (Addison-Wesley, 1991), "Interface metaphors rumble along like Rube Goldberg machines, patched and wired together every time they break, until they are so encrusted with the artifacts of repair that we can no longer interpret them or recognize their referents." It amazes me that software designers, who can finally create that dream-phone interface, give us the same old telephone simply because they were taught that a strong, global metaphor is a prerequisite to good user interface design. Of all the misconceptions to emerge from Xerox PARC, the global metaphor myth is the most debilitating and unfortunate.

Idiomatic design is the future of user interface design. Using this paradigm, we depend on the natural ability of humans to learn easily and quickly as long as we don't force them to understand how and why. There is an infinity of idioms waiting to be invented, but only a limited set of metaphors waiting to be discovered. Metaphors give first-timers a penny's worth of value but cost them many dollars' worth of problems as they continue to use the software. It is always better to design idiomatically, only using metaphors when one falls in our lap.

Manual affordances

Donald Norman, in *The Psychology of Everyday Things* (Basic Books, 1988), has given us the fine term **affordance**, which he defines as "the perceived and actual properties of the thing, primarily those fundamental properties that determine just how the thing could possibly be used."

This definition is fine as far as it goes, but it omits the key connection: *how* do we know what those properties offer us? If you look at something and understand how to use it—you comprehend its affordances—you must be using some method for making the mental connection.

I would alter Norman's definition by omitting the phrase "and actual." By doing this, affordance becomes a purely cognitive term, referring to what we *think* the object can do rather than what it can actually do. If a push-button is placed on the wall next to the front door of a residence, its affordances are 100% doorbell. If, when we push it, it causes a trapdoor to open beneath us and we fall into it, it turns out that it wasn't a doorbell, but that doesn't change its affordance as one.

So how do we know it's a doorbell? Simply because we have learned about doorbells and door etiquette and push-buttons from our complex and lengthy socialization and maturation process. We have learned about this class of push-able things by exposure to electrical and electronic devices in our environs and because—years ago—we stood on doorsteps with our parents, learning how to approach another person's abode.

But there is another force at work here, too. If we see a push-button in an unlikely place like the hood of a car, we cannot imagine what its purpose is, but we can recognize that it is a finger-pushable object. How do we know this? I don't think we know it instinctively, because a small child wouldn't necessarily recognize it as such; certainly not the way she would recognize claws or fangs. I believe that we recognize it as a pushable object because of our tool-manipulating nature. We, as a species (genus, actually), see things that are finger-sized, placed at finger-height, and we automatically push them. We see things that are long and round, and we wrap our fingers around them and grasp them like handles. I think this is what Norman was getting at with his "affordance." For clarity, though, I call this instinctive understanding of how things are manipulated with our hands **manual affordance**. When things are clearly shaped to fit our hands or feet, we recognize that they are directly manipulable and we need no written instructions.

In fact, Norman makes much of how [manual] affordances are much more compelling than written instructions. A typical example he uses is a door that must be pushed open with a metal bar for a handle. The bar is just the right shape, height and position to be grasped by the human hand. The manual affordances of the door scream "pull me." No matter how often someone uses this diabolical door, he will always attempt to pull it open, because the affordances are strong enough to drown out any number of signs affixed to the door saying "PUSH."

There are only a few manual affordances. We pull handle-shaped things with our hands and, if they are small, we pull them with our fingers. We push flat plates with our hands or fingers. If they are on the floor we push them with our feet. We rotate round things, using our fingers for small ones—like dials—and both hands on larger ones, like steering wheels. Such manual affordances are the basis for much of our visual user interface design.

The popular three-dimensional design of systems like Windows 95, NeXT and Motif rely on shading and highlighting to make screen images appear to "pop out." These images offer manual affordances of button-like images that say "push me" to our tool-manipulating natures.

Understanding what it means

What is missing from a manual affordance is any idea of what the thing really does. We can see that it looks like a button, but how do we know what it will accomplish when we press it? For that we begin to rely on text and pictures, but most of all we rely on previous learning. The manual affordance of the scrollbar clearly shows that it is manipulable, but the only things about it that tell us what it does are the arrows, which hint at its directionality. In order to know that a scrollbar controls our position in a document, we have to either be taught or learn by ourselves through experimentation.

In the canonical vocabulary (described in Chapter 4), manual affordances have no meaning in the uppermost tier, in idioms. This is why gizmos must have writing on them to make sense. If the answer isn't written directly on the gizmo, we can only learn what it does by one of two methods: experimentation or training. Either we try it to see what happens, or someone who has already tried it tells us. We get no help from our instinct or intuition. We can only rely on the empirical.

Fulfilling the contract

In the real world, a thing does what it can do. A saw can cut wood because it is sharp and flat and has a handle. However, in the digital world, a thing does what it can do because some programmer imbued it with the power to do something. Our tool-using nature can tell us a lot about how a saw works merely by inspection, and it can't easily be fooled by what it sees. On a computer screen, though, we can see a raised, three-dimensional rectangle that clearly wants to be pushed like a button, but this doesn't necessarily mean that it *should* be pushed. We can be fooled because there is no natural connection— as there is in the real world—between what we see on the screen and what lies behind it. In other words, we may not know how to work a saw, and we may even be frustrated by our inability to manipulate it effectively, but we will never be fooled by it. It makes no representations that it doesn't manifestly live up to. On computer screens, canards and false impressions are very easy to create.

When we render a button on the screen, we are making a contract with the user that that button will visually change when we push it: that it will appear to depress when the mouse button is clicked over it. Further, the contract states that the button will perform some reasonable work that is accurately described by its legend. This may sound obvious, but I am constantly astonished by the number of programs I see that offer bait-and-switch visual affordances. This is relatively rare for push-buttons, but extremely common for text fields.

An Irreverent History
of Rectangles on
the Screen

Any book on Windows user interface design must devote considerable space to windows-with-a-lower-case-w. I consider it necessary to place these omnipresent rectangles in some historical perspective to keep the reader from imbuing too much intrinsic value in them.

Xerox PARC

Microsoft's Windows derives its appearance either from the Apple Macintosh or from the Alto, an experimental desktop computer system developed in the late '70s at Xerox PARC. This is, however, a distinction without a difference, since the Macintosh was derived directly from the Alto.

Xerox PARC and the Alto contributed many significant innovations to the vernacular of desktop computing. These include several things we now regard as commonplace: the mouse, the rectangular window, the scrollbar, the pushbutton, the "desktop metaphor," object-oriented programming, pulldown menus and Ethernet.

PARC's effect on the industry and contemporary computing was profound. Both Steve Jobs and Bill Gates, chairmen of

Apple Computer and Microsoft, respectively, saw the Alto at PARC and were indelibly impressed.

Xerox tried to commercialize the Alto with a computer system called Star, but it was expensive, complex, agonizingly slow and a commercial failure. The brain trust at PARC, realizing that Xerox had blown an opportunity of legendary proportions, began an exodus that greatly enriched other software companies, particularly Apple and Microsoft.

Steve Jobs and his PARC refugees immediately tried to duplicate the Alto/Star with the Lisa. In many ways they succeeded, including copying the Star's failure to deal with reality. The Lisa was remarkable, accessible, exciting, too expensive and frustratingly slow. Even though it was a decisive commercial failure, it ignited the imagination of many people in the small but booming microcomputer industry.

Bill Gates was less impressed by the sexy "graphicalness" of the Alto/Star than he was by the more systemic advantages of an object-oriented presentation and communication model. Software produced by Microsoft in the early eighties, notably the spreadsheet Multiplan (the forerunner of Excel), reflected this thinking.

Steve Jobs wasn't deterred by the failure of the Lisa. He was convinced that its lack of success was due to compromises in its design and that PARC's vision of a truly graphical personal computer was an idea whose time had come. He added to his cadre of PARC refugees by raiding Apple's various departments for skilled and energetic individuals, then set up a "skunk works" to develop a commercially viable incarnation of the Alto. The result was the legendary Macintosh, a machine that has had enormous influence on our computing technology, design and culture. The Mac single-handedly brought an awareness of design and aesthetics to the industry. It not only raised the standards for user-friendliness, but it also enfranchised a whole population of skilled individuals from disparate fields who were previously locked out of computing because of the industry's self-absorption in techno-trivia.

The almost-religious aura surrounding the Macintosh was also associated with many aspects of the Mac's user interface. The pull-down menus, metaphors, dialog boxes, rectangular overlapping windows and other elements all became part of the mystique. Unfortunately, because its design has acquired these heroic proportions, its failings have often gone unexamined.

PARC's Principles

One of the ideas that emerged from PARC was the visual metaphor. At PARC, the global visual metaphor was considered critical to the user's ability to understand the system, and thus critical to the success of the product and its concept. In the last chapter I wrote at length about the problems of such metaphoric design.

Modes

Another principle associated with the modern GUI is the notion that modes are bad. A **mode** is a state the program can enter where the effects of a user's action changes from the norm—essentially a behavioral detour.

For example, older programs would demand that you shifted into a special state to enter records, then shift into another state to print them out. These behavioral states are modes, and they can be extremely confusing and frustrating. Former PARC staffer and current Chief Scientist at Apple, Larry Tesler, was an early advocate of eliminating modes from software and was pictured in an influential magazine wearing a T-shirt with the bold legend "Don't mode me in." His license plate reads "NOMODES." In a command-line environment, modes are indeed poison. However, in the object-verb world of a GUI, they aren't inherently bad. Unfortunately, the don't-mode-me-in principle has become an unquestioned part of our design vernacular.

Arguably, the most influential program on the Macintosh was MacPaint, a program with a thoroughly modal interface. This program enables the user to draw pixel-by-pixel on the computer screen. The user selects one tool from a palette of a dozen or so and then draws on the screen with it. Each tool is a mode, because it restricts the program to behave in one way. When a tool is selected, the behavior of the program conforms, modally, to the attributes of that tool.

Of course, the PARC researchers weren't wrong, just misunderstood. The user interface benefits of MacPaint compared with contemporary programs were great, but they didn't accrue from its imagined modelessness. Rather, they resulted from the ease with which the user could see which mode the program was in and the effortlessness of changing that mode.

Generally, modes based on the implementation model are confusing modes. "Edit" mode versus "Print" mode is convenient only for the program, not the user. But modes based on the user's mental model are often harmless. The "Spray can" mode or the "Paint brush" mode, for example.

Overlapping Windows

Another Mac fundamental that emerged from PARC (and which has metasta-sized in Microsoft Windows) is the idea of overlapping rectangular windows. The rectangular theme of modern GUIs is so dominating and omnipresent that it is somehow seen as vital to the success of visual interaction. Actually, it is a by-product of the technology: of our TV-screen-like video display terminals. They are excellent devices for showing rectangles, but much less efficient for manipulating non-orthogonal shapes. Rectangles are an effect rather than a cause of GUI design.

Overlapping windows demonstrated clearly that there are other, and better, ways to transfer control between concurrently running programs than typing in obscure commands.

Overlapping rectangular windows were intended to represent overlapping sheets of paper on the user's desktop. Okay, I'll buy that, but why? The stated reason is that it makes it easy to see which programs are running and to shift between them, but if this were true, Microsoft wouldn't be offering us the button-lined, program-changer tool called the Startbar in Windows 95. The overlapping window *concept* is good, but its execution is impractical in the real world. The number of pixels on today's video screens is way too small and users can't afford to waste them. Leaving an edge of one application's rectangle peeking out from behind the active window is an egregious waste of precious pixels.

The overlapping-sheets-of-paper metaphor starts to suffer when you get three or more applications on the screen—it just doesn't scale up well. The idiom has other problems, too. A user who clicks the mouse just one pixel away from where he thought he was can find his program disappearing, to be replaced by another one. User testing at Microsoft has shown that a typical user might launch the same word processor several times in the mistaken belief that he has somehow "lost" the program and must start over.

Part of the confusion regarding overlapping windows comes from several other idioms that happen to be implemented using an overlapping window. The familiar dialog box is one, as are all menus and tool palettes. Such overlapping within a single application is completely natural and a well-formed idiom. It even has a faint metaphoric trace: that of your faithful secretary handing you an important note.

We have windows largely because rectangular objects are very easy to draw and to manage on a raster scan device—a video screen. We have rectangular windows because they are the easiest to program, not because they offer cognitive superiority or information-management leverage.

In the grand tradition of focusing on a trivial aspect of the new PARC GUI, Bill Gates named his hastily cobbled together response to the Macintosh's success "Windows." Ever since then, the eponymous rectangle has dominated the development of our commercial products. It has been taken for granted in many circles that would otherwise be questioning such accidental dominance.

Tiling

The first version of Microsoft Windows diverged somewhat from the pattern established by Xerox and Apple. Instead of using overlapping rectangular windows to represent the overlapping sheets of paper on one's desktop, Windows 1.0 relied on what was called "tiling" to allow the user to have more than one application on screen at a time. Tiling meant that applications would divide up the available pixels in a uniform, rectilinear tessellation, evenly parsing out the available space to running programs. I suspect that tiling was invented as an idealistic way to solve the orientation and navigation problems caused by overlapping windows. Navigation with tiled windows is much easier than with overlapped ones, but the cost in pixels is horrendous. Tiling died as a mainstream idiom, although it can still be found in the most interesting places: try right clicking on the Windows 95 Startbar. No doubt tiling will stage a comeback when computer screens grow to six feet square and cost $50.

Overlapping windows fail to make it easy to navigate between multiple, running programs, so other vendors continue to search for new ways. For example, the "virtual desktop" on the UNIX-based OpenWindows platform extends the desktop to six times the size of the visible window. In the upper left corner of the screen is a small superimposed, black-and-white image of all six desktop spaces, all of which can be running different things simultaneously and each of which can have many open windows. You switch between these virtual desktops by clicking on the one you want to make active.

Microsoft braved a double-barreled breach-of-contract and patent infringement lawsuit from Apple to add overlapping to Windows 2.0. In all of this controversy, the basic problem seems to have been forgotten: How can the user easily navigate from one program to another? Multiple windows *sharing* a small screen—whether overlapping or tiled—is not a good solution. We are moving rapidly to a world of full-screen programs. Each application occupies the entire screen when it is "at bat." A tool like the Startbar borrows the minimum quantity of pixels from the running application to provide a visual method of changing the lineup. This solution is much more pixel-friendly, and the day of the overlapping main window is waning fast.

Much contemporary software design begins with the assumption that the user interface will consist of a series of overlapping windows, without modes, informed by a global metaphor. The PARC legacy is a strong one. Most of what we know about modern graphical user interface design came from these origins, whether right or wrong. But the well-tempered designer will push the myths aside and approach software design from a fresh viewpoint, using history as a guide, not as a dictator.

Windows-with-a-Small-w

Our programs are constructed of two kinds of windows: main windows and subordinate windows (like documents and dialog boxes). Determining which windows to use for a program is a primary step in determining its look and feel. If we expect to create an effective user interface, we cannot simply guess at which windows to use. We must choose them carefully and understand *why* we make our choices.

Unnecessary rooms

If we imagine our program as a house, we can picture each window as a separate room. The house itself is represented by the program's main window, and each room is a document window or dialog box. In real life, we don't add a room to our house unless it has a purpose that cannot be served by other rooms. Similarly, we shouldn't add windows to our program unless they have a special purpose that can't or shouldn't be served by existing windows.

"Purpose" is a goal-directed term. It implies that using a room is associated with a goal, but not necessarily with a particular task or function. For example, you might shake

73

someone's hand at your front door, but it will probably have quite different connotations (or goals) than shaking someone's hand in the kitchen or bedroom.

If I held out my hand and asked you to shake, you would certainly think it odd if I suddenly jerked it away and said, "Wait! Let's go into this other room to shake." It doesn't matter what room we are in, since we both understand the motivations behind the handshake, but having to move to another room to do it is incongruous. There can be no good reason for changing rooms just to shake hands because, regardless of where we are, the task can be performed just as well. It is especially ridiculous if, after shaking in the other room, we trudge back into the first room to continue what we're doing.

If you think of dialog boxes as rooms, you can easily find examples of programs that change rooms to shake hands. The WinFax program you saw back in Figure 3-2 is one. When I use the program, it is certain that I am going to send a fax, but it sends me to another room to select a previously recorded fax number, and to yet another room to record a new fax number. WinFax LITE is a one-room program, but it divides its interface into several unnecessary rooms.

A dialog box is another room. Have a good reason to go there

In most drawing programs, for example, the depth of a drop-shadow is usually set by selecting a menu item that triggers a dialog box. A winder, text field or similar gizmo on the dialog then sets the shadow depth. After the setting is made, the program returns to the main screen that contains the drawing. This sequence is so commonplace that it is completely unremarkable, and yet it is undeniably bad design. In a drawing program, changing the image is the primary task. The image is in the main window, so that's where the tools that affect it should be also. Setting the depth of a drop-shadow isn't a tangential task but one quite integral to the drawing process. If the drawing were being done with pencil on paper, the artist might bring a new tool to bear—an eraser—but he would not shift to a different table or sheet of paper just to change the depth of the drop-shadow. The drop-shadow depth could be set with a gizmo right on the toolbar, for example, or—better yet—the user could click on the shadow with the mouse and just drag it to a new position.

Putting functions in a dialog box emphasizes their separateness from the main task. Putting the drop-shadow adjustment in a dialog box works just fine, but it creates an interaction that is stilted and rough. Going into an adjacent room to shake hands works fine, too, but it is a distracting waste of effort.

From the programmer's point of view, changing the drop-shadow is a separate function, so it seems natural to treat it like one. From the user's point of view, however, it is an integral function and should be integrated into the main window.

> **Design tip:** Build function controls into the window where they are used

This is one of the most frequently violated tips in user interface design. Because the construction of programs is so function-centric, the user interface is often constructed in close parallel. Combine this with the incredible ease with which we can build dialog boxes, and the result is one (or more) dialog box per function. Our modern GUI-building tools tend to make dialogs easy to create, but adding gizmos to the surface of a document window or creating direct-manipulation idioms is generally not supported by these handy tools. The developer who wants to create a better user interface often must roll-his-own without much help from the tool vendors.

Necessary rooms

When it is time to go swimming, you'll think it odd if I offer you the crowded living room to change your clothes. Decorum and modesty are excellent reasons for you to want a separate room in which to change. It is entirely inappropriate for me not to provide a separate room when one is needed.

When I want to perform a function that is out of the normal sequence of events for a particular program, that program should provide a special place in which to perform it. For example, purging a database is not a normal activity. It involves setting up and using features and facilities that are not part of the normal operation of the database program. The more prosaic parts of the program will support daily tasks like entering and examining records, but erasing records en masse is not an everyday occurrence. The purge facility correctly belongs in a separate dialog box. It is entirely appropriate for the program to shunt me into a separate room—a window—to handle that function.

Using goal-directed thinking, we can examine each function to good effect. If the user is using a graphics program to develop a drawing, his goal is to create an appealing and effective image. All of the drawing tools are directly related to this goal, but the various pencils and sprayers and erasers are the most tightly connected functions. These tools should be intimately integrated into the workspace itself in the same way that the conventional artist will arrange his pencils, pens, knives, tweezers, erasers and other drawing equipment right on his drawing board, close at hand. The tools are ready for immediate use without having to reach far, let alone having to get up and walk into the next room. In the program, equivalent drawing tools should be arrayed on the edges of the drawing space, available with a single click of the mouse. The user shouldn't have to go to the menu or to dialog boxes to accomplish these tasks. The new Version 3 of Fractal Design Painter arranges artists' tools in trays, and lets you move the things that you use frequently to the front of the tray. While you can hide the various trays and palettes if you want, they appear as the default and are part of the main drawing window. They can be positioned anywhere on the window, as well. And if you create a brush that is, for example, thin charcoal in a particular shade of red that you're going to need again, you simply "tear it off" the palette and place it wherever you want on your workspace—just like laying that charcoal in the tray on your easel. This tool selection design closely mimics the way we manipulate tools while working with most software.

If the user decides to import a piece of clip art, the function is still closely related to the goal of ending up with a good drawing, but the tools to be used are different and somewhat unrelated to drawing. Clip art is usually held in a directory of pre-recorded art and may include a facility for previewing and selecting the desired piece. The clip art directory is clearly not congruent with the user's goal of drawing—it is only a means to an end. The conventional artist probably does not keep a book of clip art right on his drawing board, but you can expect that it is close by, probably on a bookshelf adjacent to the drawing board and available without even getting up. In the program, the clip art facility should be very easy to access but, because it involves a whole suite of tools that aren't normally needed, should be placed in a separate facility: a dialog box.

When the user is done creating the artwork, he has now achieved his initial goal of creating an effective image. At this point, his goals change. His new goal is to preserve the picture, protect it, and communicate with it. The need for pens and pencils is over. The need for clip art is over. Leaving these tools behind now is no hardship. The conventional artist would now unpin the drawing from his board, take it into the hall and spray it with fixative, then roll it up and put it in a mailing tube. He purposely leaves behind his drawing tools—he doesn't want them affected by fixative overspray and doesn't want accidents with paint or charcoal to mar the finished work. Mailing tubes are used infrequently and are sufficiently unrelated to the drawing process that he stores them in a closet. In the software equivalent of this process, the user ends the drawing program, puts away his drawing tools, finds an appropriate place on the hard disk to store the image, and sends it to someone else via electronic mail. These functions are clearly separated from the drawing process by the goals of the user and are well-suited to residing in their own dialog box.

By examining the user's goals, we are naturally guided to an appropriate form for the program. Instead of merely putting every function in a dialog box, we can see that some functions shouldn't be enclosed in a dialog at all, others should be put into a dialog that is integral to the main body of the interface, and still other functions should be completely removed from the program.

Windows pollution

Some designers take the approach that each dialog box should embody a single function. It is unclear to me why they think this. What they end up with is what some call **windows pollution**.

Achieving many user goals involves executing a series of functions. If there is a single dialog box for each function, things can quickly get visually crowded and navigationally confusing. The CompuServe Navigator (Version 1.0.1) program, shown in Figure 7-1, is a case in point.

Adding a squirt of oil to my bicycle makes it pedal easier, but it doesn't mean that dumping a gallon of oil all over it will make it pedal itself. It seems to me as though the designer of Navigator was on a mission to put more windows in our lives in the mistaken belief that windows are inherently good. He certainly

A gallon of oil won't make
a bicycle pedal itself

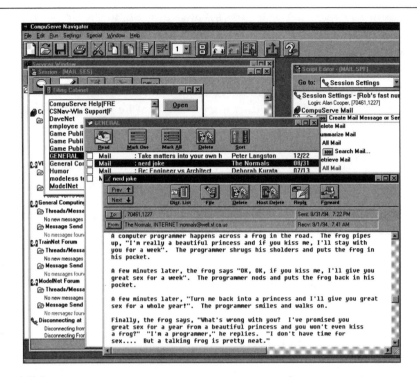

Figure 7-1

Version 1.0.1 of CompuServe Navigator suffers from tragic windows pollution. Just normal downloading of my mail requires that three windows be open. To examine a filed message demands that I open three more windows in turn. First, I get the "Filing Cabinet"; then I call up the "GENERAL" window. Finally, I can open a particular mail message in its own separate window. This is all one integral function and should occupy one integral window. But the worst is yet to come: I must put each window away separately in the reverse order of opening them.

succeeded in putting lots of windows in my life, but he didn't make things any better.

From the user's point of view, examining a saved piece of email is not three functions, but one. One dialog would not only be perfectly sufficient to accomplish this task, it would also more closely correspond to the user's goal of "viewing an email." It would also correspond more closely to the user's mental model of what is happening inside the computer. The designer has instead faithfully rendered the actual processing to the user, sort of like forcing the driver to turn two steering wheels, one for each front wheel, instead of combining the two functions into a single, conceptual whole.

A much better solution to the Navigator problem would have been to create a single "mail" box, with tools strategically positioned along the top row—a toolbar would be perfect—for managing searches. Intermediate results of the search could be shown in the window along with the final message itself. One goal—finding and reading a message—should be implemented as one dialog box.

There is no way to show the connections between lots of windows, so don't create lots of windows. Modal dialogs, however, always get you back immediately to the point of departure, so they don't count against you. This is a particularly annoying problem with Visual Basic (VB) where it is easy to create "forms." Forms are independent, top-level windows. In terms of behavior, they are the same as modeless dialog boxes. Creating applications as collections of several modeless dialog boxes is a questionable strategy that was never very common until VB made it easy to do. And, as I've said before, just because it's easy to do doesn't mean it is good design.

Each added window contributes more to the user's burden of window management excise. This overhead can grow to be really obnoxious if the program is used daily. If your program has a couple of dozen windows because you honestly feel that each of those windows moves the user towards that many different goals, then you should divide up your program into several smaller ones, each one true to its own goal. A program shouldn't have more than two or three goals, which means it shouldn't have more than two or three windows.

A VB programmer once explained to me proudly that his program was especially difficult to design because it had 57 forms. No program can be used effectively with 57 forms. Each form may be excellent in its own right, but collectively, it's simply too many. It's like saying you're going to taste 57 vintage Chardonnays at a sitting, or test-drive 57 sedans on Saturday.

Lord of the Files

If you have ever tried to teach your Mom how to use a computer, you will know that "difficult" doesn't really do the problem justice. Things start out all right: you fire up the word processor and key in a letter. She's with you all the way. When you are finally done, you press the Close button and up pops that mutant ninja turtle of a dialog box asking "Do you want to save changes?" and you and Mom hit the wall together. She looks at you and asks, "What does this mean? What changes? Is everything OK?" How can you answer her?

The tragedy of the file system

The part of modern computer systems that is the most difficult to understand is the file system, the facility that stores programs and data files on disk. Telling the uninitiated about disks is very difficult. The difference between "main memory" and "disk storage" is not clear to most people. Unfortunately, the way we design our software forces users—even your Mom—to know the difference. Every program exists in two places at once: in memory and on disk. The same is true of every file, but many users never quite grasp the difference. When that "Save Changes?" dialog box, shown in Figure 8-1, comes up, they just suppress a twinge of fear and confusion and press the YES button out of habit. A dialog box that is always answered the same way is a redundant dialog box that should be eliminated.

The Save Changes dialog box is based on a bad assumption. The very presence of the dialog assumes that saving and not saving are equally probable. The dialog gives equal weight to these two options, even though the YES button is pressed orders of magnitude more frequently than the NO button. As I discuss in Chapter 11, this is a case of putting might on will. The user *might* say no, but the user *will* almost always say yes.

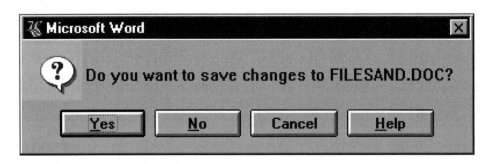

Figure 8-1

This is the question Word asks me when I close a file after I have edited it. Yes, of course I want to save it; otherwise, I wouldn't have made the changes in the first place. The origin of this dialog box is not the user's mental model, but rather the programmer's manifestation of the implementation model. In other words, the physical characteristics of the disk system are imposed on the user's work habits. This dialog is so unexpected for new users that they often say "No" inadvertently.

There is another odd thing about the dialog, and Mom will probably wonder about it. Why does it ask about saving changes when you are all done? Why didn't it ask when you actually made them? The connection between closing a document and saving changes isn't all that natural, even though we power-users have gotten quite familiar with it.

Mom is thinking "If I didn't want those changes, I would have undone them long ago." To her, the question is absurd. The program issues the dialog box when the user requests CLOSE or QUIT because that is the time when it has to reconcile the differences between the copy of the document in memory with the copy on disk. The way the technology actually implements the facility associates changes with the CLOSE and QUIT operations, but the user doesn't naturally see the connection. When we leave a room, we don't consider discarding all of the changes we made while we were there. When we put a book back on the shelf, we don't first erase any comments we wrote in the margins.

Computer geeks are very familiar with the connection between saving changes and closing or quitting. They don't want to lose this ability because it is familiar to them, but familiarity is a really bad design rationale. We don't want to keep repairing our car just because we are familiar with the shop. We don't want to keep getting root canals just because we are familiar with the drill.

As experienced users, we have learned to use this dialog box for purposes for which it was never intended. There is no other easy way to undo massive amounts of changes, so we just use the Save Changes dialog and answer it with a NO. If you discover yourself making big changes to the wrong file, you use this dialog as a kind of escape valve to return things to the status quo.

The problems caused by disks

The computer's file system is the tool it uses to manage data and programs stored on disk. This means the big hard disks where most of your information resides, but it also includes your floppy drives and your CD-ROM if you have one. The File Manager program in Windows 3.x and the Explorer in Windows 95 graphically represent the file system. Without a doubt, the file system—and the disk storage facility it manages—is the primary cause of disaffection with computers for non-computer-professionals.

Disks and files make users crazy

Even though the file system is an internal facility that shouldn't—by all rights—even affect the user, it creates a large problem because the influence of the file system on the interface of most programs is very deep. The most intractable problems facing user interface designers usually concern the file system and its demands. It affects our menus, our dialogs, even the procedural framework of our programs, and this influence is likely to continue indefinitely unless we make a concerted effort to stop it.

Currently, most software treats the file system in much the same way that the operating system shell does (Explorer, File Manager). This is tantamount to you dealing with your car the same way your mechanic does. Even though this approach is tragically bad, it is an established, de facto standard and there is considerable resistance to improving it.

Following the implementation model

Before I go any further, let me make clear that the file systems on modern personal computer operating systems, like Windows 95, are technically excellent. I have no gripe with the way they are implemented. The problem stems from the simple mistake of rendering that implementation model to the user.

The implementation model of the file system runs contrary to the mental model almost all users bring to it. In other words, they picture files or documents as typical documents in the real world, and they imbue them with the behavioral characteristics of those real objects. In the simplest terms, users visualize two salient facts about all documents: First, there is only one document, and second, it belongs to the user. The file system's implementation model violates both of these rules: There are always at least two copies of the document, and both belong to the program.

Saying that someone is "computer literate" is really a euphemism meaning that he has been indoctrinated and trained in the irrational and counter-intuitive way that file systems work, and once you have been properly subverted into thinking like a computer nerd, the obvious ridiculousness of the way the file system presents itself to the user doesn't seem so foolish.

Every data file, every document and every program, while in use by the computer, exists in a minimum of two places at once: on disk and in main memory. The user, though, imagines his document as a book on a shelf. Let's say it is a journal he is keeping. Occasionally, it comes down off the shelf to have some words added to it. There is only one journal, and it either resides on the shelf or it resides in the user's hands. On the computer, the disk drive is the shelf, and main memory is the place where editing takes place, equivalent to the user's hands. But in the computer world, the journal doesn't come "off the shelf." Instead a copy is made, and that *copy* is what resides inside the computer. As the user makes changes to the document, he is actually making changes to the in-memory copy, while the original remains untouched on disk. When the user is done and closes the document, the program is faced with a decision. It must decide whether to replace the original on disk with the changed copy from memory. From the programmer's point of view, equally concerned with all possibilities, this choice could go either way. From the software's implementation model point of view, the choice is the same either way. However, from the user's point of view, there is rarely a decision to be made at all. He made his changes already; now he is just putting the document away. If this were happening with a paper journal in the physical world, the user would have pulled it off the shelf, pencilled in some additions, and is now replacing it on the shelf. It's as if the shelf suddenly spoke up, asking if he really wants to keep those changes!

Right now, the seriously computer-holic readers are beginning to squirm in their seats. They are thinking that I'm treading on holy ground, and a pristine copy on disk is a wonderful thing and that I had better not be advocating getting rid of it. Relax! As I said before, there is nothing wrong with our file systems. I am only advocating that we hide its existence from the user. We can still offer to him all of the advantages of that extra copy on disk without exploding his mental model. I'll show you how.

Dispensing with the disk model

If we begin to render the file system according to the user's mental model, we achieve a significant advantage. The primary one is that we can all teach our Moms how to use computers. We won't have to answer her challenging questions about the inexplicable behavior of the interface. We can show her the program and explain how it allows her to work on the document and, upon completion, she can store the document on the disk as though it were a journal on a shelf. Our sensible explanation won't be interrupted by that "Save changes?" dialog. Not to put too fine a point on this, but I'm just using Mom as a surrogate representing the mass market of computer buyers.

The other big advantage is that software user interface designers won't have to incorporate clumsy file-system awareness into their products. We can structure the commands in our programs according to the goals of the user instead of according to the needs of the operating system.

We no longer need to call the left-most menu the "File" menu. This older nomenclature is a bold reminder of how the technology pokes through the facade of our programs. We can label this menu after the type of document we are processing—for example, we can call it "Spreadsheet," "Invoice," or "Picture." Alternatively, we can give it a more generic name like "Document," which is a reasonable choice for horizontal programs like word processors or spreadsheets.

Changing the name and contents of the "File" menu violates an established standard. I recognize the impact of this proposal and don't make it lightly. I have tremendous respect for standards, unless they are wrong. This one is wrong, and it's existence makes life more difficult than it has to be for every user of computers, particularly newcomers and casual users. The benefits will far outweigh any dislocation the change might cause. There will certainly be an initial cost as experienced users get used to the new presentation, but it will be far less than you might suppose. This is because these power-users have already shown their ability and tolerance by learning the implementation model. For them, learning the better model will be a slam-dunk, and there will be no loss of functionality.

The advantage for new users will be immediate and big. We computer professionals forget how tall the mountain is once we've climbed it, but everyday newcomers approach the base of this Everest of knowledge we sit atop and are severely discouraged. Anything we can do to lower the height can make a big difference, and this step removes a considerable obstacle.

Designing software with the proper model

Properly designed software will always treat documents as single instances, never as a copy on disk and a copy in memory. I call this the **unified file model**.

Saving

One of the most important functions every computer user must learn is how to "save." Invoking this function means taking whatever changes the user has made to the in-memory copy and writing them onto the on-disk copy of the document. In the unified model, we abolish all user-interface recognition of the two copies, so the "save" function disappears completely from the mainstream interface. Of course, that doesn't mean that it disappears from the program. It is still a very necessary operation.

The program will automatically save the document. At the very least, when the user is done with the document and requests the close function, the program will merely go ahead and write the changes out to disk without stopping to ask for confirmation with the "Save Changes" dialog box.

In a perfect world, that would be enough, but computers and software can crash, power can fail, and other unpredictable, catastrophic events can conspire to erase your work. If the power fails before you have pressed CLOSE, all of your changes will be lost as the memory containing them scrambles. The original copy on disk will be all right, but hours of work can still be lost. To keep this from happening, the program must also save the document at intervals during the user session. Ideally, the program will save every single little change as soon as the user makes it. In other words, after each keystroke. For most programs on modern computers, this is quite feasible. Only certain programs—word processors leap to mind—would find difficulty with this level of saving (but the solution would still not be impossible). Most documents can be saved to the hard disk in just a fraction of a second, so generally this is not a problem. Still, this is a sensitive area, because the program will hesitate noticeably in a very disturbing way. Word has a facility for automatically saving files to disk, and I never use it for that reason. The problem is caused by the save facility's logic, not because the principle of automatic saving is bad. Word automatically saves the file according to a countdown clock, and you can set the delay to any number of minutes. If you ask for a save every two minutes, for example, after precisely two minutes the program stops accepting your input to write your changes out to disk, regardless of what you are doing at the time. If you are typing when the save begins, it just clamps shut in a very realistic and disconcerting imitation of a broken program. It is a very unpleasant experience. If the algorithm would pay attention to the user instead of the clock, the problem would disappear. Nobody types continuously. Everybody stops to gather his thoughts, or flip a page, or take a sip of coffee. All the program needs to do is wait until the user stops typing for a couple of seconds and *then* save.

This automatic saving every few minutes and at CLOSE time will be adequate for everybody except the really twisted computer-freaks who have been using computers since Bill Gates was just a thousandaire. I include myself in this group. I'm so paranoid about my computer crashing and losing data that I habitually press the CTRL-S key after every paragraph I type, and sometimes after every sentence. (Pressing CTRL-S is the keyboard accelerator for the SAVE function.) I'll typically save a document—like a chapter in this book—more than 1,000* times before it's done! There is no way in the world I would even use a program that didn't provide such manual save capabilities, and all programs should have them. I just don't think that my compulsive behavior should be forced on new or occasional users who are writing the occasional letter or spreadsheet and haven't begun writing a book yet.

---

* Using the revision number feature of Microsoft Word, I print the exact number of saves at the bottom of all of my drafts. I'm not exaggerating.

Right now in Word, the SAVE function is prominently placed in-your-face on the primary program menu. The SAVE dialog is forced on all users when they ask to close the document or to QUIT or EXIT the program. These artifacts must go away, but the SAVE functionality can remain in place exactly as it is now.

Closing

There is no inherent connection between closing and saving in my unified model because there is no concept of saving.

We computer geeks are conditioned to think that CLOSE is the time and place for abandoning unwanted changes if we made some error or were just what-if-ing. This is not correct, though, because the proper time to reject changes is when the changes are made. We even have a well-established idiom to support this. The UNDO function is the proper facility for eradicating changes. We have bent and contorted our thinking so much to accommodate the implementation model that I often hear people bleat in protest over losing the ability to refuse a request to "save changes."

In Chapter 30, "Undo," I'll talk about some more sophisticated variants of undo that allow us to create multiple versions of a document. Currently, savvy computer users who understand the technology can accomplish this by working cleverly with the file system. A better interface could offer these desirable features directly and explicitly.

When you answer YES to the Save changes dialog, virtually every program then presents you with the "Save As" dialog box. A typical example is shown in Figure 8-2.

Neither the typical user nor the unified file model recognizes the concept of manual saving, so, from their point of view, the name of this dialog box doesn't make much sense. Functionally, this dialog offers the user two things. It lets you name your file, and it lets you choose which directory you wish to place it in. Both of these functions demand intimate knowledge of the file system. The user must know how to formulate a file name and how to navigate through the directory tree. I know of many users who have mastered the name portion but who have completely given up on understanding the directory tree. They put all their documents in whatever directory the program chooses for a default. All of their files associated with a particular program are stored in a single directory. Occasionally, some action will cause the program to forget its default directory, and these users must call in an expert to find their files for them. My next door neighbor, Bill, calls me about every six months to help him find his Lotus 1-2-3

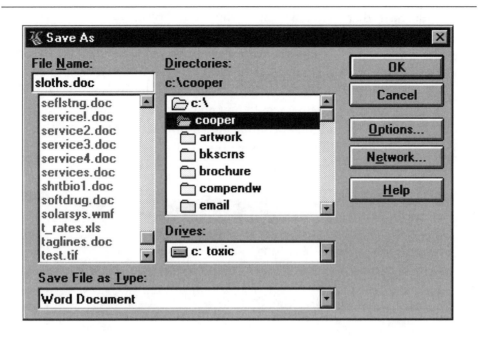

Figure 8-2

The Save As dialog box offers two functions: It lets you name your file, and it lets you place it in the directory of your choice. From the user's perspective, remember, he has no concept of "saving," so the name of this dialog is incorrect. Also, if a dialog enables me to name and place a document, shouldn't it also allow me to rename and replace the document? I certainly think so.

files. The first time he called, I asked him where he normally keeps his spreadsheets. He answered innocently "In 1-2-3." Bill's mental model is very different from the software's implementation model and, ultimately, Bill is right.

The Save As dialog needs to decide what its purpose is. If it exists to name and place files, then it does a very bad job of it. Once the user has named and placed a file, he cannot then change its name or directory. At least he can't with this dialog that purports to offer naming and placing privileges. Nor with any other tool in the application itself.

Beginners are out of luck, but experienced users learn the hard way that they can close the document, change to the Explorer, rename the file, return to the application, summon the Open File dialog, and reopen the document. In case you were wondering, the Open File dialog doesn't allow renaming or repositioning either.

Forcing the user to go to the Explorer to rename the document is a minor hardship, but therein lies a hidden trap; its teeth sharp and its spring strong. The bait is the fact that Windows easily supports several applications running simultaneously. Attracted by this feature, the user tries to rename the file in the Explorer without first closing the document in the application. This very reasonable action triggers the trap, and the steel jaws clamp down hard on his leg. He is rebuffed with a rude error message box shown in Figure 8-3. He didn't first close the document—how would he know? Trying to rename an open file is a sharing violation, and the operating system summarily rejects it with a truly frightening and unhelpful error message box.

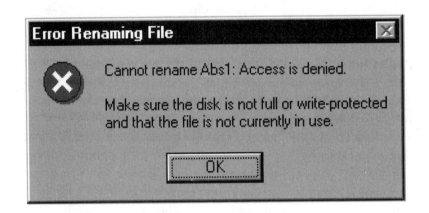

Figure 8-3

If the user attempts to rename a file using the Explorer while it is still being edited by Word, the Explorer is too stupid to get around the problem and make it work. It is also too stupid to figure out what happened so it can report it correctly. It is also too rude to be nice about it, and it puts up this frightening error message box. Rebuffed by both the program and the Explorer, it is easy for a new user to imagine that a document cannot be renamed at all.

The innocent user is merely trying to name his document, and he finds himself lost in an archipelago of operating-system arcana. Ironically, the one program that has both the authority and the responsibility to change the document's name while it is still open is the application itself, yet it refuses to even try.

Archiving

There is no explicit function for making a copy of, or archiving, a document. The user must accomplish this with the Save As dialog, and doing so is as clear as mud. Even if there were a "Copy" command, users visualize this function in different ways. If we are working, for example, on a document called "Alpha," some people imagine that we would create a file called "Copy of Alpha" and store it away. Others imagine that we put Alpha away and continue work on Copy of Alpha.

I suspect that the latter option will only occur to those who are already experienced with the implementation model of file systems. That is, of course, how we would do it today with the Save As dialog: you have already saved the file as Alpha; then you explicitly call up the Save As dialog and change the name. Alpha will be closed and put away on disk, and the new copy will be the version being edited. This action makes very little sense from the single-document viewpoint of the world, and it also offers a really nasty trap for the user.

Here is the completely reasonable scenario that leads to trouble: Let's say that I have been editing Alpha for the last twenty minutes and now wish to make an archival copy of it on disk so I can make some big, but experimental, changes to the original. I call up the Save As dialog box and change the file name to "New Alpha." The program puts Alpha away on disk leaving me to edit New Alpha. Ahhh, but Alpha was never "Saved," so it gets written to disk without the changes I made in the last twenty minutes! Those changes only exist in the "New Alpha" copy that is currently in memory—in the program. As I begin cutting and pasting in New Alpha—trusting that my handiwork is backed up by "Alpha"—I am actually trashing the sole copy of this information.

Everybody knows that you can use a hammer to drive a screw or a pliers to bash in a nail, but any skilled craftsperson knows that using the wrong tool for the job will eventually catch up with you. The tool will break or the work will be hopelessly ruined. The Save As dialog is the wrong tool for making and managing copies, and it is the user who will eventually have to pick up the pieces caused by the developer's laziness.

Unify the file model

The application program refuses to rename and reposition the file out of respect for the file system. The file system is the facility whose job it is to manage information that is not in main memory, and it does so by maintaining a second copy on disk. This method is correct, but it is an implementation detail that only confuses the user. Application software should conspire with the file system to hide this unsettling detail from the user.

If the file system is going to show the user a file that cannot be changed because it is in use by another program, the file system should indicate this to the user.

Showing the file name in red, or with a special icon next to it would be suffi-cient. A new user might still get that awful message in Figure 8-3, but at least some visual clues would be present to show him that there is a *reason* why that error cropped up.

Not only are there two copies of all data files but, when they are running, there are two copies of all programs. When I go to the Startbar's Start menu and launch my word processor, a button corresponding to Word appears on the Startbar. But if I return to the Start menu, Word is still there! From the user's point of view, I have pulled my hammer out of my toolbox, only to find that my hammer is still in my toolbox!

I'm not saying that this should not be the case. After all, one of the great strengths of the computer is its ability to have multiple copies of software run-ning simultaneously. I do think that the software should help the user to under-stand this very non-intuitive action, however. Maybe the Start menu could make some reference to the already-running program.

Document management

The established standard suite of file management for most applications con-sists of the Save As dialog, the Save Changes dialog, and the Open File dialog. Collectively, these dialogs are, as I've shown, confusing for some tasks, and completely incapable for others. Here is how I would design an application that really managed documents according to the user's mental model.

Besides rendering the document as a single entity, there are several goal-directed functions that the user may need, and each one should have its own corresponding function.

- Creating a copy of the document

- Creating a milestone copy of the document

- Naming and renaming the document

- Placing and repositioning the document

- Specifying the stored format of the document

- Reversing some changes

- Abandoning all changes

Creating a copy of the document

This should be an explicit function called "Make Snapshot Copy." The word "snapshot" makes it clear that the copy is identical to the original, while also making it clear that the copy is not tied to the original in any way. That is, subsequent changes to the original will have no effect on the copy. The new copy should be given a name with a standard form like "Copy of Alpha," where "Alpha" is the name of the original document. If there is already a document with that name, the new copy should be named "Second Copy of Alpha." The copy should be placed in the same directory as the original.

It is very tempting to envision the dialog box that accompanies this command, but there should be no such interruption. The program should take its action quietly and efficiently and sensibly, without badgering the user with silly questions. Make a copy. In the user's mind, it is a simple command. If there are any anomalies, the program should make a constructive decision on its own authority.

Naming and renaming the document

The name of the document should be shown right on the application's toolbar. If the user decides to rename the document, he can just click on it and edit it in place. What could be simpler and more direct than that?

Placing and repositioning the document

Most documents that are edited already exist. They are opened, rather than created from scratch. This means that their position in the file system is already established. Although we think of establishing the home directory for a document at either the moment of creation or the moment of first saving, neither of these events is particularly meaningful outside the implementation model. The new file should be put somewhere reasonable where the user can find it again.

If the user wants to explicitly place the document somewhere in the file-system hierarchy, he can request this function from the menu. A relative of the Save As dialog appears with the current document highlighted. The user can then move the file to any desired location. Essentially, all files are placed automatically by the program, and this dialog is used only to reposition them.

Specifying the stored format of the document

There is an additional function implemented on the Save As dialog in Figure 8-2. The combobox at the bottom of the dialog allows the user to specify the physical format of the file. This function should not be located here. By tying the physical format to the act of saving, the user is confronted with additional, unnecessary complexity. Saving should be a very simple act. In Word, if the user innocently changes the format, both the save function and any subsequent close action are accompanied by a frightening and unexpected confirmation box.

From the user's point of view, the physical format of the document—whether it is rich text, ASCII, or Word format, for example—is a characteristic of the document rather than of the disk file, so specifying the format shouldn't be associated with the act of saving the file to disk. It belongs more properly in a "Document Properties" dialog.

Overriding the physical format of a file is a rare occurrence. Saving a file is a very common occurrence. These two functions should not be combined.

The physical format of the document should be specified by way of a small dialog box callable from the main menu. This dialog box should have cautions built into its interface to make it clear to the user that the function can involve significant data loss.

Reversing some changes

If the user inadvertently makes changes to the document that must be reversed, the tool already exists for correcting these actions: undo. The file system should not be called in as a surrogate for undo. The file system may be the mechanism for supporting the function, but that doesn't mean it should be rendered to the user in those terms. The concept of going directly to the file system to undo changes merely undermines the undo function.

The milestone function (description follows) tells how a file-centric vision of undo can be implemented so that it works well with the unified file model.

Abandoning all changes

It is not uncommon for the user to decide that he wants to discard all of the changes he has made since opening or creating a document, so this action should be explicitly supported. Rather than forcing the user to understand the file system to achieve his goal, a simple "Abandon" function on the main menu would suffice. Because this function involves significant data loss, it should be protected by clear warning signs. Additionally, making this function undoable for a week or two would be relatively easy to implement and appreciated more than you might imagine.

Creating a milestone copy of the document

Making a milestone is very similar to using the copy command.

The difference between them is that the milestone copy is managed by the application after it is made. The user can call up a "Milestone" dialog box that lists each milestone copy along with various statistics about it, like the time it was recorded and its length. With a click, the user can select a milestone copy and, by doing so, immediately return to it as the active document. The version that was current at the time of the reversion will be milestoned itself, for example, under the name "Displaced by Milestone of Alpha 12/17/97, 13:53."

The new menu

Our new File menu now looks like the one shown in Figure 8-4.

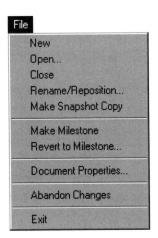

Figure 8-4

The revised File menu now reflects the user's mental model instead of the programmer's implementation model. There is only one file and the user owns it. If he wants, he can clone it, discard any changes he has made to it or change its format. He doesn't have to worry about the copy in RAM and the copy on disk.

"New" and "Open" function as before, but "Close" will just quietly close the document without a dialog box or any fuss, after assuring that it is completely saved. "Rename/Reposition..." brings up a small dialog box that lets the user rename the current file and/or move it to another directory. "Make Snapshot Copy" quietly creates a new file that is a copy of the current document. "Make Milestone" does the same thing, except that the program manages these copies by way of the dialog box summonable with the "Revert to Milestone" item. "Document Properties" also brings up a dialog box that lets the user change the physical format of the document. The final item is "Abandon Changes" and it discards all changes made to the document since it was opened or created.

File menu?

Of course, now that we are manifesting a monolithic model of storage instead of the bifurcated implementation model of disk and RAM, we no longer need to call the left-most menu the "File" menu. This older nomenclature is a bold reminder of how the technology has been inflicted on the user instead of the user's model being reflected in the technology. There are two pretty good alternatives to solving this problem.

As I said earlier, we can label the menu after the type of document we are processing. For example, a spreadsheet might label its left-most menu "Sheet." An invoicing program might label it "Invoice." I designed a patent management program for a client, and in that program we called it "Patent."

Alternatively, we can give the left-most menu a more generic label like "Document." This is certainly a reasonable choice for broad programs like word processors and spreadsheets, but is less appropriate for narrower programs like the patent manager.

Conversely, those few programs that do represent the contents of disks as files—generally operating system shells and utilities—*should* have a "File" menu, because they are addressing files with a studied ignorance of their contents.

How did we get here?

If you are still not convinced that disks and their file system are the cause of great user interface confusion, I'd like to show how our disks came to have such a profound effect on our software.

From the user's point of view, there is no reason for disks to exist. From the computer engineer's point of view, there are three:

1. Disks are cheaper than solid-state memory.

2. Once written to, disks don't forget when the power is off.

3. Disks provide a physical means of moving information from one computer to another.

Reasons number two and three are certainly useful but are not the exclusive domain of disks. Other technologies work as well or better. There are varieties of RAM that don't forget their data when the power is turned off. CMOS memory is solid state, yet it retains its setting without external power.

Networks and phone lines can be used to physically transport data to other sites, often more easily than with removable disks.

Reason number one—cost—is the *real* reason why disks exist. CMOS is a lot more expensive than disk drives. Reliable, high-bandwidth networks haven't been around as long as removable disks, and they are still more expensive.

Disk drives have many drawbacks when compared to RAM. Disk drives have always been much slower than solid-state memory. They are much less reliable, too, since they depend on moving parts. They consume more power and can take up more space, as well. The real whammy when it comes to disks, though, is that computers, the actual CPU, can't really read or write to them! Data must first be brought into main, solid-state memory by the CPU's helpers before the CPU can work with it. When the processor is done, the helpers must once again step in to move the data back out to the disk! This means that all processing involving disks is necessarily orders of magnitude slower and more complex than working in plain RAM.

Disks are a hack, not a design feature

The time and complexity penalty for using disks is so severe that nothing short of enormous cost-differential could compel us to rely on them. Disk drives are a cost-saving hack. Mind you, there is nothing wrong with using this sophisticated technology to save money, but keep in mind that the technology isn't there to provide us with services we couldn't get in other ways. This means that any changes we make to our interfaces to adjust to the disk technology are likely to be inappropriate from a goal-directed point of view.

So we can see that disks are not a law of nature; they are not architectural features that make computers better, more powerful, faster or easier to use. Instead, they make computers weaker, slower and more complex. They are a compromise, a dilution, an adulteration, a corruption of the pure architecture of digital computers. If early computer designers could have economically used RAM instead of disks, they would have done so without hesitation. Whatever other problems RAM exhibited could have been overcome with technologies simpler than the complexity of disk drives.

The difference between RAM and disk is merely a matter of economics, much like the way you go to a lending library instead of personally owning copies of every book. This means that wherever disk technology has left its mark on the design of our software, it has done so purely for implementation purposes and not for any goal-directed design rationale. While this difference should be of interest only to programmers, in reality, it is imposed on nearly every program and users are forced to master it. Any construction that supports disks is for the convenience of the programmer and the computer, and not to help the user.

The pervasiveness of the file system in our thinking and our design of software is as though refrigeration technology dominated the design of every room in our houses. Certainly, the invention of cheap mechanical refrigeration affected our domestic lives, but we don't turn our houses into shrines to Freon. Yet this is largely what we have done on our desktop computers.

It is one thing to weave a technology invisibly into our lives. It is another thing altogether to allow our lives to be dominated by that technology. Refrigeration plays a big part in our lives in many ways, including food preparation, the production and storage of some medicines and air conditioning, yet we don't usually find ourselves expressing our desires in terms of it. We don't go into a restaurant and say, "I'll have the salmon. It's been refrigerated, hasn't it?" We don't say, "You'll love working here, it's air conditioned." Omnipresent technologies don't have to intrude on our conscious thoughts to work well for us. Unfortunately, this realization hasn't yet dawned on the computer industry, and we remain sadly dependent on the file-system model.

The last gasp

There are only two arguments that can be mounted in favor of application software implemented in the file-system model: Our software is already designed and built that way, and users are used to it.

Neither of these arguments holds water, though. The first one is irrelevant because new programs written with a unified file model can freely coexist with the older implementation model applications. The underlying file system doesn't change at all. In much the same way that toolbars have invaded the interfaces of most Windows applications in the last few years accompanied only by cheers and encouragement, the unified file model could also be implemented.

The second argument is more insidious, because its proponents are placing the user community in front of them like a shield. What's more, if you ask the users themselves, they will reject the new solution because they abhor change, particularly when that change affects something they have already worked hard to master—like the file system. In the '80s, the Chrysler company showed car-buyers early sketches of a dramatically new automobile design: the minivan. The buyers were asked if they would be interested in this new vehicle, and the public uniformly gave a thumbs-down to the new design. Chrysler went ahead and produced the Caravan anyway, convinced that the design was superior. They were right, and those same people who rejected the design have not only made the Caravan the best-selling minivan, but have made the minivan the most popular new automotive archetype since the convertible.

People will gladly give up painful, poorly designed software for easier, better software even if they don't understand the explanations. After all, users aren't software designers and they cannot be expected to visualize the larger effect of the change. Saying that users want to keep their familiar file-system model is like saying you want to break your leg again so you can return to the hospital because the food was so good the last time you were in there.

Storage and Retrieval Systems

The document is a well-established concept in the mechanical world. It is an object that can be read by those who care to, and it often can be manipulated with writing or drawing instruments. Beyond that, a document can be transported, owned and stored. These latter qualities exist even if the former do not. In other words, I can hold or own a book on calculus even though I have never learned calculus. Our disk file systems are not so forgiving. A program can do little with a PowerPoint file, for example, unless it is intimately familiar with how to process PowerPoint slides. Our document-centric systems are really just file-centric systems and are harder to understand and use—and in some ways less powerful—than our manual systems.

Storing versus finding

In the physical world, storing and retrieving an item are inextricably linked; putting an item on a shelf (storing it) also gives us the means to find it later (retrieving it). In the digital world, the only thing linking these two concepts is our faulty thinking. Computers will enable remarkably sophisticated retrieval techniques if only we break our thinking out of its traditional box.

101

A storage system is a tool for placing goods into a repository for safekeeping. It is composed of a physical container and the tools necessary to put objects in and take them back out again.

A retrieval system is a method for finding goods in a repository. It is a logical system that allows the goods to be located according to some abstract value, like its name, position or some aspect of its contents.

As we saw in the last chapter, disks and files are usually rendered in implementation terms, rather than in accord with the user's mental model of how information is stored. This is even more true in the methods we use for *finding* information after it has been stored. This is extremely unfortunate, because the computer is the one tool capable of providing us with significantly better methods of finding information than is physically possible from mechanical systems.

In the real world of books and paper on library shelves, we have at least three indices: author, subject and title. Although our desktop computers can handle hundreds of different indices, we ignore this capability and have no indices at all pointing into the files stored on our disks. Instead, we have to remember where we put our files and what we called them before we can find them again. This omission is one of the most destructive backward steps in modern software design. This failure can be attributed to the interdependence of files and the organizational systems in which they exist, an interdependence that doesn't exist in the mechanical world.

We can own a book or a hammer without giving it a name or a permanent place of residence in our houses. A book can be identified by characteristics other than a name—a color or a shape, for example. Even if we do assign a "proper place" for a physical tool, it often resides away from that place for stretches of time. A volume may properly reside on our bookshelf, but when it is being read, it may be left on night stands and coffee tables, or stuffed into briefcases or purses, and it still serves us well. Of course, these places merely act as temporary locations for the book.

For the book or the hammer, it is important that there be a proper place for them, because that is how we find them when we need them. We can't just whistle and expect them to find us; we must know where they are, then go there and fetch them. In the physical world, the actual location of a thing is the means to finding it. In the real world, where the systems of storage and retrieval are the same, remembering where we put something—its address—is vital both to putting it away and to finding it again. When we want to find a spoon, for example, we go to the place where we keep our spoons. We don't find the spoon by referring to any inherent characteristic of the spoon itself. Similarly, when we look for a book, we either go to where we left the book, or we guess that it is stored with other books. We don't find the book by association. That is, we don't find the book by referring to its contents.

Retrieval methods

There are three fundamental ways to find a document. You can find it by remembering where you left it, which I call **positional retrieval**. You can find it by remembering its identifying name, which I call **identity retrieval**. The third method, which I call **associative retrieval**, is based on the ability to search for a document based on some inherent quality of the document itself.

For example, if I wanted to find a book with a red cover, or one that discusses light rail transit systems, or one that contains photographs of steam locomotives, or one that mentions Theodore Judah, the method I must use is associative.

Both positional and identity retrieval are methods that also function as storage systems. Associative retrieval is the one method that is not also a storage system. If our retrieval system is based solely on storage methods, we deny ourselves any associative searching and we must depend on the user's memory. He must know what information he wants and where it is stored in order to find it. To find the spreadsheet in which he calculated the amortization of his home loan, he has to know that he stored it in the directory called "home" and that it was called "amort1." If he doesn't remember either of these factoids, finding the document can become quite difficult.

The document and the system it lives in

In the physical world, a complex case like a library might have many thousands or millions of objects to store. To handle this, we assign books proper places somewhere on the shelves and then concoct other schemes for finding them based on some associative value: a characteristic of the book itself.

A book doesn't have to have a place on a shelf in order to exist. Books and the physical systems we store them in, shelves, are not physically dependent on each other. The book can just as easily exist without participating in any storage system.

A file on a disk, on the other hand, is not separate from the organizational structure of its filing system. What defines that file is not its contents but its presence in the filing system. *A disk file cannot exist outside of the filing system in which it lives.*

We can own, read and pass a book between us without ever entering it into a book filing system such as the Dewey Decimal system or a specific library. In order to own, read or pass on a computer "document," it must first be entered into the computer's file system.

There is no such concept as a collection of data—a document—other than as a participant in the host file system. The file systems in Windows, DOS, Macintosh and UNIX are the same in this respect: None support the existence of independent documents, only the existence of files tied intimately to their storage systems.

An independent book or document in the physical world doesn't need to have any identifying information; its physical presence is sufficient. Usually each book or document is given a title, but this is not a requirement for its existence. In order to be stored in a manual or electronic filing system, however, it must have a unique identifier (usually its name, though bigger collections require more specific identifiers).

Indexing

In libraries, where names can be too disparate or insufficiently unique or otherwise confusing, each book is also assigned a unique serial number, called a Dewey Decimal number. The book is then stored in sequence according to this number. This numbering scheme is very convenient for storing the books but, by itself, doesn't help in their retrieval. For that, we need a separate index: the traditional card catalog.

Libraries usually provide three indices: author, subject and title. Each index is associative, allowing the user to find the book according to an inherent property of the book other than its identifying number or its location on the shelf. When the book is entered into the library system and assigned a number, three index cards are created for the book, including all particulars and the serial number. Each card is headed by either the author's name, the subject or the title. These cards are then placed in their respective indices in alphabetical order. When you want to find a book, you look it up in one of the indices and find its number. You then find the row of shelves that contain books with numbers in the same range as your target, by examining signs. You then search those particular shelves, narrowing your view down by the lexical order of the numbers until you find the one you want.

You *actually, physically* retrieve the book by participating in the system of storage, but you *conceptually, logically* find the book you want by participating in a system of retrieval. The shelves and numbers are the storage system. The card indices are the retrieval system. You identify the desired book with one and fetch it with the other. In a typical university or professional library, customers are not allowed into the stacks. As a customer, you identify the book you want by using only the retrieval system. The librarian then fetches the book for you by participating only in the storage system. The unique serial number is the bridge between these two interdependent systems. In the physical world, both the retrieval system and the storage system may be very labor intensive. Particularly in older, non-computerized libraries, they are both inflexible. Adding a fourth index based on acquisition date, for example, would be prohibitively difficult in the library.

Conversely, it's not all that hard to add an index in the computer. Ironically, in a system where easily implementing dynamic, associative retrieval mechanisms is at last possible, we often don't implement *any* retrieval system. Astonishingly, we don't use indices at all.

In most of today's computer systems, there is no retrieval system other than the storage system. If you want to find a file on disk, you need to know its name and its place. It's as if we went into the library, burned the card catalog, and told the patrons that they could easily find what they want by just remembering the little numbers painted on the spines of the books. We have put 100% of the burden of file retrieval on the user's memory while the CPU just sits there idling, executing billions of NOP instructions.

An associative retrieval system

We have rendered the retrieval system in strict adherence to the implementation model of the storage system, ignoring the power and ease-of-use of a system for *finding* files that is distinct from the system for *keeping* files.

An associative retrieval system would enable us to find documents by their contents. For example, we could find all documents that contain the text string "superelevation." For such a search system to really be effective, it should know where all documents can be found, so the user doesn't have to say "Go look in such-and-such a directory and find all documents that mention superelevation." This system would, of course, know a little bit about the domain of its search, so it wouldn't try to search the entire Internet, for example, for "super-elevation" unless we insisted.

An associative retrieval system would also help the user create temporary or permanent groups of documents and use them as the basis for searches. For example, I frequently like to search for passages in the manuscript for this book, which is stored as dozens of small text files. I would like to first search for all documents containing the phrase "About Face" and have the program remember that set of files as the *book* set. Then, when I wanted to find the discussion of associative file retrieval systems, I could search the *book* set for occurrences of the phrase "associative" and gain the performance advantage of a restricted search without knowing anything about where my chapters were physically stored.

A well-crafted associative retrieval system would also enable the user to browse by synonym or related topics or by assigning attributes to individual documents. The user can then dynamically define sets of documents having these overlapping attributes. For example, imagine a consulting business where each potential client is sent a proposal letter. Each of these letters is different and is naturally grouped with the files pertinent to that client. However, there is a definite relationship between each of these letters because they all serve the same function: proposing a business relationship. It would be very convenient if a user could find and gather up all such proposal letters while each one can still retain its uniqueness and association with its particular client. A file system based on place—on its single storage location—must, of necessity, store each document by a single attribute rather than multiple characteristics.

The system can learn a lot about each document just by keeping its eyes and ears open. If the associative retrieval system remembered some of this information, much of the setup burden on the user would be made unnecessary. The program could, for example, easily remember such things as

- The program that created the document

- The type of document: words, numbers, tables, graphics

- The program that last opened the document

- If the document is exceptionally large or small

- If the document has been untouched for a long time

- The length of time the document was last open

- The amount of information that was added or deleted during the last edit

- Whether the document has been edited by more than one type of program

- Whether the document contains embedded objects from other programs

- Whether the document was created from scratch or cloned from another

- If the document is frequently edited

- If the document is frequently viewed but rarely edited

- Whether the document has been printed and where

- How often the document has been printed, and whether changes were made to it each time immediately before printing

- Whether the document has been faxed and to whom

- Whether the document has been emailed and to whom

The retrieval system could find documents for the user based on these facts without the user ever having to explicitly record anything in advance. Can you think of other useful attributes the system could remember?

There is nothing wrong with the disk file storage systems we have created for ourselves. The only problem is that we have failed to create disk file *retrieval* systems. Instead we hand the user the storage system and call it a retrieval system. This is like handing him a bag of groceries and calling it a gourmet dinner. There is no reason to change our file storage systems. The UNIX model is fine. Our programs can easily remember the names and locations of the files they have worked on, so they aren't the ones who need a retrieval system: That's just for us human users.

It ain't document-centric

The purveyors of GUIs, Microsoft Windows included, often allow themselves the conceit that we have a "document-centric" view of the world. It would be more accurate to say that we have a "file-centric" view of the world. Our so-called documents behave exactly like files and not much like documents.

When software vendors claim to have a "document-based" product, I interpret it to mean that their software supports documents independent of the supporting file system. None of the software I have seen does this.

Some programs, like those in Microsoft's Office suite, implement an associative searching system that operates outside of, and in parallel to, the normal file system, but it doesn't replace the need to work within the file system. Microsoft's solution is weak because it still demands so much advance effort by the user.

In a document-centric world, documents are naturally at the center of things, and are independent of any particular program. Instead of *Word* documents or *WordPerfect* documents or *1-2-3* documents, we would have generic documents that could be worked on by any spreadsheet or word processor program.

Of course, vendors have developed a myriad of proprietary file formats that make exchanging data problematic. But the divergence of file formats is an effect, not a cause, of the failure of document-centricity. The file systems of our popular operating systems have so punted on the issue of retrieval (and management) of documents, that vendors felt unconstrained to use any kind of common form or format ... even on UNIX which actually did have a common format: ASCII. The only elements that remain common from file to file are those two lowest common denominator retrieval tools that are part of the storage system, too: name and position.

It isn't even necessary for a company to abandon its own custom file formats. In just the same way that I can hold and own a book written in German—even though I can't read German—WordPerfect should be able to own and hold a 1-2-3 file without necessarily having the ability to read it.

In a document-centric world, applications would be less monolithic. Instead of a giant word processor with hundreds of built-in functions, we'd have programs with more tightly targeted feature sets: chartwriters and graphwriters and tablewriters and CADwriters and animationwriters. In fact, we would find that programs could get even smaller and more specialized, yet still work well together. Imagine a heterogeneity of inventive tools like pencils, inks, erasers, animators, sound recorders, fonts, undo-ers, margin controllers, spraypainters and rubber stamps that could be freely applied to any of our documents. We wouldn't have to wait for Microsoft or WordPerfect to think of it and decide to include it in the next release of their program. Nor would we be constrained to work on words in one program and images in another. We could combine these tools in one program based on our work habits rather than on one vendor's specialties. We would buy each tool from a different vendor, choosing the one whose product was best for the desired function. The result would be a program containing all of our favorite tools, all working together the way we want them to. We wouldn't be forced to use the tools from someone else's toolbox.

A utopian vision?

For this happy situation to occur, we'd have to have a standard document format independent of any one particular program. This would mean that the industry would have to reach a general agreement on the characteristics of a document—not an easy task in our competitive buisness world, where each player thinks the world should rally around its particular flag. SGML is an emerging standard that many vendors have adopted. It is gaining momentum as a common format, and this is a significant contribution to the industry. It may even grow into the utopian vision someday. Actually, we have an excellent model of an independent document standard in the UNIX world where streaming ASCII files are considered a generic, common file format that hundreds of programs know how to read, process and write.

In UNIX, any program can read or write an ASCII file regardless of which program created the file. The format of the file is common, rather than proprietary. UNIX is justifiably famous for the benefits of this standard. Programs are smaller and more powerful because they can concentrate on the function they do best. The system is egalitarian and open, and the suite of available tools comes from a wide variety of sources, both commercial and non-profit. Streaming ASCII files on UNIX are a model of what a true document-centric environment can produce.

Unfortunately, streaming ASCII is a pretty weak file format. It is a lowest-common-denominator format, lacking an internal structure of any kind. Vendors, in their endless quest to achieve a market edge with their product, abandon standards and create files in a proprietary format, but this has the effect of removing them from the ranks of open systems. From that point on, if they want to add functionality to their system, they must do it themselves and they will not be able to count on competitors adapting to their format. They have pretty-much closed off the avenue for third party add-ons.

The bottom line is whether a vendor owns the file format or if it is a common format owned by no one in particular. If the format is common, a document-centric architecture exists. If the format is proprietary, it is not document-centric. The issue hinges on the ownership of files. If a program "owns" a file because of its format, the system is closed. According to this definition, only SGML ranks as a document-centric design. Almost every application currently running on Windows uses proprietary file formats, including all of those from Microsoft. We have seen over the years how open systems thrive. The only closed systems that avoid a swift and painful death in the open marketplace are those which can offer significantly better value than the competition. This is why Microsoft is working towards a common document architecture with its OLE standard.

Unfortunately, OLE is just a baby-step in this direction, and it comes with some significant flaws. In particular, OLE doesn't address the file-ownership problem. With OLE, other objects can be embedded in a document, or it can be embedded in others, but it remains strictly cast according to its type—its owner. OLE attempts to create an interchange standard by defining complex methods for programs to talk and work with each other, instead of defining a common document architecture and letting the programs do as they please. Instead of creating a network of roads, OLE tries to connect everybody's houses with one long hallway.

There are other problems with the file-centric model besides file ownership. There are countless cases where a user wants to organize his information in groups other than documents. For example, this book is a "document," but it is composed of dozens of smaller documents, each represented by a file. The word processor that I used to create each document in the book understands how to deal with each one, but it is quite weak when it comes to handling the bigger "document," the book itself. There are no global commands, so I can't change the phrase "abysmally bad design" to "dunderheaded design" throughout the book by using a single command. Neither is there a way to tell what number this page will have when it is part of the full book. Microsoft is aware of the problem but can't seem to solve it decently. The "Master Document" feature in Word is a game attempt, but anyone who has used it on a large document will immediately see how inadequate it is. Of course, my point isn't that word processor manufacturers can't solve this problem. Programs like Interleaf or FrameMaker can handle it. It is just that our file-centric vision tends to blind us to cross-file or multi-file problems, and they usually don't receive the attention they deserve.

System designers don't seem to be aware of these tradeoffs and, consequently, many of our most cherished notions about system design are based on tradition rather than on sensible design. We have been doing files the same way for so long that nobody questions our methods. And these methods shape our thinking and, ultimately, shape our user interfaces.

Choosing Platforms

The very first strategic choice you will wrestle with as a designer will probably concern platforms. You must decide whether to write for UNIX, the Macintosh or the Intel/Microsoft platform—or for all of them. You also must decide whether to support the older, weaker hardware out there. These decisions are very difficult because they combine the messy uncertainties of real-world considerations with the clean, pure world of software construction. If you apply physical-world logic to these decisions, you will usually get left behind by the technology. If you use pure software logic for them, you will upset and alienate your customers. The correct answer is to blend the two, remaining aware that the proper proportions of each change daily. Here are my thoughts on resolving the platform issues. I expect you will temper them with the demands of your particular situation.

Software is the expensive part

Modern desktop computers are consumables, like paper clips and stationery, rather than fixed assets or durable goods, like buildings or desks. The problem isn't that computers can't perform or aren't valuable after a year or two, but that the technology moves ahead so rapidly that the resulting interaction problems detract significantly from productivity. Keeping older desktop computers in critical roles in your mainstream business environment any longer than appropriate is like making your employees take the bus on their cross-country business trips instead of flying: it is penny-wise and pound-foolish.

Every aspect of software is more expensive than hardware. You might think this isn't true because you have 1,000 computers but only have to develop an application once. Let's say it takes $350,000 to develop a program and those computers cost $3,000 each for a total of $3,000,000; it seems like your point is proven. But the comparison is not really between $350,000 and $3,000,000. Yes, the cost of the hardware is $3,000,000, but the cost of the software also includes the cost of installing, training and supporting 1,000 users of it. It may take a week to get each person up to speed on the program. If we assume that each employee makes $200 per day, their combined salary for the week is $1,000,000. Then you add about $500 per user for the teaching costs. Now don't forget the opportunity cost! While each person is learning about the program, he is *not* generating income for the company. If each employee normally generates $5,000 worth of business for the company each week, that revenue is lost. So far, the cost of implementing the software is hovering around $6,500 per user. You can get a pretty classy computer for that much money. The software cost of installing our 1,000 computers is now $6,500,000!

The half-life of a desktop computer

Much of today's business wisdom regarding computers was learned in the '60s and '70s in the data-processing centers with their giant mainframes. Those machines were large, long-term, corporate assets tended to by dozens of technicians. The technicians came and went, but the mainframe was permanent. The modern desktop computer is architecturally very similar to the mainframe, but in every other respect is quite a different animal.

The desktop PC is to the mainframe as a wild lion is to a house cat. The capability and flexibility of the PC make it the king of the jungle, while the mainframe was weak as a pussycat unless it had hordes of technicians working to keep it purring. They share many physical characteristics, but one is a domesticated animal and the other is a savage beast. To treat them the same would be dangerous. The desktop PC came from a different branch of the evolutionary tree than mainframes did, and it has dramatically different purposes, goals, usage and responsibilities. Those who treat PCs as durable goods are persisting in thinking of them as little mainframes; as permanent investments that support operations or generate revenue. But desktop PCs are, as I've said before, consumables, not investments. To be economically efficient, they must be treated as such. I'm not suggesting that you wrangle with the IRS over it (although someone should), but this is the way you should consider computers in your planning.

Think of your desktop PCs the way that Hertz thinks of their cars: certainly cars are a fundamental part of their business, but Hertz doesn't get sentimental about them. Instead, they do the math. The half-life of the price of a fleet car is about two years. That is, a car that cost $20,000 new can be resold for $10,000 in 24 months. I would guess that a modern desktop PC that can be purchased for $3,000 today can be sold for $1,500 within 12 months, because the pace of computer technology is faster than automotive technology. Hertz sells off the bulk of its fleet before they have reached their price half-life, yet most businesses won't sell off their personal computers for as long as four years; 400% of their price half-life. Are desktop computers less important for conducting your business than Hertz's cars are to them? I doubt it.

That Hertz or Avis sells its fleet cars after a year isn't an accident. These companies have performed detailed financial studies to determine the optimum amount of time to keep their cars so that their yield from resale is best with respect to the amount of rental revenues they can generate from each one. Just because Hertz sells off their fleet cars after a year doesn't mean that you can't get ten or more good years out of your family car, but it takes a considerable amount of care and attention to do so. Care and attention is expensive in business, and in today's service economy they are more effectively lavished on customers than on inanimate objects. Similarly, you can keep your family's old 386/16 with 640×480×16 VGA monitor going for several years past its prime, and it will still serve you well. You can devote the time and attention to it that it needs. In the business environment, however, you can't afford to lavish that time and attention on your office equipment. Opportunity cost is extremely expensive in modern business, and while you are baby-sitting cantankerous hardware, your competition is out stealing your market share.

Personal computers are not cars, and the dislocation involved in upgrading from one model to another is much greater than just buying a new car—it's more akin to buying a new office—so the analogy isn't precise. The point, though, is that we must begin to regard our desktop computers more like fleet cars and less like mainframes.

PCs are not little mainframes; they are unique business tools that don't age gracefully. There are enormous costs associated with keeping computers beyond their useful and most productive times. The main costs arise from interaction problems. A typical PC will have dozens of major hardware and software components, and the probability for incompatibilities between them grows exponentially as the system ages and new components are added. When you buy a brand-new computer, you start the clock ticking again at zero, and the probability for interaction problems is reduced again to a manageable level.

The potential for error inside a given modem, for example, is really small. Most hardware vendors are reputable and test their product well. However, the odds that the particular brand of modem you own is fully tested with a particular serial communications chip and a particular serial communications driver software decreases as these three products diverge in time.

Almost any mouse sold in 1995 will work with almost any computer sold in 1995. But the chances of strange, unpredictable interaction problems between that mouse and an otherwise perfectly functional computer sold in 1992 are quite high. Even the standard plugs for mice have changed between 1992 and 1995, from a seven pin DIN connector to a five-pin mini-DIN. How much will it cost your company in lost productivity to have an executive stopped from doing her job while a technician hunts down the proper connector? Is it more or less than the cost to replace her computer with a more modern one?

If the cost of keeping older desktop PCs in service is higher than their replacement cost, it makes good business sense to upgrade them. If, based on resale value, the optimal sell-off date for a computer is 10 months, you can expect that the residual value will reach zero sometime before four years have elapsed. I contend that the optimal interval to keep a computer before replacing it is roughly 24 to 30 months from the initial purchase. Before that, you pay too much in disruption. After that, you pay too much in obsolescence.

Choosing a development platform

The computer industry often makes a further miscalculation that makes keeping old computers around past their prime seem harmless by comparison. I'm referring, of course, to the decisions regarding target platforms for software development. Many development teams create software that will accommodate all existing hardware. Their management usually colludes in this error by encouraging them to support the five-, six- or seven-year-old computers that are still ticking away in corporate offices, arguing that it would be too expensive to replace all of those computers. This ignores the fact that the cost of developing software to support both old and new hardware is generally significantly greater than the cost of purchasing and supporting the more powerful new hardware. This means that, if the software is written to accommodate those old computers, it will save money on the hardware just to spend it on the software, resulting in much stupider software at greater cost. It should be the responsibility of management to assure that the computers on desktops throughout the company are as modern as can be when the new software is ready.

To develop software for modern platforms, you must design for hardware that will be readily available six to twelve months after the product first ships. Don't forget that it might take a year to develop the software, and another six months for it to penetrate your organization, and the state-of-the-market computers will be even more powerful than today.

> **Design tip:** The program should perform optimally on hardware that doesn't exist yet.

If you develop software for a target hardware platform that is any older than next year's standard, you are firmly anchoring your business in the past. If any of your competitors make the more intelligent choice, you will be quickly overtaken. The cost of programming is extremely high compared to the cost of hardware, but you will have to accept this development cost regardless of the hardware platform you write for, so this isn't the real problem. Instead, the problem lies in the desire to fully amortize the investment in the software by assuring that it covers all platforms. The trap is that by covering all existing platforms, you reach backwards, shutting yourself out of future platforms. And only the future platforms have, well, a future.

Just like the desire to fully amortize your investment in the hardware caused the problem, it also compounds the problem by forcing you into building weaker, less-effective software and then insisting on getting your money's worth from it, too. The unsuspecting businessperson can be trapped by his own parsimony into weakening the company's ability to perform its fundamental business.

The insight here is to never let software decisions be swayed significantly by the limitations of existing hardware. The software should, of course, be able to run on state-of-the-art computers when it is released, but it should have to stoop a bit to do so. The product should be designed to behave optimally with the hardware that will be state-of-the-art 6 to 12 months after the software is first released.

This is a lot less important for operating system software (OSs) or language compilers, where the performance leverage is enormous and always works against you. But in the world of applications, where user interaction is intense and performance is usually measured by how productive users feel rather than by more objective measures, don't compromise software for hardware.

Controlling the hardware

If you are creating specialized software or vertical-market programs that will be sold to customers for several thousands of dollars or more, you can certainly dictate the hardware it should run on. A larger proportion of the user's budget will go for software than for hardware.

Users will inevitably argue this point. Since the beginning of the microcomputer revolution, no axiom has been truer yet more frequently violated than this one:

Purchase the right software; then buy the computer that runs it

Most users will buy a computer and then look for software that solves their problem and—by the way—also runs on their computer hardware. This attitude is a carryover from the mainframe days, and often informs the thinking of software developers as much as it influences software buyers. To make a sale, developers are quick to adapt to a specific hardware platform. Yes, the realities of business sometimes dictate such choices and an adulteration of our practices, but this doesn't for a minute mean that these decisions make for good design. Software is the key, not the hardware. In a few more years, when the cost of computing machinery drops by another couple of orders of magnitude, this natural order will be apparent to all. Good designers will anticipate it.

Simultaneous Multiplatform Development

As tantalizing as it is to want to kill two birds with one stone, don't do simultaneous multiplatform development. It isn't worth it. Instead, develop only for your primary market. Then use the revenue from this product to port to your secondary platforms.

There are two ways to do simultaneous multiplatform development and both of them are bad. You can make the code more complicated, or you can homogenize the interface.

Design tip: Build the program to run on only one platform at a time.

Anything that increases the complexity of source code should be avoided at all costs. It will magnify the time it takes both to write and to debug. The main job of the software development manager is to avoid uncertainty and delay. Simultaneous multiplatform development generates more uncertainty and delay than any other tactic you might use. The compromises and confusion will ultimately result in the quality of your product suffering.

In the quiet of the office it seems so harmless, so easy to add a few "if-else" statements to the source code and magically reap the benefits of supporting an extra hardware platform. Don't be fooled. Everything in the already-problematic discipline of software development becomes harder and more complex. Each design decision must now be made for two platforms. Compromises slip into the product to account for the disparity between the two. If writing for dual platforms increases the amount of code by only 5%, it can increase the time to market by a *third*. This is an incredibly costly bad decision that is easily avoided.

There are several commercially available libraries of code that will let you develop on multiple platforms simultaneously. In order to do so, they demand that you design for a "generic" GUI, which the library then runs on each platform. This may be good for the development team, but the users will dislike it intensely. They will immediately detect the homogenization of the interface and will not appreciate it. Macintosh users prefer programs with a Mac sensibility. Windows users won't settle for anything but a Windows application. For example, Windows users are very comfortable with multiple, complex toolbars running horizontally across the top of the program just beneath the menubar.

Many Mac aficionados consider this idiom to be about as desirable as a shark in a swimming pool.

The programming staff will probably be game to do multiplatform development. They may even be the ones pushing for it. They see it as an intellectual challenge; multiplatform development is a tournament in which to compete and win. Just remember that programmers frequently don't give a hoot about deadlines—they're in it for the brain exercise.

Finessing the problem

A much simpler, safer and more effective way to solve the problem is by developing for a single platform first: your main market. This will typically be Windows, the market leader by a wide margin. You completely avoid the complexities of multiplatform development, finish the first version with the greatest possible speed and ship it to the largest possible market.

Once you've finished the Windows version, you are generating revenue while you begin development for other platforms. Development managers take note: This is your most compelling argument for convincing others that single-platform development is the proper course to take. The needs of secondary markets shouldn't delay the needs of primary markets.

Don't hamper primary markets by serving secondary markets

This doesn't mean that you need to abandon the secondary market. On the contrary, at this point you will have a fully articulated, working model of the product—running on Windows—to use as a prototype for the versions to run on other platforms. You can hire a team of programmers with proven skills on the new platform and tell them "go forth and clone." When programmers are working from a clearly visible model, the development time can be compressed significantly because there is little time wasted going down blind design alleys. You can also hire programmers who are less experienced—and therefore less expensive—to do clone-programming because there is less design work involved. Much of the code will likely be reusable, but you now treat this as a bonus rather than as an expectation.

When I say clone, however, I mean clone functionality but not dialect. The Windows prototype will demonstrate how the program should interact with the user, but the Macintosh version must behave like a Mac program at the detail level. For that, you need local expertise. The problem is conceptually similar to localization.

The Myth of Interoperability

Windows developers often face programs with legacies as successful DOS programs. Many applications are brought to Windows after they have had a long and lucrative run in a DOS, character-based, command-line environment. Common wisdom holds that the Windows program should emulate the DOS program as closely as possible. "Thousands of satisfied customers want to move to Windows," goes the logic, "and they will be sorely disappointed if the program is different from what they already know and love." Besides, "Many of our corporate users work in heterogeneous environments and they want the Windows version to work the same way as their DOS-only systems."

This concept is called interoperability. Believers in interoperability will tell you that your DOS customers are faithful to your product because of the way your program behaves, because they have already learned your DOS product and because they can't afford the retraining costs of moving their people to a new Windows version. They will draw the irresistible word picture of the happy user entering data at a DOS machine, then cheerfully switching to the Windows computer and performing an identical task.

As compelling as this logic is, it is dead wrong. If you are going to create a Windows version of a program, go ahead and create a Windows version—don't implement a DOS version on the Windows platform. If you try for interoperability, you will only hurt your product. You will find that no one is happy, least of all you and the development staff. Your job will become increasingly difficult as you try to reconcile fundamentally irreconcilable differences.

Simply stated, Windows users use Windows because they like it and because they don't like DOS. On the other hand, DOS users use DOS because they like it and because they don't like Windows. If your program acts like DOS on Windows, DOS users will be unhappy because they'd rather be using the genuine article on DOS, and nothing you do to simulate DOS on Windows will make them happy. Conversely, all of the Windows aficionados will turn up their noses at the pathetic DOS-ness of your program and its lack of understanding of how to behave appropriately in a Windows world.

Design tip: The program should be designed expressly for the target platform.

Your DOS customers are faithful because your DOS version is sensitive to the particular needs of DOS users. They like it because it has adapted to the local customs of the DOS environment. Given the limitations of that environment, it is a satisfactory solution. It exhibits familiar DOS-like behavior that makes users experienced in a DOS environment feel warm and fuzzy. Extrapolating this to mean that the behavior of the program itself is warm and fuzzy can be fatal when you move to another platform, particularly when exercising a paradigm shift as dramatic as moving from a character-based to a graphical platform.

Most Windows users like Windows because they were dissatisfied with the level of usability available in DOS. They are here because they want something different and better; not something similar and status quo. They came here because they wanted to leave the limitations of DOS behind, and they want you to have done the same.

Windows users expect your program to conform to the local standards in exactly the same way that DOS users expected your DOS program to conform to DOS standards. Windows users will want your Windows version to look and act like other Windows applications, not like DOS applications. They will expect your program to take advantage of the tools provided by the new platform. They will expect your program to deliver something better to justify the dislocation they had to invest in order to move from DOS to Windows.

Those people who clamor for interoperability are often motivated by fear. They are afraid of the new system; of their ability to learn it and to adapt to it. They are afraid mostly of the learning curve. They worked so hard and absorbed so much pain to learn the DOS version that they fear going through the process again on Windows. By demanding interoperability, they hope that they will be able to take their hard-earned expertise straight across to the new system.

The answer for these people, of course, is that it won't be anywhere near as difficult to learn in Windows than it was in DOS. They won't believe this, so you will just have to do the right thing despite their pleas. It's like telling a child that a tetanus shot is less painful than tetanus—all the child can see is the needle. Extending the metaphor, you must be the adult even if the frightened users hold the purse strings. It is not a good career move to make your customer happy all through the development process only to eventually deliver a dud.

Of course, you have to deliver on your promises and make a graphical user interface that really is significantly easier to learn and use than the DOS version. I have no doubt that you can do it, as long as you abandon interoperable thinking and become a Windows native.

Often, the people who clamor the loudest for interoperability are the product managers, marketing managers and programmers who worked long and hard on the DOS version. They will insist that the Windows version be designed in the image of the DOS version, the company's cash cow. I have seen this situation several times. The DOS-centric forces-of-evil have the upper hand because their product makes money for the company and, for a while at least, your product merely costs the company money. They make their compelling arguments to upper management, who can't really be expected to know better, and the dictum is handed down: "Make it like the DOS version." At this point, all of the really smart people quit, the program is written, haltingly, to worship twin operating-system gods and, when it finally ships, the market emits a loud yawn. The DOS faithful remain faithful to DOS, snickering all the while about how they told you the Windows version would flop. The Windows hopefuls are very disappointed with the product because it retained its clunkiness in spite of Windows. Your competitor will release a native Windows product that was designed and written with a "when in Rome, do as the Romans do" attitude, it will begin robbing you of sales, and your company will begin its long, agonizing slide into Chapter 11. Don't let this happen to you!

The picture that I have just painted of crossing the gulf from DOS to Windows is also very true when going from the Macintosh platform to Windows. In spite of their numerous visual similarities, Mac and Windows are different cultures, and moving from one to another is not the bed of roses you might expect. If you want to sell something to Mac users and have them appreciate it, sell it to them on the Mac. Attempting to do it on a PC will just irritate Windows people and generate a yawn from the Mac folks. Macintosh users believe deeply that Macs are better than Windows. There is not much that you can do on a PC that will impress the Mac crowd, even if you adhere slavishly to Mac doctrine. The president of a prominent Mac software company once told me that "the pixels on a Mac are better than the pixels on a PC." He actually believed this, even though you can take a typical Sony or NEC video screen and plug it into either computer.

Management will make the same arguments about interoperability they always do, but the fact remains that although companies may have thousands of Macs interspersed with thousands of PCs, very few *individuals* actually spend time working on both. You can examine the market and see for yourself that there are few companies who make interoperable applications successful on both platforms. They generally have a loyal customer base on only one platform—their native one, while their customers on the *other* platform are just marking time waiting for an easier-to-use product native to *their* platform.

Part III: The Behavior
The Program's Presentation of Self

Using much of today's software is like driving a car that has previously been rolled down a cliff: You have to climb in through the window; none of the lights seem to work; the engine makes a suspicious clunking noise; great spans of sheet metal fly off at inopportune moments. Why does it seem to be a rule that the manufactured artifacts in our lives must become increasingly harder to use and understand as they incorporate more and more technology? Most software designers won't admit to themselves the scope of their collective ignorance about what really works in the field of interface design. We have many noble experiments, and many successes and failures, to observe—we even have a smattering of books to read—but we can barely agree on the details, let alone the larger issues. The bulk of what passes for user interface design today is either guesswork or imitation. The frustrating thing is, it doesn't have to be that way.

Orchestration and Flow

To make software more productive, we must make its users more productive. To make users more productive, we have to get them into a harmonious frame of mind. After all, it is the users' mental state that ultimately dictates how effectively they are using our program.

Planing on the step

Racers of lightweight sailboats seek out a condition they call "planing." A racing dingy planes by accelerating to the point that it actually rides on top of its own bow wake. A planing hull displaces only a fraction of the water it does normally, so the drag it generates is drastically reduced. This drag reduction can result in speeds increasing by as much as 50%. The transition between displacement sailing and planing is sharp; the planing boat will almost instantly surge ahead—sailors call it "getting on the step" and the experience is exhilarating. A minute or two longer on the step can spell the difference between winning and losing a race.

Humans can plane on the step, too, when they really concentrate on an activity. The state is generally called **flow**.

Tom DeMarco and Timothy Lister in their book *Peopleware, Productive Projects and Teams* (Dorset House, 1987) define flow as a "condition of deep, nearly meditative involvement." Flow often induces a "gentle sense of euphoria" and can make you unaware of the passage of time. Most significantly, a person in a state of flow can be extremely productive, especially when engaged in process-oriented tasks such as "engineering, design, development and writing." All of these tasks are typically performed on computers while interacting with software. Therefore, it behooves us to create a software interaction that promotes and enhances flow, rather than one that includes potentially flow-breaking or flow-disturbing behavior.

When a sailor makes a lubberly tack—changes the position of the sail clumsily—the dingy falls off the plane and slows like it hit a wall. The sailor now has to carefully accelerate until the boat can once again get on the step. Good sailors tack so smoothly that the boat is undisturbed, and the hull stays on the step. In the same way, we want our program's interaction to be so smooth that the user is undisturbed and can remain in the state of flow. If the program rattles the user out of flow, it may take several minutes to regain that productive state.

Techniques for inducing and maintaining flow

To create flow, our interaction with software must become transparent. There are several excellent ways to make our interfaces recede into invisibility. They are

1. Follow mental models

2. Direct, don't discuss

3. Keep tools close at hand

4. Give modeless feedback

There are other important tools for designing transparent interfaces that we will discuss in the next couple of chapters. These include "not stopping the proceedings with idiocy" (Chapter 13), and "questions aren't the same as choices" (Chapter 14). We'll tackle the others right here.

Follow mental models

I introduced the concept of mental models in Chapter 3. Different users will have different mental models of a process, but they will rarely visualize them in terms of the detailed innards of the computer process. Each user naturally forms a mental image of how the software performs its task. The mind looks for some pattern of cause and effect to gain insight into the machine's behavior.

Creators of race cars place gauges on their dashboards so they follow the driver's mental model, which goes like this: "straight up is good. Anything else is bad." The engineer twists the gauges in their mounts so that every needle points straight up when everything is normal. The gauges won't look right to tyros, but the racer understands: her peripheral vision monitors the gauges easily while staying in flow to drive. If any needle deviates from the vertical, it demands the driver's conscious attention to the problem; otherwise, up means OK, just like that thumb's-up from her pit crew.

Direct, don't discuss

Many developers imagine the ideal interface to be a two-way conversation with the user. However, most users don't see it that way. Most users would rather interact with the software in the same way they interact with, say, their car. They open the door and get in when they want to go somewhere. They press on the accelerator when they want the car to move forward and the brake when it is time to stop; they turn the wheel when they want the car to turn.

This ideal interaction is not a dialog—it's more like using a tool. When a carpenter hits nails, she doesn't discuss the nail with the hammer; she directs the hammer onto the nail. In a car, the driver—the user—gives the car direction when he wants to change the car's behavior. The driver expects direct feedback from the car and its environment in terms appropriate to the device: the view out the windshield, the readings on the various gauges on the dashboard, the sound of rushing air and tires on pavement, the feel of lateral g-forces and vibration from the road. The carpenter expects similar feedback: the feel of the nail sinking, the sound of steel striking steel, the heft of the hammer's weight.

The driver certainly doesn't expect the car to interrogate him with a dialog box, nor would the carpenter appreciate one appearing on her hammer like the one in Figure 11-1.

One of the main reasons software often aggravates and upsets users is that it doesn't act like a car or a hammer. Instead, it has the temerity to try to engage us in a dialog—to inform us of our shortcomings and to demand answers from us. From the user's point of view, the roles are reversed: it should be the user doing the demanding and the software doing the answering.

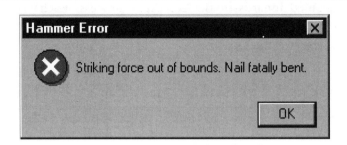

Figure 11-1

Just because programmers are accustomed to seeing messages like this doesn't mean that people from other walks of life are. Nobody wants their machines to scold them. If we guide our machines in a dunderheaded way, we expect to get a dunderheaded response. Sure, they can protect us from fatal errors, but scolding isn't the same thing as protecting.

With direct manipulation, we can point to what we want. If we want to move an object from A to B, we click on it and drag it there. As a general rule, the better, more flow-inducing interfaces are those with plentiful and sophisticated direct-manipulation idioms.

Keep tools close at hand

Most programs are too complex for one mode of direct manipulation to cover all of their features. Consequently, most programs offer a set of different tools to the user. These tools are really different modes of behavior that the program enters. Offering tools is a compromise with complexity, but we can still do a lot to make tool manipulation easy and to prevent it from disturbing the flow. Mainly, we must ensure that tool information is plentiful and easy to see and attempt to make transitions between tools quick and simple.

Tools should be close at hand, preferably on palettes or toolbars. This way, the user can see them easily and can select them with a single click. If the user must divert his attention from the application to search out a tool, his concentration will be broken. It's as if he had to get up from his desk and wander down the hall to find a pencil. And he should never have to put tools away manually.

As we manipulate tools, it's usually desirable for the program to report on their status, and on the status of the data we are manipulating with the tool. This information needs to be clearly posted and easy to see without obscuring or stopping the action.

Modern jet fighter designers go the race car designers one better in cockpit design—this is critically important when the job involves yanking and banking 40 tons of titanium at 600 miles per hour. Jet fighters have a heads-up display, or HUD, that superimposes the readings of critical instrumentation onto the forward view of the cockpit's windscreen. The pilot doesn't even have to use peripheral vision but can read vital gauges while keeping her eyes glued on the opposing fighter.

Our software should display information like a jet fighter's HUD. The program could use the edges of the display screen to show the user information about the action in the center that is being directly manipulated.

Modeless feedback

When the program has information or feedback for the user, it has several ways to present it. The most common method is to pop up a dialog box on the screen. This technique is modal: it puts the program into a mode that must be dealt with before it can return to its normal state, and before the user can continue with his task. A better way to inform the user is with **modeless feedback**.

Feedback is modeless whenever information for the user is built into the normal interface and doesn't stop the normal flow of system activities and interaction. In Word, you can see what page you are on, what section you are in, how many pages are in the current document, what position the cursor is in and what time it is modelessly just by looking at the status bar at the bottom of the screen.

If you want to know how many words are in your document, however, you have to call up the Summary Info dialog from the File menu; then you have to press a button to summon the Statistics dialog to see a word count (see Figure 11-2). I refer to the word count figure frequently when I write magazine articles (It's hard to get them short enough!). I sure wish the word count were offered modelessly.

Orchestration

If the user could achieve his goals without the program, he would. By the same token, if the user needed the program but could achieve his goals without going through its user interface, he would. Interacting with software is not an aesthetic experience. It is a pragmatic exercise that is best kept to a minimum. Don't kid yourself about your sexy new multimedia, interactive, online, social, point-and-click program. The user would rather just snap his fingers or say "abracadabra." No matter how cool your interface is, less of it would be better.

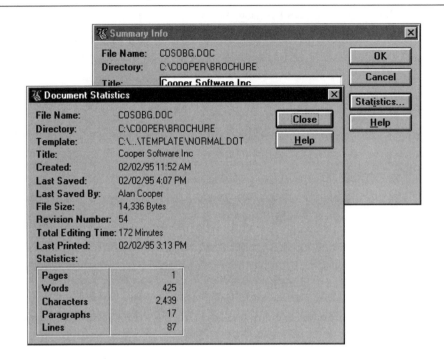

Figure 11-2

In Word, if you want to know the number of words in your document, you must first request the Summary Info dialog from the File menu. Then, by pressing the Statistics button, you call up the Document Statistics dialog box. Down in the corner, buried among other useless (for me) numbers is the one I want. After I've read it, I must press the Close key and then the Cancel key...or was it the other way around? This is the opposite of modeless feedback, and it brings whatever flow I might have had going to a screeching halt.

Directing your attention to the interaction itself puts the emphasis on the side effects of the tools rather than on the user's goals. A user interface is an artifact, not something directly related to the goals of the user. Next time you find yourself crowing about what cool interaction you've designed, just remember that the ultimate user interface is no interface at all.

No matter how cool your interface is, less of it would be better

It looks to me like the dialog boxes in Figure 11-2 were written by two different programmers. Maybe they didn't talk much with each other, but I can guarantee you that they never spoke with a designer—someone whose job it was to coordinate all of the user interface elements. The results look like what you'd get if the orchestra lacked a conductor. Each musician might know his part well, but when all seventy of them get together, they won't sound in accord.

It is vital that all of the elements work together towards a single goal. I call this process of achieving a coherent interface **orchestration**.

Webster's defines orchestration as "harmonious organization," a very reasonable phrase for what we should expect from interacting with software. Harmonious organization doesn't yield to fixed rules. You can't create guidelines like "five buttons on a dialog box are good" and "seven buttons on a dialog box are too many." Yet it is easy to see that a dialog box with 35 buttons is usually bad. The major difficulty with such analysis is that it treats the problem *in vitro*. It doesn't take into account the problem being solved; it doesn't take into account what the user is doing at the time or what he is trying to accomplish.

Finesse

In many things, the more there are, the better things are. In the world of interface design, the contrary is true, and we should constantly strive to reduce the number of elements in the interface without reducing the power of the program. In order to do this, we must do more with less; this is where careful orchestration becomes important. We must coordinate and control all of the power of our program without letting the interface become a gaggle of windows and dialogs, covered with a scattering of unrelated gizmos.

I often see dialog boxes that are complex but not very powerful. They typically allow the user to perform a single task without providing access to related tasks. For example, most programs allow the user to name and save a data file, but they never let him delete, rename or make a copy of that file while he is at it. The dialog leaves that task to the operating system. It may not be trivial to add these functions to the program, but isn't it better that the pro-grammer go through the non-trivial activities than for the user to be forced to? Today, if the user wants to do something simple like edit a new copy of file "foo," he must go through a non-trivial sequence of actions: going to the shell, selecting foo, requesting a copy from the menu, changing its name, returning to the program and then opening the new file. I'd much rather see the pro-grammer work harder and give the user a break.

It's not as hard as it looks, actually. Orchestration doesn't mean bulldozing your way through problems. It means finessing the problems, wherever possi-ble. Instead of adding the copy and rename functions to the File Open dialog box of every application, why not just discard that same slightly retarded File Open dialog box from every application and replace it with the shell program itself. When the user wants to open a file, the program calls the shell—which conveniently has all of those collateral file-munging functions built in—and the user can double-click on the desired document. That's pretty much what the File Open dialog does, except it doesn't do it so well.

Yes, the application's File Open dialog does show the user a filtered view of files (like only .DOC files in Word), but there are certainly ways to do that in the shell. I can think of several ways to do it better and easier in the shell than that old dialog does with its clunky combobox.

Following on this logic, we can also dispense with the Save As dialog, which is really the logical inverse of the File Open dialog. If every time we requested the Save As... function from our application, it wrote our file out to a temporary directory under some reasonable temporary name and then transferred control to the shell, we'd have all of those nice shell tools at our disposal to move things around or rename them.

Yes, there are access problems, but nothing that a little inter-process commu-nicating wouldn't solve. Yes, there would be a chunk of coding that program-mers would have to do, but look at the upside: Countless dialog boxes could be completely discarded. The user interfaces of thousands of programs would become more visually and functionally consistent, and all with a single design stroke. That is orchestration!

Invisibility

So much of today's software has stilted, jerky and inappropriate interactions. There seems to have been little attempt at orchestration anywhere.

When a novelist writes well, the craft of the writer becomes invisible, and the reader sees the story and characters with a clarity undisturbed by the technique of the writer. Likewise, when a program interacts well with a user, the interaction mechanics precipitate out, leaving the user face-to-face with his objectives, unaware of the intervening software. The poor writer is a visible writer, and a poor user interface designer looms with a visible presence in his software: eyes wild, hair rumpled and Jolt on his breath.

Good user interfaces are invisible

To a novelist, there is no such thing as a "good" sentence. There are no construction rules that guarantee transparent sentences. It all depends on what the protagonist is doing, or the effect the author wants to create. The writer knows to not insert an obscure word in a particularly quiet and sensitive passage, lest it sound like a sour note in a string quartet. The same goes for software. The software designer must train his ears to hear sour notes in the orchestration of software interaction.

When a program's communication with the user is well orchestrated, it becomes invisible.

Possibility versus probability

There are many cases where interaction, usually in the form of a dialog box, slips into a user interface unnecessarily. A frequent source for such clinkers is when a program is faced with a choice. That's because programmers tend to resolve choices mathematically, and it carries over to their software design. To a mathematician, if a proposition is true 999,999 times out of a million and false one time, the proposition is false—that's the way math works. However, to the rest of us, the proposition is not only not false, it is overwhelmingly true. The proposition has a *possibility* of being false, but the *probability* of it being false is minuscule to the point of irrelevancy.

Mathematicians and programmers tend to view possibilities as being the same as probabilities. For example, a user has the choice of ending the program and saving his work or ending the program and throwing away the document he has been working on for the last six hours. Mathematically, either of these choices is equally possible. Conversely, the probability of the user discarding his work is at least a thousand to one against, yet the typical program always includes a dialog box asking the user if he wants to save his changes, like the one shown in Figure 11-3.

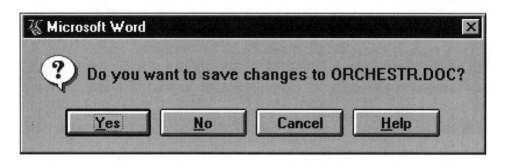

Figure 11-3

This is easily the silliest and most unnecessary dialog box in the world of GUI. Of course, I want to save my work! It is the normal course of events. Not saving it would be something out of the ordinary that should be handled by some dusty dialog box. This single dialog box does more to force the user into knowing and understanding the useless and confusing facts about RAM and disk storage than almost anything else in his entire interaction with his computer. This dialog box should never be used.

The dialog box in Figure 11-3 is completely inappropriate and should not exist. Yes, I want to save the changes to ORCHESTR.DOC. I wouldn't have bothered to name the file if I hadn't wanted to keep it. In the rare case where I change my mind and want to discard my changes and revert back to the original, the program should provide tools to do so. But these tools shouldn't be waved in my face every time I end a document. I edit a couple of hundred documents every month and I have to abandon my changes only about once a year.

Whoever designed this program confused probability with possibility, and they burden me with this irrelevancy every time I end the program. This is tantamount to my telling you not to pour your soup on your shirt every time you eat.

It is possible to argue that users have come to expect this behavior; that its absence would cause experienced users to fret that changes were being mistakenly discarded when the program ends. This rationale is like saying that a beaten dog expects to be beaten again, so we should beat it to make it happy. The time to make our programs better is now.

If a program offers a function, it ought to offer just the function and not all of its permutations. For example, when I ask to print something, I don't want a dialog box that allows me to configure the print function, I just want a simple printout of the current document. On the rare occasions when I want something special, like just a few pages, or seven copies, or sideways printing, then I should have to ask for the "Custom Print Dialog" or some such. If there is a possibility that the user might set the parameters of the function, that should be a secondary characteristic of the function itself, rather than intruding on the more probable act of invoking the function.

The print button on the Word toolbar offers immediate printing without a dialog box. This is perfect for many users, but for those with multiple printers or printers on a network, it may be offering too little information. The user may want to see which printer is selected before he either presses the button or summons the dialog to change it first. This is a good candidate for some simple modeless output placed on a toolbar or status bar.

Another good example of this confusion could be found in Microsoft Excel's older Version 4.0. When you select one or more cells and press the DELete key to clear the field, a small dialog box pops up asking what you want to delete.

The flexible little dialog box shown in Figure 11-4 conveniently allowed you the option of clearing the formats, formulas or notes from the selected cells. This dialog drove me crazy with its obtrusive uselessness. It is true that there are three types of deletion operations: format, formula and notes. However, it is also true that, although I delete formulas with great frequency, I have never in all of my spreadsheeting desired to delete formats or notes. So why does the program ignore this self-evident fact and insist on asking me through this mindless little dialog? Just because something is possible, doesn't mean that it is probable.

You *might* get hit by a bus, but you probably *will* drive safely to work this morning. Don't stay home out of fear of the killer bus. Don't let what might happen alter the way you treat what will happen. I say "Don't put might on will" to remind myself not to load up parts of a program that will get used with lots of stuff that might get used.

Programmers are judged by their ability to create software that handles the many possible but improbable conditions that crop up inside complex logical systems. This doesn't mean, however, that they should render that readiness to handle offbeat possibilities in the user interface. The presence of might-on-will

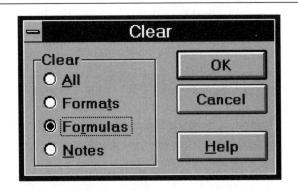

Figure 11-4

In Excel, Version 4.0, this dialog box popped up every time you pressed the DEL key. This is quite reasonable if you are a computer, but if you are a human, it means that you have to deal with the remote possibilities of deletion every time you try to do the high-probability clearing of the formula. Using Excel with this dialog was like listening to the symphony pause every time the conductor had to turn a page on the score. Thankfully, Microsoft obliterated this little gem in Excel 5.1.

Don't put might on will

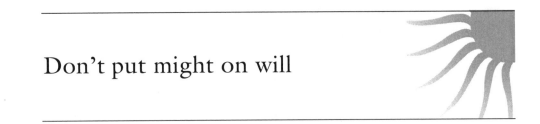

is a dead giveaway for user interfaces designed by programmers. Dialogs, controls and options that are used a hundred times a day sit side-by-side with dialogs, controls and options that are used once a year or never. One of the most potent methods for better orchestrating your user interfaces is segregating the possible from the probable.

The remedy to this situation is to create user interfaces that conform to probabilities and not to possibilities. I can easily see Excel having an advanced delete command available from a menu item that gives me access to the dialog box we just condemned. I could use it for those exceedingly rare cases where I want to delete notes or formats instead of just the formula. The program could then leave the DELete key for quickly and unobtrusively doing the obvious: deleting the contents of the field: the formula. In this case, the user interface would become quieter and less obtrusive, I would notice it less, and it would be better without taking away from the power of the program.

Quantitative information

The way that a program represents information is another way that it can obtrude noisily into a user's consciousness. One area frequently abused is the representation of quantitative, or numeric, information. If an application needs to show the amount of free space on disk, it can do what the Microsoft Windows 3.x File Manager program does and come right out and give you the number of free bytes, as shown in Figure 11-5.

Figure 11-5

This is the bottom inch or so of the Windows 3.x File Manager program. It takes great pains to tell me how much of my disk is used and how much is free down to the billionth! Does this precision help me understand whether I need to clear out space on my disk? Certainly not. Furthermore, is a number the best way to indicate the disk's status to me? Wouldn't a graphical representation that showed the space usage in a proportional manner (like a gas gauge) be more meaningful? The way this information is rendered guarantees that my concentration will be broken if I need to know it.

In the lower left corner of the program, it tells me the number of free bytes and the total number of bytes on the disk. I find these numbers very hard to read, and extremely hard to interpret. With more than a thousand million bytes of disk storage, it ceases to be important to me just how many hundreds are left, yet the display rigorously shows me down to the kilobyte how many are used and how many are left. Even while the program is telling me the state of my disk with exaggerated precision, it is failing to communicate. What I really need to know is whether or not my disk is getting full, or whether I can add a new 20 MB program and still have sufficient breathing room. Instead, I find myself concentrating on those numbers like they were Egyptian hieroglyphics trying to make sense of them. It isn't easy because the numbers don't help me to visualize the problem.

Visual presentation expert Edward Tufte says a good numeric presentation should answer the question "compared to what?" Knowing that 231,728 KB are free on my hard disk is less useful than knowing that it is 22 percent of the disk's total capacity. Another Tufte dictum is "show the data" as opposed to telling about it. A small bar or pie chart showing the used and unused portions in different colors would make it much easier to comprehend the scale and proportion of hard disk use. It would show me what 231,728 KB really means. This bar could easily be displayed where the numbers are currently shown. The numbers shouldn't go away, but they should be relegated to the status of captions on the data and not be the data itself. They should also be displayed with a more reasonable and consistent precision. The meaning of the information would be shown visually while the numbers would merely add support.

In Windows 95, Microsoft's right hand giveth while their left hand taketh away. The File Manager with the numbers (shown in Figure 11-5) is dead, replaced by the Explorer dialog box shown in Figure 11-6. This replacement is the properties dialog associated with a hard disk. The "Used space" is shown in blue, and the "Free space" is shown in magenta, making the pie chart an easy read. Now I can see at a glance the sad truth that "GRANFROMAGE" is packed to the gills.

Unfortunately, that nice pie chart isn't built into the Explorer's interface. Instead, I have to seek it out with a menu item. To see how full my disk is, I must first bring the program to a smoking halt, bring up a modal dialog box that, although it gives me the information I want, takes me away from the place where I want to know it. The Explorer is where I can see, copy, move and delete files, but it's not where I can see if things need to be deleted. That nice blue and magenta pie chart should have been built into the face of the Explorer. Besides, what if I didn't know how to find that nice pie chart dialog box? What warning would I have had that GRANFROMAGE was full?

Graphical input

Software frequently fails to present numerical information in a graphical way. Even rarer than this, though, is the ability of software to enable graphical input. A lot of software lets users enter numbers and then, on command, converts those numbers into a graph. Few products let the user enter a graph and, on command, convert that graph into a vector of numbers. By contrast, most modern word processors let you set tabs and indentations by dragging a marker on a ruler. The user can say, in effect, "Here is where I want the paragraph to start" and let the program calculate that it is precisely 1.347 inches in from the left margin instead of forcing the user to enter "1.347."

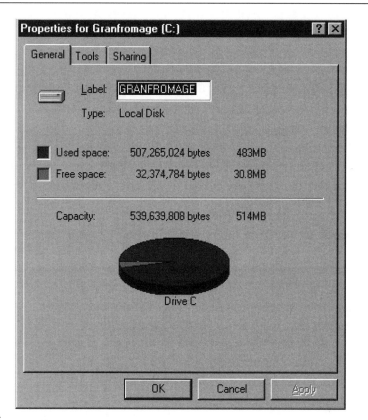

Figure 11-6

In Windows 95, Microsoft has replaced the electric chair with lethal injection. Instead of long, inscrutable numbers at the bottom of the File Manager, you can request a properties dialog box from the Explorer. The good news is that you can finally see how your disk is doing in a meaningful, graphic way with the pie chart. The bad news is that you have to stop what you're doing and open a dialog box to see fundamental information that should be readily available.

The new category of intelligent drawing programs like Shapeware's Visio are getting better at this. Each polygon that the user manipulates on screen is represented behind the scenes by a small spreadsheet, with a row for each point and a column each for the X and Y coordinates. Dragging a polygon's vertex on screen causes the values in the corresponding point in the spreadsheet, represented by the X and Y values, to change. The user can access the shape either graphically or through its spreadsheet representation.

This principle applies in a variety of situations. When items in a list need to be reordered, the user may want them ordered alphabetically, but he may also want them in order of personal preference; something no algorithm can offer.

The user should be able to drag the items into the desired order directly, without an algorithm interfering with this fundamental operation.

Reflect the status of the program

When someone is asleep, he usually looks asleep. When someone is awake, he looks awake. When someone is busy, he looks busy: his eyes are glued to his work and his body language is closed and preoccupied. When someone is unoccupied, he looks unoccupied: his body is open and moving, his eyes are questing and willing to make contact. People not only expect this kind of subtle feedback from each other, they depend on it for maintaining social order.

Our programs should work the same way. When a program is asleep, it should look asleep. When a program is awake, it should look awake, and when it's busy, it should look busy. When the computer is engaged in some significant internal action like formatting a diskette, we should see some significant external action, such as a one-inch diameter image of a diskette slowly changing from black to white. When the computer is off sending a fax, we should see a small image of the fax changing colors in horizontal lines corresponding to the bands sent. If the program is waiting for a response from a remote database, it should visually change to reflect its somnambulant state.

Lead, follow or get out of the way

I once used a program that generated tables. When I requested a table, what I got was a dialog box asking me lots of questions, but no table. I didn't ask for a big dialog. I asked for a table. Why didn't the program just give me a table? If it wasn't the table I wanted, I'd at least be motivated to see what I had to do to change it because the program clearly was willing to work with me. If it gave me a table first, then let me manipulate it to change its properties, it would be a much more effective solution.

Users—not power-users, but *normal* people—are very uncomfortable with explaining to a program what they want. Users would much rather see what the program *thinks* is right and then manipulate that to make it really right. In most cases, your program can make a fairly correct assumption based on past experience.

Don't misunderstand me. Just because I used the word "think" in conjunction with a program doesn't mean that the software should actually be intelligent and try to determine the right thing to do by reasoning. Instead, it should simply do something that has a statistically good chance of being correct, then provide the user with powerful tools for shaping that first attempt, instead of merely giving the user a blank slate and challenging him to have at it. This way the program isn't asking for permission to act, but rather asking for forgiveness after the fact.

Ask forgiveness, not permission

To most people, a blank slate is a difficult starting point. It is so much easier to begin where someone has already left off. A user can easily fine-tune an approximation provided by the program into precisely what he desires with less risk of exposure and mental effort than he would have from drafting it from nothing. As we will discuss in Chapter 14, endowing your program with a good memory is the best way to accomplish this.

Reporting to the user

For programmers, it is important to know what is happening. This goes along with being able to control all of the details of the process. For users, it is disconcerting to know all of the details of what is happening. Many people are frightened to know that the database has been updated, for example. It is better for the program to just do what has to be done, issue reassuring clues when all is well, and not burden the user with the trivia of how it was accomplished.

Many programs are quick to keep users apprised of the program's progress even though the user has neither asked nor wants to know. Programs pop up dialog boxes telling us that connections have been made, that records have been posted, that users have logged on, that 274 transactions were recorded and other useless factoids. To software engineers, these messages are equivalent to the humming of the machinery, the babbling of the brook, the white noise of the waves crashing on the beach: they tell us that all is well. To the user, however, these reports can be like eerie lights beyond the horizon, like screams in the night, like unattended objects flying about the room.

As I said before, the program should make clear that it is working hard, but the detailed feedback can be offered in a more subtle way. In particular, reporting information like this with a modal dialog box brings the interaction to a stop for no particular benefit. In Figure 11-6 we saw how Microsoft forces me to stop other things when I want to know how much space is left on my hard disk. The answer to this common question should never be relegated to a modal dialog box but should be constantly visible whenever the Explorer is running.

It is important that we not stop the proceedings to report normalcy. When some event has transpired that was supposed to have transpired, never report this fact with a dialog box. Save dialogs for events that are out of the normal course of events.

> **Design tip:** Don't use dialogs to report normalcy.

By the same token, don't stop the proceedings and bother the user with problems that are not serious. If the program is having trouble getting through a busy signal, don't put up a dialog box to report it. Instead, build a status indicator into the program so the problem is clear to the interested user but is not obtrusive to the user who is busy elsewhere.

The key to orchestrating the user interaction is to take a goal-directed approach. You must ask yourself whether a particular interaction moves the user rapidly and directly to his goal. Contemporary programs are often reluctant to take any forward motion without the user directing it in advance. But users would rather see the program take some "good enough" first step and then adjust it to what is desired. This way, the program has moved the user closer to his goal.

Where were you on the night of the sixteenth?

Programs have a proclivity for shifting into what I call interrogation mode where they begin demanding answers from the user.

They enter interrogation mode for two reasons. Sometimes they seem to feel that it is their right to demand answers from the user. In this respect, they are totally mistaken. The program should instead offer *choices* to the user. There is a big difference between offering choices and demanding answers. The second reason is that many programs can't just do what they are told but must instead demand that you micro-manage their job.

These two reasons are often combined, resulting in obnoxious dialog boxes. You ask the program to perform a function, and it takes the opportunity to demand that you explain to it in exacting detail precisely how you want it to do the function. The program should not use your request as an excuse to enter interrogation mode.

Dialog boxes have very little right to demand information from humans. They are merely digital scum, and they exist only at the sufferance of the user, and not vice versa. If you ask a program to perform a function, the program should perform that function and not begin to interrogate you about your precise demands. If you wanted to express your precise demands to the program, you would have requested the precision dialog instead.

For example, when I ask most programs to print a document, they respond by putting up a complex dialog box demanding that I specify how many copies to print, what the paper orientation is, what paper feeder to use, what margins to set, whether the output should be in monochrome or color, what scale to print it at, whether to use Postscript fonts or native fonts, whether to print the current page, the current selection or the entire document, and whether to print to a file and if so, what name should it get. Whew! All of those options sure are neat, but all I wanted was to print the document, and that is what I thought I asked for.

A much more reasonable design would be to have a command to PRINT and another command to CONFIGURE THE PRINT. The PRINT command would not issue any dialog but would just go ahead and print, either using previous settings or standard, vanilla settings. The CONFIGURE THE PRINT function would offer up all of those choices about paper and copies and fonts. It would also be very reasonable to be able to go directly from the configure dialog to printing.

There is a big difference between configuring and invoking a function. The former may include the latter, but the latter shouldn't include the former. In general, any user will want to invoke a command ten times for every one time he wants to configure it. It is better to make the user ask explicitly for the configurator one time in ten than it is to make the user reject the configurator *nine* times in ten.

The idea that "if you have available choices, they should be presented" is an expression of possibility thinking rather than the more user-centered probability thinking. Just because it is possible to fine-tune a function, it doesn't necessarily follow that there is a high probability that the user will want to.

Earlier versions of Word were notorious for this problem. I would finish editing a document, request PRINT from the menu, then get up from my chair, stretch, and walk down the hall for a cup of coffee. When I returned, expecting to find my printed document neatly stacked in the output tray of my printer, I would be frustrated to find no printout, just a mindless dialog idling peacefully in the middle of the screen waiting patiently till doomsday for me to confirm that, yes, I merely wanted one copy. I would pull my hair and press the redundant, mocking OK button, then stare disgustedly at the screen while the document slowly printed. The interrogation-mode dialog box wasn't usually needed; therefore it was not expected; therefore it was wrong. The latest version of Word still works this way, but the PRINT button on the toolbar immediately prints a single copy without presenting an intervening, unexpected dialog box—precisely what I expect.

Microsoft's printing solution is a reasonable rule of thumb. Put immediate access to functions on buttons in the toolbar and put access to function-configuration dialog boxes on menu items. The configuration dialogs are better pedagogic tools, while the buttons provide immediate action.

Sensible interaction

One of the essential parts of orchestrating a good user interface is interacting with the user in a sensible manner. This deceptively simple statement seems obvious, yet programs violate it constantly.

Many programs put dialog boxes up for no better reason than habit or programming ease. For example, in the File Manager program in Windows 3.x, if I ask to rename a file, the program puts up the dialog box shown in Figure 11-7.

The two outlined boxes are normal text-edit fields, but entering text in the top one has no effect on the file. My natural reaction to this dialog box is to directly edit the file name the program offers me in the top edit box. That is, if I want to change "WUIDABS.DOC" to "WUIDABS1.DOC," I would simply position the mouse between the s and the dot, click to get an edit caret and then enter the number 1 from the keyboard followed by an ENTER to close the dialog box. The tragic part of this story is that it is perfectly legal to take such a sequence of actions. However, if I do take those actions, nothing sensible happens! The dialog box closes, and the program continues blithely on its merry way with no acknowledgment of the fact that no change was made to the file's name.

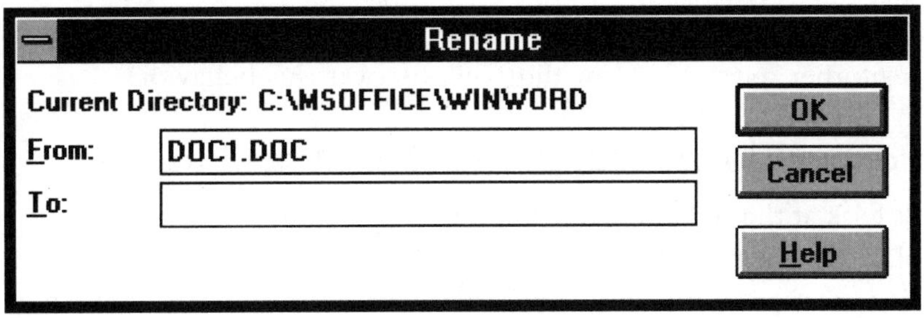

Figure 11-7

This is the File Rename dialog box from the Windows 3.x File Manager program. It violates the rule of orchestrating a good interaction with the user in numerous ways, including its very existence. Microsoft finally got rid of it in Windows 95. Are there dialogs like this one in your software?

To change the name of the file, I must enter the entire new file name in the second text edit box. I would have to enter "WUIDABS1.DOC" from the keyboard and then press ENTER to accept the change. The reaction from the program is identical to that from the first set of actions, except this time File Manager actually renames the file. Let's examine the several significant failings of the design of this dialog box.

The first field is an edit box that doesn't edit

If entering text into the topmost field is not a useful action, why did Microsoft make the field a text-entry field? The field should be for text output only, similar to the "Current Directory:" field just above it. Because the field allows text manipulation, it conveys the message to the user that text manipulation is a meaningful and effective action. If this is not true, the field should not offer such affordances. The program should not lie to the user.

I must confess that entering something into this field actually *does* have an effect. It is a nonsensical, undiscoverable and unwanted effect, but an effect nonetheless. My technical editor, Neil Rubenking, pointed it out to me, although even he can't understand what possible use it has. This is the way he explained it to me: "If you edit the text in the top line to the name of another existing file, the rename command will affect *that* file. For example, say you highlight file 'FOO' and choose File|Rename. Change 'FOO' to 'BAR' in the top box, fill in 'SNAFU' in the bottom, and you've renamed BAR to SNAFU, leaving FOO unchanged. Weird? Sure!" This begs the question: was this intentional or an accidental side effect of using an edit gizmo where an output-only text gizmo was required? Hey, Neil, wanna bet it was an accident? Actually, this begs another question: How did Neil discover this behavior?

The program doesn't fill in the second field for you

Now let's look at the second text-edit gizmo. If the lower text-edit gizmo is the proper place to construct the new filename, why doesn't the program give the user a head start by filling the field in with the current name of the file? The lack of this obvious offering is what often tricks me into trying to edit the top field. The program should be saying "here is the field as it currently exists, edit it to what you desire." Instead, it is saying "tell me exactly what you want and I don't really care if it takes extra work on your part."

Frequently, when I want to rename a file (like the word processing file in the previous example), I will only be thinking about the eight-character file name, leaving management of the three-character file extension to the discretion of the program. When I key in the new name, I will naturally forget to add the file extension, the ".DOC." Of course, the dialog box will merrily rename the file to something that my word processor will no longer recognize. Adding insult to injury, File Manager itself will now not know what to do when I double-click on the new file name—without any memory, the File Manager depends utterly on the three-character extension to know what to do. So this sequence often occurs to me: I rename a file, omitting the extension, then try to launch it with a double-click and get an error message from File Manager for my trouble. My friend Richard Schwartz at Borland has a riddle that illustrates this type of software interaction. He says, "Ask me if I'm a fish." I dutifully reply, "Are you a fish?" and he snaps out "No. Why do you ask?" Arrrrgh!

Regardless of how I use this dialog box, I will always end up with some file name in the second box; otherwise, nothing will happen. Although the range of possible entries is infinite, it is undeniably probable that I will enter *something* in the second gizmo. If the program was better prepared for the probable case, it would be bigger help to the poor user.

Design tip: Prepare for the probable case.

The appropriate way to handle this second field would be to fill it in with a copy of the current file name and then completely select the entire field. By the standard rules of behavior for selection, any single keystroke will replace the selected portion, so if I wanted to change the name to something completely different, all I would have to do would be begin typing. The old name would instantly blink out of existence and be replaced by the newly typed name. On the other hand, I could easily point with the mouse to a single location between any two characters, and the selection would become a text-entry caret for insertion or correction. The net effect would be better than it is now, with support for either choice I might make.

The program doesn't alert you to failure

When the program leads me down the garden path, teasing me with an edit field that is pointless to edit, and I fall for it, the program doesn't even have the decency to tell me. First, it doesn't say, "Hey, you can't enter text there!" Second, it doesn't say, "Hey, you made some changes in a place where their effect is meaningless." On two counts, the dialog box fails to remain aware of what is happening. The standard dialog box code doesn't support this kind of awareness—the programmer must supply it. I consider this type of failure to maintain situational awareness one of the more frustrating aspects of poorly designed software. It is like handing your secretary a folder and asking him to file it; he says, "Okay" and then awhile later you notice the folder spilled thoughtlessly on the floor. When you ask him about it, he doesn't apologize but tells *you* to pick it all up and hand it to him again. It is very aggravating because it seems like the program isn't saying, "Sorry, I can't do that," but rather saying, "I don't care about your stupid problems."

The dialog isolates the function from context

When I ask to rename a file, I really mean something less specific, like "I need to do something with this file so I can keep track of it better." There are several ways to accomplish this, but only one of them is an actual rename. This dialog box removes the function of renaming a file from the context of managing my file system, which is the purpose of the File Manager. Often, I will consider renaming a file and then decide instead to move the file to another directory. The dialog box doesn't offer any file-movement capabilities, and in fact isolates me from the file-movement tools that are in the File Manager program. If I want to rename a file, it is likely that I don't want to have the new name collide with an already-existing name in the same directory. The dialog box doesn't offer any information about the file, like when it was created, how big it is, when it was last changed or what application would be launched if I double-clicked on it. Not only that, it covers up what little information is offered by the File Manager on its main screen.

The dialog box doesn't need to exist at all

This dialog box begs the question "Why does it exist at all?" Why didn't Microsoft just make the filename in the directory display editable? I should be able to click on the name of the file (or on a trigger next to it) and get an edit cursor right in the filename display itself. This would instantly solve all of the above complaints: The relationship of edit boxes to things that are editable would be direct, one-to-one and unambiguous. I would only have to enter the changes I wanted, leaving untouched anything that I wanted to remain unchanged. The program would immediately alert me to any failure through the most efficient means possible: the same facility by which it shows me everything else it knows. The context of the file would not be hidden but would be as clearly shown as it normally is in the program. If I changed my mind and decided to move or copy the file instead, the various operations would be seamless, on the same plane and available by direct manipulation.

Whaddaya know? The Explorer in Windows 95 actually does exactly what I describe. It allows files to be renamed in place or dragged from one directory to another. All actions stay within this context. Just don't forget that three letter extension: It is still the only way Windows knows what to do with your file. The Rename dialog box is just a fading memory. My biggest complaint is that I can't use the Explorer as the File Open and Save As dialogs in my applications. Maybe in Windows 97...

Design tip: Have a reason for each idiom.

Don't create a dialog box without first assuring yourself that a dialog box is the appropriate idiom for this interaction. A dialog is a suspension of the normal course of events, and it is incorrect to use one during normal interaction. Conversely, when something out of the ordinary comes along, a dialog box calls the user's attention to the uniqueness of the occurrence.

The File Rename dialog box in Windows 3.x shows how the orchestration of user interaction can founder on something extremely simple. Often we concentrate on the bigger, more obvious complexities of interaction and forget about these simple functions. Inevitably, they are the ones that trip us up.

Posture and State

Most people, especially while they are working, have a predominant behavioral attitude: the teacher is imperious; the toll-taker is bored and invisible; the actor is shining and bigger than life; the butler is obsequious and servile. Programs, too, have a predominant manner of presenting themselves to the user.

A program may be bold or timid, bright or gray, but it should be so for a specific, goal-directed reason. Its manner shouldn't result merely from the personal preference of its designer or programmer. The presentation of the program affects the way the user relates to it, which strongly influences the usability of the product. Programs whose appearance or manner conflict with their purpose seem somehow clunky and inappropriate, like a loud, profane voice in a church or shouting from the audience during a stageplay.

Posture

The behavior of your program should reflect how it is used, rather than an arbitrary standard. If your program is used like Excel, then modeling its behavior after Excel is suitable. If not, your program runs the risk of ending up looking like Henry Kissinger dancing the hula.

151

I call a program's behavioral stance—the way it presents itself to the user—its posture.

The look and feel of your program is not as much an aesthetic choice as much as it is a behavioral choice. Your program's posture is its behavioral foundation.

I divide desktop applications into four categories of posture: sovereign, transient, daemonic and parasitic. Because each describes a different set of behavioral attributes, they also describe different types of user interaction. More importantly, they give the designer a point of departure for designing an interface. A sovereign posture program, for example, won't feel right unless it behaves in a "sovereign" way.

Sovereign Posture

I call a program that is the only one on the screen, monopolizing the user's attention for long periods of time, a sovereign posture application.

Sovereign applications travel in royal splendor, surrounded by their numerous courtiers. They offer a panoply of related functions and features, and users tend to keep them up and running continuously. Good examples of this type of application are word processors and spreadsheets. Many vertical applications are also sovereign applications, as they often deploy on the screen for long periods of time and interaction with them can be very complex and involved. Users working with sovereign programs often find themselves in a state of flow. Sovereign programs are usually used maximized (we'll talk more about window states later in this chapter). For example, it is hard to imagine using Word in a 10×15 cm window—at that size it's not really appropriate for its main job: creating and editing documents.

Sovereign programs are characteristically used for long, continuous stretches. I'm using Word to write this manuscript; it has been the only one on screen for the last hour and will remain so for many hours to come. Typical. A sovereign program dominates a process as its primary tool. PowerPoint, for example, is camped out full screen while I create a presentation from start to finish. Even if other programs are used for support tasks, PowerPoint remains in the royal role.

The implications of sovereign behavior are subtle but quite clear once you think about them. The most important implication is that users of sovereign programs are experienced users. Sure, each user will spend some time as a novice, but only for a short period of time *relative to the amount of time he will eventually spend using the product.* I'm not making light of the difficulty the new user has in getting over the painful hump of first-learning, but, seen from the perspective of the entire relationship, the time the user spends getting acquainted with the program is small.

Sovereign users are experienced users

From the designer's point of view, this means that the program should be designed for optimal use by experienced users, and not primarily for first-time users. Sacrificing speed and power in favor of clumsier but easier-to-learn idioms is out of place here. Of course, if you can offer easier idioms without compromising the interaction for experienced users, that is always best.

Between first-time users and experienced users there are many people who must use sovereign applications only on occasion. These infrequent users cannot be ignored, and the quality of the interface will be reflected in the product's acceptance by its infrequent users. However, the success of a sovereign application will still be completely dependent on its experienced, frequent users until someone else satisfies both them and the inexperienced or first-time users. WordStar, an early word processing program is a good example. It dominated the word processing marketplace in the late '70s and early '80s because it served its experienced users so well, even though it was extremely difficult for infrequent and first-time users. WordStar Corporation thrived until its competition offered the same power for experienced users while simultaneously making it much less painful for infrequent users. The WordStar company rapidly shrank to insignificance.

Take the pixels

Because the user's interaction with a sovereign program dominates his session at the computer, the program shouldn't be afraid to take as much video real estate as possible. No other program will be competing with yours, so expect to take advantage of it all. Don't ever waste space, of course, but don't be shy about taking what you need to do the job. If you need four toolbars to cover the bases, use four toolbars. In a different type of program, four toolbars may be overly complex, greedy and inappropriate, but the sovereign posture has a defensible claim on the pixels.

Generally, as I said before, you can expect that sovereign programs will be running maximized. In fact, in the absence of explicit instructions from the user, your sovereign application should always default to maximized. The program needs to be fully resizable, and must work in all manner of oddball configurations, but optimize its interface for maximization instead of the oddball stuff.

Toolbars are mostly populated with familiar, three-dimensional, rectangular push-buttons with pictographic icons on them instead of text. Naturally, I call these gizmos **buttcons**; a simple combination of buttons and icons. I introduce the term now because it is relevant to this discussion, but we'll discuss these gizmos in detail in Parts V and VI.

Because the user will stare at a sovereign application for long periods, you should take care to mute the colors and texture of the visual presentation. Keep the color palette narrow and conservative. That big red-striped gizmo may look really cool to newcomers, but it will seem garish after a couple of weeks of daily use. Tiny dots or accents of color will have more effect in the long run than big splashes, allowing you to pack controls together more tightly than you could otherwise.

Your user will stare at the same palettes, menus and toolbars for many hours, gaining an innate sense of where things are from sheer familiarity. This gives you, the designer, the freedom to do more with fewer pixels. Buttcons can be smaller than normal. Auxiliary controls like screen-splitters, rulers, scrollers and other manipulable items can be smaller and more closely spaced.

Sovereign applications are great platforms for creating an environment truly rich in visual feedback for the user. You can productively add extra little bits of information into the interface. The status bar at the bottom of the screen, the ends of the space normally occupied by scroll-bars, the caption bar and other dusty corners of the program's visible extents can be filled with graphs, numbers, indicators, simulated leds and many other visual indications of the program's status, the status of the data, the state of the system and hints for more productive user actions. While enriching the visual feedback, you must be careful not to create an interface that is hopelessly cluttered and busy.

The first-time user won't even notice such artifacts, let alone understand them, because of the subtle way they are shown on the screen. After a couple of months of steady use, though, he will begin to see them, wonder about their meaning, and explore them. At this point, the user will be willing to expend a little effort to learn more, and if you provide an easy means for him to find out what the artifacts are, he will become not only a better user, but a more satisfied user, as his power over the program grows with his understanding. Adding such richness to the interface is like adding a variety of ingredients to a meat stock—it enhances the entire meal.

In the same vein, sovereign programs benefit from rich input. Every frequently used aspect of the program should be controllable in several ways. Direct manipulation, dialog boxes, buttcons, keyboard mnemonics and keyboard accelerators are all appropriate. You can make more aggressive demands on the user's fine motor skills with direct-manipulation idioms. Sensitive areas on the screen can be just a couple of pixels across, because you can assume that the user will be established comfortably in his chair, arm positioned in a stable way on his desk, rolling his mouse firmly across a resilient mouse pad.

Go ahead and use all of the corners of the program's window for controls. In a jet cockpit, the most frequently used controls are situated directly in front of the pilot; those needed only occasionally or in an emergency are found on the armrests, overhead, and on the side panels. In Word, Microsoft has put the most frequently used functions on buttcons on the two main toolbars (see Figure 12-1). They put the frequently used but visually dislocating functions on small buttcons to the left of the horizontal scroll-bar near the bottom of the screen. These controls change the appearance of the entire visual display— NORMAL VIEW, PAGE LAYOUT VIEW and OUTLINE VIEW. They are not usually used by neophytes and, if accidentally triggered, they can be confusing. By placing them near the bottom of the screen, they become almost invisible to the new user. Their segregated positioning subtly and silently indicates that caution should be taken in their use. More experienced users, with more confidence in their understanding and control of the program will begin to notice these controls and wonder about their purpose. They will experimentally press them when they feel fully prepared for their consequence. This is a very accurate and useful mapping of control placement to usage.

Interactions that involve a delay won't be appreciated much by the user. Like a grain of sand in your shoe, a one- or two-second delay gets awfully painful when frequently repeated. It is perfectly acceptable to have procedures that take time, but they should not be ones that are frequent or repeated during the normal use of the product. If, for example, it takes more than a fraction of a

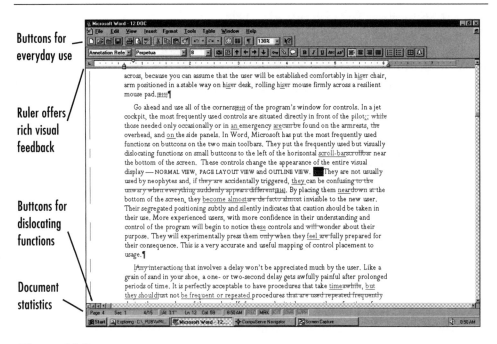

Buttons for everyday use

Ruler offers rich visual feedback

Buttons for dislocating functions

Document statistics

Figure 12-1

Microsoft Word is a classic example of a sovereign-posture application. It stays on-screen, interacting with the user for long, uninterrupted periods. Notice how Microsoft has built controls into both the top and the bottom of the application. Those at the top are more benign than those at the bottom, which are segregated because they can cause significant visual dislocation.

second to save the user's work to disk, that delay will quickly come to be viewed as unreasonable. On the other hand, inverting a matrix or changing the entire formatting style of a document can take a few seconds without causing irritation because the user can plainly see what a big evolution it is. Besides, he won't want to invoke the evolution very often.

The dictum that sovereign programs should maximize on the screen is also true of document windows within the program itself. Child windows containing documents should always be maximized inside the program unless the user explicitly instructs otherwise.

Many sovereign programs are also document-centric, making it easy to confuse the two, but they are not the same. Most of the documents we work with are

8½-by-11 inches and won't fit on a standard video screen. We strain to show as much of them as possible, which naturally demands a maximized aspect. If the document under construction were a 4-by-6 inch photograph, for example, a document-centric program wouldn't need to take the full screen. The sovereignty of a program does not come from its document-centricity nor from the size of the document—it comes from the nature of the program's use.

Transient posture

If a program manipulates a document but only does some very simple, single function, like scanning in a graphic, it isn't a sovereign application and shouldn't exhibit sovereign behavior. Such single-function applications have a posture of their own, which I call transient.

A transient-posture program comes and goes, presenting a single, high-relief function with a tightly restricted set of accompanying controls. The program is called when needed, appears, performs its job, then quickly leaves, letting the user continue his more normal activity, which is usually working with a sovereign application.

The salient characteristic of transient programs is their temporary nature. Because they don't stay on the screen for extended periods of time, the user doesn't get the chance to become very familiar with them. Consequently, the program's user interface needs to be unsubtle, presenting its controls clearly and boldly with no possibility of mistakes. The interface must spell out what it does: this is not the place for artistic-but-ambiguous images on buttcons—it *is* the place for big buttons with precise legends spelled out in big, 12-point type.

Although a transient program can certainly operate alone on your desktop, it usually acts in a supporting role to a sovereign application. For example, calling up the Explorer to locate and open a file while editing another with Word is a typical transient scenario. So is checking your email. Because the transient program borrows space at the expense of the sovereign, it must respect the sovereign by not taking more space on screen than is absolutely necessary. Where the sovereign can dig a hole and pour a concrete foundation for itself, the transient program is just on a weekend campout. It cannot deploy itself on screen either graphically or temporally. It is the Roto-Rooter truck of the software world.

While a transient program must conserve the total amount of video real estate it consumes, the gizmos on its surface can be proportionally larger than those on a sovereign application. Where such heavy-handed visual design on a sovereign program would pall within a few weeks, the transient program isn't on screen long enough for it to bother the user. On the contrary, the coarser graphics help the user to orient himself more quickly when the program pops up. The program shouldn't restrict itself to a dull corporate gray, either, but should paint itself in brighter colors to help differentiate it from the hosting sovereign, which may be more appropriately attired in gray flannel.

Transient programs should use brighter colors and bold graphics to convey their purpose—there is little time for the user to visually orient himself with conservative coloration. The user needs big, bright, reflective road signs to keep him from making the wrong turn at 100 kilometers per hour. Animated buttons are certainly not out of place here. A little bit of animation goes a long way, as our eyes are drawn to movement. A couple of pixels changing slowly is all it takes to ensure that the user notices.

Transient programs should have instructions built into their surface. The user may only see the program once a month, and will likely forget the meanings of the choices presented. Instead of a button captioned "Setup," it might be better to make the button large enough to caption it "Set Up User Preferences." The meaning is clearer, and the button more reassuring. Likewise, nothing should be abbreviated on a transient program—everything should be spelled out to avoid confusion. The user should be able to see without difficulty that the printer is busy, for example, or that the audio clip is 5 seconds long.

Once the user summons a transient program, all of the information and facilities he needs should be right there on the surface of the program's single window. Keep the user's locus of attention on that window and never force him into supporting sub-windows or dialog boxes to take care of the main function of the program. If you find yourself adding a dialog box or second view to a transient application, that's a key sign that your design needs a review.

Transient programs are not the place for tiny scroll-bars and fussy point-click-and-drag interfaces. You want to keep the demands here on the user's fine motor skills down to a minimum. Simple push-buttons for simple functions are better. Anything directly manipulable must be big enough to move to easily: at least twenty pixels square. Keep controls off the borders of the window. Don't use the window bottoms, status bars or sides in transient programs. Instead, position the controls up close and personal in the main part of the window.

You should definitely provide a keyboard interface, but it must be a simple one. It shouldn't be any fancier than ENTER, ESCAPE and TAB. You might add the arrow keys, too, but that's about it.

Of course, there are exceptions to this monothematism, although they are rare. If a transient program performs more than just a single function, the interface should communicate this visually. For example, if the program imports and exports graphics, the interface should be evenly and visually split into two halves by bold coloration or other graphics. One half could contain the controls for importing and the other half the controls for exporting. The two halves must be labeled unambiguously. Whatever you do, don't add more windows or dialogs.

Keep in mind that any given transient program may be called upon to assist in the management of some aspect of a sovereign program. This means that the transient program, as it positions itself on top of the sovereign, may obscure the very information that it is chartered to work on. This implies that the transient program must be movable, which means it must have a caption bar. Making it reshapable may also be desirable, though not mandatory.

Having said that, it is vital to remember how important it is to keep the amount of management overhead as low as possible with transient programs. All the user wants to do is call the program up, request a function and then end the program. It is completely unreasonable to force the user to add non-productive window-management tasks to this interaction. Manipulating the Windows semi-standard **multiple document interface (MDI)** is a strong example of non-productive window management.

MDI can certainly be useful in some situations, but I cannot imagine a need for it in any transient program. For example, the Program Manager in Windows 3.x is a transient program, yet it insists on using MDI. The amount of time and frustration its users spend wondering where their icons are, zooming, moving, reorganizing and managing their group windows is high in relation to the benefit. All the program really does is launch applications, which isn't demanding enough to require all of that paperwork. This high demand for bureaucratic management overhead is one of the reasons why there is such a brisk business in Windows shell replacement programs. Even Microsoft has replaced it in Windows 95.

The most appropriate way to help the user with both transient and sovereign apps is, as usual, to give the program a memory. If the transient program remembers where it was the last time it was used, the chances are excellent that the same shape and place will be appropriate next time, too. It will almost always be more apt than any default setting might chance to be. Whatever shape and position the user morphed the program into is the shape and position the program should reappear in when it is next summoned. Of course, this holds true for its logical settings, too.

On the other hand, if the use of the program is really simple and single-minded, go ahead and specify its shape—omit the thickframe, the directly resizable window border. Save yourself the work and remove the complexity from the program. I say this with some trepidation, though, as this can certainly be abused. The goal here is not to save the programmer work—that's just a collateral benefit—but to keep the user aware of as few complexities as possible. If the program's functions don't demand reshaping, and the overall size of the program is small, Occam's razor, the principle that "simpler is better," takes on more importance than usual. The Windows calculator, for example, isn't resizable. It is always the "correct" size and shape.

No doubt you have already realized that almost all dialog boxes are really transient programs. You can see that all of the above guidelines for transient programs apply equally well to the design of dialog boxes.

Daemonic Posture

I call programs that do not normally interact with the user **daemonic posture** programs. These programs serve quietly and invisibly in the background, performing possibly vital tasks without the need for human intervention. A printer driver is an excellent example.

As you might expect, any discussion of the user interface of daemonic programs will be necessarily short. Too frequently, though, programmers give daemonic programs full-screen control panels that are better suited to sovereign programs. Designing your fax manager in the image of Excel, for example, is a fatal mistake. At the other end of the spectrum, daemonic programs are too-frequently unreachable by the user, causing no end of frustration when adjustments need to be made.

Where a transient program controls the execution of a function, daemonic programs usually manage processes. Your heartbeat isn't a function that must be consciously controlled; rather, it is a process that proceeds autonomously in the background. Like the processes that regulate your heartbeat, daemonic programs generally remain completely invisible, competently performing their process as long as your computer is turned on. Unlike your heart, however, daemonic programs must occasionally be installed and removed and, also occasionally, they must be manually adjusted to deal with changing circumstances. It is at these times that the daemon talks to the user. Without exception, the interaction between the user and a daemonic program is transient in nature, and all of the imperatives of transient program design hold true here also.

The principles of transient design that are concerned with keeping the user informed of the purpose of the program and of the scope and meaning of the user's available choices become even more critical with daemonic programs. If you recognize that in many cases the user will not even be consciously (or unconsciously) aware of the existence of the daemonic program, it becomes obvious that reports about status from that program can be quite dislocating if not presented in an appropriate context. Since many of these programs perform esoteric functions—like printer drivers or communications concentrators—the messages from them must take particular care not to confuse the user or lead to misunderstandings.

A question that is often taken for granted with programs of other postures becomes very significant with daemonic programs: if the program is normally invisible, how should the user interface be summoned on those rare occasions when it is needed? One of the most frequently used methods is to represent the daemon with an on-screen program icon the way the After Dark screen savers do. Putting the icon so boldly in the user's face when it is almost never needed is a real affront, like pasting an advertisement on the windshield of somebody's car. If your daemon needs configuring less than once a day, get it off the main screen.

A better approach is to create a "control panel" application that will be found by the Windows control panel program, CONTROL.EXE, and shown in its window. The user then has a consistent place to go for access to such process-centric applications. An equally effective solution is to create a transient program that runs as a launchable application to configure the daemon.

Parasitic Posture

I call programs that blend the characteristics of sovereign and transient programs parasitic posture programs. The parasitic program is continuously present like a sovereign, but it performs only a supporting role, is small and is superimposed on another application the way a transient is. The Windows Clock and Microsoft Office Manager are two good examples of parasitic programs.

Parasitic programs typically are silent reporters of ongoing processes. In some cases, this reporting may be a function they perform in addition to actually managing that process, but this is not necessarily true. A parasite may, for example, monitor the amount of system resources either in use or available. The program constantly displays a small bar chart reflecting the current resource availability. There are many parasitic shareware applications that, for example, paint a clock on every program's caption bar, or display an icon with animated eyeballs that constantly watch the mouse cursor, or show how much memory is free.

A process-reporting parasitic program must be simple and often bold in reporting its information. It rides on top of a sovereign application, so it must be very respectful of the preeminence of that other program and should be quick to move out of the way when necessary.

Parasitic programs are not the locus of the user's attention; that distinction belongs to the host application. For example, recall the case I cited earlier of my client who has the automatic call distribution (ACD) program. An ACD is used to evenly distribute incoming calls to teams of human "agents" who are trained order-takers or customer-support representatives. Each agent has a computer running an application specific to his job. This application, because it is the primary reason for the system's existence, is always a sovereign-posture application; the ACD program is a parasite on top of it. For example, a sales agent will field calls from prospective buyers on an incoming toll-free number. The agent's order entry program is the sovereign, while the ACD program is the parasite, riding on top to feed incoming calls to the agent. The ACD program must be very conservative in its use of pixels because it always obscures some of the underlying sovereign application. It can afford to have small features because it will be on the screen for long periods of time. In other words, the gizmos on the parasite can be designed to a sovereign's sensibilities.

Other Postures

There are other program postures, but most programs you design will fall into one of these four categories. Visual Basic is a notable exception, following as it does none of the four posture paradigms. As the inventor of its somewhat oddball configuration, I feel that I should explain its genesis. The idea behind VB was to create a visual programming language that had two distinct modes: programming and running the result. The generated program would be a standalone application, not part of the VB tool suite. This, in turn, dictated the design. In programming mode, the user's program would have one or more "forms" visible on the screen, surrounded by a suite of tools. The forms are independent of the tools, rather than being enclosed in the tool application window. This enabled the next step, wherein the user could shift to "running the result" mode, and only the tools would disappear, leaving the forms untouched and visible.

The actual need for a posture like Visual Basic's is exceedingly rare, yet it is astonishing how many programs copy it. This says to me that many programmers don't know how to select their program's posture and merely copy that of the language in which it is written. Properly determining your program's posture will tell you much about its behavioral persona which, in turn, will dictate many of the important guidelines for the design process. This is much like how a novelist or screenwriter constructs a story by creating characters, putting them in a situation, then letting them act "in character." As a user interface designer, you get a lot of bang for your buck merely by assuring that your program behaves in the posture most appropriate for its behavior.

Windows states

A Microsoft Windows programmer would call an application's primary window its **top-level window**.

The intrinsic behavior of a top-level window includes the ability to overlap other top-level windows, but this is not how they are normally used. Each top-level window has the native ability to be in one of three states, depending on how they are programmed. Oddly, only two of these three states have been given names by Microsoft: **minimized** and **maximized**.

They somehow manage to avoid directly referring to the third state, which you get to by using the button labelled with both the up- and down-arrows, and the only hint of a name is on the system menu where the verb "Restore" describes the other way to get to it. This function "restores" a minimized top-level window to its previous state, either maximized or that other state. In the interests of sanity, I call this third state **pluralized**, although it has been called "restored" more than once.

The pluralized state is that in-between condition where the window is neither an icon nor maximized to cover the entire screen. When a window is pluralized, it shares the screen with icons and other pluralized windows.

In Version 1.0 of Windows, the states of minimization and maximization were called "iconized" and "zoomed," terms that were more descriptive and certainly more engaging. IBM, then enjoying a cozy relationship with Microsoft, demanded the change to corporate-speak in the mistaken impression that America's executives would feel more comfortable. The weaker appellations have stuck.

The normal state for a sovereign application is maximized. There is no reason for such a program to be pluralized, other than to support switching between programs. Some transient applications, like the File Manager or the Explorer, are appropriately run pluralized, but these transient programs are used merely as springboards for sovereign applications. Many users, however, run their sovereign programs in the pluralized state, and I don't know why (other than merely because that is the program's default and the user is too timid to change it). By definition, a sovereign application will be in use for extended periods of time, and any pixels not used by it are wasted. There aren't enough pixels to waste. I suspect that those users who run sovereign applications pluralized do so because the exercise of switching between maximized applications is too great for them to bother fussing with: it's easier to just accept the loss of video real estate. For those of us who are persistent enough to master the technique, though, maximized sovereign applications are the normal mode of operating.

Why minimize?

Any application can be minimized, but why? I can think of two reasons, but neither of them makes much sense.

You can minimize to switch from one application to another, but this is an ungainly procedure. You minimize the active program, then maximize (or pluralize) the icon of the desired program. To switch back, you reverse the sequence. You must move the mouse all over the screen and the process is slow, complicated and ungainly.

In Windows 3.x, the ALT-TAB key sequence is a much more useful method of switching between applications, but it is obscure, not visual, demands a high level of user expertise, is relatively unknown outside of the power-user community and operates unlike any other idiom in Windows. Pressing ALT-TAB moves you quickly and directly to the next running program. Holding down the ALT key and repeatedly pressing the TAB key cycles you through each running program. It does this by showing a small window in the center of the screen with the name and icon of the candidate program. The trick is that the actual selection of a program occurs when the user *releases* the ALT key! Nowhere else in Windows does an action occur on the release of a shifting key. This idiom is weird enough that most people don't know about it (I used Windows for seven years before I discovered it), and learning it can be difficult. Once the idiom is learned, though, it is remarkably powerful and clearly the best way to navigate between applications. Besides the speed of the technique for switching from program to program, the great advantage is that the various programs can each remain in their natural state, either maximized or pluralized, but usually maximized.

The ALT-TAB idiom is a classic example of how a programming staff can ingeniously solve a significant problem that baffled the experts. Many sharp software designers tried to create convenient program-switching idioms, but none are the equal of this one. The solution is brilliant but virtually undiscoverable—it's not documented and it doesn't appear on any menu, so someone must tell you about it. The solution is fabulously economical of overhead but requires a deep familiarity and dexterity with the computer, coupled with a clear sense of dominance over it—a good description of your average code-slinger. What we really needed was a more benign version of ALT-TAB that wasn't just for power-users and hackers. In Windows 95, we get this solution with the Startbar.

The Windows 95 Startbar finally acknowledges that most people want to work on one maximized sovereign application at a time, and that they want a more accessible idiom for accomplishing this. A significant percentage of the screen's real estate is devoted to this ever-present gray bar, but it is worth it for everyone but the most hard-core programmers (and they can always exercise their option of turning it off). The Startbar contains a button for every running program, regardless of its current state (except daemonic-posture programs, of course). The button for the active program is shown in its pushed-in state.

The Startbar is a simple and visual implementation of the ALT-TAB idiom: you press the button of the application you want, and it moves to the front of the screen and becomes active. If it was last in a maximized state, it will now be maximized. If it was last in a pluralized state, it will now be pluralized and in the same position it was in before. If you imagine your running programs as cards in a deck, the buttons on the Startbar cut the deck directly to the desired program with a single click of the mouse button. Or you can imagine the running programs as channels on your TV—pressing buttons jumps from channel to channel.

The other reason to minimize a program is to reduce clutter on your screen. If you run several pluralized sovereign applications, it can simplify your screen to minimize some of them. However, this is treating the symptom rather than the cause of the problem. Running several pluralized applications is far too wasteful of pixels. If each application is maximized in turn, there will be no apparent clutter, and minimizing won't be necessary, as long as you have the Startbar or the ALT-TAB to navigate between them. Within MDI programs, it also can make sense to minimize document windows, particularly in a program like Program Manager. Although minimizing helps out here, the real problem isn't the state of the document windows. It's the Program Manager itself. This program provides extremely poor tools for organizing programs, even though that is its sole job. Thankfully, it, too, has been discarded in favor of the Startbar in Windows 95.

Windows 95 removes the only two rationales for minimizing a program. Managing your programs as a deck of cards is superior when you have adequate tools. The ALT-TAB has long allowed power-users to work this way, and the Startbar finally brings the capability to the rest of us.

Minimized applications have been used in curious and innovative ways, but ultimately their usefulness is immaterial, because most sovereign applications run maximized. The icons are always covered up, and whatever clever information they were displaying is invisible. Iconic programs have shown remaining memory, remaining resource storage and the amount of disk traffic. They have pointed to the cursor's location and reported on the results of background communications processes. Several of these functions are of interest only to that rapidly shrinking population with extremely small computers, and the rest can be duplicated by using the Startbar.

Why pluralize?

Is there any reason for a program to be pluralized? Well, maybe. Sometimes situations require two or more programs to be juxtaposed, frequently in development tasks. If all the user wants to do is run one sovereign program after another, with an intersprinkling of smaller transient programs temporarily overlaid on them, pluralization is unnecessary. If the user wants to cut and paste information between sovereign programs, the clipboard will work just fine. However, if the user wishes to take advantage of the program-to-program drag-and-drop facility brought to fruition with OLE 2.0, the two programs doing the dragging-and-dropping must both be visible, sharing the screen. In other words, both programs must be pluralized.

Modern SVGA computer screens range from 640×480 pixels to 1600×1280 pixels. Arguably, 1024×768 is the most common resolution in the latter half of the '90s. In such limited physical environments, modern sovereign programs such as word processors or graphics programs are difficult and unpleasant to use when they own less than half of the screen. When giving demonstrations to the press or captains of industry, Microsoft proudly demonstrates the drag-and-drop of a spreadsheet into a word processor. The windows of the two applications are carefully posed in advance to illustrate this single function in isolation. What they don't show you is that the management overhead of pluralizing two windows and then adjusting them manually so that each one gets sufficient exposure is considerably greater than the management overhead of using the clipboard and Startbar and merely swapping between the two sovereign programs.

If you right-click on the Startbar, the context menu offers automatic control of tiling. This is certainly a boon if you want to tile, but why bother? Tiling for an SVGA screen is like a tool that allows you to put 40 people in an elevator; it's just easier and more pleasant to wait for the next one.

Program-to-program drag-and-drop is a powerful idiom, and one that we may see with increasing frequency in the future. However, we won't see it used too much between sovereign applications until our computer screens get a lot bigger, which doesn't promise to happen for several more years. However, program-to-program drag-and-drop can be a boon for moving information between a sovereign application and a transient application. For example, let's look at the process of adding a piece of clip art to a word processing document.

The word processor is the sovereign application, and it is running maximized. The clip art librarian is a transient application and would normally run as a fixed-size window approximately one-quarter of the full size of the screen (one half of the width and one half of the height). The clip art librarian could be easily positioned in the least obtrusive quadrant of the screen and, after the desired image is located, the image could be dragged directly into the appropriate place in the word processor. Another click and the clip art librarian is stored away on the Startbar and the user can proceed. Window management overhead is a mere two clicks, one to open and one to close the librarian, with a possible click-and-drag operation to move the librarian out of the way so the critical area of the word processor's display can be seen more easily. Neither application needed to be explicitly pluralized.

Modern Microsoft Windows software can be effectively built without supplying the ability to either minimize or pluralize. Programs occupying the in-between state of pluralization are dying out, and Windows 95 is helping to kill them. The programs never have to pass through the pluralized or iconized state. Of course, that doesn't mean that you can actually dispense with these options. You must be able to minimize for backwards compatibility, and every program that can maximize must be able to be pluralized for those oddball cases when a user needs to tile the screen with the application (or just in case Microsoft decides to demonstrate your program at COMDEX). Although it is difficult to guess what the case might be, experienced users will probably be upset if the application can't acquit itself of this basic expectation, even though it is more an exercise in adaptability than in practical software design. In this, it is analogous to compulsory figures in figure skating or ground-reference maneuvers for private pilots—not tremendously useful in themselves, but they show a mastery of other necessary skills.

For practical purposes, we are left with only two program configurations: maximized sovereign programs and pluralized transient programs. The sovereign programs endure while the transient programs appear briefly on top of them. When you design your application, you must make this fundamental design decision: dominant or temporary. This will dictate the type of main window you will use.

MDI

Several years ago, Microsoft began proselytizing a new method for organizing the functions in a Windows application. They called this the multiple document interface, or MDI. It satisfied a need apparent in certain categories of applications, namely those that handled multiple instances of a single type of document simultaneously. Notable examples were Excel and Word.

Microsoft backed up their new standard with code built into the operating system, so the emergence of MDI as a standard was inevitable. For a time in the late '80s and early '90s, MDI was regarded by some at Microsoft as a kind of cure-all patent medicine for user interface ills. It was prescribed liberally for all manner of ailments.

Now Microsoft seems to be turning its back on MDI and embracing something called single document interface, or SDI. It seems that MDI didn't fix all the problems after all.

If you want to copy a cell from one spreadsheet and paste it to another, the tedium of opening and closing both spreadsheets in turn is very clunky. It would be much better to have two spreadsheets open simultaneously. Well, there are two ways to accomplish this: You can have one spreadsheet program that can contain two or more spreadsheet instances inside of it. Or you can have multiple instances of the entire spreadsheet program, each one containing a single instance of a spreadsheet. The second option is technically superior, but it demands high-performance equipment.

In the early days of Windows, Microsoft chose the first option for the simple, practical reason of resource frugality. Remember, early Windows versions had to run in real mode on 286 processors. This was sort of like running an underwater sack race on Quaaludes. One program with multiple spreadsheets (documents) was more conservative of bytes and CPU cycles than multiple programs, and performance matters.

Unfortunately, the one-program-multiple-documents model violated a fundamental design rule established early on in Windows: Only one window can be "active" at a time. What was needed was a way to have one program active at a time along with one document window active at a time within it. MDI was the hack that implemented this solution.

Two conditions have emerged in the years since MDI was made a standard. First, the facility was tragically abused by well-meaning programmers. Second, our computers have gotten much more powerful—to the point where multiple instances of programs, each with a single document, are very feasible. Windows 95 with its 32-bit kernel and its preemptive multitasking make the formerly rejected model much more attractive, so Microsoft has made it clear that MDI is no longer politically correct, if not actually doomed.

The winds of change at Microsoft notwithstanding, MDI is actually a fine thing, as long as it is not abused. The main way to abuse it is to have more than one type of document window in a single program. Figure 7-1 shows what I mean. The CompuServe Navigator program offers a dozen or more different types of document windows making it very difficult to understand what is going on. This is very frequently done, and is one of the reasons why some designers would like to see the whole facility thrown out. I see nothing wrong with MDI in a sovereign application like a word processor or spreadsheet, as long as there is only one type of document. Otherwise, confusion sets in as functions lose their sharp edges. Typically, as document windows of different types are selected, the menus change to keep up. This is not an absolutely bad thing, but it is absolutely not a good thing. The user depends on the permanency of menus to help keep them oriented on the screen. Changing them bleeds away this reliability.

Everything I said in the earlier discussion about minimizing, maximizing and pluralizing windows applies to document windows inside an MDI application. If you have to zoom and move and putz with little windows, it is bad design. It is much better to go cleanly from one window to the next. Going from one fully maximized spreadsheet to another fully maximized spreadsheet is powerful and effective. In a few years, when our computers will easily run multiple copies of all of our applications, there will be little effective difference between the MDI and SDI. In MDI, you go to the "Window" menu to change from spreadsheet to spreadsheet, but you go to the Startbar to change from Excel to Word. In SDI, you will go to the Startbar to change both. SDI is clearly better just for this fact, but it's still not a lot better.

Overhead and Idiocy

Software developers often implement stunningly elegant cases of user interface foolishness. They create interactions that are top-heavy with extra work for the user and programs that exhibit really idiotic behavior. Programmers tend to do this because they focus so intently on the enabling technology that they don't see things from a goal-directed point of view. Designers often do this because much of their design work is derivative. They do it the bad way because that is the way it has always been done. But we can free ourselves from these shackles of technology and the past. All we have to do is insist on holding every interaction up to the yardstick of the user's goals.

Overhead

When I want to drive to the office, I have to open the garage door, get in, start the motor, back out and close the garage door before I even begin the forward motion that will take me to my destination. All of these actions are in support of my automobile rather than in support of getting to my destination. If I had a mental-telepathy-matter-transference module, I'd just picture my destination in my mind and then be there—no garages, no motor. My point here is not to

171

complain about the intricacies of driving, but rather to point out the difference between two types of actions we take to accomplish our daily tasks. Any large task, such as driving to the office, involves many smaller tasks. Some of these, which I call revenue tasks, work to solve the problem directly; these are tasks like steering down the road toward my office.

Other tasks, which I call excise tasks, don't contribute directly to solving the problem but are necessary to accomplishing it just the same.

Such tasks include opening and closing the garage door and starting the engine, in addition to putting oil and gas in the car and performing periodic maintenance.

Excise is the extra work that satisfies the needs of our tools as we use them to achieve our objectives. The distinction is sometimes hard to see because we get so used to the excise being part of our tasks. In the above example, this is very true. Most of us drive so frequently that differentiating the act of opening the garage door from the act of driving towards our destination is difficult. Manipulating the garage door is something we do for the car, not for us, and it doesn't move us towards our destination the way the accelerator pedal and steering wheel do.

You may complain that opening and closing the garage door is a task of such monumental trivialness that fretting over it is silly. But imagine if you had to first put air in the car's tires, drive it to the pumps and fill the fuel tank with gasoline, drive it to the oil rack and put oil in the transmission and the crankcase, drive it to the other rack and put hydraulic fluid in the power steering reservoir, brake cylinders and differential, drive it to the vacuum and clean the floor mats, drive it the repair shop and replace the headlights and align the wheels. You'd quickly come to see the difference between excise and revenue tasks. These are all tasks that we perform for the benefit of our automobiles, and not for our benefit. We don't notice them because we don't have to do them every time we need to go somewhere. We only have to change the oil every few months and sometimes we go for a year or more without touching the air in our tires. You can draw a dividing line between serving the car and serving the driver—operating the garage door is on the car side of the line.

Software, too, has a pretty clear dividing line between revenue tasks and excise tasks. Like automobiles, some software excise tasks are trivial and performing them is no great hardship. On the other hand, some software excise tasks are as obnoxious as fixing a flat tire. Installation leaps to mind here, as do such excise tasks as configuring networks, making backups, connecting to online services and installing sound cards.

The problem with excise tasks is that the effort we expend in doing them doesn't go directly towards accomplishing our goals. Instead, it goes towards satisfying the needs of the tool we use to accomplish our goal. It is overhead. It is the percentage that the house gets. It is friction in the system. Without exception, where we can eliminate the need for excise tasks, we make the user more effective and productive and improve the usability of the software. As a software designer, you should become sensitive to the presence of excise and take steps to eradicate it with the same enthusiasm a doctor would apply to curing an infection.

> *Design Tip:* Eliminating excise makes the user more effective.

Fixing a flat tire and installing software are both obviously onerous excise tasks, and eliminating them from our necessary tasks offers clear benefits. But if we can identify enough software equivalents to opening the garage door, we can streamline our interfaces significantly in many tiny increments rather than in one big leap. Indeed, there are many such instances of petty excise, particularly in GUIs. Virtually all window management falls into this category. Dragging, reshaping, resizing, reordering, tiling and cascading windows qualify as excise actions on the order of the garage door.

GUI excise

One of the main criticisms leveled at graphical user interfaces by experienced computer users—notably those trained on command-line systems—is that getting to where you want to go is made slower and more difficult by the extra effort that goes into manipulating windows and icons. They complain that with a command line, they can just type in the desired command and the computer executes it immediately. With windowing systems, they must open various folders looking for the desired file or program before they can launch it; then, once it appears on the screen, they must stretch and drag the window until it is in the desired location and configuration.

These complaints are well-founded. Extra window manipulation tasks like these are, indeed, excise. They don't move the user towards his goal; they are overhead that the programs demand before they deign to assist the user. But everybody knows that GUIs are easier to use than command-line systems. Who is right?

The confusion arises because the real issues are hidden. The command-line interface forces an even more expensive excise budget on the user: He must first memorize the commands. Also, he cannot configure his screen to his own personal requirements; the command-line program occupies the whole screen without sharing. The excise of the command-line interface becomes smaller only after the user has invested significant time and effort in learning it.

On the other hand, for the casual or first-time user, the visual explicitness of the GUI helps him navigate and learn what tasks are appropriate and when. The step-by-step nature of the GUI is a great help to users who aren't yet familiar with the task or the system. It is also a benefit to those users who have more than one task to perform and who must use more than one program at a time.

Any user willing to learn a command-line interface automatically qualifies as a power user. And, any power user of a command-line interface will quickly become a power user of any other type of interface, GUI included. These users will easily learn each nuance of the programs they use. They will start up each program with a clear idea of exactly what it is they want to do and how they want to do it. To this user, the assistance offered to the casual or first-time user is just in the way. So one person's excise task is often another person's revenue task.

One user's excise task is another user's revenue task

This axiom tells us that we must be careful when we eliminate excise. We must not remove it just to suit power users. Similarly, though, we must not force power users to pay the full price of being helpful to new or infrequent users.

Pure excise

Occasionally—actually, not so occasionally—we find actions that are excise of such purity that nobody needs them, from power users to first-timers. These include most hardware-management tasks like telling a program which IRQ or COM port to use. Any demands for such information should be struck from all user interfaces without a backward glance.

Sometimes, however, we find certain tasks like window management, that, although they are mainly for the program, are useful for occasional users or users with special preferences. In this case, the function itself can only be considered excise if it is forced on the user rather than made available at his discretion.

This brings us back to goal direction, of course. The only way to determine whether a function is excise is by comparing it to the user's goals. If the user wants to see two programs at a time on the screen in order to compare or transfer information, the ability to configure the main windows of the programs so that they share the screen space is not excise. If the user doesn't have this specific goal, any requirement that the user be able to configure the main window of either program is excise.

One of the areas where software designers can inadvertently introduce significant amounts of excise is in support for first-time or casual users. It is easy to justify adding to a program facilities that will make it easy for newer users to learn how to use the program. Unfortunately, these facilities quickly become excise as the user becomes familiar with the program. Facilities added to software for this purpose must be made so that they can be easily turned off. Training wheels are rarely needed for extended periods of time, and training wheels, while a boon to beginners, are a hindrance to advanced learning and use.

Visual metaphor excise

Designers also paint themselves into excise corners by depending on visual metaphors. Visual metaphors like desktops with telephones, copy machines, staplers and fax machines—or file cabinets with folders in drawers—are cases in point. These visual metaphors may make it easy to learn the purpose of the program and to understand the relationships between the pieces, but once these fundamentals are learned, the management of the metaphor becomes pure excise. In addition, the screen space consumed by the images becomes increasingly egregious, particularly in sovereign posture applications. The more we stare at the program from day to day, the more we resent the number of pixels it takes to tell us what we already know. The cute little telephone that so charmingly told us how to dial on that first day long ago is now a barrier to quick communications. It would be much better if we could directly select our goal, such as getting our mail or sending our outgoing letters, from a list rather than having to double-click on the telephone and then select the number to dial.

The visual metaphor that helped us learn the basics has become a significant impediment once we have learned the basics, and the metaphor really didn't teach anything beyond the barest of the basics.

Transient-posture applications can tolerate more training and explanation excise than sovereign applications. Transient-posture programs aren't used frequently, so their users will need more assistance in understanding what the program does and remembering how to control it. For sovereign-posture applications, however, the slightest excise will be like a grain of sand in your shoe: it will produce a painful blister after you've walked just a few miles.

Never make the user ask to ask

Back in the days of command lines and character-based menus, interfaces would often offer services to the user indirectly. If you wanted to change an item like your address, you had to first ask the program to change it. The program would then offer up a screen where your address could be changed. I call that first question a 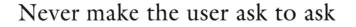meta-question, because you are not asking the question but rather asking if you can ask the question.

Meta-questions are pure excise and there is no reason for them in user interface design. If you want to ask a question, the program should let you go ahead and ask. If you want to change some value, you should go ahead and change it. You shouldn't have to ask permission to ask.

Many install programs proffer meta-questions in abundance. They say, "I will install your program in this directory" and then show you the proposed directory. If you don't like the choice shown, you can't just change it in place in that dialog box. You instead press a button that says MODIFY and then get another cascading dialog box to change it.

The program should simply let the user edit the directory name in place. It could easily track those changes, verify their validity and assure that things get installed correctly without forcing the user into the meta-question.

Another way to look at this same problem is from the input-versus-output point of view. Programs and dialogs offer bits of information in the form of

Allow input wherever you output

filenames, numeric values and selected options. If these options are modifiable by the user, he should be able to do the setting right where the program displays them. Many programs have one place where the values are displayed for output and another place where input to them is accepted from the user. This follows the implementation model, which treats input and output as different processes, but the user's mental model doesn't recognize a difference. He thinks, "There is the number; I'll just click on it and enter a new value." If the program can't accommodate this impulse, it is needlessly inserting excise into the interface.

Of course, if changing the information is dangerous or unrecoverable, inserting an interface layer can call attention to the fact that changing this information shouldn't be treated lightly.

Error and confirmation messages

There are probably no bigger excise elements than error message boxes and confirmation message dialogs. These nasty little buggers are so prevalent that eradicating them takes a lot of work. In Part VII, I devote a chapter to each of them, but for now, suffice it to say that they are high in poly-unsaturated excise and should be completely eliminated from your diet.

Other excise traps

You should be vigilant in finding and rooting out each small item of excise in your interface. The myriad little extra steps can add up to a lot of extra work in a complex program. This list should help you spot excise transgressions:

- Don't force the user to go to another window to perform a function that affects this window.

- Don't force the user to remember where he put things in the hierarchical file system.

- Don't force the user to resize windows. When a child window pops up on the screen, the program should size it appropriately for its contents. Don't make it big and empty or so small that it requires constant scrolling.

- Don't force the user to move windows. If there is open space on the desktop, put the program there instead of directly over some other already-open program.

- Don't force the user to reenter his personal settings. If he has ever set a font, a color, an indentation or a sound, make sure that he doesn't have to do it again unless he changes his mind.

- Don't force the user to fill fields to satisfy some arbitrary measure of completeness. If the user wants to omit some details from the transaction entry screen, don't force him to enter them. Assume that he has a good reason for not entering them. The completeness of some database isn't worth badgering the user.

- Don't force the user to ask permission to ask a question. This is frequently a symptom of not allowing input in the same place as output.

- Don't ask the user to confirm his actions.

- Don't let the user's actions result in an error.

Idiocy

In Chapter 11, I introduced the concept of flow, where the user enters a very productive mental state by working in harmony with his software tools. Flow is a natural state, and people will enter it without much prodding. Actually, it takes some effort to break into flow once someone is there. Interruptions like

Don't stop the proceedings with idiocy

a ringing telephone will do it, as will an error message box. Some interruptions are unavoidable, but most others are easily dispensable. For a program to include the dispensable is unforgivable.

Software can behave with awesome idiocy. It never fails to astonish me how stupidly software can behave. It will ask questions and make assertions that no self-respecting individual would ever make. And worse, the software does it with a puffed-up self-righteousness unheard of in other media. It will state unequivocally, for example, that a file doesn't exist, merely because it is too stupid to look in the right place for it, then will implicitly blame *you* for losing it! Programs will state categorically that your computer is out of memory an hour after you have beefed it up to 32 MB! A program will go catatonic executing an impossible query that will execute for either another 4.3 million years or until you reboot, whichever comes first. I call behavior like this "stopping the proceedings with idiocy," giving rise to an important axiom: "Don't stop the proceedings with idiocy."

Stopping the proceedings

You might think that "idiocy" is too harsh a word, but it isn't. Let's look at some examples. Figure 13-1 is a good place to start.

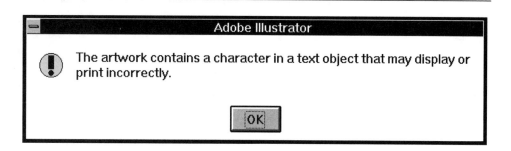

Figure 13-1

This is a totally useless error message box that stops the proceedings with idiocy. We can't verify or identify what it tells us and it gives us no options for responding other than to admit our own culpability with the OK button. This message only comes up when the program is loading; that is, when we have entrusted it to do something simple and straightforward for us. The program is so stupid that it can't even fetch a file (whose name we tell it) without help. If this program were a clerk or secretary, we'd fire it on the spot!

The typical error message box is unnecessary. It either tells the user something that he doesn't care about or demands that he fix some situation that the program could usually fix just as well. Figure 13-1 shows an error message box displayed by Adobe Illustrator (Version 4) while trying to load an image that was previously drawn with it. The message stops an already annoying and time-consuming procedure, making it take even longer. The user cannot reliably fetch a cup of coffee after telling the program to load an image, because he might return only to see the function incomplete and the program mindlessly holding up the process merely to state the ridiculous. If the issue were data integrity, why didn't the program point out the problematic character when it was entered? If the issue were important, why doesn't the program show where the offending character is? If the issue were a true inability of the program to handle the bad character, why doesn't it just remove it or replace it with a valid character?

Not to pick on Illustrator, but as Adobe was kind enough to provide us with numerous fine examples of really dunderheaded software design, it seems only appropriate that we examine them in detail. Here's how to get the "artwork versus printer format" dialog shown in Figure 13-2.

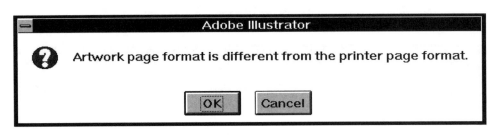

Figure 13-2

Here is another totally useless error message box that stops the proceedings with idiocy. If the program is smart enough to detect the difference, why can't it correct the problem? Why would I ever want to print with conflicting formats? The two options are insulting, telling me that I can either go ahead and shoot my dog, or admit that I shouldn't be carrying a gun. And am I canceling this warning box, or the print operation? Will it still go ahead and kill my dog? What were they thinking?

An image in Illustrator has an "orientation": landscape-oriented is wider than it is tall, and portrait-oriented is taller than it is wide. The printer can be set to either orientation, too. Most programs change the printer's orientation to match that of the image being printed, but not Illustrator. Adobe's product lets you set the orientation of your picture, but it demands that you explicitly set the orientation of the printer independently. This wouldn't be so bad if the program would at least use the image's orientation as a default setting for the printer. Instead, the program ignores the printer's setting completely. The result is that you have to configure both the orientation of the image and the orientation of the printer, and if you get them wrong, the program stops the proceedings with the idiocy shown in Figure 13-2.

There is one other problem, though. Logically, the place that you define the format of the drawing is connected to the creation of the drawing, but, oddly, the only place in the program to set the drawing's orientation is in the "*Print Setup*" dialog box, shown in Figure 13-3. Of course, the format is important when it comes to printing, but couldn't the print procedure take its cue from the picture and make the appropriate setting before it begins to print? That is, if the drawing is in landscape orientation, print it in landscape orientation, and if the drawing is in portrait orientation, print it in portrait orientation.

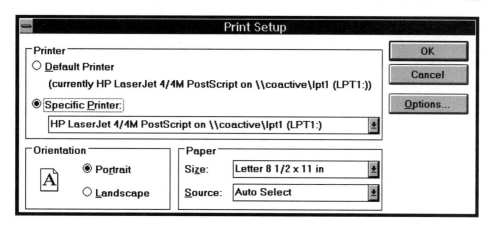

Figure 13-3

The only place to tell Adobe Illustrator what format of paper to use is in the Print Setup dialog box. The program subsequently remembers the format for drawing purposes but forgets it for printing purposes! Call me crazy, but the format of the electronic page has a lot to do with the way things are going to print out. Why would the program forget this connection? I'm used to bossing computers around, but what about the new user who is timid around computers? This program will crush his ego. It would be embarrassingly simple for the program merely to put the printer in whatever mode suits the document and finesse the entire problem.

If, for some truly bizarre reason, the user wanted to print a landscape-oriented drawing on a portrait-oriented piece of paper, he could then go to the Print Setup dialog box and request the desired specification. However, I can pretty much guarantee Adobe that this will rarely happen. Very few of their users will want to take such unusual actions, so why should all of the normal print jobs be interrupted and delayed by an obscure possibility? Sounds like a good example of putting might on will, to me.

Even if Adobe insists on keeping the silly error message box, why don't they add a button to it labeled "Change to Landscape" or "Change to Portrait" as the case dictates? This would help the user rather than just irritating him.

Protecting me from myself

Another place where the proceedings get stopped with regular idiocy is in password-protection systems. Every morning, I boot up my computer, then go fetch a cup of coffee. When I return, instead of finding the computer waiting eagerly for my instructions, it is pouting and surly, demanding that I log on with my password.

Security is a big issue in many businesses, but it doesn't mean much around here. I don't use a password to protect my computer, yet there is no way (that *I* can find) to turn off the dialog box. I wish it knew how foolish it looked, asking me for my password every morning, only to be summarily dismissed with a stroke. Why can't I make this proceedings-stopping dialog box go away? Why isn't it smart enough to see that it is neither required nor wanted?

Getting stupid

It may seem tautological, but a good way to keep your program from stopping the proceedings with idiocy is for it to not act stupid. A program gets stupid when it becomes deaf, dumb and unresponsive while going off and computing for long periods of time.

Typically, programs with a proclivity for getting stupid are those that talk to remote devices, like servers, printers, networks and modems. Don't discount the ingenuity of programmers, however; they can make a spreadsheet or accounting program get stupid by going into some kind of internal loop—what programmers call "corebound." Every program that executes potentially time-consuming tasks must make sure that it occasionally checks to see if the user is still out there, banging away on the keyboard or madly clicking on the mouse, whimpering "No, no, no, I didn't mean to reorganize the *entire* database. That will take 4.3 million years!"

The Secret Weapon
of Interface Design

If your program could predict what the user will do next, could it provide a better interaction? If your program could know which selections the user will make in a particular dialog box, couldn't that dialog box be skipped? Wouldn't you consider advance knowledge of what actions your user will take to be an awesome secret weapon of interface design?

Well, I'm here to tell you that you *can* predict what your users will do. You *can* build a sixth sense into your program that will tell it with uncanny accuracy exactly what the user will do next!

Get a memory

All you have to do is give your program a memory! I'm not talking about RAM here, but a memory like that of a human being. If your program simply remembers what the user did the last time, it can use that remembered behavior as a guide to how it should behave the next time. Actually, as we'll see later in this chapter, your program should remember even more than just one previous choice. This simple principle is one of the most effective tools available for designing the interaction, yet it is arguably the most untapped resource available.

183

You might think that bothering with a memory isn't necessary; it's easier to just ask the user. Programmers are quick to pop up a simple dialog box to request some bit of information that isn't lying conveniently around. They see nothing wrong with it, but *people don't like to be asked questions*. You know that old adage "the customer is always right?" Well, in the information age, your user is your customer. The user is always right, and asking him questions is a subtle way of expressing doubt about his authority.

Questions aren't choices

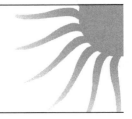

Asking questions is quite different from offering choices. The difference between them is the same as that between browsing in a store and having a job interview. The individual asking the questions is understood to be in a position superior to the individual being asked. Bosses ask their subordinates questions and the underlings respond. Judges ask defendants questions and they must respond. Parents ask their children questions and they must answer truthfully. Asking users questions makes them feel inferior and is a sure way to put them down.

Dialog boxes ask questions. Buttcons on a toolbar offer choices. The dialog box stops the proceedings, demanding an answer, and it won't leave until it gets what it wants. The buttcons, on the other hand, are always there, quietly and politely offering up their wares like a well-appointed store, offering you the luxury of selecting what you would like with just a flick of your finger.

Contrary to what many software developers think, questions and choices don't necessarily make the user feel empowered. More commonly, it makes the user feel badgered and harassed. *Would you like soup or salad?* Salad. *Would you like cole slaw or green?* Green. *Would you like French, Thousand Island or Italian?* French. *Would you like lo-cal or regular?* Stop! Just bring me soup! *Would you like chowder or chicken noodle?*

Users don't like to be asked questions. It reflects poorly on the program doing the asking by showing it to be

- Ignorant

- Forgetful

- Weak

- Lacking initiative

- Unable to fend for itself

- Fretful

These are qualities that we typically dislike in people. Why should we not dislike them in software? The program is not asking us our opinion out of intellectual curiosity, the way a friend might, say, over dinner. The program is asking us because it is stupid. I use the word "stupid" quite deliberately. (If it was a person, I wouldn't use that word so as not to hurt his feelings. But a program has no feelings, so I'm not going to pull my punch.) The program isn't interested in our opinion; it needs a fact, and chances are it didn't really need to ask the user to get it. It was just too stupid to know where to look for it. That is stupid behavior.

Software that asks fewer questions appears smarter to the user. The questions someone asks you at a cocktail party may flatter you and seem interesting, but face it, no software is ever going to make social chit-chat with its user. Software can only ask the kind of questions that, if someone asked them of you at a party, would have you making excuses and quickly heading for the dip.

One thing that users hate more than questions is questions that are asked repeatedly and unnecessarily. Do you want to save that file? Do you want to save that file *now*? Do you *really* want to save that file? Are you *sure* you want to print? Are you sure you want to print on *that* printer? Are you *absolutely* sure you want to print? Help! Somebody stop this stupid software from asking me another dumb, redundant question.

And if the already-irritated user ever fails to know the answer to a question, it also makes him feel stupid. Do you want the professional install or the beginner install? In other words, do you want something you can't handle, or are you just a wimp?

Choices are certainly good things, but there is a big difference between being free to make choices and being offered ultimatums by the program. Instead of being interrogated by the software, users would much rather direct it the way they direct their automobiles down the street. An automobile offers the user an infinity of choices without once issuing a dialog box. Imagine the scenario in Figure 14-1.

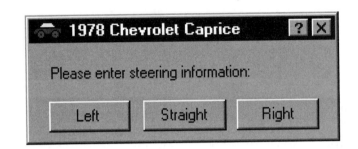

Figure 14-1

Imagine if you had to steer your car by pressing buttons on a dialog box! This will give you some idea of how normal people feel about the dialog boxes on your software. Humbling, isn't it?

Directly manipulating a steering wheel is not only a more appropriate idiom for communicating with your car, but it puts you in the superior position, directing your car where it should go. No user likes to be questioned like a suspect in a lineup, yet that is exactly what our software often demands of us.

Task coherence

The idea that you can predict what a user will do by simply remembering what he did last is based on a simple principle that I call **task coherence**. The idea is that what we do is generally the same from day to day, and this is not only true about how we brush our teeth and eat our breakfast, but also about how we use our word processors and email programs. Although Sally, for example, may use Excel in dramatically different ways than Kazu, Sally will tend to use it the same way each time she does. Although Kazu likes 9-point Times Roman and Sally prefers 12-point Helvetica, Sally will use 12-point Helvetica with dependable regularity. It isn't really necessary to ask Sally which font to use. A very reliable starting point would be 12-point Helvetica.

I devised the task coherence term by borrowing from the pioneers of computer graphics. They observed an interesting phenomenon that let them optimize their graphic computations to speed up their displays. A computer screen is composed of a "raster" of several hundred parallel horizontal lines of individual pixels. Graphics software must calculate the color value of each pixel.

Although the whole image may be changing rapidly and dramatically, the pixels in any two adjacent lines don't change very much from moment to moment. The likelihood that any given pixel will have the same value as its neighbor in the line above it is extremely high. Thus, by tracking only the changes in each line, 80 out of a 100 pixels don't have to be recalculated, because their values remain the same from line to line. This phenomenon is called "edge coherence," and it remains a fundamental optimization for graphics programming.

When we apply the task coherence principle to our software, we can realize great advantage from it. When a consumer uses your program, there is a very high-percentage chance that what he does will be the same as what he did the last time he used your program. With significant reliability, you can predict the behavior of your users by the simple expedient of remembering what they did the last time they used the program. This allows you to greatly reduce the number of questions your program asks the user.

We would all like to have an assistant who is intelligent and self-motivated—one who shows initiative and drive, who demonstrates good judgment and a keen memory. When we tell our assistant to fetch a document, we want that assistant to remember where he found it the last time we sent him off to get it. A program that makes effective use of its memory would be more like that self-motivated assistant. It would remember the settings the user specified from execution to execution. Simple things can make a big difference: The position of windows, particularly MDI children, should be remembered, so if I maximized the document last time, it should be maximized the next time. If I tiled it vertically with the on-screen window, it would be tiled vertically next time without any instruction from me.

The way to determine what information the program should remember is with a simple axiom:

If it's worth asking the user, it's worth the program remembering

Any time your program finds itself with a choice, and especially when that choice is being offered to the user, the program should remember the information from run to run. Instead of choosing a hard-wired default, the program can use the previous setting as the default, and it will have a much better chance of giving the user what he wanted. Instead of asking the user to make a determination, the program should go ahead and make the same determination the user made last time, and let the user undo it if it was wrong. Whatever options the user had set should be remembered, so that they could remain in effect until manually changed. If the user ignored facilities of the program or turned them off, they should not be offered to the user again. The user will seek them out when and if he is ready for them.

One of the most annoying effects of programs without memories is that they are so parsimonious with their assistance regarding files and disks. If there is one place where the user needs help, it's with files and disks. A program like Word remembers the last place the user looked for a file. Unfortunately, if the user always puts his files in a directory called LETTERS, then once edits a document template stored in the TEMPLATE directory, all his subsequent letters will be stored in the TEMPLATE directory rather than in the LETTERS directory. So the program must remember more than just the last place the files were accessed. It must remember the last place files *of each type* were accessed. On my computer, all template files—files with a suffix of .DOT—are stored in the template directory. Various other documents—ones with a suffix of .DOC—are stored in various other directories. When I'm editing a template file, there is no reason for the word processor to ever even suspect that it will go anywhere other than my template directory. Although this is a convention I never violate on my computer, the software takes no notice of the pattern and refuses to alter its behavior one iota. I always must explain the difference to the program. I should never have to step through the tree to a given directory more than once.

The user can benefit in several ways from a program with a good memory. Memory reduces excise, the useless effort that must be devoted to managing the tool instead of doing the work. A significant portion of the total excise of an interface is in having to explain things to the program that it should already know. For example, in my word processor, I often want to reverse-out text, making it white on black. To do this, I select some text and change the font color to white. Without altering the selection, I then set the background color to black. If the program paid enough attention, it would notice the fact that I requested two formatting steps without an intervening selection option. As far as a user is concerned, this is effectively a single operation. Wouldn't it be nice if the program, upon seeing this unique pattern, automatically created a new format style of this type, or better yet, created a new "reverse-out" toolbar buttcon?

Most mainstream programs allow their users to set defaults, but this doesn't fit the bill like a memory would. I have Microsoft Word thoroughly configured for my preferences, but a colleague of mine uses Word only occasionally and doesn't have the inclination to learn how to customize it. Every time she runs the program, though, she must manually change the font to her preferred one. If the program only remembered her actions, it would make that maddening step unnecessary.

Most of our software is incredibly forgetful, remembering little or nothing from execution to execution. If our programs are smart enough to retain information, it is usually information that makes the job easier for the *programmer* and not for the user. The program willingly discards information about the way it was used, how it was changed, where it was used, what data it processed, who used it, and whether and how frequently the various facilities of the program were used. Meanwhile, the program fills INI files with driver names, port assignments and OLE details that ease the programmer's job.

Another flagrant violator of the rules of the get-a-memory-club are dialog boxes. These modal monsters almost never remember anything from instantiation to instantiation. They don't remember where they were placed, what they did, what settings were made and what parts were untouched.

A program with a better memory can reduce the number of errors the user makes. This is true simply because the user has to enter less information. More of it will be entered automatically from the program's memory. In an invoicing program, for example, if the software enters the date, department number and other standard fields from memory, the user has less opportunity to make typing errors in these fields.

If the program remembers what the user enters and uses that information for future reasonableness checks, the program can work to keep erroneous data from being entered. Imagine a data-entry program where zip codes and city names are remembered from run to run. When the user enters a familiar city name along with an unfamiliar zip code, the field can turn yellow, indicating uncertainty about the match. And when the user enters a familiar city name with a zip code already associated with another city, the field can turn pink, indicating a more serious ambiguity. He wouldn't necessarily have to take any action because of these colors, but the warning is there if he wants it.

When the user has to tell the program about excise trivia or explain to it information that he explained to it a week ago, his thoughts can be derailed from the real task at hand, distracting him from his real goal by the program's management. He misses his subway stop because he is too busy finding a strap to hold. In the time it takes to enter the correct date into the invoice, the user can forget the meaning of the invoice.

Task coherence predicts what the user will do in the future with reasonable, but not absolute, certainty. If our program relies on this principle, it's natural to wonder about the uncertainty of our predictions. If we can reliably predict what the user will do 80% of the time, it means that 20% of the time we will be wrong. It might seem that the proper step to take here is to offer the user a choice, but this puts us right back at square one. Rather than offering a choice, the program should go ahead and do what it thinks is most appropriate and allow the user to override or undo it. If the undo facility is sufficiently easy to use and understand, the user won't be bothered by it. After all, he will have to use undo only two times out of ten instead of having to deal with a redundant dialog box eight times out of ten. This is a much better deal for humans.

A new way of thinking

A remarkable thing happens to the software design process once developers accept the power of task coherence. Designers find that their thinking takes on a whole new quality. The normally unquestioned recourse of popping up a dialog box gets replaced with a more studied process, where the designer asks questions of much greater subtlety. Questions like: How *much* should the program remember? Which aspects should be remembered? Should the program remember more than just the last setting? What constitutes a change in pattern?

They start to imagine situations like this: The user accepts the same date format 50 times in a row, then manually enters a different format once. The next time the user enters a date, which format should the program use? The 50-times format or the more-recent one-time format? How many times must the new format be specified before it becomes the default? Just because there is ambiguity here, the program still shouldn't ask the user. It must use its initiative to make a reasonable decision. The user is free to override the program's decision if it is the wrong one.

I've identified a couple of characteristic patterns in the ways people make choices that can help us resolve these more complex questions about task coherence.

People tend to reduce an infinite set of choices down to a small, finite set of choices. Even when you don't do the exact same thing each time, you will tend to choose your actions from a small, repetitive set of options. I call this principle **decision-set streamlining**.

For example, just because you went shopping at Safeway yesterday doesn't necessarily mean that you will be shopping at Safeway today, too. However, the next time you need groceries, you will probably shop at Safeway again. Or, even though your favorite Chinese restaurant has 250 items on the menu, chances are that you will usually choose from your own personal subset of five or six favorites. Or, although most people drive home from work the exact same way every evening, some people drive home a different way every night. However, these people will choose from a set of four or five different routes that rarely change. Computers, of course, can remember four or five things without breaking a sweat.

Although simply remembering the last action is better than not remembering anything, it can lead to a peculiar pathology if the decision-set consists of precisely two alternating elements. If, for example, I alternately read files from one directory and store them in another, each time the program offers me the last directory, it will be guaranteed to be wrong. The solution is to remember more than just one previous choice.

Decision-set streamlining guides us to the idea that pieces of information the program must remember about the user's choices tend to come in groups. Instead of there being one right way, there will be several options that are all correct. The program should look for more subtle clues to differentiate which one of the small set is correct. For example, if I use a check-writing program to pay my bills, the program will very quickly learn that only six or eight accounts are used regularly. But how can it determine from a given check which of the eight accounts is the most likely for it? If the payees and amounts were remembered on an account-by-account basis, that decision would be easy. Whaddaya know, every time I pay the rent, it is the exact same amount! Same with my car payment. The amount paid to the electric company varies from check to check, but it always stays within 10 or 20 percent of the last check I wrote to them.

The decisions people make tend to fall into two primary categories: important and not important. Usually, any given activity will involve hundreds of decisions, but very few of them are important. All of the rest are insignificant. I call this principle **preference thresholding**.

Once you decide to buy that car, you don't really care who finances it as long as the terms are competitive. Once you decide to buy groceries, the particular checkout aisle you select is not important. Once you decide to ride the Matterhorn, you don't really care which toboggan they seat you in.

Preference thresholding can guide us in our user interface design by showing us that asking the user for successively detailed decisions about a procedure is unnecessary. Once the user asks to print, we don't have to ask him how many copies he wants or whether the image is landscape or portrait. We can make an assumption about these things the first time out and then remember them for all subsequent invocations. If the user wants to change them, he can always request the Printer Options dialog box.

Using preference thresholding, we can easily track which facilities of the program the user likes to adjust and which are set once and ignored. With this knowledge, the program can offer choices where it has a pretty good expectation that the user will want to take control, while simultaneously not bothering the user with decisions he won't be interested in.

Questions like these soon give rise to associated issues like how to inform the user of the assumptions that the program made. If the program saves a changed file without first discussing it with the user, how does it let the user know that it took this action? When programmers and designers begin to ask questions like these, it means that they are beginning to design software for *users* instead of for programmers. These questions are all ways of serving the customer—the user—instead of concentrating on the needs of the programmer. This kind of goal-oriented thinking is bound to not only create better software, but also better software designers.

One of the main reasons our software is often so difficult to use is because its designers have made rational, logical assumptions that, unfortunately, are very wrong. They assumed that the behavior of users is random and unpredictable, and that they must be interrogated to determine the proper course of action. While human behavior certainly isn't deterministic like a digital computer, it is rarely random, and asking questions is predictably unpleasant. The next time you find your program asking your user a question, make it ask itself one instead.

Part IV: The Interaction
Pointing and Clicking

The scientists who invented computers gave us the complex symbology of language as the tool for communicating with software. It has the advantage of precision, but it is far too labor-intensive and error-prone. Pundits outside of the industry—and some inside it who should know better—advocate instead an interface based on speaking to our computers. Anyone with children, however, knows that you teach people by demonstration, not lecture. Words are for discussing actions after they have been taken. It won't be any different with software. The idea of pointing with a mouse or stylus or finger is the right one. Because these actions are more direct, we show the computer what to do, instead of telling it what to do. This is a fundamental truth about interface design, and one that deserves a close look.

Elephants, Mice and Minnies

The best way to point to something is with your finger. They're always handy; you probably have several of these convenient pointing devices nearby right now. The only real drawback they have is that their ends are too blunt for precisely pointing to SVGA screens. Because of this limitation, other pointing devices have taken their place, and each substitute has its own strengths and weaknesses. The mouse is the most omnipresent, but its days are numbered.

Why we use a mouse instead of a pen

The first computer pointing device, the light pen, was a very logical extension of the Mark I Finger. You held the light pen in your hand and pointed it at the screen like a pen. It was the perfect tool for direct manipulation, except for the tragic truth that it was completely unusable with computers.

When we use a stylus, or any other writing device, we exercise extremely fine motor control of our hand muscles to manipulate the tip of the stylus with our fingers. To do this reliably, we have to have something to rest the heel of our hand on; otherwise, our movements are cast adrift. No matter how precise our finger motions are, they drift unless we provide our hand with a firm foundation.

Computers use big, clunky cathode-ray tubes as their display screens, and these CRTs face us vertically rather than lying flat on our desks like books and papers. As easy as it is to use a stylus on a sheet of paper on a firm horizontal surface, it is terribly difficult to make precise movements with that same stylus on a vertical surface with your arm and hand in the air, unsupported. Using a light pen on a CRT squanders the fine motor control of our fingers and forces us to rely on the gross motor control of the muscles in our arms. These muscles are well suited for moving much greater distances, but they cannot give us the precision we expect for accurate pointing.

It is also extremely difficult to draw on a vertical surface while resting the ball of your hand on it—try it on your wall. Your wrist just won't bend backwards far enough. Sign painters, who must paint on the vertical surfaces of walls, doors and windows, frequently use a tool called a mahlstick—a wooden dowel a half-meter long with a padded end. The artist rests the padded end on the wall and holds the other end in her free hand. Then she rests the heel of her drawing hand on the center of the stick. The mahlstick enables her to change the relative incidence of the painting surface from pure vertical to one that is better suited to keeping her drawing hand under control. Unfortunately, a mahlstick is impractical for computer users, so we invented other tools like the mouse.

Indirect manipulation

As we roll the mouse around on our desktop, we see a visual symbol, the cursor, move around on the video screen in the same way. Move the mouse left and the cursor moves left; move the mouse up and the cursor moves up. As you first use the mouse, you immediately get the sensation that the mouse and cursor are connected, a sensation that is extremely easy to learn and equally hard to forget. This is good, because perceiving how the mouse works by inspection is nearly impossible. There is a famous scene in the movie *Star Trek IV: The Voyage Home*, where Scotty comes to twentieth-century Earth and tries to use a computer. He picks up the mouse, holds it to his mouth and speaks into it. This scene is funny because of its underlying truth: the mouse has no visual affordance that it is a pointing device until someone shows us how its movements are related to the movements of the cursor. At that point, though, understanding is instantaneous. All idioms must be learned. Good idioms need only be learned once, and the mouse is certainly a good idiom.

The motion of the mouse to the cursor is not usually one-to-one, however. Instead the motion is proportional. On most PCs, the cursor crosses an entire 30-centimeter screen in about 4 centimeters of mouse movement. With the heel of your hand resting firmly on the table top, your fingers can move the mouse with great accuracy. The fine motor control of the muscles in your hand enable you to precisely place the cursor, even with a 1:8 movement ratio. Those users who have a difficult time mastering the mouse usually don't place the heel of their palm firmly on their desk.

Although we use the term "direct manipulation" when we talk about pointing and moving things with the mouse, we are actually manipulating these things *indirectly*. A light pen points directly to the screen, and can more properly be called a direct-manipulation tool because we actually point to the object. With the mouse, however, we are only manipulating a mouse on the desk, not the object on the screen.

With a thin-bodied stylus, we can get very precise control of the point, but with the palm-sized mouse, the muscles in our fingertips don't come into play the way they can with a Scripto. This is why we cannot enter handwriting practically with a mouse. Although we utilize fine motor control with a mouse, it is nothing like the extremely detailed control we exercise with the tip of a pen. With our hand wrapped around the much larger mouse, we can easily move the cursor to a particular place, but we cannot effectively define shapes or make the continuous self-relative movements that are required either for cursive or block printing. Thus the mouse is great for pointing at things on the screen but miserable for entering graphical data. The stylus is fine for both tasks.

Mice are not here to stay

The mouse is a clever tool that allows us to point to things on a vertical screen without entangling ourselves with the drawbacks of pointing or drawing on a vertical surface. Don't for a minute imagine that the mouse is a superior tool for anything beyond this, though. In all other ways it is worse. The fact that you can enter cursive handwriting with a pen and that you cannot do so with a mouse should be clue enough that the pen is more accurately manipulable than the mouse. It is only when the writing surface goes vertical that the mouse emerges as the better tool.

When flat-panel displays become cheap and common, they will inevitably migrate down from their vertical perch to a horizontal one, like paper on a desktop. When that happens, the pen input device will have a resurgence of popularity that will ultimately place it at the top of the world of direct-manipulation devices. The mouse will go the way of acoustic modems and 8-inch floppies. This dominance will have nothing whatever to do with hand-writing recognition. Instead, it will be based on the way human bodies are constructed and how we can best point to things.

Mousing around

When you mouse around on the screen, there is a distinct dividing line between near motions and far motions. That line is, simply, whether your destination is near enough that you can keep the heel of your hand stationary on your desk-top or if you must pick it up. When the heel of your hand is down and you move the cursor from place to place, you use the fine motor skills of the muscles in your fingers. When you lift the heel of your hand from the desktop to make a larger move, you use the gross motor skills of the muscles in your arm. Gross motor skills are no faster or slower than fine motor skills, but transitioning between the two is difficult. It takes both time and concentration, because the user must integrate the two groups of muscles. Touch-typists dislike anything that forces them to move their hands from the home position on the keyboard, because it requires a transition between their muscle groups. For the same rea-son, moving the mouse cursor across the screen to manipulate a control forces a change from fine to gross to fine motor skills.

Pressing the button on the mouse also requires fine motor control—you use your finger to push it—and if your hand is not firmly planted on the desktop, you cannot press it without inadvertently moving the mouse and the cursor. This means that, while some compromise is possible between fine and gross motor control for the movement aspect of working a mouse, when it comes time to actually press the button—to pull the trigger—the user must first plant the heel of his hand, forcibly going into fine-motor-control mode. To manipu-late a gizmo with a mouse, the user must use fine motor control to precisely position the cursor over the checkbox or push-button. However, if the cursor is far away from the desired gizmo, the user must first use gross motor control to move the cursor near the gizmo, then shift to fine motor control to finish the job.

It should be obvious at this point that any program that places its clickable areas more than a few pixels apart is inviting trouble. If a given control demands a click here and then a click waaaay over there, it is a tragic mis-design of the gizmo. Yet the ubiquitous scrollbar is just such a creature. If you are trying to scroll down in a document, you press the down arrow several times, using fine motor control, until you find what you are looking for, but you are likely to press it one too many times and overrun your destination. At this point, you must press the up arrow to get back to where you want to go. Of course, to move the cursor to the up arrow, you must pick up the heel of your hand and make a gross motor movement, then place the heel of your hand back down and make a fine motor movement to precisely locate the arrow and keep the mouse firmly positioned while you press the button.

Why are the arrows on scroll-bars separated by the entire length of the bar itself? Yes, it looks visually bolder and more symmetrical this way, but it is much more difficult to use. If the two arrows were instead placed adjacent to each other at either end of the scroll-bar as shown in Figure 15-1, changing the direction of the scroll could be accomplished by a single fine motor movement, instead of by the difficult dance of fine-gross-fine.

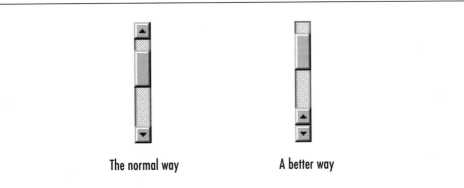

The normal way   A better way

Figure 15-1

The familiar scrollbar, shown on the left, is one of the more difficult-to-use gizmos in Windows. To go from scrolling up to scrolling down, you must transition from the fine motor control required by clicking the button to the gross motor control you need to move your hand to the opposite end of the bar, then change back to fine motor control to accurately position the mouse and press the button again. Bummer. If the scrollbar were modified only slightly, so that the two buttons were adjacent, the problem would go away. The other features, both good and bad, of the scrollbar are discussed in Part VI, "The Gizmos."

Not only do the less-manually dexterous find the mouse problematic, but many experienced computer users, particularly touch-typists, find the mouse difficult at times. For many data-intensive tasks, the keyboard is superior to the mouse. It is frustrating to have to pull your hands away from the keyboard to reposition a cursor with the mouse, only to have to return to the keyboard again. In the early days of personal computing, it was the keyboard or nothing, and today, it is often the mouse or nothing. Programs should fully support both the mouse and the keyboard for all motion and selection tasks.

Some people find it very difficult to manipulate a mouse. Their rodent fear, like that of the pachyderm's, leads me to stick my tongue in my cheek and call these people elephants.

A good percentage of computer users are elephants, so if we want to be successful, we must design our software in sympathy with them. This means that for each mouse-based idiom there should be at least one non-mouse alternative. Of course, this may not always be possible. Some very graphic-oriented actions in a drawing program, for example, would be ridiculous to try to support without a mouse, but these examples are in a clear minority. Most business or personal software lends itself pretty well to keyboard commands. Most users, even elephants, will actually use a combination of mouse and keyboard commands, sometimes starting commands with the mouse and ending them with the keyboard and vice versa.

What do you call a person who is the antithesis of an elephant? Someone who really loves mice? A minnie, of course!

The left mouse button

The inventors of the mouse tried to figure out how many buttons to put on it and couldn't agree. Some said one button was correct, while others swore by two buttons. Still others advocated a mouse with several buttons that could be clicked separately or together so that five buttons could yield up to 32 distinct combinations. I suspect that the actual decisions were made over beers at some long-forgotten sessions at a watering hole somewhere in Silicon Valley. Ultimately, though, Apple settled on one button for their Macintosh, while virtually everybody else agreed on two buttons.

Actually, one of the major drawbacks of the Macintosh is its single-button mouse. I understand that Apple's extensive user testing determined that the optimum number of buttons was one, thereby enshrining the single-button mouse in the pantheon of Apple history. This is unfortunate, as the right mouse button usually only comes into play when a person has graduated out of beginner-hood. A single button sacrifices power for the majority of computer users in exchange for simplicity for beginners.

There is less difference between the one- and two-button camps than you might think, as the established purpose of the left mouse button is tacitly defined as "the same as the single button on the Macintosh mouse." In other words, the right mouse button is widely regarded as an extra button, and the left button is the only one the user really needs. This statement is certainly true today, although it is gradually becoming less so as the Windows user interface evolves.

In general, the left mouse button is used for all of the major direct-manipulation functions of triggering controls, making selections, drawing, et cetera. By deduction, this means that the functions the left button doesn't support must be the non-major functions. The non-major functions either reside on the right mouse button or are not available by direct manipulation, residing only on menus or the keyboard.

The most common meaning of the left mouse button is activation or selection. For a control such as a push-button or checkbox, the left mouse button means pushing the button or checking the box. If you are left-clicking in data, the left mouse button generally means selecting. We'll discuss this in greater detail in the next chapter.

Right mouse button

The right mouse button was long treated as nonexistent by Microsoft and many others. Only a few brave programmers connected actions to the right mouse button, and they were generally considered to be extra, optional or advanced functions. When Borland International embraced object-orientation on a company-wide basis, they used the right mouse button as a tool for accessing a dialog box that showed an object's properties. The industry seemed ambivalent towards this action although it was, as they say, critically acclaimed. Of course, most usability critics have Macs, which only have one button, and Microsoft disdains Borland, so the concept didn't achieve the popularity it deserved. This is changing, however, with Windows 95, as Microsoft finally follows Borland's lead. The right mouse button is stepping into its best role for enabling direct access to properties as a standard *de jure*. This is, indeed, a pyrrhic victory for Borland.

In Windows 3.x, Microsoft tentatively defined the right mouse button as the "shortcut" button. That is, operations that are also available via other idioms are the only ones allowed on the right mouse button (though they weren't shy about breaking their own rule). This stemmed from Microsoft's assumption that one-button mice would have a role to play on the PC. Since this latter assumption has proven to be baseless, Microsoft has restated their position in the Windows 95 style guide, attributing to the right button "context-specific actions" (a clever way to say "properties").

Middle mouse button

Although application vendors can confidently expect a right mouse button, they can't depend on the presence of a middle mouse button. Because of this, no vendor can use the button as anything other than a shortcut. In fact, in its style guide, Microsoft states that the middle button "should be assigned to operations or functions already in the interface," a definition they once reserved for the right mouse button. I agree.

I use a two-button mouse most of the time, but my other computer has a three-button Logitech mouse. I never find myself reaching for extra functionality on the middle button. I have some friends who do use the middle button. Actually, they swear by it. Mostly, they use it as a shortcut for double-clicking with the left mouse button—a feature they create by configuring the mouse driver software, and of which trickery the application remains blissfully ignorant.

Things you can do with a mouse

Physically, there aren't a lot of things that you can do with a mouse. You can move it around to point to different things and press the buttons. These are the primitives of the vocabulary as discussed in Chapter 4. Any further mouse actions beyond pointing and clicking will be made up of a combination of one or more of those actions, called compounds. The vocabulary of mouse actions is canonically formed, and this is a significant reason why mice make such good computer peripherals.

Mouse actions can also be altered by using the meta-keys: CTRL, SHIFT and ALT. We will discuss these keys later in this chapter. The complete set of mouse actions that can be accomplished without using meta-keys is summarized in the following list. For the sake of discussion, I have assigned a short name to each of the actions (shown in parenthesis). These names may not be standard (what is?), but they are brief and unique.

1. Point (Point)

2. Point, click, release (Click)

3. Point, click, drag, release (Click-and-drag)

4. Point, click, release, click, release (Double-click)

5. Point, click, click other button, release, release (Chord-click)

6. Point, click, release, click, release, click, release (Triple-click)

7. Point, click, release, click, drag, release (Double-drag)

Of course, each of these actions (except chord-clicking, of course) can be performed on either button of a two-button mouse. It's theoretically possible to quadruple-click, quintuple-click, and so on, but even triple-clicking takes a steady and practiced hand, and just trying to double-click can often demoralize an elephant.

Any self-respecting minnie will easily perform all seven actions, while only the first five items on the list are within the scope of normal users. Of these, only the first three can be considered reasonable actions for elephants. Windows 95 is designed to be 100% workable with only the first three actions. Of course, to avoid double-clicking, the user of Windows 95 may have to take circuitous routes to perform their desired tasks, but at least the access is possible.

Pointing

This simple operation is a cornerstone of the graphical user interface and is the basis for all mouse operations. The user moves the mouse until its corresponding on-screen cursor is pointing to, or placed over, the desired object.

Clicking

While the user holds the mouse in a steady position, he clicks the button down and releases it. In general, this action is defined as triggering a state change in a gizmo, or selecting an object. In a matrix of text or cells, the click means "bring the selection point over here." For a push-button gizmo, a state change means that while the mouse button is down and directly over the gizmo, the button will enter and remain in the pushed state. When the mouse button is released, the button is triggered, and its associated action occurs.

Design tip: Single-click selects data or changes the gizmo state.

If, however, the user, while still holding the mouse button down, moves the cursor off the gizmo, the push-button gizmo returns to its unpushed state. When the user then releases the mouse button, nothing happens. This provides a convenient escape route if the user changes his mind.

The drawback to this escape route is that it consumes one of the cooler idioms: dragging a push-button somewhere. The button or buttcon could be dragable, so an idiom could be created that would allow a verb-object grammar in addition to the normal object-verb form. For example, the user could click on the Justified Text button in Word and drag it onto a paragraph of text. The margins of the paragraph would immediately change to justified. Instead of the user having to select the paragraph and then press the buttcon, the user would have the freedom to do the operation in reverse.

Clicking-and-dragging

This versatile operation has many common uses including selecting, reshaping, repositioning, drawing and dragging-and-dropping. We'll discuss all of these in the remaining chapters of this part.

Double-clicking

If double-clicking is composed of single-clicking twice, then it seems logical that the first thing a double-click should do is the same thing that a single-click does. This is indeed its meaning when the mouse is pointing into data. Single-clicking selects something; double-clicking selects something and then takes action on it.

Design tip: Double-click means a single-click plus action.

This fundamental interpretation comes from the Alto/Star by way of the Macintosh, and it remains a standard in all contemporary GUI applications. The fact that double-clicking is difficult for elephants—painful for some and impossible for a few—was largely ignored. But since Microsoft has embraced user testing, they have had to confront this awful truth. Despite mixed feelings, the double-click has assumed a significantly diminished role in Windows 95. I, too, have very mixed feelings about this role reduction for double-clicking. While a significant number of users are undoubtedly elephants, the majority of users have no trouble double-clicking and working comfortably with the mouse. We should not penalize the majority for the limitations of the elephants. The answer is to go ahead and include double-click idioms, while assuring that their functions have corresponding single-click idioms.

While double-clicking on data is well-defined, double-clicking on most gizmos has no meaning (I class icons as data, not gizmos), and the extra click is discarded. Many gizmos don't discard the extra click but just ignore it. If the gizmo stays in place, it will be interpreted as a second click on it. Depending on the gizmo, this can be benign or problematic. If the gizmo is a toggle button, you may find that you've just returned it to the state it started in (rapidly turning it on, then off). If the gizmo is one that goes away after the first click, like the OK button in a dialog box, for example, the results can be quite unpredictable—whatever was directly below the push-button gets the second button-down message.

Chord-clicking

Chord-clicking means pressing two buttons simultaneously, although they don't really have to be either pressed or released at precisely the same time. To qualify as a chord-click, the second mouse button must be pressed at some point before the first mouse button is released.

There are two variants to chord-clicking. The first is the simplest, whereby the user merely points to something and presses both buttons at the same time. This idiom is very clumsy and has not found much currency in existing software, although some creatively desperate programmers have implemented it as a substitute for a shift key on selection.

The second variant is using chord-clicking to terminate a drag. The drag begins as a simple, one-button drag; then the user adds the second button. Although this technique sounds more obscure than the first variant, it actually has found wider acceptance in the industry, and it is one of my personal favorites, because it is perfectly suited for canceling drag operations. I'll discuss it in more detail in the next chapter.

Triple-clicking

Believe it or not, some otherwise-respectable programs have actions that involve triple-clicking. Triple-clicking can challenge even those minnies with a high level of manual dexterity. In Word, triple-clicking is used to select entire paragraphs. The logic is simple: a single-click selects a character; a double-click selects a word; a triple-click selects a paragraph. But this idiom is so difficult to perform reliably, let alone to communicate to the user, that it is only useful for those who spend the majority of their time using the program (like authors of user interface design books).

For horizontal, sovereign applications with extremely broad user populations, like word processors and spreadsheets, triple-clicking can be worth implementing. For any program used less frequently than several hours each day, it is silly. In any case, by the time you resort to such an idiom, you should also have provided the user with several other methods of accomplishing the same task. To select a paragraph in Word without triple-clicking, for example, you can

- Double-click in the left-hand margin

- Click in the left-hand margin beside the first line and drag down to the last line

- Click at the beginning of the first word and drag to the end of the last word

- Click at the beginning of the first word and CTRL-SHIFT-RIGHT-ARROW until all of the words in the paragraph are selected

- Click at the beginning of the first word and CTRL-SHIFT-PAGEDOWN

- Double-click anywhere in the first word and drag to the end of the last word

Double-dragging

Double-dragging is another minnie-only idiom. Faultlessly executing a double-click-and-drag can be like patting your head and rubbing your stomach at the same time. Like triple-clicking, it is useful only in mainstream, horizontal sovereign applications. Use it as a variant of selection extension.

I use double-dragging in Word all of the time as a selection tool. You can double-click in text to select an entire word, so, expanding that function, you can extend the selection word-by-word by double-dragging. When I want to delete a phrase from the middle of a sentence, for example, I double-click in the middle of the first word, then drag until the phrase is selected. This is hard to do, and Microsoft has added a feature to Word that *automatically* extends your selection to word boundaries by default. Evidently, some subjects in their user testing liked this feature. I don't, so I turn it off and tolerate double-dragging.

In a big, horizontal, sovereign application that has many permutations of selection, idioms like this one are appropriate. But unless you are creating such a monster, I suggest you stick with the basic mouse actions.

Up and down events

Each time the user presses a mouse button, the program must deal with two discrete events: the button-down event and the button-up event. With the bold lack of consistency exhibited elsewhere in the world of mouse management, the definitions of the actions to be taken on button-down and button-up can vary with the context and from program to program. These actions should be made rigidly consistent.

When you're selecting an object, the selection should always take place on the button-down. This is so because the button-down may be the first step in a dragging sequence. By definition, you cannot drag something without first selecting it, so the selection *must* take place on the button-down. If not, the user would have to perform the demanding double-drag.

Design tip: Button–down means select over data.

On the other hand, if the cursor is positioned over a gizmo rather than selectable data, the action on the button-down event is to *tentatively* activate the gizmo's state transition. When the gizmo finally sees the button-up event, it then commits to the state transition.

Design tip: Button–down means propose action; button–up means commit to action over gizmos.

This is the mechanism that allows the user to gracefully bow out of an inadvertent click. In a push-button, for example, the user can just move the mouse outside of the button and the selection is deactivated even though the mouse button is still down. For a checkbox, the meaning is similar: on button-down, the checkbox visually shows that it has been activated, but the check doesn't actually appear until the button-up transition.

The cursor

The cursor is the visible representation on the screen of the mouse's position. By convention, it is normally a small arrow pointing slightly West of North, but under program control it can change to any shape as long as it stays relatively small: 32×32 pixels. Because the cursor frequently must resolve to a single pixel—pointing to things that may occupy only a single pixel—there must be some way for the cursor to indicate precisely which pixel is the one pointed to. This is accomplished by always designating one single pixel of any cursor as the actual locus of pointing, called the hotspot. For the standard arrow, the hotspot is, logically, the tip of the arrow. Regardless of the shape the cursor assumes, it always has a single hotspot pixel.

As you move the mouse across the screen, some things that the mouse points to are inert: clicking the mouse button while the cursor's hotspot is over them provokes no reaction. Other, more interesting things, react when you click on them. Any object or area on the screen that reacts to a mouse action I call pliant. A push-button gizmo is pliant because it can be "pushed" by the mouse cursor. Any object that can be picked up and dragged is pliant, thus any directory or file icon in the File Manager or Explorer is pliant. In fact, every cell in a spreadsheet and every character in text is pliant.

When objects on the screen are pliant, this fact must be communicated to the user. If this fact isn't made clear, the idiom ceases to be useful to any user other than experts (conceivably, this could be useful, but in general, the more information we can communicate to the user the better).

Visually hint at pliancy

Hinting

There are three basic ways to communicate the pliancy of an object to the user: by the static visual affordances of the object itself, its dynamically changing visual affordances, or by changing the visual affordances of the cursor as it passes over the object. If the pliancy of the object is communicated by the static visual affordance of the object itself, I call that static visual hinting.

Static visual hinting merely indicates the way the object is drawn on the screen. For example, the three-dimensional sculpting of a push-button is static visual hinting because of its manual affordance for pushing.

Some visual objects that are pliant are not obviously so, either because they are too small or because they are hidden. If the directly manipulable object is out of the central area of the program's face, the side posts, scrollbars or status bar at the bottom of the screen, for example, the user simply may not understand that the object is directly manipulable. This case calls for more aggressive visual hinting, which I call **active visual hinting**.

It works like this: When the cursor passes over the pliant object, the object changes its appearance with an animated motion. Remember, this action occurs merely when the cursor passes over the object, before any mouse buttons are pressed. LucasArts' X-Wing does this with great wit and panache: When the cursor passes over the doors to different elements of the program—the missions, training, or briefing room—the door itself slides smoothly upward with a sibilant pneumatic hiss to reveal the room beyond. Active visual hinting at this level is powerful enough to act as a training device, in addition to merely reminding the user of where the pliant spots are. I'm not suggesting that a business program be as bold as an arcade-game style program, but a more subtle implementation of active visual hinting could be just the ticket for bringing an important but latent idiom to the user's attention. There is remarkably little active visual hinting in the world of business and productivity software. Too bad. The edutainment field uses it often, and their software is better for it.

Cursor hinting

If the pliancy of the object is communicated by a change in the cursor as it passes over, I call that **cursor hinting**.

Because the cursor is dynamically changing, all cursor hinting is *active* cursor hinting.

Most popular software intermixes visual hinting and cursor hinting freely, and we think nothing of it. For example, push-buttons are rendered three-dimensionally, and the shading clearly indicates that the object is raised and affords to be pushed; when the cursor passes over the raised button, however, it doesn't change. On the other hand, when the cursor passes over a pluralized window's thickframe, the cursor changes to a double-ended arrow showing the axis in which the window edge can be stretched. This is the only definite visual affordance that the thickframe can be stretched. In Windows 3.x, the thick-frame is a visually distinct area, so it has some visual hinting, but in the redesigned Windows 95, that hinting is attenuated significantly.

In a broad generalization, gizmos usually offer static visual hinting, while pliant data more frequently offers cursor hinting. We'll talk more about hinting in Chapter 18, "Drag-and-Drop."

> **Design tip:** Indicating pliancy is the most important role of cursor hinting.

Although cursor hinting usually involves changing the cursor to some shape that indicates what type of direct-manipulation action is acceptable, its most important role is in making it clear to the user that the object is pliant. It is difficult to make data visually hint at its pliancy without disturbing its normal representation, so cursor hinting is the most effective method. Some gizmos are small and difficult for users to spot as readily as a button or buttcon, and cursor hinting is vital for the success of such gizmos. The column dividers and screen splitters in Microsoft's Excel are good examples, as you can see in Figure 15-2.

Wait cursor hinting

Actually, there is a third variant of cursor hinting, called **wait cursor hinting**. Whenever the program is doing something that takes significant amounts of time in human terms—like accessing the disk or rebuilding directories—the program changes the cursor into a visual indication that the program has gone stupid. In Windows, this image is the familiar hourglass. Other operating systems have used wristwatches, spinning balls and steaming cups of coffee. Informing the user when the program becomes stupid is a good idea, but the cursor isn't the right tool for the job. After all, the cursor belongs to everybody, and not to any particular program. Too bad the idiom has wide currency as a standard and will undoubtedly live on for many years.

The user interface problem arises because the cursor belongs to the system and is just "borrowed" by a program when it invades that program's airspace. In a non-preemptive system like Windows 3.x, using the cursor to indicate the wait is a reasonable idiom because when one program gets stupid, they all get stupid.

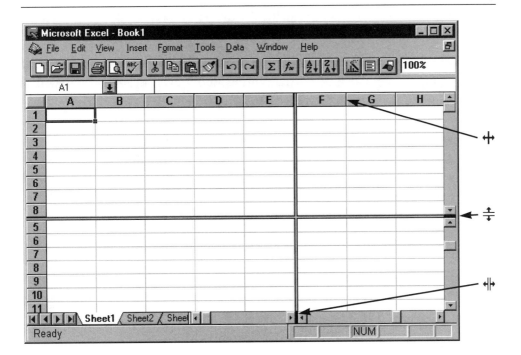

Figure 15-2

Microsoft Excel for Windows uses cursor hinting to highlight several gizmos that, by visual inspection, are not obviously pliant. The width of the individual columns can be set by dragging on the short vertical lines between each pair of columns, so the cursor changes to a two-headed horizontal arrow hinting at both the pliancy and indicating the permissible drag direction. The same is true for the two screen-splitter controls. The short, dark lines in the scroll-bars are fatter than those dividing each column, and the corresponding cursor is slightly different, using a double line, but the meaning is substantially the same.

In the *preemptive* multi-tasking world of Windows 95, when one program gets stupid, it won't necessarily make other running programs get stupid, and, if the user points to one of them, it will need to use the cursor. Therefore, the cursor cannot be used to indicate a busy state for any single program.

If the program must turn a blind eye and deaf ear to the user while it scratches some digital itch, it should make this known through an indicator on its own video real estate, leaving the cursor alone. It can graphically indicate the corresponding function and show its progress either on its main window, or in a dialog box that appears for the duration of the procedure. It's also important to offer the user a means to cancel the operation. (We'll discuss this more in

Chapter 21, "Dialog Boxes." Actually, the dialog box is a weaker implementation than drawing the same graphics right on the main window of the program.

Windows 95 forced Microsoft to rethink the wait cursor. Clearly, they wanted to maintain the familiar wait cursor hinting idiom even though the new dispatching algorithm meant it would probably be lying to the user. They decided that programs will only show the hourglass cursor within their own windows, which is logically correct. However, the result of this fix means the program that is busy now offers no visual feedback of its state of stupidity. If the user inadvertently moves the cursor off a busy program's main window and onto that of another—running—program, the cursor will revert to a normal arrow. The visual hinting is all wrong.

I don't believe that Microsoft has solved the problem with their compromise. Ultimately, each program must indicate its busy state by some visual change to its own visage. Using the cursor to indicate a busy state doesn't work if that busy state depends on where the cursor is pointing. Preemptive multi-tasking will kill the idea of the wait cursor. May it rest in peace.

Focus

Focus is an obscure technical state that is so complex it has confounded more than one erstwhile Windows programming expert. One of them, after a particularly grueling and fruitless week of focus programming, declared to me in disgust that focus was actually a contraction of two words, the second one being "us."

Windows is a multi-tasking system, which means that more than one program can be performing useful work at any given time. Despite allegations to the contrary, Windows has *always* been a multi-tasking system; Windows 95 is merely the first version of it that multi-tasks *preemptively*. Regardless of the dispatching algorithm, though, no matter how many programs are running concurrently, only one program can be in direct contact with the user at a time. That is why the concept of focus was derived. Focus indicates which program will receive the next input from the user. For the purposes of our discussion here, we can think of focus as being the same as "activation," as in, there is only one program active at a time. This is purely from the user's point of view. Programmers will generally have to do more homework. The active program is the one with the most prominent caption bar (it's usually dark blue or whatever color you have personalized your desktop to show).

In its simplest case, the program with the focus will receive the next keystroke. Because a normal keystroke has no location component, the focus cannot change because of it, but a mouse button press does have a location component and can cause the focus to change as a side effect of its normal command. I call a mouse click that changes the focus a **new-focus click**.

However, if you click the mouse somewhere in a window that already has the focus, an action that I call an **in-focus click**, there is no change to the focus.

An in-focus click is the normal case, and the program will deal with it as just another mouse click, selecting some data, moving the insertion point or invoking a command. The conundrum arises for the new-focus click: what should the program do with it? Should the program discard it (from a functional standpoint) after it has performed its job of transferring the focus, or should it do double-duty, first transferring the focus and then performing its normal task within the application?

For example, let's assume that both File Manager and Program Manager are pluralized and visible on the screen simultaneously. Only one of them can be active, so let's make it the Program Manager. By definition, if it is active, it has the focus and visibly indicates this with a highlighted caption bar. Pressing keys sends messages only to Program Manager. Mouse clicks inside the already-active Program Manager are in-focus and go only to the Program Manager. Now, if you move the mouse cursor over to the File Manager window and click the mouse, you are telling Windows that you want File Manager to become the active window and take over the focus. This new-focus click causes both caption bars to change color, indicating that the File Manager is active and the Program Manager is inactive. Now the question arises: should the File Manager interpret that new-focus click within its own context? Let's say that new-focus click was on a visible filename. Should that filename also become selected or should the click be discarded after transferring the focus? If File Manager were already active and I in-focus clicked on that same filename, the filename would be selected. As a matter of fact, in real life, the filename *does* get selected. Both File Manager and Program Manager interpret the new-focus click as a valid in-focus click.

Windows interprets new-focus clicks as in-focus clicks with some uniformity. For instance, if I change focus to Word by clicking and dragging on its caption bar, Word not only gets the focus but is repositioned, too. Ah, but here is where it gets sticky! If I change the focus to Word by clicking on a document inside Word, Word gets the focus, but the click is discarded—it is *not* also inter-preted as an in-focus click within the document. Adobe Illustrator for Windows and Microsoft's Excel also discard the new-focus click in this manner.

The Microsoft style guide weighs in on this point to say that "The reactivation of a window or pane does not affect any pre-existing selection there; the selec-tion and focus are restored to the state that existed when the window or pane was last active." But just because it says so in the guide doesn't necessarily mean that Microsoft won't completely refute this in their next release. Nor does the guide blush over the fact that Program Manager, File Manager and the Explorer have blatantly violated the statement since they first shipped.

I suspect that the guide author looked more towards Microsoft's applications for archetypes than towards its operating systems. I know experts who strongly hold contradictory positions on this issue, so neither policy is necessarily "right." Generally, I think ignoring the new-focus click is a safer and more con-servative course of action. On the other hand, I am loathe to demand extra clicks from the user. If you do choose to ignore the click, like Word and Excel do, it is difficult to explain the contradiction that a new-focus click in any non-client areas will be also used as an in-focus click, even though it somehow *feels* right.

Meta-keys

Direct-manipulation idioms can be extended by using one of the various meta-keys in conjunction with the mouse. Meta-keys include the CONTROL key, the ALT key and either of the two SHIFT keys.

There is a slightly sacrilegious joke floating around Silicon Valley: God must have loved standards because he gave us so many of them. In the Windows world, no single voice articulated user interface standards with the iron will that Apple did for the Macintosh, and the result was chaos in some important areas. This is certainly evident when we look at meta-key usage. Although Microsoft has finally articulated meta-key standards with Windows 95, their efforts now are about as futile as trying to eliminate kudzu from Alabama roadsides.

Even Microsoft freely violates their own standards for meta-keys. Each program tends to roll its own, but some meanings predominate, usually those that were first firmly defined by Apple. Unfortunately, the mapping isn't exactly the same. Apples have a CLOVER key and an APPLE key that roughly correspond to the CTRL and ALT keys, respectively. Keep in mind that the choice of which meta-key to use, or which program to model your choices after, is less important than remaining consistent within your own interface.

Meta-key cursor hinting

Using cursor hinting to show the meanings of meta-keys is an all-around good idea and more programs should do it. This is something that must be done dynamically, too. As the meta-key goes down, the cursor should change immediately to reflect the new intention of the idiom.

Design tip: Use cursor hinting to show meta-key meanings.

ALT meta-key

The ALT meta-key is the problem-child of the family. Microsoft has studiously avoided imbuing it with meaning, so it has been rather a rudderless ship adrift in a sea of clever programmers, who use it as the whim strikes and ignore it otherwise. Doubtless, someone at Microsoft will latch onto it for some favorite idiom, and it will then grow into a de facto standard.

At one time, I favored using it to indicate a two-application drag-and-drop operation. However, first the ALT-TAB idiom and now the Startbar have gone a long way to disabuse me of the idea that two-application drag-and-drop will be the Next-Big-Thing. As a result, I'm just as adrift on the ALT key as Microsoft is. I'll probably come to regret that statement.

I will discuss the specific meanings and usage of the CONTROL and SHIFT meta-keys and how they affect selection and drag-and-drop in their respective chapters.

Selection

There are basically only two things you can do with a mouse: Choose something, and choose something to do to what you've chosen. These choosing actions are referred to as **selection**, and they have many nuances.

Object-verb

A fundamental issue in user interfaces is the sequence in which commands are issued. Most every command has an operation and one or more operands. The operation describes what action will occur, and the operands are the target of that operation. "Operation" and "operand" are programmer's terms; interface designers prefer to borrow linguistic terminology, referring to the operation as the **verb**, and the operand as the **object**.

You can specify the verb first, followed by the object, or you can specify the object first, followed by the verb. These are commonly called **verb-object** and **object-verb** orders, respectively. Either order is good, and modern user interfaces typically use both.

In the days when language compilers like COBOL and FORTRAN were the bee's knees in high technology, all computer languages used verb-object ordering. A typical statement went like this: PERFORM ACTION ON X AND Y. The verb, PERFORM ACTION, came before the objects, X and Y. This ordering was intended to follow the natural formations of the English language. In the world of linguistic processing, though, this actually wasn't all that convenient, as the computer doesn't like this notation. Compiler-writers put considerable effort into swapping things around, making it easier to turn the human-readable source code into machine-readable executable code. But there was never any question that verb-object ordering was the right way to present things to the user—the programmer—because it was clear and natural and effective for written, text-oriented communications with the computer.

When graphical user interfaces emerged, it became clear that verb-object ordering created a problem. In an interactive interface, if the user chooses a verb, the system must then enter a state—a mode—that differs from the norm: waiting for an object. Normally, the user will then choose an object and all will be well. However, if the user wants to act on more than one object, how does the system know this? It can only know if the user tells it in advance how many operands he will enter, which violates the axiom of not requiring the user to ask permission to ask a question. Otherwise, the program must accept all operands until the user enters some special object-list-termination-command, also a very clumsy idiom. See the problem? What works just fine in a highly structured, linguistic environment falls apart completely in the looser universe of interactivity.

By swapping the command order to object-verb, we don't need all of that complex termination stuff. The user merely selects which objects will be operated upon and then indicates which verb to execute on them. The software very simply executes the indicated function on the selected data. Notice, though, that a new concept has crept into the equation that didn't exist—wasn't needed—in a verb-object world. That new concept is called **selection**.

Rather than the program remembering the verb while the user specifies one or more objects, we are asking the program to remember one or more objects while the user chooses the verb. This way, however, we need a mechanism for identifying, marking and remembering the chosen operands. Selection is the mechanism by which the user informs the program which objects to remember.

The object-verb model can be difficult to understand intellectually, but selection is an idiom that is very easy to grasp and, once shown, rarely forgotten.

Explained through the linguistic context of the English language, it is non-sensical that we must choose an object first. On the other hand, we use this model frequently in our non-linguistic actions. We purchase groceries by first selecting the objects—by placing them in our shopping cart—then specifying the operation to execute on them—by bringing the cart up to the checkout counter and expressing our desire to purchase. But we never say "Corn flakes, buy" in English conversation.

In a non-interactive interface, like a modal dialog box, the concept of selection isn't always needed. Dialog boxes naturally come with one of those object-list-termination-commands: the OK button. The user can choose a function first and an object second or vice versa because the whole operation won't actually occur until the confirming OK button is pressed. This is not to say that object-verb ordering isn't used in most dialog boxes. It merely shows that no particular command ordering has a divine right; the two orderings have strengths and weaknesses that complement each other in the complex world of user inter-faces. Both are powerful tools for the software designer and should be used where they are best suited.

In its simplest variant, selection is trivial: The user points to a data object with the mouse cursor, clicks and the object is selected. However, this operation is deceptively simple and, in practice, many interesting variants are exposed.

Concrete and discrete data

Users select data, not verbs. When you invoke a verb, you may do it with the same type of click action you used to select the data, though, so don't get con-fused. The basic variants of selection, then, depend on the basic variants of selectable data, and there are two broad categories of data.

Some programs represent data as distinct visual objects that can be manipul-ated independently of other objects. The icons in the Program Manager and graphic objects in draw programs are examples. These objects are also selected independently of each other. They are discrete data, and I call selection within them discrete selection. Discrete data is not necessarily homogeneous, and discrete selection is not necessarily contiguous.

Conversely, some programs represent their data as a matrix of many little con-tiguous pieces of data. The text in a word processor or the cells in a spreadsheet are concretions of hundreds or thousands of similar little objects that together form a coherent whole. These objects are often selected in solid groups, so I call them **concrete data** and selection within them **concrete selection**.

Both concrete and discrete selection support both single-click selection and click-and-drag selection. Single clicking selects the smallest possible discrete amount, and clicking-and-dragging selects some larger quantity, but there are significant differences.

The nature of discrete selection is discontiguous, while that of concrete selection is contiguous. I'll show you what I mean: There is a natural order to the text in a word processor's document—concrete data. Scrambling the order of the letters destroys the sense of it. The characters flow from the beginning to the end in a meaningful continuum; selecting a word or paragraph makes sense in the context of the data, while random, disconnected selections are generally meaningless. Although it is theoretically possible to allow a discontiguous selection—several disconnected paragraphs, for example—the user's task of visualizing the selections and avoiding inadvertent, unwanted operations on them is more trouble than it is worth. Generally, if the data can be scrolled off screen, it shouldn't be discontiguously selectable.

Discrete data, on the other hand, has no inherent order; like peas on your plate, the order in which you select and eat them is irrelevant. In a drawing program, where various graphic objects reside on the screen, the objects are independent. No relationship is integral to their meaning, and even the z-order, the order in which they overlay each other on the screen, is only significant if they directly cover each other. Scrambling the order of the objects might have no effect whatsoever on the collective image (again, except where objects overlay each other). Because there is no inherent order in these objects, contiguous selection has no meaning in this context, and each object is selected discretely.

Most drawing programs offer a grouping facility which allows more than one discrete object to be logically grouped together to form a single, new discrete object. That group object now behaves as though it were a single discrete object regardless of the number of component pieces it contains.

Of course, you can always select more than one discrete object, but it remains a series of independent selections rather than as a subset of ordered data.

Insertion and replacement

As we've established, selection indicates which data the next function will operate on. If that next function is a write command, the incoming data (keystrokes or a PASTE command) writes onto the selected data. In discrete selection, one or more discrete objects are selected, and the incoming data is handed to the selected discrete objects which process them in their own way. This may cause a **replacement** action, where the incoming data replaces the selected object. Alternatively, the selected object may treat the incoming data as fodder for some standard function. In PowerPoint, for example, incoming keystrokes with a shape selected result in a text annotation of the selected shape.

In concrete selection, however, the incoming data always replaces the currently selected data. In a word processor, when you type, you replace what is selected with what you are typing. Concrete selection exhibits a unique quirk related to insertion, where the selection can shrink down to a single point that indicates a place *in between* two bits of data, rather than one or more bits of data. This in-between place is called the **insertion point**.

In a word processor, the blinking caret (usually a dark, vertical line indicating where the next character will go) is essentially the least amount of concrete selection available: a location only. It just indicates a position in the data, between two atomic elements, without actually selecting either one of them. By pointing and clicking anywhere else, you can easily move the caret, but if you drag to extend the selection, the blinking caret disappears and is replaced by the contiguous selection.

Another way to think of the insertion point is as a null selection. By definition, typing into a selection replaces that selection with the new characters, but if the selection is null, the new characters replace nothing; they are merely inserted. In other words, insertion is the trivial case of replacement.

Even though spreadsheets use concrete selection, they are different from word processors. The selection is concrete because the cells form a contiguous matrix of data, but there is no concept of selecting the space between two cells. In the spreadsheet, a single-click will select exactly one whole cell. There is currently no concept of an insertion point in a spreadsheet, although the design possibilities are intriguing.

A blend of these two idioms is implementable as well. In PowerPoint's slide-sorter view, insertion-point selection is allowed, but single slides can be selected, too. If you click on a slide, that slide is selected, but if you click in between two slides, a blinking insertion-point caret is placed there.

If a program allows an insertion point as a selection, objects themselves are selected by clicking and dragging across them. Even to select a single character in a word processor, the mouse must be dragged across it. This means that the user will be doing quite a bit of clicking-and-dragging in the normal course of using the program, with the side effect that any drag-and-drop idiom will be more difficult to express. You can see this in Word, where dragging-and-dropping text involves first a click-and-drag operation to make the selection, then another mouse move back into the selection to click-and-drag again for the actual move. To do the same thing, Excel makes you find a special pliant zone that is only a pixel or two wide on the border of the desired cell. In discrete selection, all the user must do is click-and-drag on the object in a single motion.

To relieve the click-and-drag burden of selection in word processors, other direct-manipulation shortcuts are also implemented, like double-clicking to select a word.

Mutual exclusion

Generally, when a selection is made, any previous selection is unmade. This behavior is called **mutual exclusion**, as the selection of one excludes the selection of the other. Typically, the user clicks on an object, and it becomes selected. That object remains selected until the user selects something else. Mutual exclusion is the rule in both discrete and concrete selection.

Some discrete systems allow a selected object to be deselected by clicking on it a second, canceling, time. This can lead to a curious condition in which nothing at all is selected, and there is no insertion point. You must decide whether this condition is appropriate for your program.

Additive selection

I cannot imagine a concrete-selection program without mutual exclusion, because the user cannot see or know what effect his actions will have if his selections can readily be scrolled off the screen. Imagine being able to select several independent paragraphs of text in a long document. It might be useful, but it certainly isn't controllable. The problem is caused by the scrolling, not the concrete selection, but most programs with concrete-selectable data *are* scrollable.

However, if mutual exclusion is turned off in discrete selection, you have the simple case where many independent objects can be selected merely by clicking on more than one in turn. I call this **additive selection**. A listbox, for example, can allow the user to make as many selections as desired. An entry is then de-selected by clicking it a second time. Once the user has selected the desired objects, the terminating verb acts on them collectively.

Most discrete-selection systems implement mutual exclusion by default and allow additive selection only by using a meta-key. The SHIFT meta-key is used most frequently for this. In a draw program, for example, after you've clicked to select one graphical object, you typically can add another one to your selection by SHIFT-clicking.

Concrete selection systems should never allow additive selection because there should never be more than a single selection in a concrete system. However, concrete-selection systems do need to enable their single allowable selection to be extended, and again, meta-keys are used. Unfortunately, there is little consensus regarding whether it should be the CTRL or the SHIFT key that performs this role. In Word, the SHIFT key causes everything between the initial selection and the SHIFTED-click to be selected. It is easy to find programs with similar additive selection functions that have made different choices of meta-key variations. There is little practical difference between choices, so this is an area where following the market leader is best because it offers the user the small-but-real advantage of consistency.

Group selection

The click-and-drag operation is also the basis for group selection. In a matrix of text or cells, it means "extend the selection" from the mouse-down point to the mouse-up point. This can also be modified with meta-keys. In Word, for example, CTRL-click selects a complete sentence, so a CTRL-drag extends the selection sentence-by-sentence. Sovereign applications should rightly enrich their interaction with as many of these variants as possible. Experienced users will eventually come to memorize and use them, as long as the variants are manually simple.

In a collection of discrete objects, the click-and-drag operation generally begins a drag-and-drop move. If the mouse button is pressed in the open area between objects, rather than on any specific object, however, it has a special meaning. It creates a dragrect, shown in Figure 16-1.

A dragrect is a dynamic gray rectangle whose upper left corner is the mouse-down point and whose lower right corner is the mouse-up point. When the mouse button is released, any and all objects enclosed within the dragrect are selected as a group.

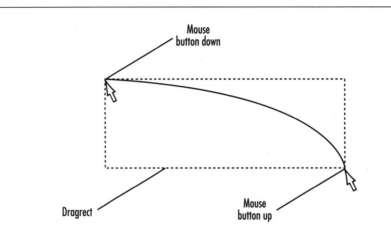

Mouse button down

Dragrect

Mouse button up

Figure 16-1

The simple click-and-drag operation, when the cursor is not on any particular object at mouse-down time, normally creates a dragrect that selects any object that is wholly enclosed in it when the mouse button is released. This is a familiar idiom to users of drawing programs and many word processors.

Visual indication of selection

It is critical that you visually indicate to the user when something is selected. The selected state must be easy to spot on a crowded screen, unambiguous, and must not obscure the object or what it is.

Design tip: Make selection visually bold and unambiguous.

The old Norton Utilities for DOS were infamous for putting up a dialog box with two push-button choices, the selected one in gray and the unselected one in blue—or was it the unselected one in gray and the selected one in blue? I couldn't tell, and neither could anybody else. Pressing the ENTER key was a gamble because the selection was ambiguous. Particularly if there are only two selectable objects on the screen, you must be careful about what you choose to indicate selection. You must assure that anyone can easily tell by visual inspection which one is selected and which isn't. It's not good enough just to be able to see that they are different. In Windows, it's harder to pull a stunt like that, but the lesson is still valid. Also, a significant portion of the population is color-blind, so color alone is insufficient to distinguish between selections.

The performance hack for indicating selection

Traditionally, selection is accomplished by inversion—by inverting the pixels of the selected object.

On a monochrome screen, this means turning all of the white pixels black and all of the black pixels white, but how many of you are still using black-and-white monitors? When the original Macintosh was released in 1984, it was a monochrome computer in spirit as well as in hardware. Because of this, Apple felt justified in using the inversion technique for indicating selections. Inversion was accomplished by the expedient of exclusive-ORing (or XORing) the pixels of the selected object with all 1 bits (or all 0 bits, depending on the processor). The XOR happens to be one of the fastest operations a CPU can execute, and with the limited computing power available in 1984, this was an easily justifiable choice. XORs are not only naturally fast but, by a curious quirk of digital circuitry, the action of an XOR can be undone merely by repeating the identical XOR. Fast! Microsoft continued the XOR technique in the first releases of Windows even though it was never a monochrome system in thought or in deed.

The hidden gotcha is that the result of the XOR operation is only defined when its operands are binary: on or off, one or zero, white pixels or black pixels. Color, however, is represented by more than a single bit. A 256-color screen uses eight bits. When the XOR is used on these more-complex numbers, the individual bits invert reliably, but a problem arises when the new value is sent to the physical video screen. Different video drivers interpret those bits in very different ways. The number may be split into smaller pieces to control individual red, green or blue bits, or they may result in a subscript for a color-table lookup. The result is that, although the XOR operation will be consistently represented on your computer, it may well be represented completely differently on another computer. XOR really is undefined for color video. Sure, it works, but the colors you get are defined only by accidents of hardware and not by any standard. What is the inverse of blue? In art class, it's yellow, but in Boolean algebra: who knows? In Windows, the bits are reasonably standard and the colors are generally predictable, but this technology is an accident waiting to happen.

Word processors and spreadsheets almost always show black text on a white background, so it is reasonable to use the XOR inversion shortcut to show selection. When colors are used, inversion still works, but the results may be aesthetically lacking. For example, in Windows 1 and 2, if you used the Control Panel program to configure your screen colors, and you set your menus to yellow instead of gray, they inverted to blue. This was certainly noticeable but not necessarily desirable.

Microsoft acknowledged this problem in Windows 3.0 by defining two new system color settings: COLOR_HIGHLIGHT and COLOR_HIGHLIGHTTEXT. Of course, these manifest constants merely represent changeable colors rather than some fixed color. Each user can change these variable definitions, which then remain constant for all of their applications. Along with these new colors came a corresponding standard for use: When an object is selected, its color changes to whatever color is represented by COLOR_HIGHLIGHT. Any text or other contrasting pixels within the selected object change to whatever color is represented by COLOR_HIGHLIGHTTEXT. If the selection is concrete, as in a word processor, the background becomes COLOR_HIGHLIGHT and the foreground text becomes COLOR_HIGHLIGHTTEXT. This new standard normalizes the visual behavior of selection on a color platform. It is an excellent idea on Microsoft's part and should be followed widely.

> *Design tip:* Use COLOR_HIGHLIGHT and COLOR_HIGHLIGHT-TEXT to show selection.

It is easy to see what colors these two constants represent simply by pulling down any menu in any program. The standard menu system in Windows uses COLOR_HIGHLIGHT and COLOR_HIGHLIGHTTEXT in the prescribed way. Of course, it is also interesting to look at a program like Excel or Word and notice what colors they use to indicate selection within cells or text. Yup, you guessed it: They invert instead of using the new standard selection colors.

Modern computing power makes the performance-hack of inversion moot. It just isn't that time-consuming anymore to use defined, consistent selection colors. I look forward to seeing the first word processor program to have a COLOR_HIGHLIGHT edit caret and, when dragging to select some text, have the selection background in COLOR_HIGHLIGHT and the text characters in COLOR_HIGHLIGHTTEXT. If you are responsible for a selection-intensive program like a word processor or spreadsheet, you might take the expedient route and use XOR inversion to indicate selection. If, however, you want to do it right and show the world your skill, use COLOR_HIGHLIGHT and watch the delighted faces.

Selecting multi-color objects

In drawing, painting, animation and presentation programs, where we deal with multi-color objects, the only decent solution I can see is to *add* selection indicators to the image, rather than by changing the selected image's color, whether by inversion or COLOR_HIGHLIGHT. Inversion can obscure details like accompanying text, while using the single system colors forces the program to reduce the selected image to two colors, foreground and background. This will likely obscure many details in multi-color objects.

Microsoft's PowerPoint is very color-intensive, and the slide view is rarely monochrome. I suspect that the authors tried to outwit the problems of inversion selection in multi-color objects by experimenting with the internal Boolean operations. When characters within text objects are selected for editing, the background turns black and the actual characters are inverted. The consistent black background can be reassuring, while the inverted pixels are otherwise fine. However, when the text is white (as it commonly is), its background turns black and the characters are inverted from white to, ta-da, black, and this makes for very difficult editing. The authors were caught by their own cleverness and created an idiom with significant areas of failure. I'm not impressed. I would rather have seen them force the background black and the foreground white. It would have been less clever but a lot better for the user.

Whatever color you choose, in a richly colored environment the selection can get visually lost. The solution is to instead highlight the selection with an additional graphic that shows its outline. This is often done with grapples (discussed in the next chapter): little boxes that surround the selected object. Grapples can still get lost in the clutter, particularly with modern, powerful image-manipulation programs. There is, however, one way to assure that the selection will always be visible regardless of the colors used: indicate the selection by movement.

One of the first programs on the Macintosh, MacPaint, had a wonderful idiom where a selected object was outlined with a simple dashed line, except that the dashes all moved in synchrony around the object. The dashes looked like ants in a column; thus, it earned the colorful sobriquet **marching ants**.

Unfortunately, this idiom has had little currency on the Windows platform. The animation is not hard to do, although it takes some care to get it right, and it works regardless of the color mix and intensity of the background. Adobe's PhotoShop uses this idiom to show selected regions of photographs, and it works very well. I'd really like to see this idiom used more widely on Windows applications. I suspect the increase in multimedia applications will accelerate its arrival. Besides, subtle animation adds a very desirable sense of engagement and humanity to the interface.

Direct Manipulation

B en Shneiderman coined the term direct manipulation in 1974. Here is my paraphrase of its three elements:

○ Visual representation of the manipulated objects

○ Physical actions instead of text entry

○ Immediately visible impact of the operation

A less-rigorous definition would say that direct manipulation is clicking-and-dragging things, and although this is true, it can easily miss the point that Shneiderman subtly makes. Notice that of his three points, two of them concern the visual feedback the program offers the user, and only the second point concerns the user's actions. It might be more accurate to call it "visual manipulation" because of the importance of what we see during the process. Unfortunately, I've seen many instances of direct-manipulation idioms implemented without adequate visual feedback, and these idioms fail to satisfy the definition of effective direct manipulation.

A rich visual interaction is the key to successful direct manipulation

Yet another observation about direct manipulation—one that is hidden by its obviousness—is that we can only directly manipulate information that is already displayed by the program; it must be visible for us to manipulate it, which again emphasizes the visual nature of direct manipulation. If you want to create effective direct-manipulation idioms in your software, you must take care to render data, objects, gizmos and cursors with good graphic detail and richness.

Direct manipulation is simple, straightforward, easy to use and easy to remember. Unfortunately, when users are first exposed to a given direct-manipulation idiom, they generally cannot intuit it or discover it independently. Direct manipulation should be taught, but the teaching of it is trivial—usually consisting of merely pointing it out—and, once taught, is never forgotten. It is a classic and archetypal example of idiomatic design. Adding metaphoric images may help, but you cannot depend on finding an appropriate one, and if you do, you cannot depend on it communicating clearly to all users. Resign yourself to the burden of teaching idioms. Console yourself with the ease of that teaching.

Apple's guide to human interaction says, with regard to direct manipulation, that "users want to feel that they are in charge of the computer's activities." Both these published guidelines and the Macintosh user interface make clear that Apple believes in direct manipulation as a fundamental tenet of good user interface design. However, cognitive psychology guru, Don Norman, says, "But direct manipulation, first-person systems have their drawbacks. Although they are often easy to use, fun, and entertaining, it is often difficult to do a really good job with them. They require the user to do the task directly, and the user may not be very good at it." Norman goes on to describe the inappropriateness of giving him a drawing program with great direct-manipulation idioms because he is such a poor artist. Which of these two contradictory statements should we believe?

The answer, of course, is both of them. As Apple says, direct manipulation is an extremely powerful tool, and as Norman says, the tool must be put into the hands of someone qualified to use it.

This contradiction should illustrate the differences between the various direct-manipulation types. Pushing a button is direct manipulation, and so is drawing with the pen tool in a paint program. Any normal user can push a button, but few are capable of drawing well with the pen tool. These examples illustrate the two variants of direct manipulation: management and content. Management includes gizmo-manipulation like button pushing and scrolling, and is generally accessible to all users. Content is drawing, and although it can be performed by anyone, its results will always be commensurate with the artistic talent of the manipulator.

All text and image manipulations such as those you find in programs like Corel Draw!, Adobe PhotoShop or Paint are drawing operations. Programs like ABC Flowcharter and Visio strain the definition, but even their more-structured interfaces are still content-centered and require some graphic talent from the user. Drawing will be discussed in detail in the next chapter.

In the management category, we find five varieties of direct manipulation:

○ Making selections

○ Dragging-and-dropping

○ Manipulating gizmos

○ Resizing, reshaping and repositioning

○ Arrowing

Selection was discussed in Chapter 16, and drag-and-drop will be discussed in Chapter 18, so I'd like to address the remaining three direct-manipulation idioms here, making some general observations along the way.

Manipulating gizmos

We can further divide up the types of direct manipulation by which mouse action they require: clicking or clicking-and-dragging.

Most gizmos—like buttcons, push-buttons, checkboxes and radio buttons—merely require the user to move the cursor over them and click the mouse button once. In terms of gizmo variants, these are a minority; but in terms of the number of actions a user will take in the average execution of a typical application, single clicking on buttcons and push-buttons is likely to be a majority.

Single-button click operations are the simplest of direct-manipulation idioms and the ones that work best with gizmos that specify operations immediately. Naturally, these functions are the ones that fall into the user's working set and will be invoked most frequently.

Beyond these simple gizmos, most direct-manipulation idioms demand a click-and-drag operation. This is a fundamental building block of visual interaction, and we will explore it in some detail.

Anatomy of a drag

A drag begins when the user presses the mouse button and then moves it without releasing the button. The set of cursor screen coordinates when the user first presses the mouse button is called the **mouse-down point** and that when the user releases the button is called the **mouse-up point**. The mouse-down point is a known quantity throughout any direct-manipulation operation. The mouse-up point only becomes known at the end of the process.

Once a drag begins, the entire interaction between the user and the computer enters a special state I call **capture**.

In programmer lingo, we say that all interaction between the system and the user is captured, meaning that no other program can interact with the user until the drag is completed. Any actions the user might take with the mouse or keyboard or any other input device go directly to the program—technically, the window—in which the mouse button first went down. I call this window that owns the mouse-down point the **master object**. If this master object is concrete data or a gizmo, the drag will likely indicate a selection extension or a gizmo state change. However, if the master object is a discrete object, it more likely indicates the beginning of a direct-manipulation operation like drag-and-drop, and capture will play an important part.

Technically, a state of capture exists the instant the user presses the mouse button, and it doesn't end until that mouse button is released, regardless of the distance the mouse moves between the two button actions. To the human, a simple click-and-release without motion seems instantaneous, but to the program, hundreds of thousands of instructions can be executed in the time it takes to press and release the button. If the user inadvertently moves the mouse before releasing the button, capture protects him from wildly triggering adjacent controls. The master object will simply reject such spurious commands.

Escaping from capture

One of the most important—yet most frequently ignored—parts of a drag is a mechanism for getting out of it. The user not only needs a way to abort the drag, if he does, he needs to have solid assurance that he did so successfully.

If the latter condition is met, the former idiom can be a lot more effective. That is, if the communication to the user that the drag action was canceled is clear, bold and unambiguous, he will be reassured and confident in using the cancel idiom, whatever it may be. Most applications, though, have no means of drag cancellation whatsoever. This is a grave lapse in user interface terms, as any good interface provides consistent and reliable ways out of a user's ill-starred action.

Provide an escape from dragging, and inform the user

At a minimum, the ESCAPE key on the keyboard should always be recognized as a general-purpose cancel mechanism for any mouse operation, either clicking or dragging. If the user presses the ESCAPE key while holding down the mouse button, the system should abandon the state of capture and return the system to the state it was in before the mouse button was pressed. When the user subsequently releases the mouse button, the program must remember to discard that mouse-up input before it has any side effect.

Because the meta-keys are often the only keys that have any meaning during drags, we could actually use any non-meta-keystroke to cancel a mouse stroke, rather than offering up only the ESCAPE. However, some programs allow the use of the arrow keys in conjunction with the mouse (we'll discuss this in the next chapter), so there are some exceptions to work around.

My personal favorite cancel idiom is the chord-click, where the user presses both mouse buttons simultaneously. Typically, the user likely begins a drag with the left mouse button, then discovers that he doesn't really want to finish what he has begun. He presses the right mouse button, then safely releases both. The idiom is insensitive to the timing or sequence of the release, and works equally well if the drag was begun with the right mouse button.

Design tip: Cancel drags on chord-click.

Microsoft used chord-clicking for drag cancel in their Word for DOS software, but unfortunately discarded the idiom when it went to Windows. Admittedly, the idiom is for minnies, but it is bad design to hobble an interface for minnies simply to pander to elephants. At least the current version of Word recognizes the ESCAPE key as a drag cancel.

Sad to say, the chord-click action is not defined in the Windows API. There is no system call to test for it, and no message is generated when the user chord-clicks. The messages are there for the asking, but it's hard for Visual Basic programmers to get them. However it is not difficult to code if you are writing in C or C++, and a DLL for VB would be easy to create.

Because Microsoft was so tentative in committing to the presence of a second mouse button, it is only fitting that they were reluctant to commit the chord-click to a cancel idiom. But now that Microsoft seems to have admitted, in Windows 95, that all of their users will have at least two mouse buttons, adopting the chord-click as a universal cancel idiom would only make good sense. Write your congressperson today.

Informing the user

If your program is well-designed and enables the user to cancel out of a drag operation with an ESCAPE key or a chord-click, the problem still remains of assuring the user that he is now safe. The cursor may have been changed to indicate that a drag was in progress, or an outline of the dragged object may have been moving with the cursor. The cancellation makes these visual hints go away, but the user may still wonder if he is truly safe. A user may have pressed the ESCAPE key, but is still holding the mouse button down, unsure whether it is entirely safe to let go of it. It is cruel and unusual punishment to leave him in this state. It is imperative that he be informed that the operation has been effectively canceled and that releasing the mouse button is OK. It can't hurt—and can only help—to make sure that he gets a reassuring message.

The message should clearly state that the drag is harmlessly over. I designed such an idiom for one of my clients that looked—and sounded—like a big, red, rubber stamp saying "Drag Canceled" had been thumped down in the middle of the screen. You can see this in Figure 17-1. At the instant the user cancels the drag, a bitmap about six by ten centimeters appears, centered on the screen, and remains there for two seconds. The moment it appears, a prerecorded sound of a rubber stamp striking paper is played on the optional sound system. Users went crazy over this idiom, often starting drags just so they could joyously abort them.

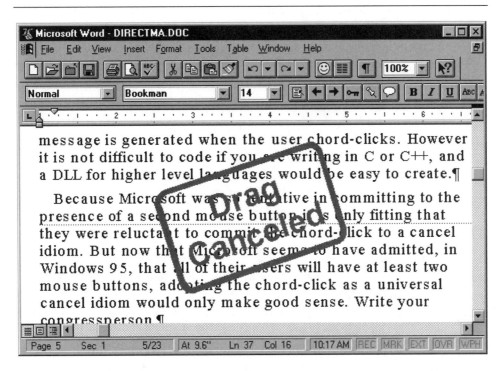

Figure 17-1

When the user cancels an unintended drag operation, they need to know positively and immediately that the operation has, indeed, been safely canceled. What could be better than the big, red, rubber stamp of implacable bureaucracy assuring them that the airplane has been grounded, the factory shut down, the train stopped, the groundwater cleaned, the nuke decontaminated, the forest saved, the criminal apprehended. Now, life can go on, happily ever after. And don't forget to add that satisfying "Thump" sound effect!

Let's go back to the drag itself: Once the drag begins, the meaning of the user's actions varies depending on the type of drag action. The drag action depends on the program, the context and the master object.

In the simplest case, concrete data, the drag means to extend the selection. The text or cells or whatever are selected contiguously from the mouse-down point to the mouse-up point.

If the mouse goes down inside a gizmo, the gizmo must visually show that it is poised to undergo a state change. This action is important and is often neglected by those who create their own gizmos. It is a form of active visual hinting that I call the **pliant response**.

A push-button needs to change from a visually outdented state to a visually indented state; a checkbox should highlight its box but not show a check just yet. The pliant response is an important feedback mechanism for any gizmo that either invokes an action or changes its state, letting the user know that some action is forthcoming if he releases the mouse button. The pliant response is also an important part of the cancel mechanism. When the user clicks down on a button, that button responds by indenting. If the user moves the mouse away from that button while still holding the button down, the button should return to its quiescent, outdented state. If the user then releases the mouse, the button will not be activated (as is consistent with the missing pliant response).

Dragging gizmos

Many gizmos, particularly menus, require the moderately difficult motion of a click-and-drag rather than a mere click. This direct-manipulation operation is more demanding of the user because of its juxtaposition of fine motions with gross motions to click, drag and then release the mouse button. Although menus are not used as frequently as toolbar gizmos, they are still used very often, particularly by new or infrequent users. Thus, we find one of the more intractable conundrums of GUI design: The menu is the primary gizmo for beginners, yet it is one of the more difficult gizmos to physically operate. I know of no solution to this problem other than to provide additional idioms to accomplish the same task. If a function is available from the menu and it is one that will be used more than just rarely, make sure to provide other idioms for invoking the function—idioms that don't require a click-and-drag operation.

One of the nice features of Windows 3.x is the ability to work its menus with a series of single clicks rather than clicking-and-dragging. You click on the menu and it drops down. You point to the desired item and click once to select it and close the menu. I find it remarkable that Apple hasn't included this idiom in their interface. In Windows 95, Microsoft has extended this idea even further by putting the program into a sort-of "menu mode" as soon as you click once on any menu. When in menu mode, all of the top-level menus in the program and all of the items on those menus are active, just as though you were clicking-and-dragging. As you move the mouse around, each menu in turn drops down without having to use the mouse button at all. This can be disconcerting if you are unfamiliar with it, but after the initial shock has worn off, the action is generally more pleasant, mostly because it is easier on the wrist.

There are other types of click-and-drag gizmos. **Cascading menus** are another variant.

In a cascading menu, you pull down a menu in the normal way, then launch a secondary menu from an item on the first menu by dragging the mouse to the right. Cascading menus, like the one shown in Figure 17-2, can be stacked up so there are more than one. They form a hierarchy of menus.

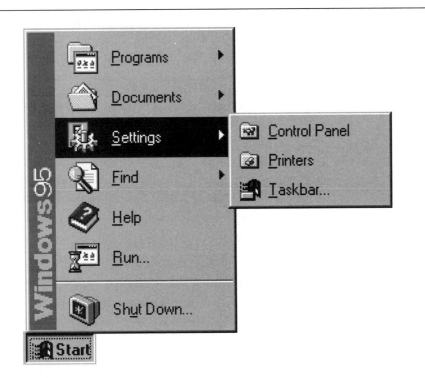

Figure 17-2

In Windows 95, Microsoft implemented the Startbar, with its rich array of cascading menus, for the avowed purpose of making life easier for neophytes and elephants. Physically navigating cascading menus is tough, and logically they are a hierarchy—one of the more difficult concepts for non-programmers to grasp. The Startbar is clearly a winner, and the new "menu-mode" certainly helps, but will cascades prove popular with elephants? Only time will tell.

Cascading menus demand a fair amount of skill by the mouse user, because any false move that causes the cursor to detour outside of the enclosing menu rectangle will cause one or another of the menus to disappear. Cascades can be a frustrating gizmo to manipulate, and although they have their place in interface design, I recommend against using them for frequently used functions. Of course, Microsoft and I are clearly not in agreement on that point, as Windows 95 makes extensive use of cascading menus throughout its interface. I suspect that the new "menu-mode" has convinced the designers in Redmond that the problems with cascades are eliminated. I doubt they are right, and a straw poll of my colleagues indicates agreement with my conclusion.

Repositioning

Gizmos that depend on click-and-drag motions include icons and the various repositioning, resizing and reshaping idioms. We'll address icons when we discuss drag-and-drop in the next chapter. Repositioning is the simple act of clicking on an object and dragging it to another location.

The most significant design issue regarding repositioning is that it usurps the place of other direct-manipulation idioms. Repositioning is a form of direct manipulation that takes place on a higher conceptual level than that occupied by the object you are repositioning. That is, you are not manipulating some aspect of the object, but simply manipulating the placement of the object in space. This action consumes the click-and-drag action, making it unavailable for other purposes. If the object is repositionable, the meaning of click-and-drag is taken and cannot be devoted to some other action within the object itself, like a button press.

The most general solution to this conflict is to dedicate a specific physical area of the object to the repositioning function. For example, you can reposition a window in Windows or on the Macintosh by clicking-and-dragging its caption bar. The rest of the window is not pliant for repositioning, so the click-and-drag idiom is available for more application-specific functions, as you would expect. The only hint of the window's draggability is the color of the caption bar, a subtle visual hint that is purely idiomatic: there is no way to intuit the presence of the idiom. But the idiom is very effective, and it merely proves the efficacy of idiomatic interface design. Generally, though, you need to provide some more-explicit visual hinting of an area's pliancy. The cost of this solution is the number of pixels devoted to the caption bar. Mitigating this is the fact that the caption bar does double-duty as a program identifier, active status indicator and repository for certain other system-standard controls such as the minimize, maximize and close functions, as well as the system menu.

To move an object, it must first be selected. This is why selection must take place on the mouse-down transition: the user can drag without having to first click-and-release on an object to select it, then click-and-drag on it to reposition it. It feels so much more natural to simply click it and then drag it to where you want it in one easy motion. When you pick up a book or a pencil, you select and move it in one combined action, rather than having to pick it up to select it, put it back, then pick it up again to move it. And yet, in Word, Microsoft has given us this clumsy click-wait-click operation to drag chunks of text. You must click-and-drag to select a section of text, then wait a second or so and click-and-drag again to move it. This idiom is very clumsy, but there is really no way around it in concrete selection. If Microsoft were willing to dispense with their meta-key idioms for extending the selection, those same meta-keys could be used to, say, select a sentence and drag it in a single movement. But this still wouldn't solve the problem of selecting and moving some arbitrary hunk of text.

Resizing and reshaping

When referring to the "desktop" of Windows and other similar GUIs, there isn't really any functional difference between resizing and reshaping. The user adjusts a rectangular window's size and aspect ratio at the same time and with the same control by clicking-and-dragging on a dedicated gizmo. On the Macintosh, there is a special resizing control on each window in the lower right corner, frequently nestled into the space between the application's vertical and horizontal scrollbars. Dragging this control allows the user to change both the height and width of the rectangle. Windows 3.x eschewed this idiom in favor of the thickframe surrounding each window. The thickframe is an excellent solution. It offers both generous visual hinting and cursor hinting, so it is easily discovered. Its shortcoming is the amount of real estate it consumes. It may only be four or five pixels wide (you can adjust it down to two pixels), but multiply that by the sum of the lengths of the four sides of the window, and you'll see that thickframes are expensive.

Windows 95 institutes a new reshaping-resizing gizmo that is remarkably like the Macintosh's lower-right-corner reshaper/resizer. The gizmo is a little triangle with 45°, 3D ribbing, which you can see in Figure 17-3. I've christened this new gizmo with a contraction of the words shaper and triangle: Shangle. The shangle still occupies a square of space on the window, but most Windows 95 programs have a status bar of some sort across their bottoms, and the reshaper-resizer borrows space from it rather than from the client area of the window.

Windows 95 still retains the thickframe and its cursor hinting, but it has dramatically changed so that virtually no visual hinting of the frame remains, although the cursor hinting remains. The user interface gurus in Redmond are clearly Mac-influenced, and the new shangle gizmo and the visual attenuation of the thickframe are prime evidence of this swing. I suspect that the thickframe will now begin to lose currency in favor of the shangle.

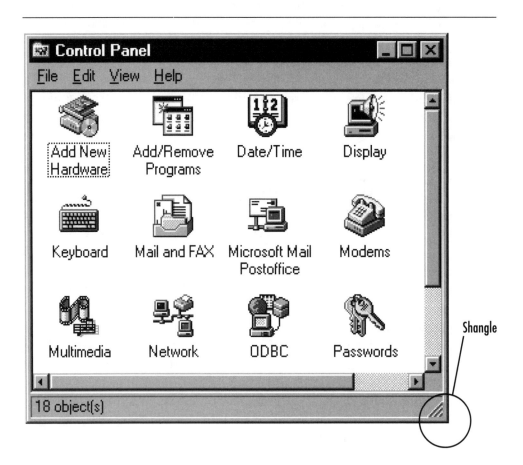

Shangle

Figure 17-3

I call the new-for-Windows-95 reshaper/resizer gizmo a shangle (a contraction of shaper and triangle). You can see an example of it in the lower right corner of the window. Notice that the shangle resides on the bottom status bar and not in the wasted square between the two scrollbars, as is normal on the Macintosh. The pliant area is actually a square, because rectangles are much more programmer-friendly in Windows than triangles are, but the effect is negligible. Actually, in this program, the thickframe is still active but has become invisible.

Thickframes and shangles are fine for resizing windows, but when the object to be resized is a graphical element in a painting or drawing program, it is not acceptable to permanently superimpose controls onto it. A resizing idiom for graphical objects must be visually bold to differentiate itself from parts of the drawing, especially the object it controls, and it must be respectful of the user's view of the object and the space it swims in. The resizer must not obscure the resizing action. There is a popular idiom that accomplishes these goals. It consists of eight little black squares positioned one at each corner of a rectangular object and one centered on each side. These little black squares, shown in Figure 17-4, are often called "handles," but that word is so overbooked in the programming world that I prefer to call them grapples to avoid confusion.

Grapples are a boon to designers because they can also indicate selection. This is a naturally symbiotic relationship, as an object must usually be selected to be resizable.

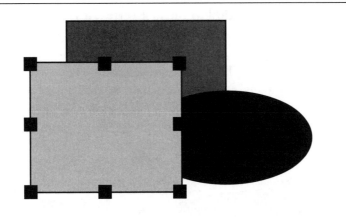

Figure 17-4

The selected object has eight grapples, one at each corner and one centered on each side. The grapples indicate selection, and are a convenient idiom for resizing and reshaping the object. Grapples are sometimes implemented with pixel inversion, but in a multi-color universe they can get lost in the clutter.

The grapple centered on each side moves only that side, while the other sides remain motionless. The grapples on the corners simultaneously move both of the sides they touch. Wow, is that logical!

Grapples tend to obscure the object they represent, so they don't make very good permanent controls. This is why we don't see them on top-level resizable windows. For that situation, the thickframe or shangle is a better idiom. If the selected object is larger than the screen, the grapples may not be visible. If they are hidden off screen, not only are they unavailable for direct manipulation, but they are useless as indicators of selection.

Notice that the assumption in this entire discussion of grapples is that the object under scrutiny is rectangular or can be easily bounded by a rectangle. Certainly in the Windows world, things that are rectangular are easy for programs to handle and non-rectangular things are best handled by enclosing them in a bounding rectangle. If the user is creating an organization chart, this may be fine, but what about reshaping more complex objects? There is a very powerful and useful variant of the grapple, which I call a **vertex grapple**.

Many programs draw objects on the screen with polylines. A **polyline** is a graphic programmer's term for a multi-segment line defined by an array of vertices. If the last vertex is identical to the first vertex, it is a closed form and the polyline is a polygon. When the object is selected, the program, rather than placing eight grapples as it does on a rectangle, places one grapple on top of every vertex of the polyline. The user can then drag any vertex of the polyline independently and actually change one small aspect of the object's internal shape rather than affecting it as a whole. This is shown in Figure 17-5.

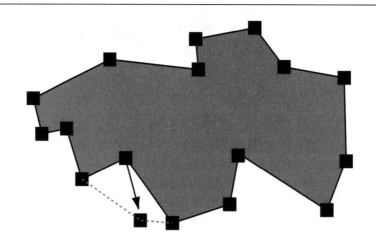

Figure 17-5

These are vertex grapples, so named because there is one grapple for each vertex of the polygon. The user can click and drag any grapple to reshape the polygon one segment at a time. This idiom is useful for drawing programs, but it may have application in desktop productivity programs, too.

Many objects in PowerPoint, including polygons, are rendered with polylines. If you click on a polygon, it is given a bounding rectangle with the standard eight grapples. If you double-click on the polygon, the bounding rectangle disappears and vertex grapples appear instead. It is important that both of these idioms are available, as the former is necessary to scale the image in proportion, while the latter is necessary to fine-tune the shape.

Resizing and reshaping meta-key variants

In the context of dragging, a meta-key is often used to constrain the drag to an orthogonal direction. This type of drag is called a **constrained drag**, and is shown in Figure 17-6.

A constrained drag is one that stays on a 90° or 45° axis regardless of how the user might veer off a straight line with the mouse. Usually, the SHIFT meta-key is used, but this convention varies from program to program. Constrained drags are extremely helpful in drawing programs, particularly when drawing business graphics, which are generally neat diagrams. The angle of the drag is determined by the predominant motion of the first few millimeters of the drag. If the user begins dragging on a predominantly horizontal axis, for example, the drag will henceforth be constrained to the horizontal axis. Some programs interpret constraints differently, letting the user shift axes in mid-drag by dragging the mouse across a threshold. Either way is fine.

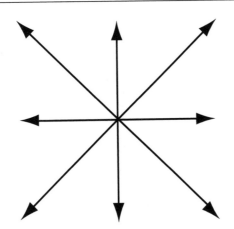

Figure 17-6

When a drag is constrained, usually by holding down the SHIFT key, the object is only dragged along one of the four axes shown here. The program selects which one by the direction of the initial movement of the mouse, an implementation of the drag threshold discussed later in the chapter.

The Paint program that comes with Windows 95 doesn't constrain drags when moving an object around, but it does constrain the drawing of a few shapes, like lines and circles. Most drawing programs (like PowerPoint) that treat their graphics as objects instead of as bits (like Paint) allow constrained drags.

The use of meta-keys gives rise to a curious question: where in the drag does the meta-key become meaningful? In other words, must the meta-key be held down when the drag begins—when the mouse button descends—or is it merely necessary for the meta-key to be pressed at some point during the drag? Or should the meta-key be pressed at the time the user releases the mouse button? In general, the answer is the latter case: If the computer detects that the meta-key is held down at the instant when the mouse button is released, the effect is considered valid. This is true in PowerPoint and Paint, for example.

Arrowing

A direct-manipulation idiom that can be very powerful in some applications is what I call arrowing, in which the user clicks-and-drags from one object to another, but instead of dragging the first object onto the second, an arrow is drawn from the first object to the second one.

If you use project management or organization chart programs, you are undoubtedly familiar with this idiom. For example, to connect one task box in a project manager's network diagram (often called a PERT chart) with another, you click-and-drag an arrow between them. The direction of the arrowing is significant: the task where the mouse button went down is the "from" task, and where the mouse button is released is the "to" task.

The visual arrows generally behave in a manner best described as rubber-banding.

Rubber-banding is where the arrow forms a line that extends from the exact mouse-down point to the current cursor position. The line is animated, so as the user moves the cursor, the position of the cursor-end of the line is constantly pivoting on the anchored end of the line (from the mouse-down point). Once the user releases the mouse button, the mouse-up point is known, and the program can decide whether it was within a valid target location. If so, the program draws a more permanent visual arrow between the two objects. Generally, it also links them logically.

As the user drags the end of the arrow around the screen, input is captured, and the rules of dragging in discrete data apply.

The arrowing function can't normally be triggered by the left button because it would collide with selection and repositioning. In some programs, it is triggered by the right button, but Windows 95 makes that problematic with its usurpation of the right click for the context menu. Hey! Is that ALT meta-key still unused?

Arrowing doesn't require cursor hinting as much as other idioms because the rubber-banding effect is so clearly visible. However, it would be a big help, in programs where objects are connected logically, to show which objects currently pointed-to are valid targets for the arrow. In other words, if the user drags an arrow until it points to some icon or widget on the screen, how can he tell if that icon or widget can legally be arrowed to? The answer, of course, is to have the potential target object engage in some active visual hinting.

What is indisputably vital, however, is a convenient means of canceling the action. Chord-clicking still works for this one.

Direct-manipulation visual feedback

As I said at the beginning of this chapter, the key to successful direct manipulation is rich visual feedback. Let's take a more detailed look at some visual feedback methods.

First off, we can divide the direct-manipulation process into three distinct phases:

1. *Free Phase*: Before the user takes any action

2. *Captive Phase*: Once the user has begun the drag

3. *Termination Phase*: After the user releases the mouse button

In the free phase, our job is to indicate direct-manipulation pliancy.

In the captive phase, we have two tasks. We must positively indicate that the direct-manipulation process has begun, and we must visually identify the potential participants in the action.

In the termination phase, we must plainly indicate to the user that the action has terminated and show exactly what the result is. We'll talk more about the captive and termination phases in the next chapter, "Drag-and-Drop."

Depending on which direct manipulation phase we are in, there are two variants of cursor hinting. During the free phase, I call any visual change the cursor makes as it merely passes over something on the screen free cursor hinting. Once the captive phase has begun, I call changes to the cursor captive cursor hinting.

Microsoft Word uses the clever free cursor hint of reversing the angle of the arrow when the cursor is to the left of text to indicate that selection will be line-by-line or paragraph-by-paragraph instead of character-by-character as it normally is within the text itself. Many other programs use a hand-shaped cursor to indicate that the document itself, rather than the information in it, is draggable.

Microsoft is using captive cursor hinting more and more as they discover its usefulness. Dragging-and-dropping text in Word or cells in Excel are accompanied by cursor changes indicating precisely what the action is and whether the objects are being moved or copied. In Windows 95, when you drag a file in the Explorer, you actually drag the text of the name of the file from one place to another.

When something is dragged, the cursor must drag either the thing or some simulacrum of that thing. In a drawing program, for example, when you drag a complex visual element from one position to another, it may be too difficult for the program to actually drag the image (due to the computer's performance limitations), so it often just drags an outline of the object. If you are holding down the CTRL key during the drag to drag away a copy of the object instead of the object itself, the cursor may change from an arrow to an arrow with a little plus sign over it to indicate that the operation is a copy rather than a move. This is a clear example of captive cursor hinting.

Drag-and-Drop

Of all the direct-manipulation idioms characteristic of the GUI, nothing defines it more than the drag-and-drop operation, clicking and holding the button while moving some object across the screen. Surprisingly, drag-and-drop isn't used as widely as we imagine, and it certainly hasn't lived up to its full potential.

Whither drag-and-drop?

Any mouse action is very efficient because it combines two command components in a single user action: a geographical location and a specific function. Drag-and-drop is doubly efficient because, in a single, smooth action, it adds a second geographical location. Although drag-and-drop was accepted immediately as a cornerstone of the modern GUI, it is remarkable that drag-and-drop is found so rarely outside of programs that specialize in drawing and painting. Thankfully, this seems to be changing, as more programs add this idiom.

There are several variations of drag-and-drop, and they are only a subset of the many forms of direct manipulation. The characteristics of drag-and-drop are fuzzy and difficult to define exactly. We might define it as "clicking on some object and moving it elsewhere," although that is a pretty good description of repositioning, too. A more accurate description of drag-and-drop is "clicking on some object and moving it to imply a transformation."

The Macintosh was the first successful system to offer drag-and-drop. A lot of expectations were raised with the Mac's drag-and-drop that were never truly realized for two simple reasons:

1. Drag-and-drop wasn't a system-wide facility, but rather an artifact of the Finder, a single program.

2. As a single-tasking computer, the concept of drag-and-drop between applications didn't surface as an issue for many years.

To Apple's credit, they described drag-and-drop in their first user interface standards guide. On the other side of the fence, Microsoft not only didn't put drag-and-drop aids in their system, but it wasn't described in their programmer documentation. Nor was it implemented in their Finder equivalent, the notoriously brain-dead MSDOS.EXE, the first Windows shell. The only drag-and-drop anywhere in Windows was in the simple paint utility distributed with the system. Yet again, Microsoft shipped an operating system—a standard-defining tool—but abdicated their responsibility for adequately defining collateral standards. I'm not ungrateful, as Windows was still by far the best thing around on the PC platform. Still, had Microsoft defined even some rudimentary standards, the drag-and-drop world would have evolved stronger and more rapidly.

It wasn't until Windows 3.0 that any drag-and-drop outside of MSPAINT.EXE appeared. The new File Manager and Program Manager programs supported a rudimentary form of drag-and-drop. You could drag icons around in the Program Manager and files and directories around in the File Manager. Wonder of wonders, you could also drag an EXE file* from the File Manager into the Program Manager and create an icon, although few users knew this. This disappointing lack of design leadership has resulted in an industry-wide sluggishness to embrace drag-and-drop, much to our software's detriment.

After ten years, though, Windows is finally getting a drag-and-drop standard. It is not strictly a part of Windows, but rather a part of the OLE 2.0

---

*Or any other file, for that matter.

specification. To get a community of third-party developers to adopt a technology, there is something even better than having a defined standard: having a solid set of library routines that enable them to implement features in their applications without having to invent the technology themselves. No such libraries have ever been made available in the Windows environment. OLE 2.0 is so large and frustratingly complex that there is some peril that the drag-and-drop standard will become either lost or bastardized in various proprietary implementations. This unfortunate bind will only be resolved when some clever vendor encapsulates the functionality of drag-and-drop in a powerful, flexible and easy-to-program package, then makes it widely available to applications developers.

I find it amusing that the Microsoft style guide treats drag-and-drop so lightly. It makes it sound like a simple and commonly known process, as though it was describing how to put on your shoes in the morning. Sorry, it's just not that easy.

Dragging where?

Fundamentally, you can drag-and-drop something from one place to another inside your program, or you can drag-and-drop something from inside your program into some other program. I call these variants **interior drag-and-drop** and **exterior drag-and-drop**, respectively.

Interior drag-and-drop can be made pretty simple, both from a conceptual and from a coding point of view. Exterior drag-and-drop demands significantly more sophisticated support because both programs must subscribe to the same concepts, and they must be implemented in compatible ways. We'll talk more about the exterior variant after we get a look at the basics of drag-and-drop.

I classified repositioning as a direct-manipulation idiom and discussed it in the last chapter. Now we will discuss the remaining drag-and-drop variants. Primarily, there are two: master-and-target and tool manipulation.

Master-and-target

When the user clicks on a discrete object and drags it to another discrete object in order to perform a function, I call it **master-and-target**.

The object within which the dragging originates controls the entire process, so it is the master object, which will be a window. If you are dragging an icon, that icon is a window. If you are dragging a paragraph of text, the enclosing editor is the window. When the user ultimately releases the mouse button, whatever was dragged is dropped on some target object.

The main purpose of the term "master-and-target" is to differentiate this operation from the kind of drag-and-drop operations we find in drawing and painting programs, where tools and graphical objects are dragged around on an open canvas. Master-and-target is a more function-oriented idiom, where manipulating logical objects represents some behind-the-scenes processes. The most familiar form of master-and-target drag-and-drop is rearranging icons in the Program Manager or in the Macintosh Finder.

Dragging data to functions

Instead of dragging a file or folder to another folder, you can drag it to a gizmo that represents a function. This idiom is arguably the most famous expression of direct manipulation because of the Macintosh's familiar trashcan. Windows 95 copies this familiar idiom with its "recycle bin." Someday, as we build software with better object-orientation, we'll be able to drag-and-drop objects onto gizmos representing functions other than just delete. Imagine targets representing a cloner, an archiver, a file compressor, a faxer or a contents-indexer.

Notice that all of the idioms in the above paragraph involve exterior drag-and-drop, because the target objects are separate programs. Within a single program, the code knows what objects are draggable—usually one type—and any function gizmo that it gets dropped on will easily handle it. In an exterior drop, the master object can come from any program, and the target gizmo may well not have any direct knowledge of the originating program or the dropped object. The target must be able to handle the unknown object in some reasonable way without necessarily understanding what it is or what is in it. The Program Manager, for example, can do this because it knows that it will only be handed files. What would it do if it were handed a paragraph of dragged text from a word processor, for example? If it can't handle the text, it isn't truly exterior capable. To Microsoft's credit, the Recycle Bin in Windows 95 can actually accept paragraphs of text dragged from Word or cells dragged from Excel. I have not yet been able to determine whether these are generic operations or just code specific to Microsoft applications.

To be truly exterior capable, an object must be able to accept a drop of anything from any other object, regardless of the originating program. At first, this sounds like a dauntingly complex implementation problem, but it doesn't have to be. Mostly, it's a matter of defining interface standards. When data is dragged to an object, all the target object has to say is "yes, I can accept the drop" to the master object. The two objects then must negotiate over formats, because it is unreasonable to expect every object to accept data in every other program's proprietary formats. If the master object is Excel, say, it may initially offer the data in its internal format. Another Microsoft program may know how to decipher this format, but a Brand X product might not. So the Brand X target object politely demurs—not to the drop, but to the *format* of the drop's contents. Excel, the master, must then re-offer the data in successively more generic formats: SYLK, CSV, ASCII. The target object can turn up its nose at SYLK or CSV, but by convention, it must accept ASCII; it is the lowest common denominator format on all platforms. Every exterior capable object must minimally accept ASCII, simple bitmaps, pointers to files and, as we'll see, functions. Objects that hope to become successful in the open market will accept many more formats than that, but these four guarantee compatibility with everything. Even an audio file, for example, can ultimately be passed as a simple pointer to a disk file. I call exterior drag-and-drop protocols that support this type of haggling over formats **negotiated drag-and-drop**.

I call protocols like those in the Windows 3.x File Manager and Program Manager, which don't negotiate formats, **known-format drag-and-drop**.

Dragging functions to data

Proper, negotiated, exterior drag-and-drop capability includes dragging-and-dropping functions onto data as well as dragging-and-dropping data onto functions. Defining the scope of such actions can be problematic when working in concrete data, but it can still be generally quite useful. For example, a user could click on the italic buttton on the toolbar and drag it down onto a cell in a spreadsheet. Clearly, the user's intent in this action is to turn the content in that cell to italic. Part of the format negotiation includes being able to recognize a function as a valid drop value. Conceptually, there is little difference between the function "delete" and the function "italic." In one, the target program deletes its internal copy of the data and hands it to the master. In the other, the target program hands a copy of the data to the italic function, which converts the text to italic and hands it back. This way the italic buttton in Excel's window can be dragged onto text in Word's window, and Word will know what to do with it. Or, more meaningfully, the Brand X buttton can be dragged onto the text in Microsoft Word. Once this interface is in place, little companies can begin to chip away at the big, monopolistic, mega-applications.

For now, there is no standard exterior drag-and-drop protocol, although OLE purports to offer one. Certainly, there is no negotiated drag-and-drop protocol.* A given protocol may allow format negotiation or function dragging. Your mileage may vary.

How master-and-target works

A well-designed master object will visually hint at its pliancy, either statically in the way it is drawn, or actively, by animating as the cursor passes over it.

The idea that an object is dragable is easily learned idiomatically. It is difficult to forget that an icon, selected text or other distinct object is directly manipulable, once the user has been shown this. He may forget the details of the action, so other feedback forms are very important *after* the user clicks on the object, but the fact of direct-manipulation pliancy itself is easy to remember. The first-timer or very infrequent user will probably require some additional help. This help will come either through additional training programs or by advice built right into the interface. In general, a program with a forgiving interaction encourages users to try direct manipulation on various objects in the program.

As soon as the user presses the mouse button over an object, that object becomes the master object for the duration of the drag-and-drop. On the other hand, there is no corresponding target object because the mouse-up point hasn't yet been determined: it could be on another object or in the open space between objects. However, as the user moves the mouse around with the button held down—remember, this is called the captive phase—the cursor may pass over a variety of objects inside or outside the master object's program. If these objects are drag-and-drop compliant, they are possible targets, and I call them **drop candidates**.

There can only be one master and one target in a drag, but there may be many drop candidates. Depending on the drag-and-drop protocol, the drop candidate may not know how to accept the particular dropped value, it just has to know how to accept the offered drop protocol. Other protocols may require that the drop candidate recognize immediately whether it can do anything useful with the offered master object. The latter method is slower but offers much better feedback to the user. Remember, this operation is under direct human control, and the master object may pass quickly over dozens of drop candidates before the user positions it over the desired one. If the protocol requires

---

*I offered the first (and possibly only) one several years ago called SPIDR (Standard PIck up and DRop). It was adopted by only a few major companies.

extensive conversing between the master object and each drop candidate, the interaction can be sluggish, at which point it isn't worth the game.

Visual indications

The only task of each drop candidate is to visually indicate that the hotspot of the captive cursor is over it, meaning that it will accept the drop—or at least comprehend it—if the user releases the mouse button. Such an indication is, by its nature, active visual hinting.

> *Design tip:* The drop candidate must visually indicate its dropability.

The weakest way to offer the visual indication of dropability is by changing the cursor. It is the job of the cursor to represent what is being dragged and leave all indications of drop candidacy to the drop candidate itself.

> *Design tip:* The drag cursor must visually indicate the master object.

It is important that these two visual functions not be confused. Unfortunately, Microsoft seems to have done so in both Windows 3.x and Windows 95. I suspect this decision was made more for the ease of coding than for any design considerations. It is much easier to change the cursor than it is to have drop candidates highlight to show their dropability. The role of the cursor is to represent the master, the dragged object. It should not be used to represent the drop candidate.

As if that weren't bad enough, Microsoft performs cursor hinting with the detestable circle with bend sinister, which I call a **sinister-circle**.

The sinister-circle is not a pleasant idiom because it tells users what they can't do. It is negative feedback. The sinister-circle is an idiom for "don't do it," and a user can easily construe its meaning to be "don't let go of the mouse now or you'll do some irreversible damage" instead of "go ahead and let go now and nothing will happen." Adding the sinister-circle to cursor hinting is a sad combination of two weak idioms and should be avoided, regardless of what the Microsoft style guide says.

Once the user finally releases the mouse button, the current drop candidate becomes the *target*. If the user releases the mouse button in the interstice between valid drop candidates, or over an invalid drop candidate, there is no target and the drag-and-drop operation ends with no action. Silence, or visual inactivity, is a good way to indicate this termination. It isn't a cancellation, exactly, so there is no need to show a cancel stamp.

Indicating drag pliancy

Active cursor hinting to indicate drag pliancy is a problematic solution. In an increasingly object-oriented world, more things can be dragged than not. A cursor flicking and changing rapidly can be more of a visual distraction than a help. One solution is to just assume that things can be dragged and let the user experiment. This method is reasonably successful in the Program Manager, the File Manager and the Explorer. Without cursor hinting, drag pliancy can be a hard-to-discover idiom, so you might consider building some other indication into the interface, maybe a textual hint or a ToolTip-style popup.

Once the master object is picked up and the drag operation begins, there must be some visual indication of this. The most visually rich method is to fully animate the drag operation, showing the entire master object moving in real-time. This method is hard to implement, can be annoyingly slow and very probably isn't the proper solution. The problem is that a master-and-target operation requires a pretty precise pointer. For example, the master object may be 6 centimeters square, but it must be dropped on a target that is 1 centimeter square. The master object must not obscure the target, and, because the master object is big enough to span multiple drop candidates, we need to use a cursor hotspot to precisely indicate which candidate it will be dropped on. What this means is that, in master-and-target, dragging a transparent outline of the object may be much better than actually dragging a fully animated, exact image of the master object. It also means that the dragged object can't obscure the normal arrow cursor either. The tip of the arrow is needed to indicate the exact hotspot.

Dragging an outline also is appropriate for most repositioning, as the outline can be moved relative to the master object, which is still visible in its original position.

Indicating drop candidacy

As the cursor traverses the screen, carrying with it an outline of the master object, it passes over one drop candidate after another. These drop candidates must visually indicate that they are aware of being considered as potential drop targets. By visually changing, the drop candidate alerts the user that it can do something constructive with the dropped object.

A point so obvious as to be difficult to see is that the only objects that can be drop candidates are those that are currently visible. A running application doesn't have to worry about visually indicating its readiness to be a target if it isn't visible. Usually, the number of objects occupying screen real estate is very small— a couple of dozen at most. This means that the implementation burden should not be overwhelming.

Internally, the master object should be communicating with each drop candidate as it passes over it. A brief conversation should occur, where the master asks the target whether it can accept a drop. If it can, the target indicates it with visual hinting.

Microsoft not only doesn't insist on drop candidate visual hinting, it suggests that changing the cursor is sufficient. I believe that they do the industry a major disservice by taking this route. Certainly, it is easier to program this way, but in every user-centered way it is worse. It is difficult to understand what is being dragged, what the target is and whether the target can make sense of the drop. In Windows 95, at least on the desktop, icons now correctly indicate their drop candidacy by visually inverting. But I worry that this is just a shallow imitation of the Macintosh Finder specific only to the Window's desktop and not a new, system-wide standard for how master-and-target drag-and-drop should work.

Completing the drag-and-drop operation

When the master object is finally dropped on a drop candidate, the candidate becomes a bona fide target. At this point, the master and target must engage in a more detailed conversation than the brief one that occurred between the master and all of the other drop candidates. After all, the user has committed, and we now know the target. The target may know how to accept the drop, but that does not necessarily mean that it can swallow the particular master object dropped in this specific operation. This distinction is generally not important in interior drag-and-drop, but in exterior drag-and-drop, it is doubtful that there is enough time to resolve this issue during the captive phase. Of course, this is still a performance hack, and faster computers will someday allow sufficient communications detail during real-time drags.

The implication of this more-detailed conversation is that the transfer may fail. That is okay. It is better to show dropability and choke on the actual drop than it is to not indicate dropability. (If minimum common format standards are adhered to, after all, there should never be a physical failure.) If the drag-and-drop is negotiated, the format of the transfer remains to be resolved. If information is transferred, the master-and-target may wish to negotiate whether the transfer will be in some proprietary format known to both, or whether the data will have to be reduced in resolution to some weaker but more common format, like ASCII text.

Visual indication of completion

If the target and the master can agree, the appropriate operation then takes place. A vital step at this point is the visual indication that the operation has occurred. If the operation is a transfer, the master object must disappear from its source and reappear in the target. If the target represents a function rather than a container (such as a print icon), the icon must visually hint that it received the drop and is now printing. It can do this with an animation, or by changing its visual state.

A richly visual master-and-target drag-and-drop operation is one of the most powerful operations in the GUI designer's bag of tricks. I know that if this idiom is better supported by tool vendors, it will grow in popularity with application developers. Users will be the beneficiaries.

Tool-manipulation drag-and-drop

In drawing and painting programs, the user manipulates tools with drag-and-drop, where a tool or shape is dragged onto a canvas and used as a drawing tool. There are two basic variants of this that I call modal tool and charged cursor.

Modal tool

In **modal tool**, the user selects a tool from a list, usually called a toolbox or palette. The program is now completely in the mode of that tool: it will only do that one tool's job. The cursor usually changes to indicate the active tool.

When the user clicks-and-drags with the tool on the drawing area, the tool does its thing. If the active tool is a spray can, for example, the program enters "spray can mode" and it can only spray. The tool can be used over and over, spraying as much ink as desired until the user clicks on a different tool. If the user wants to use some other tool on the graphic, like an eraser, he must return to the tool-box and select the eraser tool. The program then enters "eraser mode" and can only erase things until another tool is chosen. There is usually a just-plain-cursor tool on the palette to let the user return the cursor to a general-purpose pointer.

Modal tool works for both tools that perform actions on drawings—like an eraser—or for shapes that can be drawn—like ellipses. The cursor can become an eraser tool and erase anything previously entered, or it can become an ellipse tool and draw any number of new ellipses.

Modal tool is not bothersome in a program like Paint, where the number of drawing tools is very small. In a more advanced drawing program such as Adobe Illustrator, however, the modality is very disruptive because, as the user gets more facile with the cursor and the tools, the percentage of time and motion devoted to selecting and deselecting tools—the excise—increases dramatically. Modal tools are excellent idioms for introducing users to the range of features of such a program, but they don't usually scale well for experienced users of more sophisticated programs.

The difficulty of managing a modal tool application isn't caused by the modality as much as it is by the sheer quantity of tools. Or, more precisely, the efficiencies break down when the quantity of tools in the user's working set gets too large. A working set of more than about five modal tools tends to get hard to manage. If the number of necessary tools in Adobe Illustrator could be reduced from 24 to 8, for example, its user interface problems might diminish below the threshold of user pain.

To compensate for the profusion of modal tools, products like Adobe Illustrator use meta-keys to modify the various modes. The SHIFT key is commonly used for constrained drags, but Illustrator adds many non-standard meta-keys and uses them in non-standard ways. For example, holding down the ALT key while dragging an object drags away a *copy* of that object, but the ALT key is also used to promote the selector tool from single vertex selection to object selection. The distinction between these uses is subtle: If you click on something, then press the ALT key, you drag away a copy of it. Alternately, if you press the ALT key and *then* click on something, you select all of it, rather than a single vertex of it. But then, to further confuse matters, you must *release* the ALT key, or you will drag away a copy of the entire object. To do something as simple as selecting an entire object and dragging it to a new position, you must press the ALT key, point to the object, press and hold the mouse button without moving the mouse, release the ALT key, then drag the object to the desired position! What were these people thinking?

Admittedly, the possible combinations are powerful, but they are very hard to learn, hard to remember and hard to use. If you are a graphic arts professional working with Illustrator for eight hours a day, you can turn these shortcomings into benefits in the same way that a race car driver can turn the cantankerous behavior of a car into an asset on the track. The casual user of Illustrator, however, is like the average driver behind the wheel of an Indy car: way out of his depth with a temperamental and unsuitable tool.

Adobe Illustrator is firmly rooted in the Macintosh world. One of the major errors that Adobe made in their Windows interface design was a refusal to take advantage of the benefits of the two-button mouse, something that comes cheap or free with Windows. Illustrator doesn't use the right mouse button at all. I suspect that someone in the company felt that interoperability with the Mac was more important—a bad notion, as I've discussed before. Adobe could have put all selection tools on the left button and all drawing tools on the right button, just for an example. Users could then go back and forth between drawing things and manipulating them just by deciding which mouse button to use, and, even better, each button would then have available to it three meta-keys: ALT, CTRL and SHIFT. Not taking advantage of the right mouse button was an error on their part.

Charged cursor

The second tool-manipulation drag-and-drop technique is what I call **charged cursor**.

With charged cursor, the user again selects a tool or shape from a palette, but this time the cursor, rather than becoming an object of the selected type, becomes loaded—or charged—with a single instance of the selected object. When the user clicks once on the drawing surface, an instance of the object is created—dropped, if you will—on the surface at the mouse-up point. Charged cursor doesn't work too well for tools, but it is nicely suited for graphic objects. PowerPoint, for example, uses it extensively. The user selects a rectangle from the graphics palette and the cursor then becomes a modal rectangle tool charged with exactly one rectangle.

Many common drawing programs work this way, but it is also very popular for graphic direct-manipulation idioms in programs that aren't normally thought of as drawing programs. A good example is Visual Basic. When the user clicks on one of the gizmos on the tool palette, the cursor becomes charged with that gizmo. The user then clicks again to create a single instance of it on a form. Borland's Delphi uses charged cursor too, but if you SHIFT-click on a gizmo in the palette, you get a modal tool instead for creating multiple instances of a gizmo. Nice touch.

In many charged cursor programs like PowerPoint, the user cannot always deposit the object with a simple click but must drag a bounding rectangle to determine the size of the deposited object. Some programs, like Visual Basic, allow either method. A single click of a charged cursor creates a single instance of the object in a standard size. The new object is created in a state of selection, so it is surrounded by grapples and ready for immediate precision reshaping and resizing. This dual-mode, allowing either a single click for a default-sized object or dragging a rectangle for a custom-sized object is certainly the most flexible and discoverable, and will satisfy most users.

I have seen charged cursor programs that forget to change the appearance of the cursor. For example, although Visual Basic changes the cursor to crosshairs when it's charged, Delphi doesn't change it at all. This is really silly: if the cursor has assumed a modal behavior—if clicking it somewhere will create something—it is imperative that it visually indicate this state. Charged cursor also absolutely demands good cancel idioms; otherwise, how do you harmlessly discharge the cursor?

Bomb sighting

As the user drags a master object around the screen, each drop candidate visually changes as it is pointed to, which indicates its ability to accept the drop. In some programs, the master object can instead be dropped in the spaces between other objects. I call this variant of drag-and-drop **bombardier**. Dragging text in Word, for example, is a bombardier operation, as are most rearranging operations.

The vital visual feedback of bombardier drag-and-drop is showing where the master object will fall if the user releases the mouse button. In master-and-target, the drop candidate becomes visually highlighted to indicate the potential drop, but in bombardier, the potential drop will be in some space where there is no object at all. The visual hinting is something drawn on the background of the program or in its concrete data. I call this visual hint the **bombsight**.

Rearranging slides in PowerPoint's slide-sorter view is a good example of this type of drag-and-drop. The user can pick up a slide and drag it into a different presentation order. As you drag, the bombsight, a vertical black bar that looks like a big text edit caret, appears between slides. Word, too, shows a bombsight when you drag text. Not only is the loaded cursor moving, but you see a vertical gray bar showing the precise location, in between characters, where the dropped text will land.

One of my clients has a report generation program. You can rearrange the left-to-right order of the columns by clicking-and-dragging one of them. As you drag the outline of the column, a thick vertical-line bombsight shows up between the other columns, indicating where the column will be dropped.

Whenever something can be dragged-and-dropped on the space between other objects, the program must show a bombsight. Just like a drop candidate in master-and-target, it must visually indicate its candidacy.

Drag-and-drop problems and solutions

When we are first exposed to the drag-and-drop idiom, it seems pretty simple, but for frequent users and in some special conditions, it can exhibit problems and difficulties that are not so simple. As usual, the iterative refinement process of software design has exposed these shortcomings, and in the spirit of invention, clever designers have devised equally clever solutions.

Autoscroll

What interpretation should the program make when the selected object is dragged beyond the border of the enclosing application rectangle? The correct interpretation is, of course, that the object is being dragged to a new position, but is that new position inside or outside of the enclosing rectangle?

Let's take Microsoft Word for example. When a piece of selected text is dragged outside the visible text window, is the user saying, "I want to put this piece of text into another program" or is he saying, "I want to put this piece of text somewhere else in this same document, but that place is currently scrolled off the screen"? If the former, things are easy. If the latter, the application must scroll in the direction of the drag to reposition the selection at a distant, not-currently-visible location in the same document. I call such scrolling **autoscroll**.

Autoscroll is a very important adjunct to drag-and-drop. Where you implement one, you will likely have to implement the other. Wherever the drop target can possibly be scrolled off screen, the program requires autoscroll.

> ***Design tip:*** Any scrollable drag-and-drop target must auto-scroll.

In early implementations, autoscrolling worked if you dragged outside the application's window. This had two fatal flaws, though. First, if the application was maximized, how could you get the cursor outside the app? And second, if you want to drag the object to another program, how can the app tell the difference between that and the desire to autoscroll?

Microsoft developed a very intelligent solution to this problem. Basically, they begin autoscrolling just *inside* the application's border instead of just *outside* the border. As the drag cursor approaches the borders of the scrollable window—but is still inside it—a scroll in the direction of the drag is initiated. If the drag cursor comes within three or four millimeters of the bottom of the text window, Word begins to scroll the window's contents upward. If the drag cursor comes equally close to the top edge of the text window, Word scrolls down. Unfortunately, Word's implementation doesn't take into account the power of the microprocessor, and the action occurs too fast to be useful on my (relatively slow) 486/66. Besides compensating for processor speed, a better way to implement this same idiom would be to use a variable autoscroll rate as shown in Figure 18-1, where the automatic scrolling increases in speed as the cursor gets closer to the window edge. For example, when the cursor is five millimeters from the upper edge, the text would scroll down at one line per second. At four millimeters, the text would scroll at two lines per second, and so on. This gives the user sufficient control over the autoscroll to make it useful. The autoscroll should never be unconstrained; computers are only getting faster.

Another important detail required by autoscrolling is a time delay. If autoscrolling begins as soon as the cursor enters the sensitive zone around the edges, it is too easy for a slow-moving user to inadvertently autoscroll. To cure this, autoscrolling should only begin after the drag cursor has been in the auto-scroll zone for some reasonable time cushion—about a half-second.

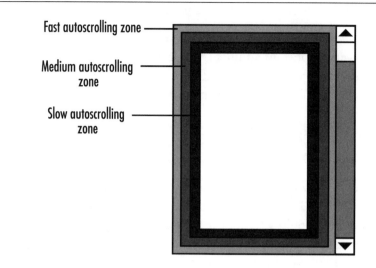

Fast autoscrolling zone

Medium autoscrolling zone

Slow autoscrolling zone

Figure 18-1

Microsoft unfortunately lets the scrolling go forth at whatever speed the computer is capable of, which is too fast to be useful, even on my 486/66. Not only should they put a maximum scroll limit on autoscroll, they should also make it graduated and user-controllable. It should autoscroll faster the closer the user gets to the edge of the window. To their credit, Microsoft's idea of autoscrolling as the cursor approaches the inside edges of the enclosing scrollbox, rather than the outside, is very clever indeed.

If the user drags the cursor completely outside the application's scrollable text window, no autoscrolling occurs. Instead, the repositioning operation will terminate in a program other than Word. For example, if the drag cursor goes outside Word and is positioned over PowerPoint when the user releases the mouse button, the selection will be pasted into the PowerPoint slide at the position indicated by the mouse. Furthermore, if the drag cursor moves within three or four millimeters of any of the borders of the PowerPoint edit window, PowerPoint begins autoscrolling in the appropriate direction. This is a very convenient feature, as the tight confines of contemporary video screens mean that we often find ourselves with a loaded drag cursor and no place to drop its contents—a very frustrating state and one that makes drag-and-drop less appealing in general.

Avoiding drag-and-drop twitchiness

When an object can be either selected or dragged, it is vital that the mouse be biased towards the selection operation. Because it is so difficult to click on something without inadvertently moving the cursor a pixel or two, the frequent act of selecting something must not accidentally cause the program to misinterpret the action as the beginning of a drag-and-drop operation. The user rarely wants to drag an object one or two pixels across the screen. The time it takes to perform a drag is usually much greater than the time it takes to perform a selection, and the drag is often accompanied by a repaint, so objects on the screen will flash and flicker. This unexpected visual paroxysm can be very disturbing to users expecting a simple selection. Additionally, the object is now displaced by a couple of pixels. The user probably had the object just where he wanted it, so having it displaced by even one pixel will not please him. And to fix it, he'll have to drag the object back one pixel, a very demanding operation.

In the hardware world, controls like push-buttons that have mechanical contacts can exhibit what engineers call "bounce," in which the tiny metal contacts of the switch literally bounce when someone presses them. For electrical circuits like doorbells, the milliseconds the bounce takes aren't meaningful, but in modern electronics, those extra clicks can be significant. The circuitry backing up such switches has special logic to ignore extra transitions if they occur within a few milliseconds of the first one. This keeps your stereo from turning back off a thousandth of a second after you've turned it on. This situation is analogous to the oversensitive mouse problem, and the solution is to copy switch makers and **debounce** the mouse.

To avoid this situation, programs should establish what I call a **drag threshold**.

Essentially, all mouse-movement messages that arrive after the mouse button goes down and capture begins are ignored unless the movement exceeds some small threshold amount, say three pixels. This provides some protection against initiating an inadvertent drag operation. If the user can keep the mouse button within three pixels of the mouse-down point, the entire click action is interpreted as a selection command, and all tiny, spurious moves are ignored. The object has been debounced. As soon as the mouse moves beyond the three-pixel threshold, the program can confidently change the operation to a drag. This is shown in Figure 18-2. Anytime you have a situation where an object can be selected and dragged, the drag operation should be debounced.

Design tip: Debounce all drags.

The Program Manager in Windows 3.x has a one-pixel drag threshold, which is too small. It is far too easy to accidentally move an icon out of position when all you want to do is select it. Icons on the Windows 95 desktop appear to have a four-pixel debounce threshold.

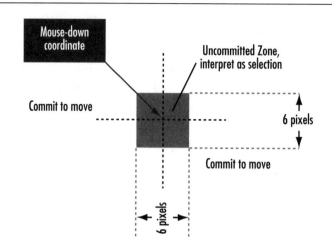

Figure 18-2

Any object that can be both selected and dragged must be "debounced." When the user clicks on the object, the action must be interpreted as a selection rather than a drag, even if the user accidentally moves the mouse a pixel or two between the click and the release. The program must ignore any mouse movement as long as it stays within the uncommitted zone, which extends three pixels in each direction. Once the cursor moves more than three pixels away from the mouse-down coordinate, the action changes to a drag, and the object is considered "in play." This is called a drag threshold, and it is used to debounce the mouse.

My report-generator client (for whom we developed the column-reposition bombsight) required more-complex drag threshold handling. The user could reposition columns on the report by dragging them horizontally. The user could put the FIRSTNAME column to the left of the LASTNAME column just by dragging it into position. This was, by far, the most frequently used drag-and-drop idiom. There was, however, another seldom-used technique. This one allowed the values in one column to be interspersed *vertically* with the values of another column, as shown in Figure 18-3. We wanted to follow the user's mental model and enable him to drag the values of one column on top of the values of another to perform this stacking operation, but this conflicted with the simple horizontal reordering of columns. We solved the problem by differentiating between horizontal drags and vertical drags. If the user dragged the column left or right, it meant that he was repositioning the column as a unit. If the user dragged the column up or down, it meant that he was interspersing the values of one column with the values of another.

Because the horizontal drag was the predominant user action and vertical drags were rare, we biased the drag threshold towards the horizontal axis. Instead of

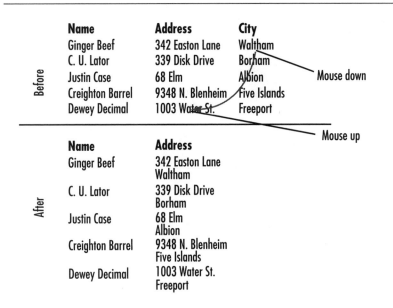

Figure 18-3

This report-generator program offered an interesting feature that enabled the contents of one column to be interspersed with the contents of another by merely dragging-and-dropping it. This direct-manipulation action conflicted with the more-frequent drag-and-drop action of reordering the columns (like moving City to the left of Address). We used a special, two-axis drag threshold to accomplish this.

a square uncommitted zone, we created the spool-shaped zone shown in Figure 18-4. By setting the horizontal-motion threshold at four pixels, it didn't take a big movement to commit the user to the normal horizontal move, while still insulating the user from an inadvertent vertical move. To commit to the far-less-frequent vertical move, the user had to move the cursor eight pixels on the vertical axis without deviating more than four pixels left or right. The motion is quite natural and easily learned.

This two-dimensional thresholding can be used in other ways, too. Visio implements something similar to differentiate between drawing a straight and a curved line.

Mouse vernier

The weakness of the mouse as a precision pointing tool is readily apparent, particularly when dragging objects around in drawing programs. It is darned hard to drag something to the exact desired spot, especially when the screen resolution is 100 or more pixels-per-inch and the mouse is running at a six-to-one

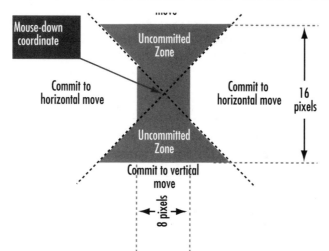

Figure 18-4

This spool-shaped drag threshold allowed me to create a bias toward horizontal dragging in a client's program. Horizontal dragging was, by far, the most frequently used type of drag in this application. This drag threshold made it difficult for the user to inadvertently begin a vertical drag. However, if the user really wanted to drag vertically, a bold move either up or down would cause the program to commit to the vertical mode with a minimum of excise. Before this method was instituted, a vertical move involved a nasty semi-permanent mode change by using a buttcon.

ratio to the screen. To move the cursor one pixel, you must move the mouse precisely one six-hundredth of an inch. Not easy to do.

This is solved by adding what I call a **mouse vernier** function, where the user can quickly shift into a mode that allows much finer-resolution for mouse-based manipulation of objects.

During a drag, if the user decides that he needs more precise maneuvering, he can change the ratio of the mouse's movement relative to the object's movement on the screen. Any program that might demand precise alignment must offer a vernier facility. This includes at a minimum all drawing and painting programs, presentation programs and image-manipulation programs.

> *Design tip:* Any program that demands precise alignment must offer a vernier.

There are several acceptable variants of this idiom. A button can be pressed during the drag operation, like the ENTER key, and the mouse would shift into vernier mode. In vernier mode, each ten pixels of mouse movement would be interpreted as a single pixel of object movement.

One method that seems popular is to make the arrow keys active during a drag operation. While holding down the mouse button, the user can manipulate the arrow keys to move the selection up, down, left or right one pixel at a time. The drag operation is still terminated by releasing the mouse button.

The problem with such a vernier is that the simple act of releasing the mouse button can often cause the user's hand shift a pixel or two, making the perfectly placed object slip out of alignment just at the moment of acceptance. The solution to this is, upon receipt of the first vernier keystroke, to "desensitize" the mouse. This is accomplished by making the mouse ignore all subsequent movements under some reasonable threshold, say five pixels. This means that the user can make the initial gross movements with the mouse, then make a final, precise placement with the arrow keys, and release the mouse button without disturbing the placement. If the user wanted to make additional gross movements after beginning the vernier, he would simply move the mouse beyond the threshold, and the system would shift back out of vernier mode.

If the arrow keys are not otherwise spoken for in the interface, as in a drawing program, they can be used to control vernier movement of the selected object without having to hold the mouse button down. This is nicely done in PowerPoint: the arrow keys move the selected object one step on the grid—about two millimeters using the default grid settings. If you hold the ALT key down while arrowing, the movement is one pixel per arrow click.

Part V: The Cast
The Actors in the Drama

Windows, menus, dialogs and push-buttons are the most visible trappings of the modern graphical user interface, but they are effects, rather than causes, of good design. They serve a purpose, and we have to understand how they fit into the designer's toolbox. More importantly, though, we must understand why each component exists and what purpose and effect they each have before we can profitably fit them into our creations.

The Meaning of Menus

19

The modern GUI with its pulldown menus and dialog boxes hasn't been around all that long—only since 1984—as a mainstream design idiom. Still, it is so ubiquitous that it is easy to take for granted. It is worthwhile for us to peer backwards and see the path we've taken in the development of the modern dialog and menu interface, not just to see how far we've come, but also to see how far we have yet to go.

The command-line interface

If you wanted to talk to an IBM mainframe computer in the 1970s, you had to manually keypunch a deck of computer cards, use an obscure language called JCL (job control language) to tell the computer how to read your program, and submit this deck of cards to the system through a noisy, mechanical card reader. Each line of JCL or program had to be punched onto a separate card. Even the first microcomputers, small, slow and stupid, running a primitive operating system called CP/M, had a much better conversational style than those hulking dinosaurs in their refrigerated glass houses. You could communicate directly with microcomputers running CP/M merely by typing commands into a standard keyboard. What a miracle! The program issued a prompt on the computer screen that looked like this:

```
A>
```

You could then type in the names of programs, which were stored as files, as commands, and CP/M would run them. We called it the command-line interface, and it was widely considered a great leap forward in man-machine communications.

The only catch is that you had to know what to type. For frequent users, who at that time were mostly programmers, the command-line prompt was very powerful and effective because it offered the quickest and most efficient route to getting the desired task done. With his hands on the keyboard in the best tradition of touch-typists, the knowledgeable user could rip out "`copy a:*.* b:`" and the disk was copied. And today, if you possess the knowledge, the command line is still faster than using a mouse for many operations.

The command-line interface really separated the men from the nerds. The programmers of early desktop computers mostly just shrugged their shoulders and thought "if you wanna make an omelet, ya gotta break some eggs." As software got more powerful and complex, however, the memorization demands that the command-line interface made on users were just too great, and it had to give way to something better.

The hierarchical menu interface

Finally, sometime in the late '70s, some very clever programmer came up with the idea of offering the user a list of choices. He could read the list and select an item from it the way that you choose a dish at a restaurant by reading the menu. The appellation stuck, and the age of the hierarchical menu began.

The hierarchical menu enabled the user to forget many of the commands and option details required by the command-line interface. Instead of keeping the details in his head, he could read them off the screen. Another miracle! Circa 1979, your program was judged heavily on whether or not it was "menu-based." Those vendors stuck in the command-line world fell by the wayside in favor of the modern paradigm.

Although the paradigm was called "menu-based" at the time, I call it *hierarchical* menu-based to differentiate it from the menus in widespread use today. The old pre-GUI menus were deeply hierarchical: after making a selection from one menu, you would be presented with another, then another and so on, drilling down into a tall tree of commands. Such menu-based interfaces would be judged terrible by today's standards. Their chief failing was the necessary depth of the hierarchy. This was coupled with a striking lack of flexibility and clarity in dealing with their users.

A typical menu would offer a half-dozen choices, each indicated by an ordinal from 1 to 6; the user would enter the number to select the corresponding option. Once the user made his selection, it was set in concrete—there was no going back. People, of course, made mistakes all of the time, so the more progressive developers of the day added confirmation menus. The program would accept the user's choice as before, then issue another menu to enquire: "Press the ESCAPE key to change your selection, otherwise press ENTER to proceed." This was an incredible pain in the butt, regardless of your choice. If you made a mistake and wanted to change your selection, you had to navigate through this clumsy meta-question, asking permission to ask a question. On the other hand, if you entered your response correctly, you still had to navigate through this clumsy meta-question.

Because only one menu at a time could be placed on the screen, and also because software at that time was still very heavily influenced by the batch-and-JCL style of mainframe computing, the hierarchical menu paradigm was very sequential in behavior. The user was presented with a high-level menu for choosing between major functions, for example:

1. Enter transactions

2. Close books for month

3. Print Income Statement

4. Print Balance Sheet

5. Exit

Once the user chose "1. Enter Transactions," he would then be prompted with another menu, subordinate to his choice from the first one, such as

1. Enter invoices

2. Enter payments

3. Enter invoice corrections

4. Enter payment corrections

5. Exit

The user would choose from this list and, most likely, be confronted with a couple more such menus before the actual work would begin. Then the "Exit" option would take him up only one level in the hierarchy. This meant that navigating through the menu tree was a real chore.

Still better than command lines, where you had to remember each operand, this technique lightened the user's memorization burden but forced him to laboriously navigate an archipelago of confusing choices and options, and it, too, had to give way to something better.

The Lotus 1-2-3 interface

The next great advance in user-interface technology came in 1979 from Lotus Corporation, with the original 1-2-3 spreadsheet program. 1-2-3 was still controlled by a deeply hierarchical menuing interface, but they added their own twist to it that helped make it the most successful piece of software ever sold up to that point. I call it a **visible hierarchical menu**.

Remember that computer screens in those days weren't capable of displaying high-resolution graphics the way they are today. In 1979, a computer screen offered exactly 2000 characters per screen, arranged in 25 horizontal rows of 80 characters each. 1-2-3 presented its menu horizontally along the top of the screen, where it consumed only two rows out of the 25 available. Take a look at Figure 19-1. This meant that the menu could coexist on the screen with the actual spreadsheet program. Unlike the hierarchical menu programs that came before it, the user didn't have to leave a productive screen to see a menu. He could enter a menu command right there.

Lotus used their new menu idiom with great abandon, creating a hierarchical menu structure of remarkable proportions, both in width and depth. There were dozens of nodes in the menu tree, and several hundred individual choices available. Each one could be found by looking at the top line of the screen and tabbing over and down to the desired selection. The program differentiated between data for the spreadsheet and a command for the menu by detecting the presence of a "/." If the user entered a slash, the keystrokes that

```
B38: (,3) [W11] +B26-B35
Line █████ XY  Stacked-Bar  Pie                                    █████
Bar graph
          A             B            C            D            E            F
   Profit and Loss Statement

   (in millions)     --------Actual----------      -- Projected --
                      1983         1984         1985         1986         1987
                     -----------------------------------------------------------
   Revenues          3.551        5.300        6.170        6.787        7.465

   Expenses
      Labor          0.300        0.370        0.550        0.616        0.727
      Energy         0.165        0.284        0.350        0.392        0.462
      Materials      1.108        1.626        2.513        2.814        3.321
      Administration 0.317        0.365        0.388        0.435        0.513
      Other          0.447        0.491        0.523        0.586        0.691

      Total Expenses 2.337        3.136        4.323        4.842        5.714
                     -----------------------------------------------------------
   Profit (Loss)    █1.215█       2.163        1.846        1.944        1.751
                     -----------------------------------------------------------
   Inflation                                   10.0%        12.0%        10.0%
28-Apr-86  09:48 AM
```

Figure 19-1

The original Lotus 1-2-3, which first shipped in 1979, exhibited a remarkable new menu structure that actually coexisted with the working screen of the program. You can see the menu at the second line down from the top of the screen. The highlighted word "Bar" is the currently selected menu item. All other menu-based programs at that time forced you to leave the working screen to make menu selections. Like all great ideas, this one was invisible in foresight and obvious in hindsight.

followed were interpreted as menu commands rather than data. To select an item on the menu, all you had to do was read it and type in its first letter. Sub-menus then replaced the main menu on the top line.

Frequent users quickly realized that the patterns were memorable, and they didn't necessarily have to read the menu. They could just type "SLASH-S" to save their work to disk. They could just type "SLASH-C-G-X" to add up a column of numbers. They could, in essence, bypass the use of the menu entirely. They became power-users, memorizing the letter commands and gloating over their knowledge of obscure functions.

It seems silly now, but it illustrates a very powerful point: that a good user interface enables its users to move in an ad hoc, piecemeal fashion from beginner to expert. A given power-user of 1-2-3 might be on intimate terms with a couple of dozen functions, while simultaneously being completely ignorant of several dozen others. If he has memorized a particular slash-key sequence, he can go ahead and access it immediately. Otherwise, he can read the menu to find those less frequently used ones that he hasn't committed to memory.

But 1-2-3's hierarchical menu was hideously complex. There were simply too many commands, and every one of them had to fit into the single hierarchical menu idiom. The program's designers bent over backwards to make logical connections between functions in an attempt to justify the way they had apportioned the commands in the hierarchy. In the delirium of revolutionary success and market dominance, such details were easily ignored.

As you might imagine, 1-2-3's success in the mid '80s led to a time of widespread 1-2-3 cloning. The always-visible, hierarchical menu found its way into numerous programs, but the idiom was really the last gasp of the character-based user interface in the same way that the great, articulated steam locomotives of the late 1940s were the final and finest expression of a doomed technology. As surely as diesel locomotives completely eliminated all steam power within the span of a decade, the GUI eliminated the 1-2-3-style hierarchical menu within a few short years.

Monocline grouping

Hierarchies are one of the programmer's most durable tools. Much of the data inside programs, along with much of the code that manipulates it, is in hierarchical form, and many programmers offer hierarchies to the user in the interface. The early menus of personal software were hierarchical. But hierarchies are generally very difficult for users to understand and use. This basic fact is often difficult for programmers to grasp, as comfortable as they are with hierarchies.

Humans are familiar with hierarchies in their relationships, but they are not natural concepts for them when it comes to storing and retrieving information. Most storage systems outside of computers are very simple, composed either of a single sequence of stored objects, like a bookshelf, or a series of sequences, each one level deep, like a file cabinet. This method of organizing things into a single layer of groups is extremely common and can be found everywhere in your home and office. Because it never exceeds a single level of nesting, I call this storage technique **monocline grouping**.

Programmers are very comfortable with nested systems where an instance of an object is stored in another instance of the same object. Humans, on the other hand, generally have a very difficult time with the idea. Personally, I *love* hierarchies, but most users don't like them or work comfortably with them. Really complex manual storage systems get around this by comprising each level from a very different technology. In a file cabinet, you never see folders inside folders, Pendaflexes inside Pendaflexes or file drawers inside file drawers. Even the dissimilar nesting of folder-inside-Pendaflex-inside-cabinet rarely exceeds two levels of nesting.

Many people store their papers in a series of stacks based on some common characteristic: The Acme papers go here; the Project M papers go there; personal stuff goes in the drawer. Donald Norman, in *Things That Make Us Smart*, calls this a "pile cabinet." Normally, only inside computers would we put the Project M papers inside the Active Clients box, which, in turn, is stored inside the Clients box, stored inside the Business cabinet.

Computer science gives us the hierarchy as a tool to solve the very real problems of managing massive quantities of data. But when programmers render this implementation model as the manifest model, users get confused because it conflicts with their mental model of storage systems. Monocline grouping is the mental model the user typically brings to the software. Monocline grouping is so dominant outside the computer that the software designer violates it at his peril.

Admittedly, monocline grouping is an inadequate system for managing the large quantities of data we commonly find on computers, but that doesn't mean it is a bad *model*. The solution to this conundrum is to render the model as the user imagines it—as monocline grouping—but to provide the search and access tools that only a hierarchical organization can offer.

The Popup Menu

Many concepts and technologies had to come together to make the GUI possible: notably the mouse, memory-mapped video, powerful processors and popup windows. A popup window is a rectangle on the screen that appears, overlapping and obscuring the main part of the screen, until it has completed its work, whereupon it disappears, leaving the original screen behind, untouched. The popup window is the mechanism used to implement both pull-down menus and dialog boxes.

In a GUI, the menus are visible across the top row of the screen just like Lotus 1-2-3's visible hierarchical menu, but the resemblance ends there. The user points and clicks on a menu, and its directly subordinate list of options immediately appears in a small window just below it. This is called a popup menu.

The user makes a single choice from the popup menu by clicking once or by dragging and releasing. There's nothing remarkable about that, except that the menus generally go no deeper than this. The selection the user makes at the popup menu level either takes immediate effect or calls up a dialog box. The hierarchy of menus has been flattened down until it is only one level deep. In other words, it has finally become monocline grouping.

Arguably the most significant advance of the GUI menu was this retreat from the hierarchical form into monocline grouping. The dialog box, another use of the popup window, was the tool that simplified the menu. The dialog box enabled the software designer to encapsulate all of the sub-choices of any one menu option in a single, interactive container. With dialogs, the menu could flatten out tremendously, gathering all of the niggling details from further down the menu tree into a single dialog. The deeply hierarchical menu was a thing of the past.

Enough choices could be displayed on the main menu bar to organize all of the program's functions into about a half-dozen meaningful groups, each group represented by a one-word menu title. The menu for each group could be roomy enough to include all of the related functions. The need to go to additional levels of menus was made superfluous.

Of course, philistines and reprobates are always with us, and they have created methods for turning pulldown menus back into hierarchical menus. They are called pull-rights or cascading menus and, although they are occasionally useful, more often they merely tempt the weaker souls in the development community to gum up their menus for little gain. I'll discuss these in more detail in the next chapter.

The pedagogic vector

As the modern GUI evolved, two idioms developed that fundamentally changed the role of the menu in the user interface. These two idioms are direct manipulation and toolbars. The development of direct-manipulation idioms has been a slow and steady progression from the first days of graphical user interfaces. Conversely, the toolbar was an innovation that swept the industry around 1989. Within a couple of years, virtually every Windows program sold had a toolbar covered with buttons. Only a few years before, nobody had seen a toolbar.

I call each distinct technique for issuing instructions to the program a **command vector**. Menus are a command vector, as are direct manipulation and toolbar buttons. Good user interfaces will conscientiously provide what I call **multiple command vectors**, where each function in the program has menu commands, toolbar commands, keyboard commands and direct-manipulation commands, each with the parallel ability to invoke a given command. This enables users of different skill sets and preferences to command the program according to their desires and abilities.

Both direct-manipulation and toolbar-buttcon command vectors have the property of being **immediate vectors**. There is no delay between pressing a buttcon and seeing the results of the function. Direct manipulation also has an immediate effect on the information without any intermediary. Neither menus nor dialog boxes have this immediate property. Each one requires an intermediate step, sometimes more than one.

In the same way that a stranger to town may take a roundabout route to her destination while a native will always proceed on the most economical path, experienced users of a program will commonly invoke a function with the most immediate command rather than one that requires intermediate steps. Naturally, the most frequently used commands in a program are those that migrate onto buttons on the toolbar. These functions are still supported by items on the menu—the menu command vector—where their use becomes increasingly the purview of beginners. Experienced users, however, gravitate toward the immediate vectors of buttons and direct manipulation.

This bifurcation of usage along lines of experience is an important characteristic of software usage, and it affects how menus and dialog boxes are used. They are needed less and less for daily use, and have instead become a teaching tool for first-time and infrequent users.

The buttons and other gizmos on the toolbar are usually redundant with respect to commands on the menu. Buttons are immediate, while menu commands remain relatively slow and clunky. Menu commands have a great advantage, however, in their English descriptions of the functions, and the detailed controls and data that appear on corresponding dialog boxes. This detailed data makes the menu/dialog command vector the most useful one for teaching purposes, which is why I call it the **pedagogic vector**.

One required element of effective pedagogy is the ability to examine and experiment without fear of commitment. The CANCEL button on each dialog box supports this well. Contrary to the user interface paradigms of just a few years ago, menus and dialog boxes have ceased to be the main method by which normal users perform everyday functions. Many programmers and designers haven't realized this fact yet, and they continue to confuse the purpose of the menu command vector. Its role is simply to teach new users and to remind those who have forgotten.

Design tip: Menus and dialogs are the pedagogic vector.

When a user looks at a program for the first time, it is often difficult for him to size up what that program can do. An excellent way to get an impression of the power and purpose of an application is to glance at the set of available functions by way of its menus and dialogs. We do this in the same way we look at a restaurant's menu posted at its entrance to get an idea of the type of food, the presentation, the setting and the price.

Understanding the scope of what a program can and can't do is one of the fundamental aspects of creating an atmosphere conducive to learning. Many otherwise easy-to-use programs put the user off because there is no simple, unthreatening way for him to find out just what the program is capable of doing.

The toolbar and other direct-manipulation idioms can be too inscrutable for the first-time user to understand or to even fit into a framework of possibilities, but the textual nature of the menus serves to explain the functions. Reading "Borders and Shading" is a heck of a lot more enlightening to the new user than trying to interpret a buttcon that looks like this:

For infrequent users who are somewhat familiar with the program, the menu/dialog vector's main task is as an index to tools: a place to look when he knows there is a function but can't remember where it is or what it is called. This works the same way as its namesake brother, the restaurant menu, permits him to rediscover that delightful fish curry thing he ordered a year ago, without having to remember its precise name; the pulldown menu lets him rediscover functions whose name he's forgotten. He doesn't have to keep such trivia in his head but can depend on the menu to keep it for him, available when he needs it.

If the main purpose of menus were to execute commands, terseness would be a virtue. But because the main justification of their existence is to teach us about what is available, how to get it and what shortcuts are available, terseness is really the exact opposite of what we need. Our menus have to explain what a given function does, not just where to invoke it. Because of this, it behooves us to be more verbose in our menu item text. We shouldn't say "Open..." but rather "Open the Report...." We shouldn't say "Auto-arrange" but rather "Auto-arrange the icons." We should stay far away from jargon, as our menu's users won't yet be acquainted with it.

Many programs also use the status bar that goes across the bottom of their main window to display an even-longer line of explanatory text associated with the currently selected menu item. This idiom certainly enhances the teaching value of the command vector.

The pedagogic vector also means that menus must be complete, offering a full selection of the actions and facilities available in the program. Every dialog box in the program should be accessible from some menu option. A scan of the menus should make clear the scope of the program and the depth and breadth of its various facilities.

Another teaching purpose is served by providing hints pointing to other command vectors in the menu itself. Putting hints in that describe keyboard equivalents teaches users, as they work with the program more frequently, about quicker command methods that are available. By putting this information right in the menu, the user sees it subconsciously. It won't intrude upon his conscious thoughts until he is ready to learn it, and then he will find it readily available and already familiar.

Menus

20

In the last chapter, we discussed how menus fit into the grand scheme of user interface idioms. Now let's take a closer look at menus and talk about specifics.

Standard menus

Menus are just about the hoariest idiom in the GUI universe—revered and surrounded by superstition and lore. We accept without question that traditional menu design is correct, because so many existing programs attest to its excellence. But this belief is like snapping your fingers to keep the tigers away. There aren't any tigers here, you say? See, it works!

Most every GUI these days has at least a "File" and an "Edit" menu in its two leftmost positions and a "Help" menu all the way over to the right. The Windows style guide states that these File, Edit and Help menus are standard. You might also think that this de facto cross-platform standard is a strong indication of the proven correctness of the idiom. Wrong! It is a strong indication of the development community's willingness to blithely accept bad design, changing it only when the competition forces us to do better. My *least* favorite menus are the File, Edit and Help menus. The File menu is named after an accident of the way our operating systems work. The Edit menu is based on the very weak clipboard. And the Help menu is frequently the least helpful source of insight and information for the befuddled user.

The conventions of these three menus trap us into weak user interfaces for some pretty vital parts of our programs. Now, I'm not saying that we should discard conventions and scramble our menus on a whim. Rather, I think of changing these menus as life-saving surgery. I don't think that the fear of surgery should keep us away from the doctor too long.

I can hear the screaming already, programmers saying "How can you change something that has become a standard? People *expect* the File menu!" My answer is a simple one: People may get used to pain and suffering, but that is no reason to perpetuate it. Sure, prisoners of war often have a hard time adjusting to freedom after their release, but ask any former POW if he'd like to return to the camp and he'll laugh in your face. Users will adapt without significant problems if we change the File menu so that it delivers a better, more meaningful model. Changing only the menu items without accompanying this with significant changes to the model would indeed be the big mistake these programmers worry about.

Pathological manifest models aside, it is a Good Thing to group your program's functions into one of these more-or-less standard menus. As in all interface things, however, blindly following hard-and-fast rules will only make things worse. Microsoft did this in their latest release of their Office suite, falling victim to the Style Nazis. Every program has nearly identical menus. Their intent was good, but they went a little too far. In particular, PowerPoint suffered. It just doesn't gain much from having a menu structure similar to Excel and Word, and it loses quite a bit of its native ease-of-use by conforming to an alien structure. Face it, a presentation program just isn't the same as a word processor—forcing its menu to look like one can't be much help.

After the Windows style guide declares the File, Edit and Help menus as "standard," it then proceeds to mostly ignore several other de facto menu standards, like "Window," "View," "Insert," "Format," "Tools" and "Options." Just because they aren't common to all programs doesn't mean that they aren't standard. The simple fact that the user has seen one of these menus before tells him something about the meaning of this instance's contents. This contributes to the trustworthiness of the application, which in turn encourages the user to explore and learn; and learning is the main purpose of the menu system.

The menus on most of our programs may be familiar, but are they good ways to organize functions? Words like "View," "Insert," "Format," "Tools" and "Options" sound like tools and functions, not goals. Why not organize the facilities in a more goal-directed way?

The correct menus

So what is the correct set of menus to have? What is the right way to classify the functions on them? I certainly wish I could answer these questions definitively, but I don't think anyone can. First, I don't believe that a definite answer exists. Second, you must consider the individual needs of the program under consideration. Third, we are fighting against the massive weight of established convention. Fourth, it would take years of development and iterative refinement to arrive at perfection. I do know, though, that our current standards are not even close yet.

But since I asked the question, it's only fair that I go out on a limb and present a framework for rethinking menus. It may not be right, but it should get your creative juices flowing, and who knows? Maybe we'll see some movement in menu design. We are close, but we are not yet where we should be.

Using every spatial and visual hint at our disposal, we should arrange the menus from left to right in some meaningful order. We could put Help in the far left position because it may well be used first. I don't think that is good, however, because we will generally not use it much after we get acquainted with the program. So putting Help in the far right position is better. We can depend on its location from program to program, where the menus to its left will certainly be different.

A reasonable sequence for the other menus would be to order them according to their scope: The most global items on the left, getting more and more specific as we move to the right. If we assume a document-centric program, we will find, in descending order of their scope, these topics: The *program*, the *document* and *pieces* of the document. For each of these components, we might have *properties*, *views*, *functions* and *access* to the outside world. Using this structure as a framework, we would have a menu system that looks like the schematic in Figure 20-1.

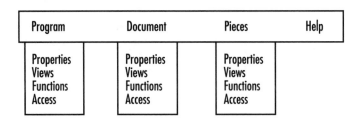

Figure 20-1

This is a highly stylized schematic of a suggested menu structure. On the far left is the topic of broadest scope: the program. Moving to the right, with diminishing scope as we go, is first the document, then the pieces that comprise the document. In descending order of importance are the four aspects of each component: Their properties, views of them, functions that operate on them and their access to the "outside world." In the Program menu, we can probably dispense with Views and Access. There is no reason that these schematic menus can't be productively broken into two or more menus. The Document menu, for example, could have Properties and Views on one and Functions and Access on another.

The program menus

The properties of a program include its default settings, what templates are available, and what modes it is in. It would include the configuration of standard interface idioms like toolbars. It would also include personalization items like colors and graphics.

Most likely, the menus for Views and Access could be omitted for the program, although if your program needed them, this would be the place to have them. Access might include items to save and restore program-wide settings.

The document menus

The next menu would cover the document under construction: what we are working on. The prime menu items would deal with the properties of the currently active document. This would include things like its size and type, its margin setup and page orientation.

Documents can certainly have different views, and this would be the place to set them. Things like draft versus presentation views; whether to show temporary guidelines, and what resolution to render images. This is also the place where we would select which of the multiple open documents we wish to look at.

Next come functions that operate on an entire document at once. This would include operations like calculating spreadsheets and formatting text.

Access to the outside world at the document level is currently served by the top five items on most File menus. In our new framework, the bottom of the Document menu is the place where the user would go to open and close documents. The "outside world" includes the printer, fax and email, so access to those functions should reside here, as well.

This would also be the logical place to maintain the **most recently used** list of documents that we frequently see on the bottom of the File menu.

As you can see, the document menu is a big one, so most likely it would be broken into two or more popups. We could put properties and views on the first menu and functions and access on the second document menu.

Pieces of the document

The next menu to the right would cover the objects embedded in the document. If there are tables or images in the document, here is where the menu items that control them would reside. These menu items would only be active when the particular object they relate to is selected. And these objects don't necessarily have to be embedded by another program. In a drawing program, for example, they would be things like rectangles, ellipses and polylines. In a word processor, they would be the paragraphs of text and the headings, and the controls on this menu would be the "style sheets," and formatting controls.

Again, the first items cover properties of the object, such as its size and orientation. Control of its different views would follow. Often, objects have many possible transformations like formatting and rotation, and items for these functions would be next.

Last on this menu would be the ability to load and save objects from other documents or to and from disk.

The last menu, of course, would be the one that summons help for all or any of the others. Some programs would require another menu in between the Program and Document menus. Called "Group," it would house functions that operated on groups of documents. Assembling, formatting and printing chapters in a book would be an example of its power.

Meanwhile, back on Planet Earth

I don't have any illusions about the likelihood of seeing my new menu model getting implemented soon, so I'll return to reality and give you some more practical advice.

The File menu

In Chapter 8, I described a better "File" menu that was shown in Figure 8-4. Although I removed the SAVE function from the menu, I wouldn't dispense with it entirely. I'd just put it in some inconspicuous place for more advanced users to find. The program should save automatically for everyone else. The save function doesn't necessarily have to overwrite the original copy on disk the way it does now. It just needs to save the data in an easily recoverable way that is independent and invisible from within the application.

If we change from a file-centric view to this document-centric view, we should also change the name of the menu from "File" to "Document."

The Most Recently Used (MRU) list on Microsoft applications is an excellent shortcut idea and I recommend it. You can see it in Figure 20-2.

The Edit menu

The Edit menu contains facilities for cutting and pasting and importing and exporting. Don't use it as a catchall for functions that don't seem to fit anywhere else. Instead, gather them up into an Options or Preferences dialog that is accessible from the Tools menu.

The Windows menu

The Windows menu is for MDI only, providing a means for switching between MDI documents. It also offers tools for arranging multiple documents on screen simultaneously. Nothing else should go on this menu.

The Help menu

Today's Help menus are poorly designed reflections of poor help systems. We'll talk about help in Part VIII, but I would mention here that the Help menu sorely needs an item labeled "Shortcuts..." that would explain how to go beyond relying on the menus. It could offer pointers on more immediate idioms such as accelerators, toolbar buttons and direct-manipulation idioms.

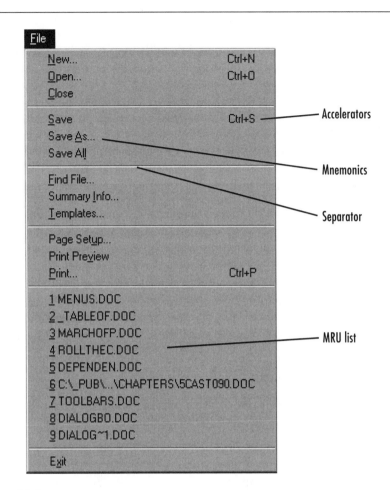

Figure 20-2

The File menu from Microsoft Word shows off the excellent Most Recently Used (MRU) list. In Chapter 8, I showed you how to reconstruct the first six items so that they better reflect the user's mental model, rather than following the technically faithful implementation model as shown here.

Optional menus

The View menu

The View menu should contain all options that influence the way the user looks at the program's data. Additionally, any optional visual items like rulers, templates or palettes should be controlled here.

The Insert menu

The Insert menu is really an extension of the Edit menu. If you only have one or two Insert items, consider putting them on the Edit menu instead and omitting the Insert menu entirely.

The Settings menu

If you have a Settings menu in your application, you are making a commitment to the user that anytime he wants to alter a setting in the program he will find the way to do it here. Don't offer up a Settings menu and then scatter other setting items or dialogs on other menus. This rule includes printer settings, which are often erroneously found on the File menu.

The Format menu

The Format menu is one of the weakest of the optional menus, as it deals almost exclusively with properties of visual objects and not functions. In a more object-oriented world, properties of visual objects are controlled by more-visual direct-manipulation idioms, and not by functions. The menu serves its pedagogic purpose, but you might consider omitting it entirely if you've implemented a more object-oriented format property scheme.

The page setup stuff that normally resides on the File menu should be placed here. Notice that page setup is very different from printer setup.

The Tools menu

The Tools menu, sometimes called options or functions, is where big, powerful transforms go. Functions like spell-checkers and goal-finders are considered tools. Also, the Tool menu is where what I call the hard-hat items go.

Hard-hat items are the functions that should only be used by real power users. These include various advanced settings. For example, a client/server database program has easy-to-use direct-manipulation idioms for building a query, while behind the scenes the program is composing the appropriate SQL statement to create the report. Giving power users a way to edit the SQL statement directly is most definitely a hard-hat function! Functions like these can be dangerous or dislocating, so they must be visually set off from the more benign tools available. In the past, I've segregated them from the other menu items and highlighted them with little hard-hat icons to indicate that they are for experts only.

Menu item variants

Disabling menu items

A defined Windows standard is to disable—or gray out—menu items when they are not relevant to the selected data item. Menus have robust facilities that make it easy to gray them out when their corresponding function is not valid, and you should take every advantage of this. The user will be well-served to know that the enabling and disabling of menu items reflects their appropriate use. This function helps the menu become an even more robust teaching tool.

Design tip: Disable menu items when they are moot.

It is important that each menu item clearly show when it is or isn't valid to fulfull its role as a teacher. Don't omit this detail.

Cascading menus

There is a variant of menus where a secondary menu can be made to pop up alongside a top-level popup menu. This technique, called **cascading menus**, was added to Windows in Version 3.1, so it has had only moderate penetration in interface design.

Where popup menus provide nice, monocline grouping, cascading menus move us into the nasty territory of nesting and hierarchies. Hierarchies are so natural to the mathematically inclined, but they are quite unnatural to the rest of us. The temptation to make menus hierarchical is nearly unavoidable for most programmers, who have a mathematical bent.

In the last chapter, we talked about how the modern GUI allowed us to leave hierarchical menus behind. It seems tragic to me that programmers would want to revive an idiom that lies happily in its grave. Cascading menus do serve a purpose: they allow lots of functions to be crammed onto a menu that would otherwise be way too long. There are occasionally enough items on a menu to justify putting some of the more obscure ones onto a second level, but I would consider it an idiom of last resort. I would make sure not to use cascading menus for anything that might be used frequently.

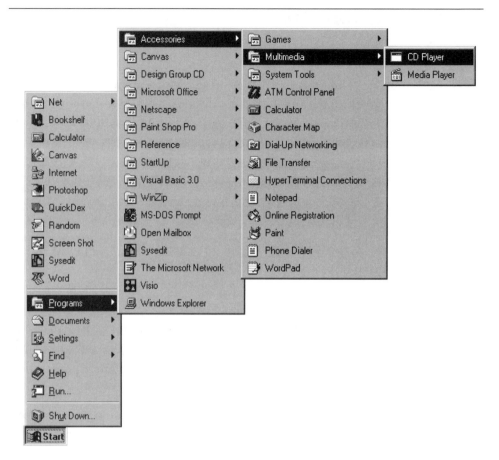

Figure 20-3

Here is a typical cascading menu on the Windows 95 Startbar. It's not very user friendly, but is quite software.dot.dweeb friendly. Hierarchies make logical sense to the programmers but rarely to users. Cascades also demand considerable skill with a mouse—putting them into real minnie territory—and this will frustrate infrequent users.

In Windows, it is difficult to say categorically that an idiom should not be used because the range of possible application software is so huge. Cascading menus, however, are a weak idiom, one that can be used as needed, but that should not be chosen before first considering other ways to solve the problem.

Windows 95 makes a tragically widespread use of cascading menus in the Startbar. The poor Start button is so overloaded with hierarchical menus that even I find it jerky and unresponsive, and I'm a pretty good mouser. It really seems that Microsoft went to an incredible extreme to make double-clicks unnecessary. Figure 20-3 shows just how silly the cascading menus on the Windows 95 Startbar can get.

Flip-flop menu items

If the menu choice being offered is a binary one, that is, one that will be in either of two states, you might take advantage of a trick for saving menu space. For example, if you have two items, one called "Display Tools," and the other called "Hide Tools," you can create a single menu item that alternates between the two values, always showing the one currently *not* chosen. I call this technique a **flip-flop**.

This method saves space because otherwise it would require two menu items with mutually exclusive checkmarks. The flip-flop is a sucker's bet. As instructional clarity is the goal for menus, anything that obscures understanding is bad, and flip-flops can be very confusing for one simple reason: you can't tell if it is offering a choice or describing a state. If it says "Display Tools," does that mean tools are now being displayed or does it mean that by selecting the option you can begin displaying them? By combining roles, we make the meaning ambiguous. Although a menu is a list of functions and not a status display, a neophyte user can still easily get confused. If you can't label the states more unambiguously—"Display Tools Now"—then solve your space problem another way.

Graphics on menus

Visual symbols next to text items help the user to differentiate between them without having to read, so the items are understood faster. Because of this, adding small graphics to menu items can really speed users up. They also provide a helpful visual connection to other gizmos that do the same task. In particular, a menu item should show the same image as its corresponding toolbar buttcon.

Design tip: Parallel visual symbols on parallel
command vectors

Microsoft Windows provides powerful tools for putting graphics in menus. Too few programs take advantage of this opportunity for providing an easy, visual learning trick. For example, the applications in Microsoft's Office suite all use a sheet of paper as an icon on a toolbar button to indicate the "New" function. Microsoft could put that same sheet of paper on the "File" menu next to the "New" menu item. The user would soon make the connection, probably without even thinking about it.

Microsoft PowerPoint has done an excellent job of incorporating teaching graphics into their menus in their latest release (4.0) as shown in Figure 20-4. Too bad Microsoft was only brave enough to use this excellent idiom on cascading menus and not on the normal popups, too.

Bang menu items

In the early days of Windows, a few smaller programs were shipped with a menu variant that has fallen out of favor, and for good reason. I'm referring to the top-level immediate menu item. Just as its name implies, it is a top-level menu item—on the horizontal menubar—that behaves like an immediate menu item on a popup; rather than displaying a popup menu for a subsequent selection, the immediate item causes the function to be executed right now! For example, an immediate menu item to compile some source code would be called "Compile!" In programmer's jargon, an exclamation mark is a "bang," and, by convention, top-level immediate menu items were always followed with a bang. Naturally, I call it a **bang menu item**, and bang it does!

Its behavior is so unexpected that it usually generates instant anger. The bang menu item has virtually no instructional value. It is dislocating and disconcerting. The same immediacy on a toolbar buttcon bothers nobody, though, and that is where immediate commands should stay. Surprisingly, this idiom resurfaces every once in a while.

> **Design tip:** Don't use bang menu items.

Buttcons on a toolbar behave just like bang menu items: they are immediate and top-level. The difference is that buttcons on a toolbar advertise their immediacy because they are *buttons*. Menu items are things we trust to help us learn.

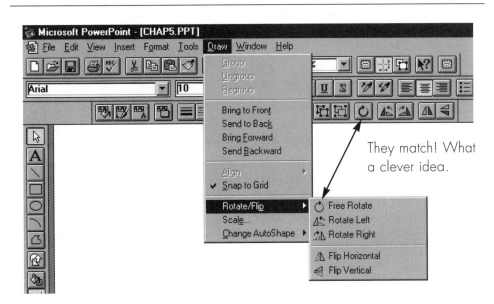

They match! What a clever idea.

Figure 20-4

Microsoft PowerPoint offers us a regular smorgasbord of menu idioms. Most are tooth-some, but some are a bit gamey. The Draw menu shows us disabled items, separators, cascades, menumonics, checks and vectors. The use of graphics on the little Rotate/Flip cascade menu is a nice implementation of visually linking menu items to other command vectors. The little graphic images are the same as those on the buttons that perform the identical tasks. What a wonderful way to build learning into the interface without it seem-ing pedantic or intruding on everyday usage. I'm sure Microsoft put those graphics in to better explain the functions and only inadvertently achieved the benefit of accelerating the user's growth to expertise by echoing the buttcon images. It's too bad they didn't put these cool little graphic dingbats on every menu item that has a corresponding buttcon.

So don't betray that trust by using bang menu items, please. Beware, however, because the capability to add them is still present in Windows.

Accelerators

Accelerators provide an additional, optional way to invoke a function from the keyboard. Accelerators are the keystrokes, which usually are a function key (like F9) or activated with a "CTRL," "ALT" or "SHIFT" prefix, that are shown on the right side of some popup menus. They are a defined Windows standard, but their implementation is up to the individual designer and they are often forgotten.

There are three tips for successfully creating good accelerators.

○ Follow standards

○ Provide for their daily use

○ Show how to access them

Where standard accelerators exist, use them. In particular this refers to the standard editing set as shown on the "Edit" menu. Users quickly learn how much easier it is to type CTRL+C and CTRL+V than it is to remove their mouse hand from the home row to pull down the Edit menu, select "Copy," then pull it down again and select "Paste." Don't disappoint them when they use your program. Don't forget standards like CTRL+P for print and CTRL+S for save.

Identifying the set of commands that will comprise those needed for daily use is the tricky part. You must select the functions likely to be used frequently and assure that those menu items are given accelerators. The good news is that this set won't be large. The bad news is that it can vary significantly from user to user.

The solution is to perform a triage operation on the available functions. Divide them into three groups: those that are definitely part of everyone's daily use; those that are definitely not part of anyone's daily use; and everything else. The first group must have accelerators, and the second group must not. The final group will be the toughest to configure, and it will inevitably be the largest. You can perform a subsequent triage on this group and assign the best accelerators, like F2, F3, F4 and so on to the winners of this group. More obscure accelerators, like ALT+7 should go to those least likely to be part of someone's everyday commands.

Don't forget to show the accelerator in the menu. An accelerator isn't going to do anyone any good if he has to go to the manual or online help to find it. Put it right there in the menu on the right side. Users won't notice it at first, but eventually they will and they will be happy to make the discovery. It will give them a sense of accomplishment and a feeling of being an insider. These are both good feelings well worth inducing in your customers.

Mnemonics

Mnemonics are another Windows standard for adding keystroke commands in parallel to the direct manipulation of menus and dialogs.

The Microsoft style guide covers both mnemonics and accelerators in detail, so I will just take this opportunity to stress that they should not be overlooked. Mnemonics are the underlined letter in a menu item. Entering this letter shifted with the ALT meta-key executes the menu item. The main purpose of mnemonics is to provide a keyboard equivalent of each menu command. For this reason, mnemonics should be complete, particularly for text-oriented programs. Don't think of them as a convenience so much as a pipeline to the keyboard. Keep in mind that your most experienced users will rely heavily on their keyboards, so to keep them loyal, assure that the mnemonics are consistent and thoroughly thought-out. Mnemonics are not optional.

For those designers among you who don't use mnemonics (I confess to be one, also), it is easy to put in bad mnemonics; to have non-unique characters within a menu, or to use really inappropriate and difficult-to-remember (thus becoming, by definition, non-mnemonic mnemonics) letters. Make sure that someone on the development or design team actually uses and refines the mnemonics.

The system menu

The **system menu** (inexplicably referred to as the "Control" menu in the style guide) is that standard little menu available in the upper left-hand corner of all independent windows. Curiously, it doesn't really do much. In Windows 3.x, there was a little box with a horizontal bar in it. In Windows 95, it is replaced by the program's icon.

Of all the menus, Microsoft has declared this one the most sacred: changing it is considered not, well, illegal, but akin to breaking the glass and ringing the fire alarm: You'd better have a darn good reason for it! Although I can't think of a single reason for changing it, I can imagine getting rid of it altogether.

Programs that use MDI give us two system menus because the document qualifies as a window and can be moved, minimized, maximized and so on just like its parent window.

Neil Rubenking claims that, in Windows 3.x, the horizontal bar in the main window's system menu box is actually a picture of the spacebar. You press ALT+SPACE to invoke it. He also says that the shorter horizontal bar in the MDI document window's system menu box is a picture of a hyphen, and—you guessed it—you can press ALT+HYPHEN to invoke it. If this is true, it is an example of out-clevering yourself. The idea is a good one, but the execution fails badly. In Windows 95, the little bars are thankfully replaced by icons.

The irony of this sacred relic is just that: It is a relic. It serves no useful purpose. Originally, it was to be the home of system-level window management commands, but all of the initial ones have migrated to immediate gizmos on the other end of the caption bar, and no new ones have been added. I don't think that users actually *use* the system menu anymore, particularly since Windows 95 arrived with its handy immediate close box. The sole remaining purpose for the system menu is as a programming support for equivalent keyboard commands for moving, resizing, maximizing and minimizing the window. It would be no loss to the interface if the system menu were eliminated (as long as the keyboard commands were retained).

Further, the very existence of the system menu contributes to the general level of ambient confusion; It's just another lever on the mechanism with no evident purpose except to generate worry in the user's mind. When MDI programs give us two of these confusion generators, the uninitiated can be doubly misled.

Windows itself puts this menu on top-level and MDI windows, so the application designer doesn't really have much choice about it. But it would be nice if someone pointed out to the designers of Windows how truly useless this little appendix is.

Dialog Boxes

21

Dialog boxes are not part of the main program. If the program is the kitchen, the dialog box is its pantry. The pantry plays a secondary role, as does the dialog box. They are supporting actors rather than lead players, and although they may ratchet the action forward, they are not the engines of motion.

Suspension of normal interaction

Dialog boxes are superimposed over the main window of the owning program. The dialog box engages the user in a conversation by offering information and requesting some input. When the user has finished viewing or changing the information presented, he has the option of accepting or rejecting his changes. The dialog box then disappears and returns the user to the main program.

Many users and practitioners think of dialog boxes as the primary user interface idiom of the GUI. Many applications have dialogs that provide the main method of interaction with the program (I'm not speaking of those smaller programs that are composed of just a single dialog box; in those cases, the dialog assumes the role of a main window). The user is constantly bouncing back and forth between the program's main window and its dialog boxes for no apparent reason.

When the application presents a dialog box, it is temporarily moving the action out of the mainstream; abandoning the main plot to develop a secondary issue. It is taking the focus of the dinner party away from the table and turning it onto the preparation of the food. It may be crucial, but it is not the main point.

Put primary interaction on the primary window

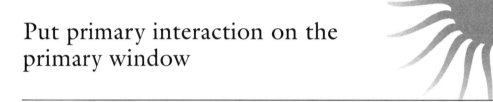

This understanding that dialog boxes are suspensions of normal processing is the key to their proper design. The main interaction of the program should be developed right on the main window of the program, while dialog boxes should be used only for secondary interaction.

If you asked your dinner party to temporarily abandon their soup and step into the kitchen, the smooth flow of conversation and warm friendship would be broken. In the same way, a dialog box breaks the smooth flow of rapport between a user and the program. Dialogs, for good or ill, interrupt the interaction and make the user react to the program instead of driving it.

Design tip: Dialogs break flow.

Dialogs boxes are appropriate for any functions or features that are out of the mainstream of interaction. Anything that is confusing, dangerous or rarely used can profitably be placed on a dialog box. I use the term **dislocating** to describe functions that make immediate and gross changes to the screen image. Such changes can be visually disturbing to the user and should be cordoned off from users unfamiliar with them. For this reason, dialogs are tools well-suited to managing dislocating actions.

Dialog boxes are good for presenting infrequently used functions and settings. The dialog box serves to isolate them from the more frequently used functions and settings. The dialog box is generally a roomier setting to present controls than toolbars or other primary control venues, so you can take a more leisurely approach to arranging and showing buttons and other gizmos. You have more space for explanatory labels than you do in a toolbar, for example.

Dialog boxes are also well-suited for concentrating information related to a single subject, such as the properties of an object in an application—an invoice or customer, for example. They can also gather together all information relevant to a function performed by a program—printing reports, for example. The dialog box, when used in this way, becomes an encapsulation tool, enabling you to box up and remove functions and settings that might have a dislocating or dangerous effect on the program from the normal flow of events. For example, a dialog box that allows wholesale reformatting of a document should be considered a dislocating action. The dialog helps prevent this from being invoked accidentally by assuring that a big, friendly CANCEL button is always present, and also by providing the space to show more protective and explanatory information along with the risky controls. The dialog can graphically show the user the potential effects of the function with a picture of what the changes will look like.

Most dialogs are invoked from a menu, so there is a natural kinship between menus and dialogs. As discussed in the last chapter, menus provide the pedagogic command vector—their primary purpose is to teach users about the program. By extension, dialog boxes also frequently play a part in the pedagogic vector.

Dialog boxes serve two masters: the frequent user who is familiar with the program and uses them to control its more advanced or dangerous facilities; and the infrequent user who is unfamiliar with the scope and use of the program and who is using dialogs to learn the basics. This dual nature means that dialog boxes must be compact and powerful, speedy and smooth, and yet be clear and self-explanatory in use. These two goals may seem to contradict each other, but they can actually be useful complements. A dialog's speedy and powerful nature can contribute directly to its power of self-explanation.

Dialog box basics

Most dialogs have buttons, comboboxes and other gizmos on their surface and, although there are some rudimentary conventions, generally the designer places them as she sees fit and not according to any conventional plan. The dialog's window may or may not have a caption bar or thickframe.

All dialog boxes have an owner. Normally, this owner is an application program—usually the one that created it—but it can also be the Windows system itself. Dialog boxes are always placed visually on top of their owning program, although the windows of other programs may obscure them.

Every dialog box has at least one **terminating command**, a control that, when activated, causes the dialog box to shut down and go away.

Generally, most dialogs will offer at least two push-buttons as terminating commands, OK and CANCEL, although the closebox in the upper right corner (upper left corner in Windows 3.x) is also a terminating command idiom.

It is technically possible for dialogs to not have terminating commands. Some dialogs are unilaterally erected and removed by the program—for reporting on the progress of a time-consuming function, for example—so their designers may have omitted terminating commands. This is bad design for a variety of reasons, as we will see.

Modal dialog boxes

There are two types of dialog boxes: modal and modeless. **Modal dialog boxes** are, by far, the most common variety.

Once the box comes up, the owning program cannot continue until the dialog box is closed. It stops the proceedings, which is how it got its name. Clicking on any other window belonging to the program will get the user only a rude "beep" for his trouble. All of the controls and objects on the surface of the owning application are deactivated for the duration of the modal dialog box. Of course, the user can activate *other* programs while a modal dialog box is up, but the dialog box will stay there indefinitely. And, when the owning program is reactivated, the modal dialog box will still be there waiting.

In general, modal dialogs are the easiest for users (and designers) to understand. The operation of a modal dialog is quite clear, saying to the user, "Stop what you are doing and deal with me now. When you are done, you can return to what you were doing." It is a classic subroutine: a PERFORM, a GOSUB, a FUNCTION call. It is thus ideally suited for most functions like summarizing and printing. The rigidly defined behavior of the modal dialog means that, although it may be abused, it will rarely be misunderstood. There may be too many of them and they may be generally weak or stupid, but their purpose and scope will usually be clear to the user. Like death and taxes, you may not like modal dialog boxes, but you grasp their meaning.

If a modal dialog box is function-oriented, it usually operates on the entire program or on the entire active document. If the modal dialog box is process- or property-oriented, it usually operates on the current selection. In any case, you can't change the selection once you've summoned the dialog. This is the biggest difference between modal and modeless dialogs.

Actually, because modal dialog boxes only stop their owning application, they are more precisely named **application modal**.

It is also possible to create a dialog box, called **system modal**, that brings every program in the system to a halt. No application program should ever create one of these. Their only purpose is to report truly catastrophic occurrences that affect the entire system, such as the hard disk melting.

Design tip: Never create a system modal dialog box.

Modeless dialog boxes

The other variety of dialog box is called **modeless**. They are less common than their modal siblings, and they are more misunderstood, too.

Once the modeless box comes up, the owning program continues without interruption. It does not stop the proceedings, and the application does not freeze. The various facilities and controls, menus and toolbars of the main program remain active and functional. Modeless dialogs have terminating commands, too, although the conventions for them are far weaker and more confusing than for modal dialogs.

A modeless dialog box is a much more difficult beast to use and understand, mostly because the scope of its operation is unclear. It appears when you summon it, but you can go back to operating the main program while it stays around. This means that you can change the selection while the modeless dialog box is still visible. If the dialog acts on the current selection, you can select, change, select, change, select, change all you want.

In some cases, you can also drag objects between the main window and a modal dialog box. This characteristic makes them really effective as tool or object palettes in drawing-type programs.

The modeless dialog problem

I am unhappy with the way most modeless dialogs are currently implemented. Their behavior is inconsistent and confusing. They are visually very close to modal dialog boxes but are functionally very different. There are few established behavioral conventions for them, particularly with respect to terminating commands, and Microsoft is setting a disturbing precedent with terminating buttons that change legends contextually a poor construct.

Most of the confusion arises because we are more familiar with the modal form—and because of inconsistencies that arise in the way we use dialogs. When we see a dialog box, we assume that it is modal and has modal behavior. If it is modeless, users must tentatively poke and prod at it to determine how it behaves. There is just no clear archetype for it.

More confusion creeps into the situation because users are so familiar with the behavior of modal dialogs. A modal dialog can fine-tune itself for the selection in the program's main window at the instant it was summoned. It can do this with the sublime assurance that the selection won't change during its lifetime. Conversely, the selection is quite likely to change during the lifetime of a modeless dialog box. Then what should the dialog do? For example, if the modeless dialog box modifies text, what should it do if we now select some non-text object on the main window? Should gizmos on the dialog box gray out? Freeze up? Disappear? Should the dialog box just stay there with all of its gizmos "active" but having no effect if they are pushed? All of these options have been tried, and although each one has advantages, it is not clear which help and which hinder us. We'll take a closer look in the next few pages.

Modeless dialog boxes also lead us into situations that aren't, well, right. For example, in Word, request the modeless Find dialog box from the Edit menu. Now, from the Format menu request the modal Font dialog. Voilá! You now have a *modal* dialog box sitting on top of a *modeless* dialog box, each supporting its own, totally unrelated, functions. The modeless Find dialog is function-oriented, while the modal Font dialog is property-oriented. Functionally, there is nothing wrong about this situation, but visually—comprehensibly—it is a nonsensical juxtaposition of unrelated dialogs. Is this helpful? Should such a circumstance be allowed to arise? I can't categorically say no, but I do think it is weak and confusing. The simple answer would be to eliminate modeless dialog boxes entirely, but that would be cutting off our nose to spite our face.

Two solutions

I'll take a stand right here and say that a solution must be found for the modeless dialog box problem. In fact, I'll offer two solutions. The first one is easy to swallow—an evolutionary step forward from our present peccadillo. The second one is more radical—a revolutionary leap. As you might suspect, the first solution is less thorough and effective than the second one. You might also guess—correctly—that I'm more fond of the revolutionary leap.

The evolutionary solution

In the evolutionary solution, we leave modeless dialog boxes pretty much the way they are, but we adopt two guiding principles and apply them consistently to all modeless dialog boxes. The first principle says that we must visually differentiate modeless dialog boxes from modal ones. The second principle says that we must adopt consistent and correct conventions for the terminating commands.

> **Design tip:** Visually differentiate modeless dialogs from modal dialogs.

If a programmer uses the standard modeless dialog box facility in the Windows API, the resultant dialog is visually indistinguishable from a modal one. We must break this habit. The designer must assure that all modeless dialog boxes are rendered with a clearly noticeable visual difference. A good method would be to use a distinctive hue for the dialog's background, or to add a pattern to it like desktop wallpaper. You can provide a colored border around the window or insert a colored stripe across its corner. You can change all of the buttons to visually distinct buttcons: make them a different shape or color or use a distinctive font.

You can visually differentiate a modeless dialog box by radically changing its shape: orient them all vertically instead of the usual horizontal shape. There are things you can do to the caption bar to set it apart visually, things like making it thicker or thinner, adding symbols or patterns to it, or animating it.

Whatever method you choose, you must stick with it consistently. It would be nice if vendors used a standard common to all, but that is wishful thinking. It will still be a significant improvement if each vendor adheres to his own, company-wide, standards for modeless dialog boxes.

Design tip: Give modeless dialog boxes consistent terminating commands.

The other area where developers must follow consistent conventions is in the design of modeless dialog box terminating commands. Currently, this is one of the most inconsistent areas. It seems that each vendor, sometimes each programmer, uses a different technique on each individual dialog box. I simply do not see any reason for this cacophony of methods. Some dialogs say CLOSE, some say APPLY, some use DONE, while some DISMISS, ACCEPT, YES, and some even use OK. The variety is endless. Still others dispense with terminating buttons altogether and rely only upon the close box in the upper right corner (upper left corner in Windows 3.x). Terminating a modeless dialog box should be a simple, easy, consistent idiom, very similar—if not exactly the same—from program to program.

One of the most obnoxious constructions I've seen is terminating buttons that change their legend from CANCEL to APPLY, or from CANCEL to CLOSE depending on whether the user has taken action with the modeless dialog box. Microsoft's applications do this with frightening frequency. This changing is, at best, disconcerting and hard to interpret and, at worst, frightening and inscrutable. These legends should *never* change. If the user hasn't selected a valid option but presses OK anyway, the dialog box should assume the user means "dismiss the box without taking any action," for the simple reason that that is what the user actually did. Modal dialog boxes offer us the ability to cancel our actions directly, with the CANCEL button. Modeless dialogs don't usually allow this direct idiom—we must resort to UNDO—so changing the legends to warn the user just confuses things.

Design tip: Never change terminating button captions.

The cornerstone of the cognitive strength of modal dialog boxes are their rigidly consistent OK and CANCEL buttons. The problem is that there is no equivalent for modeless dialog boxes. Modally, the OK button means "accept my input and close the dialog." Because the controls on a modeless dialog box are always live, their equivalent concept is clouded in confusion. The user doesn't conditionally configure changes in anticipation of a terminal "execute" command like he does for a modal dialog box. Modally, the CANCEL button means "abandon my input and close the dialog." But because the changes made from a modeless dialog box are immediate—occurring as soon as an activating button is pressed—there is no concept of "cancel all of my actions." There may have been hundreds of separate actions on a number of selections. The proper idiom for this is the UNDO function, which resides on the toolbar or Edit menu and is active application-wide for all modeless dialog boxes. This all fits together logically, because the UNDO function is unavailable if a modal dialog box is up, but is still usable with modeless ones.

The only consistent terminating action for modeless dialog boxes is CLOSE or GO AWAY. Every modeless dialog box should have a CLOSE button placed in a consistent location like the lower right corner. It would have to be consistent from dialog to dialog: in the exact same place and with the exact same caption. Not to put too fine a point on this, but the word CLOSE is the one to use, and it should never deactivate or change its caption.

If the CLOSE button activates a function in addition to shutting the dialog, you have created a modal dialog box, and it should follow the conventions for that idiom instead.

Don't forget that modeless dialog boxes will frequently have several buttons that immediately invoke various functions. The dialog box should not close when one of these function buttons is pressed. It is modeless because it stays around for repetitive use and should only close when the single, consistently placed CLOSE button is pressed.

Another point is that modeless dialog boxes must be incredibly conservative of pixels. They will be staying around on the screen, occupying the front and center location, so they must be extra careful not to waste pixels on anything unnecessary.

A more radical, but better, solution

What I proposed earlier was a series of baby steps; an interim solution. What I will now propose is a more sweeping and radical solution, but one that delivers us from the full panoply of modeless-dialog maladies in one fell swoop. As I describe this solution, remember that idioms like toolbars and tabbed dialogs were perceived as quite radical when they first appeared, but they are now widely accepted as normal. Here goes...

We currently have two modeless tool facilities in common use. The modeless dialog box is the older of them, but it is a clumsy and ineffectual one for all of the reasons outlined above.

The other modeless tool facility is a newcomer on the user interface scene, but it has achieved an unprecedented success. I'm referring, of course, to toolbars and buttcons. The toolbar idiom is only about five years old, but it has achieved a widespread success because of its demonstrable quality and convenience. *Well, it is nothing more than a modeless dialog box permanently attached to the top of the program's main window.*

The modelessness of toolbar buttcons is perfectly acceptable because they are not delivered to us in the familiar visual form of the dialog. Instead, they are visually presented as something clearly different. The row of omnipresent tools surrounding the workspace, without the usual trappings of dialog boxes, assures that they won't be confused with modal dialog boxes.

The buttcons and other tools on the toolbar are happy in their modeless role. We select something—text, say—and press the ITALIC buttcon; then we select something else, press ITALIC, select, press, select, press. We have no trouble understanding their scope even though it often confounds us when the same thing is positioned on a modeless dialog box.

If—depending on what is currently selected—a menu item can have no effect, it grays-out and deactivates. Toolbar buttcons can do the same, or they can merely take the "just ignore it" approach. However, when a buttcon's function becomes meaningless in the context, it should at least become unresponsive by not offering the pliant response. In other words, the buttcon should not visually depress.

Toolbars are just as modeless as modeless dialog boxes, but they don't intro- duce the conundrums that the dialogs do. They offer two characteristics that modeless dialog boxes don't: They are visually different from dialog boxes, and they have a consistent idiom for coming and going. They solve our other big problems, too. Toolbars are incredibly efficient in video space, particularly compared to dialog boxes.

I'm a firm believer in the principle that things that behave differently should look different. GUIs communicate visually, and we squander opportunity when we don't visually differentiate different things.

Things that behave differently should look different

If we make modeless dialog boxes look very different from modal dialog boxes, we will have solved half of our problem. Making our modeless dialog boxes into toolbars accomplishes this very effectively.

Now, you are probably thinking that the toolbar idea is good as far as it goes, but modeless dialog boxes are free-floating things that the user can position on the screen wherever he likes. Our friends in Redmond have created the perfect solution for this problem: the **floating toolbar**, sometimes called a **floater**. In all of Microsoft's current crop of applications, you can click-and-drag on any toolbar and pull it out away from the edge of the program, and it will instantly convert into a floater. A floater is a toolbar that isn't **docked** on one of the four edges of the program's main window.

A floater looks exactly like a docked toolbar, except that it has a thickframe for resizing and a **mini-caption bar**. A mini-caption bar is just what it sounds like: a caption bar that isn't as tall as a regular caption bar. It is about half the height of a normal one but is otherwise identical in operation and appearance.

The mini-caption bar, as shown in Figure 21-1, first appeared on Visual Basic's tool palette. The mini-caption bar hasn't achieved much currency in the industry for several reasons. First, it isn't standard and there is no easy way to get one. In code, you have to descend to the event-loop level and subclass the window, then perform some undocumented and non-standard actions to fool Windows into imagining that everything is normal. Because of the implementation hurdles and the lack of generally accepted usage conventions, no one is compelled to employ the idiom.

Figure 21-1

Here's a picture of a floating toolbar from Microsoft Word. But wait! This is a modeless dialog box! The mini-caption bar gives it a visual appearance distinct from modal dialog boxes, and the apparent conundrum of contextually inactive buttcons is bothersome to nobody. If all modeless dialog boxes were rendered this way, much of their confusion would disappear. What's more, if you drag this floating toolbar to an edge of the application, it docks on that edge as a familiar, fixed toolbar. Imagine if you could do that with any modeless dialog box—the Find dialog, for example?

If we went ahead and gave all modeless dialog boxes mini-caption bars, we would immediately solve the visual differentiation problem. Look again at Figure 21-1. Notice that it is just a toolbar from Microsoft Word that has been undocked. It is normally docked in a horizontal row at the top of the main window, just below the menu bar. Floating toolbars can be docked merely by dragging them to one edge of the main window, whereupon they attach themselves to it as a fixed toolbar, and the mini-caption bar disappears.

Now let's turn the tables. Imagine Word's Find dialog, shown in Figure 21-2, rendered as a floating toolbar. It would have a mini-caption bar instead of its normal one. It would lack a terminating button, relying instead on the close box in the mini-caption bar. What would happen if we were to drag this new Find dialog to the upper edge of the main window? If its behavior were consistent, it would dock: the gizmos on the surface of the Find dialog would distribute themselves in a horizontal toolbar the way the Format toolbar does. If it works for all of those Format buttcons and comboboxes, why can't it work for the Find dialog? Why can't we have a toolbar with a buttcon for FIND NEXT and with checkboxes for the various options?

Microsoft has made the floating/docking toolbar idiom a standard in the latest release of its Office suite. The programs all include a facility for customizing the toolbars to the user's taste. I not only think that this is a fine step in developing the user interface but that it should be used as the new idiom for replacing modeless dialog boxes.

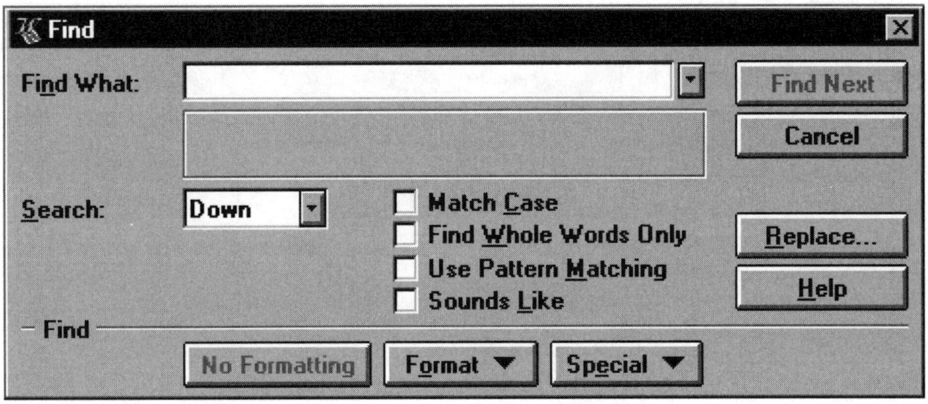

Figure 21-2

Here's a typical, state-of-the-art modeless dialog box. What a mess! It is big, obscures the text it needs to search within, and its buttons are clear as mud. That CANCEL one, for example: what does it cancel? Where can I tell this box to go away? Why can't functions like FIND be built into the main window interface, anyway? These aren't merely rhetorical questions; read the text for some real answers.

Property dialog boxes

The concepts of modal and modeless are derived from programmers' terms. They affect our design, but we must also examine dialogs from a goal-directed point of view. In that light, there are four fundamental varieties of dialog box which I call property, function, bulletin and process.

A **property dialog box** presents the user with the settings or characteristics of a selected object and enables the user to make changes to these characteristics. Sometimes the characteristics may relate to the entire application or document, rather than just one object.

The Font dialog box in Word, shown in Figure 21-3 is a good example. The user selects some characters, then requests the dialog box from the menu. The dialog enables the user to change font-related characteristics of the selected characters. You can think of property dialogs as a control panel with exposed configuration controls for the selected object. Property dialog boxes are usually modal. However, it is not uncommon for them to be modeless.

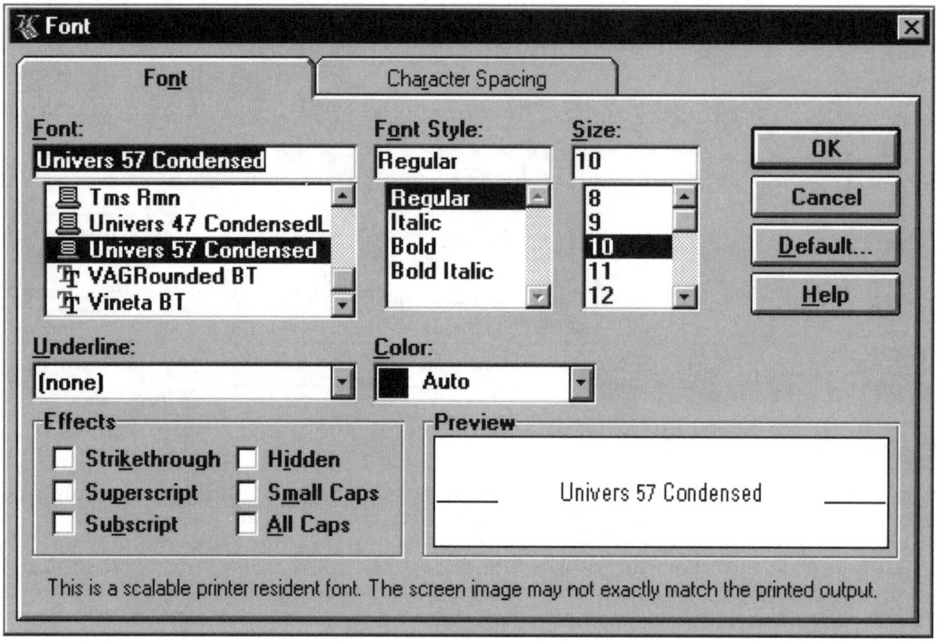

Figure 21-3

The Font dialog box in Word is a properties dialog. It reflects all of the characteristics of the current selection, as they relate to typography. When the user changes something on this dialog, the text qualities of the selection will change, but no functions are executed. The process is essentially a passive, configuring one, rather than an active, process-oriented one. This dialog reflects the best and worst of contemporary dialog design. The preview box is great, but why can't the font combobox in the upper left corner use the actual fonts, too? The OK and CANCEL buttons are in the upper right corner, an emerging Microsoft standard. Upper right corner?! English-speaking people and many others read from upper left to lower right, so the terminating command buttons should be in the lower right corner. Another big mistake is that the terminating buttons are on the panes rather than on the common dialog background. This arrangement is ambiguous. Does the OK button mean to accept this pane or accept the entire dialog box? All terminating buttons should be placed outside any tabbed panes.

It is easy to think of "properties" as an artifact of object-oriented programming because, in that world, that is how we refer to the characteristics of things. But properties are just the aspects of any artifact in a program—the characteristics of a document or chunk of data.

A properties dialog box generally controls the current selection. This follows the object-verb form: The user selects the object and then, via the property dialog, selects new settings for the selection.

Function dialog boxes

Function dialog boxes are usually summoned from the menu. They are most frequently modal dialog boxes, and they control a single function like printing, inserting or spell checking.

Function dialog boxes not only allow the user to launch an action, but they often also enable the user to configure the details of the action's behavior. In many programs, for example, when the user requests printing, the user uses the print dialog to specify which pages to print, the number of copies to print, which printer to output to and other settings directly relating to the print function. The terminating OK button on the dialog not only closes the dialog but also initiates the print operation.

This technique, though common, combines two functions into one: configuring the function and invoking it. Just because a function *can* be configured, however, doesn't necessarily mean that a user will *want* to configure it before every invocation. I prefer to see these two functions accessible separately.

Many functions available from modern software are quite complicated and have many configurable options. Their controlling dialog boxes are correspondingly complicated, too.

The example shown in Figure 21-4 is from PowerPoint. The user first configures the operation by choosing a file, then executes the configured command by pressing the terminating command button: OK. It is very tempting to make that terminating button say PRINT instead. Fight the urge. It may seem more logical, but the loss of a consistently captioned terminating command button is too great a price to pay. If the dialog's caption bar text is appropriate, it will read like an English phrase, telling the user exactly what will happen: "Print the document".....OK.

Bulletin dialog boxes

The **bulletin dialog box** is a devilishly simple little artifact that is arguably the most abused part of the graphic user interface.

The bulletin is best characterized by the ubiquitous error message box. There are well-defined conventions for how these dialogs should look and work, primarily because the MessageBox call has been present in the Windows API since Version 1.0. Normally, the issuing program's name is shown in the caption bar, and a very brief text description of the problem is displayed in the body. A

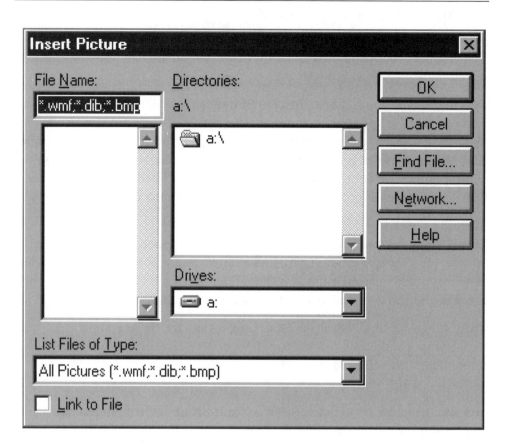

Figure 21-4

The Insert Picture dialog box from PowerPoint is a function dialog box. It is quintessentially modal, allowing the user to first configure the function by choosing a file. Nothing happens, however, until the OK button is pressed. The dialog does not have an effect on an object but rather performs an operation.

graphic icon that indicates the class or severity of the problem along with an OK button usually completes the ensemble. Sometimes a button to summon online help is added. An example from Word is shown in Figure 21-5.

Both property and function dialog boxes are always intentionally requested by the user—they serve the user. Bulletins, on the other hand, are always issued unilaterally by the program—they serve the program. Both error and confirmation messages are bulletins, and we will cover both variants in detail in Part VII, "The Guardian."

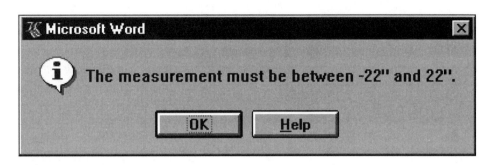

Figure 21-5

Here's a typical bulletin dialog box. It is never requested by the user but is always issued unilaterally by the program when it fails to do its job. The program simply decides that it is easier to blame the user than it is to go ahead and solve the problem. Users interpret this as saying "The measurement must be between -22 inches and 22 inches, and you are an incredible buffoon for not knowing that basic, fundamental fact. You are so stupid, in fact, that I'm not even going to change it for you!"

Process dialog boxes

Process dialog boxes, like bulletins, are erected at the program's discretion rather than at the user's request. They indicate to the user that the program is busy with some internal function and that it has become stupid.

The process dialog box alerts the user to the program's inability to respond normally. It also warns the user not to be overcome with impatience and to resist banging on the keyboard to get the program's attention.

All of today's desktop computers have a single-microprocessor central processing unit, or CPU. CPUs can only do one thing at a time, although through concurrency—where the CPU does a tiny bit of work on several programs in a kind of round-robin—they can seemingly execute multiple software threads at the same time. A problem arises when hardware becomes part of the equation. The CPU cannot use concurrent programming techniques if a chunk of hardware ties down the system for a long time. What this means is that when the computer must access the disk or the network, it cannot continue with other processing until the hardware responds. If the CPU requests something big from the disk—something that takes ten seconds, say—the entire computer comes to a grinding halt for the entire ten seconds; the computer gets stupid. This is true even in a preemptive multi-tasking environment like Windows 95.

The CPU can preempt software threads, but it still cannot preempt a hardware process.

Software that makes significant use of slower hardware, like networks, disks or tapes, will always become stupid, sometimes for relatively long periods of time. Software can also get stupid without accessing hardware. Programs that must perform billions of instructions before they can interact with users—anachronistically named "corebound" programs—frequently get stupid during their calculations.

In any case, when a program begins a process that will take perceptible quantities of time, as measured by the human user, the program must make it clear that it is busy and not just being rude. If the program does not indicate this, the user will interpret it as rudeness at best, or at worst, will assume the program has crashed and take drastic action.

Design tip: The program must inform the user when it gets stupid.

As we discussed in Chapter 15, many programs rely on active wait cursor hinting, turning the cursor into an hourglass. This solution springs big leaks in the multi-threaded world of Windows 95, and a better solution is a process dialog box (better yet, an equivalent progress meter built directly into the program's main window).

Each process dialog box has four tasks:

❍ Make clear to the user that a time-consuming process is happening

❍ Make clear to the user that things are completely normal

❍ Make clear to the user how much more time the process will take

❍ Provide a way for the user to cancel the operation

The mere presence of the process dialog box satisfies the first requirement, alerting the user to the fact that some process is occurring. Satisfying the third requirement can be accomplished with a **progress meter** of some sort, showing the relative percentage of work performed and how much is yet to go. Satisfying the second requirement is the tough one. The program can crash and leave the dialog box up, lying mutely to the user about the status of the operation. The process dialog box must continually show, via time-related movement, that things are progressing normally. The meter should show the progress relative to the total time the process will consume rather than the total size of the process. Fifty percent of one process may be radically different in time than 50% of the next process.

The user's mental model of the computer executing a time-consuming process will quite reasonably be that of a machine turning or reciprocating. A static dialog box that merely announces that the computer is "Reading disk" may *tell* the user that a time-consuming process is happening, but it doesn't *show* that this is true. The best way to show the process is with some animation on the dialog box. In the Explorer in Windows 95, when files are moved, copied or deleted, a process dialog box shows a small animated cartoon of papers flying from one folder to another folder or the wastebasket (see Figure 21-6). The effect is remarkable: the user gets the sense that the computer is really *doing* something. The sensation that things are working normally is visceral rather than cerebral, and users, even expert users, are reassured. The progress bar of blue squares satisfies—barely—the third requirement by hinting at the amount of time remaining in the process. Although this is one of the best designed features in Windows 95, it can still use some improvement. There is one dialog box per operation, but the operation can affect many files. The dialog should also show an animated countdown of the number of files in the operation. Right now, the blue squares in the progress bar just show the progress of the single file currently being transferred. Regardless, I'm tickled that Microsoft got this one so right.

Notice that the copy dialog in Figure 21-6 also has a CANCEL button. Ostensibly, this satisfies requirement number four, that there be a way to cancel the operation. The user may have second thoughts about the amount of time the operation will take and decide to postpone it, so the CANCEL button allows him to do so. However, if the user realizes that he issued the wrong command and wishes to cancel the operation, he will not only want the operation to stop but will want all trace of the operation to be obliterated.

If the user drags 25 files from directory Alpha to directory Bravo, and halfway through the move realizes that he really wanted them placed in directory Charlie, he can push the CANCEL button. Unfortunately, all that does is *stop* the move at its current state and abandons the remainder of the moves. In other words, if the user presses the CANCEL button after 10 files have been copied, the remaining 15 files are still in directory Alpha, but the first 10 are now in

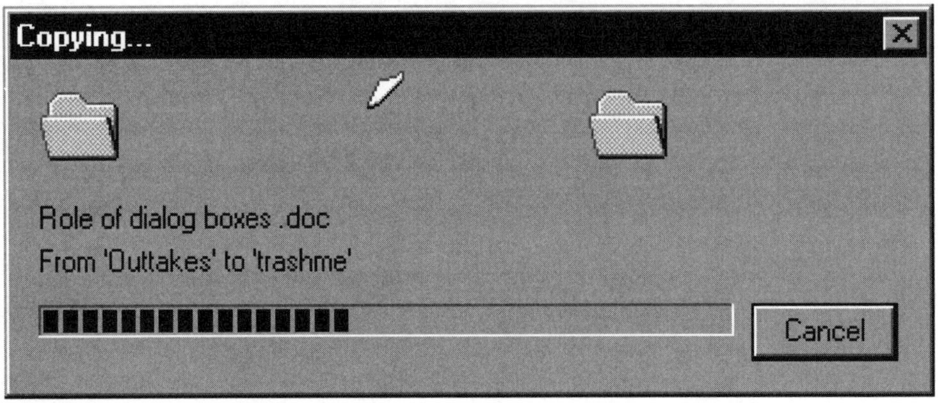

Figure 21-6

Hooray, Microsoft! They really got this one right. For any move, copy or delete operation in the Explorer, they show a well-designed process dialog box. The dialog uses animation to show paper documents flying out of the folder on the left into the folder (or wastebasket) on the right. The user's mental model is one of the things moving inside the computer, and this little gem actually shows things moving. It is refreshing to see the outside of the computer reflect the inside of the computer in users' terms for once. The only thing that worries me is whether Microsoft merely spawns an animation thread or actually ties the animation to the copy—in other words, if the program crashes, does the animation stop, too? Or will pages just keep on flying from one folder to another forever?

directory Bravo. This is *not* what the user wants. If the button says CANCEL, it should mean *cancel*, and that means "I don't want any of this to have any effect." If the button were to accurately represent its current action, it would say ABANDON, ABORT or STOP. Instead, it says CANCEL, so cancel is what it should do.

If the user pressed the CANCEL button, the program should really *cancel* the effects of the operation by undoing the already-done part. This may mean some significant buffering is needed, and the cancel operation could easily take more time than the original move, copy or delete. But isn't this rare event one when the time required is easily justified? In the Explorer, the program can completely undo a copy, move or delete (attaboy!), so there is no reason why the CANCEL button couldn't also undo the portion that had already been performed.

A good alternative would be to have two buttons on the dialog, one labeled CANCEL and the other labeled ABANDON. The user could then choose the one he really wants.

Dialog Box Etiquette

22

In the last chapter, we discussed the larger design issues concerning dialog boxes. In this chapter, we zoom in closer to examine the way well-behaved dialogs should act. Even an appropriate dialog box can exhibit behavior that is unexpected or irritating. By attending to the details, we can change them from rude interrupters to polite and helpful attendants.

You rang?

If you recall, we divided dialog boxes into four types: property, function, bulletin and process. One of the most important differences between these types is the way they are summoned. The first two are shown only at the user's explicit request, while the latter two are issued unilaterally by the program. When you say, "Jeeves, come in here," you expect the butler to step smartly into the room and plainly and immediately offer his services. On the other hand, when Jeeves wants to ask for a raise, you want him to wait obsequiously until you are relaxing in a pleasant mood before interrupting your reverie to impose his own needs. In this butlerian spirit, bulletin and process dialogs should show much more deference than property or function dialogs. Unfortunately, the opposite is often true.

A user-requested dialog may be large and place itself front-and-center on the screen. No unrequested dialog should be so brassy, however. It should be smaller, more compact in its use of space, and should appear off to one side of the screen so as not to obstruct the user's view of things.

Who's processing?

Actually, the need for bulletin and process dialog boxes is unclear. They are as common as weeds in contemporary software, and about as useful, too. In Chapters 28 and 29, we'll discuss ways of eliminating bulletin dialog boxes, but what can we do with process dialogs?

The answer to that question is found by asking who is doing the processing. Because a dialog is a separate room, we must ask whether the process reported by the dialog is a function separate from that on the main window. If the function is an integral part of what is shown on the main window, then the status of that function should be shown on the main window instead. For example, the Windows 95 flying pages dialog that was shown in Figure 21-6 is attractive and appropriate, but isn't copying a file fundamental to what the Explorer does? The animation in this case could have been built right into the main Explorer window. The little pages could fly across the status bar, or they could fly directly across the main window from directory to directory.

Process dialogs are, of course, much easier to program than building animation right into the main window of a program. They also provide a convenient place for the CANCEL button, so it is a very reasonable compromise to fling up a process dialog for the duration of a time-consuming task. But don't lose sight of the fact that by doing this we are still going to another room for a this-room function. It is an easy solution, but not the correct solution.

The caption bar

If a dialog box doesn't have a caption bar, it cannot be moved. All dialog boxes should be movable so they don't obscure the contents of the windows they overlap. Therefore, all dialog boxes should have caption bars. Is that clear? Even the Windows style guide almost agrees on this point, saying, "In general, an application should use only movable dialog boxes."

Design tip: All dialog boxes should have caption bars.

There seems to be some belief that system modal messages (which, of course, you will *never* create) don't have to have caption bars, because they are often used to report fatal errors. I guess the programmer's reasoning goes: "Well, the system is crashed, so why bother to let them move the dialog around?" Of course, when your system crashes is precisely the time you might need to get a good look at what was on your screen before you reboot. After all, you will probably lose whatever was there.

There also seems to be widespread confusion about what text string to put in the caption bar of a dialog box. Some people think it should be the name of the function, while others think it should be the name of the program. The belt-and-suspenders crew tends to use both. The correct answer is very simple: neither of these.

If the dialog box is a function dialog, the caption bar should have the name of the function—the verb, if you will. For example, if you request "Break" from the "Insert" menu, the caption bar of the dialog should say "Insert Break." What are we doing? We are *inserting a break*! We are not "breaking," so the caption bar should not say "Break." A word like that could easily scare or confuse somebody.

Design tip: Use verbs in function dialog caption bars.

I would go so far as to say that when the function will operate on some selection, the caption bar should indicate what is selected to the best of its ability. For example, if you select a sentence "Smilin' Ed is dead," and invoke the "Font" item from the "Format" menu, the dialog's caption bar should say "Format font for 'Smilin' Ed is dead.'" If you've selected text that's too big to fit on the caption bar, it should show the first and last couple of words of the selection separated by ellipses. If nothing is selected, the caption should say "Format font for future text."

Design tip: Use object names in property dialog caption bars.

If the dialog box is a property dialog, the caption bar should have the name or description of the object whose properties we are setting. The properties dialogs in Windows 95 work this way. When I request the Properties dialog for a directory named "Backup," the caption bar says "Properties for Backup."

Transient posture

If dialog boxes were independent programs, they would be transient-posture programs. As you might expect, dialog boxes should then look and behave like transient programs, with bold, visual idioms, bright colors and large buttons. On the other hand, transient programs borrow their pixels from sovereign applications, so they must never be wasteful of pixels. The imperative to be large is constantly at war with the imperative to be small. One solution is to make each of the individual gizmos slightly larger, but to make sure that the dialog itself wastes no additional space.

> ***Design tip:*** Dialogs should be as small as possible, but no smaller.

A few years ago, Borland International popularized a standard by creating extra-large buttons with bitmapped symbols on their faces: a large red "X" for CANCEL, a large green checkmark for OK, and a big blue question mark for HELP. They were cleverly designed and very attractive—at first. Most people now find them wasteful of space and with good reason. The icons on the buttons worked well to visually identify themselves, well enough that the extra size wasn't necessary. Borland now uses the same bitmaps on buttons of a more conventional size, which is a much better solution. The visual images accomplished the job just fine without the need to waste precious pixels.

Obscuring the parent window can be avoided by always being conservative of space. Dialog boxes should never take more room than they need. Pixels remain the most limited resource in modern desktop computers, and dialog boxes can easily overstep the boundaries of good taste by sprawling across the screen. Compare the space efficiency of the CompuServe Navigator dialog in Figure 22-1 to the one from Word in Figure 22-2.

Checkboxes are a relatively space-inefficient gizmo: the accompanying text requires a lot of dedicated space. Compared to the text of checkboxes, buttons can be crammed together like sardines.

Reduce excise

Dialog boxes can be a burden on the user if they require a lot of excise—unnecessary overhead, which we discussed in Chapter 13. The user will soon tire of having to always reposition or reconfigure a dialog box every time it appears.

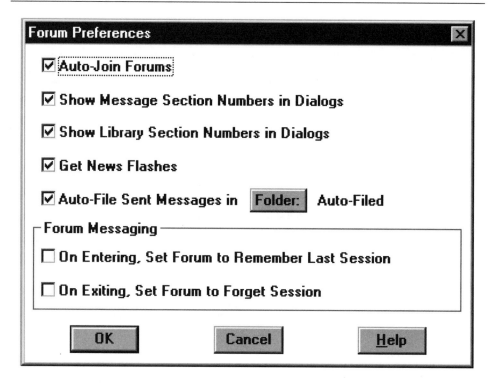

Figure 22-1

Here is a properties dialog box from CompuServe Navigator for Windows (Version 1.0). The sprawling checkboxes consume a lot of space. At least it has a caption bar, so you can move it out of the way.

The duty of the dialog box designer is to assure that the excise is kept to a bare minimum, particularly because dialog boxes are only supporting actors in the interactive drama.

The most usual areas where dialog boxes fail to reduce excise are in their geographical placement and their state. Dialogs should always remember where they were placed the last time, and they should return to that place automatically. Most dialogs also start out fresh each time they are invoked, remembering nothing from their last run. This is an artifact of the way they are implemented: as subroutines with dynamic storage. We should not let these implementation details so deeply affect the way our programs behave. Dialogs should always remember what state they were in the last time they were invoked and return to that same state. If the dialog was expanded or a certain tab was

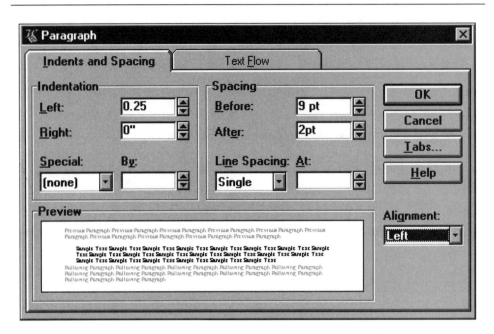

Figure 22-2

A typical function dialog box from Microsoft Word shows an excellent use of space. The controls are compact and very conservative of space. Compare this with the previous figure (Figure 22-1). Notice, also, their willingness to use graphic objects instead of just canned, text-based gizmos like edit fields, checkboxes and push-buttons.

selected, the dialog should return the exact same way on subsequent visits. In Chapter 14, I talked in more detail about how to apply memory to this type of problem.

The same idea can be applied to the contents of input fields. If a checkbox was checked last time, the dialog box should remember and come up with the box checked next time. Chances are good that the settings used the last time will be used the next time, too.

Know if you are needed

The most effective way that a dialog box can reduce excise is to not even bother appearing if it is not needed. If there is some way for the dialog box to be smart enough to know whether it is really necessary, the program should—by all means—determine this and prevent the user from having to merely dismiss the unneeded box: an action that is pure excise.

For example, in Word, I always save my document just before I print it, and I often print it just before closing it. In other words, I frequently want to SAVE, PRINT and CLOSE a document. Unfortunately the repagination involved in printing inadvertently marks the document as changed. This means that the program always asks me if I want to save it when I issue the CLOSE command, even though I just did! The program should pay attention! Of course, I want to save the document before closing. Not only should it not ask this question at all, it should be able to see from my actions that *I* didn't change it, the *program* did. The entire invocation of this dialog box is excise.

The same thing is true of bulletin dialogs that tell me that the program has completed some function normally. If it was so normal, the program shouldn't need to resort to the excise of a dialog box that stops the proceedings with idiocy.

If a program uses a dialog box to offer me a selection of options every time I ask for a certain function, and I always use the same options, the program shouldn't bother to even put up the dialog box. It should be able to recognize the pattern and remove the unnecessary step. Of course, it would have to inform me first, so I am not surprised, and it should give me the option to override its decision.

Terminating commands for modal dialog boxes

Every modal dialog box has one or more terminating commands. Most modal dialog boxes have three: the OK and CANCEL buttons and the close box on the caption bar. The OK button means "accept any changes I have made, then close the dialog and go away." The CANCEL button means "reject any changes I have made, then close the dialog and go away." This is such a simple and obvious formula, such a well-established standard, that it is inconceivable that anyone would vary from its familiar, trustworthy, well-trod path. Yet, for inexplicable reasons, many user interface designers do diverge from this simple formula, always to the detriment of their product and the despair of their users.

The modal dialog box makes a contract with the user that it will offer services on approval—the OK button—and a bold and simple way to get out without hurting anything—the CANCEL button. These two buttons cannot be omitted without violating the contract, and doing so deflates any trust the user might have had in the program. It is extremely expensive in terms of stretching the user's tolerance. Never omit these two buttons or change their legends.

Design tip: Offer OK and CANCEL buttons on all modal dialog boxes.

A colleague countered this tip by suggesting that a dialog box asking if the user wants to "Cancel Reservation?" would cause problems when it appears with an OK and CANCEL button. What does it mean to say CANCEL to Cancel? Good question, and the solution to the problem is to never ask questions like that. The example is a particularly ugly one for several reasons, notably because it is a confirmation dialog. Besides, if you ever need to ask a question like that—and you shouldn't—don't express it using the same words that are in the termination keys. With "Cancel Reservation?" the user must respond with the word CANCEL to avoid canceling. Confusing? You bet! Instead, the question should be stated like this: "Discard the Reservation?" Better yet, we'll talk about how to eliminate confirmation dialogs entirely in Part VII.

Design tip: Never use terminating words in dialogs.

The design tip "Offer OK and CANCEL buttons on all modal dialog boxes" applies to function and property types. Bulletin dialogs reporting errors—those hateful things—can get away with just an OK button (as if the user wants to collude in the program's failure!). Process dialogs only need a CANCEL button so the user can end a time-consuming process.

The OK and CANCEL buttons are the most important controls on any dialog box. These two buttons must be immediately identifiable visually, standing out from the other controls on the dialog box, and particularly from other action buttons. This means that lining up several, visually-identical buttons, including OK and CANCEL is *not* the right thing to do, regardless of how frequently it is done (id est: the stack of buttons in Figure 21-4). Even from companies who should know better, the OK and CANCEL buttons are buried in groups of other, unrelated buttons, and their familiar legends change with depressing frequency.

The CANCEL button, in particular, is crucial to the dialog box's ability to serve its pedagogic purpose. As the new user browses the program, he will want to examine the dialogs to learn their scope and purpose, then CANCEL them so as not to get into any trouble. For the more experienced user, the OK button begins to assume greater import than the CANCEL button. The user calls the dialog box, makes his changes, and exits with a confirming push of the OK button.

Lately, Microsoft has shown off a new standard for terminating buttons. They demand that the OK button be in the upper right corner of the dialog and that the CANCEL button be positioned immediately below it, with the HELP button below that. Unfortunately, Microsoft's style troopers have chosen poorly: The majority of users read from upper left to lower right, so the terminating buttons make more sense in the lower right of the dialog box. Microsoft has also gone for the executive gray look, and the terminating buttons are not visually identified by any unique color, bitmaps or even a unique font or typesize. They just blend right in with the other buttons on the dialog—too bad.

I'm much more concerned with consistency in placement of these buttons than I am in the particular location they occupy. However, I'm not indifferent to their placement. The OK button should be placed in the lower right corner of the dialog box, and the CANCEL button should be placed immediately to its left (or immediately above it). The user can then dependably know that an affirmative ending of the dialog can be had by going to the extreme lower-right corner.

The close box

Because dialog boxes are windows with caption bars, they have another terminating idiom. Clicking in the closebox in the upper right corner (or double-clicking the system menu box in the upper left corner in Windows 3.x) terminates the dialog box. The problem with this idiom is that the disposition of the user's changes is unclear: Were the changes accepted or rejected? Was it the equivalent of an OK or a CANCEL? Because of the potential for confusion, there is only one possible way for programs to interpret the idiom: as CANCEL. Unfortunately, this conflicts with its meaning on a modeless dialog, where it is the same as a CLOSE command. The close box is needed on a modeless dialog but not on a modal dialog box. So, to avoid confusion, the close box should *not* be included in modal dialogs.

Design tip: Don't put close boxes on modal dialogs.

If the user expects an OK and gets a CANCEL, he will be surprised and will have to do the work over—and he will learn. On the other hand, if the user expects a CANCEL and gets an OK, he will still have to do the work over, but this time he will be angry. Don't let this situation arise.

The HELP button requests context-sensitive help but doesn't terminate the dialog, so it isn't a terminating button. It is so often grouped with the terminating buttons that it has assumed the same importance by association. Online help, however, is not as important as the terminating commands. Putting help adjacent to them is weak, but not harmful, and it has the power of a familiar standard. In Windows 95, Microsoft is showing that they understand this problem. As you can see in Figure 22-3, they are beginning to move help away from the OK and CANCEL terminating buttons, putting it on the caption bar. Up there, it is on an area common to all dialogs but clearly separated from the very special terminating commands.

Keyboard shortcuts

Many dialogs offer services that are frequently used or used repetitively, like those for REPLACE or FIND. As users gain experience with the program, they will appreciate the presence of keyboard shortcuts for these frequently used dialogs. There are usually enough keys to go around, and there is no reason why a given function should have just a single keyboard shortcut. A function like FIND should be callable with a CTRL+F keystroke as well as a special function key, like F2. REPLACE could be CTRL+R and F3.

Users learn these shortcuts either from the help system or from the menus. Usually, these shortcuts go unnoticed until they are desired. New users go directly to the menus, and it is only after they find themselves actively searching for faster ways to operate that they discover them. And they will then be grateful that you had the foresight to put those shortcuts in for them. It can really please the power-user crowd, and this crowd will have a big influence over new users.

Tabbed dialogs

The latest user interface idiom to take the world of commercial software by storm is the **tabbed dialog**, sometimes called a "multi-pane dialog." In less than two years, tabbed dialogs, as shown in Figure 22-4, have gone from a virtually unknown idiom to a well-established standard. When an idiom has merit, it is widely copied, and the tab gizmo has been such a blessing to dialog box

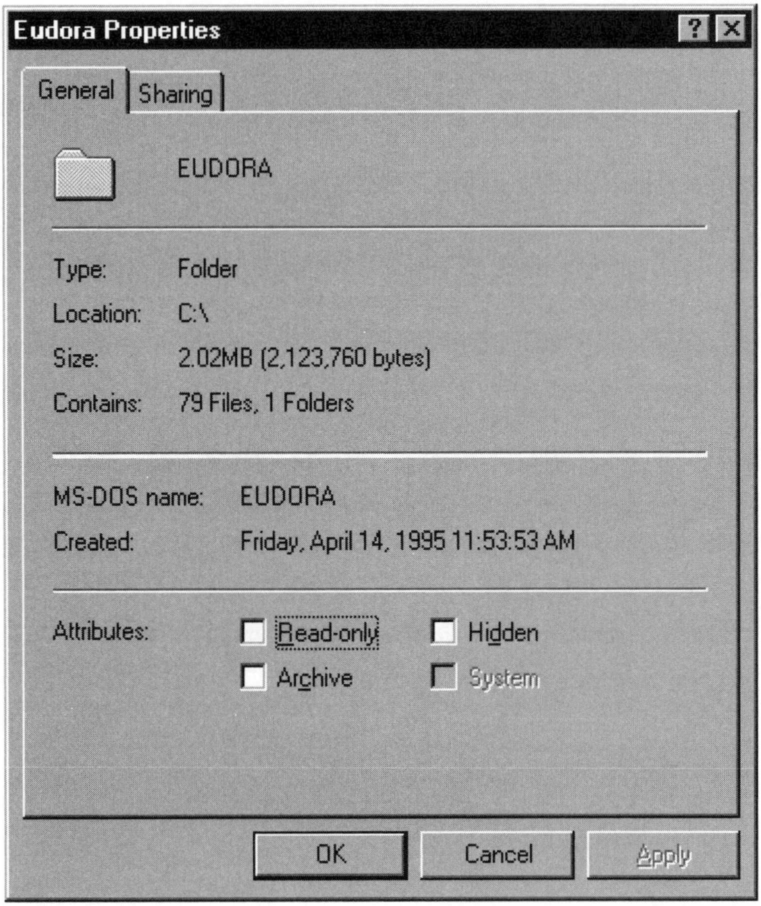

Figure 22-3

This properties modal dialog box from Windows 95 shows how Microsoft has finally realized that Help is not a terminating command. They removed it from the suite of terminating buttons and put it on the caption bar near the close box. This is certainly an improvement, but then they went ahead and added a newcomer to the terminating-button row: Apply. There is no use for an apply function on this pane, but it is applicable on the other pane, Sharing. Why not put the Apply button on the pane where it means something and keep it out of the way of the terminating buttons?

designers that it has become a standard part of Windows 95. We can expect that developers will soon embrace it with even more vigor than they already have.

Tabbed dialogs allow all or part of a dialog to be set aside in a series of fully overlapping **panes**, each one with a protruding, identifying **tab**.

Pressing a tab brings its associated pane to the foreground, hiding the others. The tabs can run horizontally across the top or the bottom of the panes or vertically down either side.

Many objects with numerous properties can now have correspondingly rich property dialog boxes without making those boxes excessively large and crowded with gizmos. Many function dialogs that were also jam-packed with gizmos now make better use of their space. Before tabbed dialogs, the problem

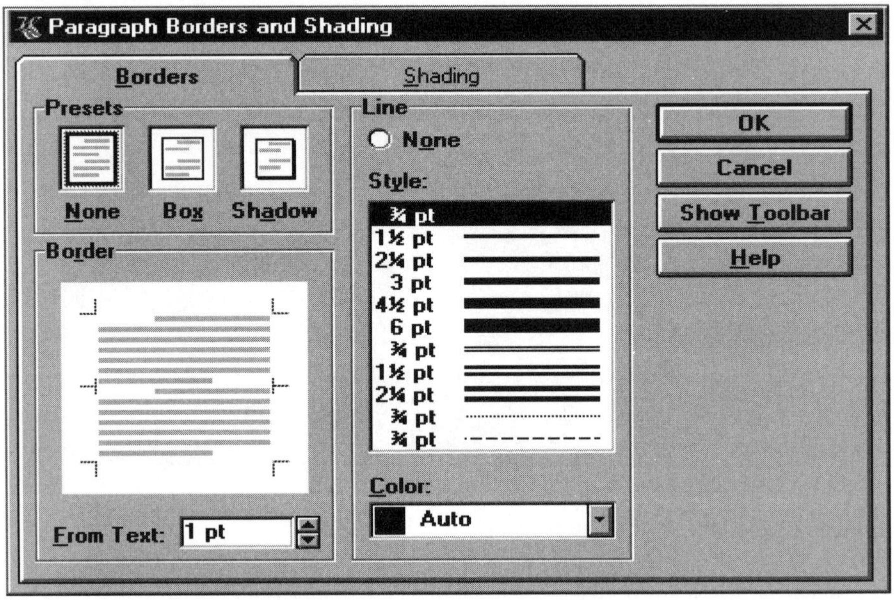

Figure 22-4

This is a tabbed dialog box from Microsoft Word. Combining borders and shading on one dialog box makes sense, if you have a convenient way to do it. Tabbing provides that way. Notice that Microsoft hasn't yet learned to put the terminating command buttons on the background instead of the pane. Putting them on the pane can confuse the user over whether he is canceling the pane or the entire dialog.

was clumsily solved with expanding and cascading dialogs, which I'll discuss shortly.

I believe that the tabbed dialog box is having such success because it follows the user's mental model of how things are normally stored: in a monocline grouping. The various gizmos are grouped in several parallel panes, one level deep.

A tabbed dialog allows you to cram more gizmos onto a single dialog box, but more gizmos doesn't necessarily mean that the user will find it better. The contents of the various panes on the dialog must have a meaningful rationale for being together; otherwise, this capability just degrades to what is good for the programmer, rather than what is good for the user.

The various panes on a dialog can be organized to manage increased depth or increased breadth. For more breadth, each pane covers additional aspects of the main topic, the way borders and shading, in Figure 22-4, both address ways that text is enhanced. For more depth, each pane probes the same aspect of one topic in greater depth. For example, the cascading dialog in Figure 22-7 could be implemented as a tabbed dialog with the custom color factory as a separate pane.

Every tabbed dialog box is divided into two parts, the stack of panes, which I call the tabbed area, and the remainder of the dialog outside the panes, which I call the untabbed area.

The terminating command buttons must be placed on the untabbed area. If the terminating buttons are placed directly on the tabbed area, even if they don't change position from pane to pane, their meaning is ambiguous. The user may well ask "if I press the CANCEL button, am I canceling just the changes made on *this* pane or all of the changes made on *all* of the panes?" By removing the buttons from the panes and placing them on the untabbed area, their scope becomes visually clear. Microsoft's Office suite has many terminating buttons incorrectly placed in the tabbed area, but the new Windows 95 has them correctly placed in the untabbed area. Expect to see them migrate off the panes in subsequent releases of Office.

Design tip: Put terminating buttons on untabbed area.

Multi-pane dialogs have been around for a while, implemented with a row of push-buttons, radio buttons or other common idioms for switching panes. The new tab gizmo that comes standard with Windows 95 has powerful visual affordances that the other idioms lack. The fact that Microsoft is supporting the standard with code will make it the idiom of choice for dialog box designers.

Because you can cram so many gizmos into a tabbed dialog, the temptation is great to add more and more panes to a dialog. The Options dialog in Microsoft Word, shown in Figure 22-5, is a clear example of this problem. The twelve tabs

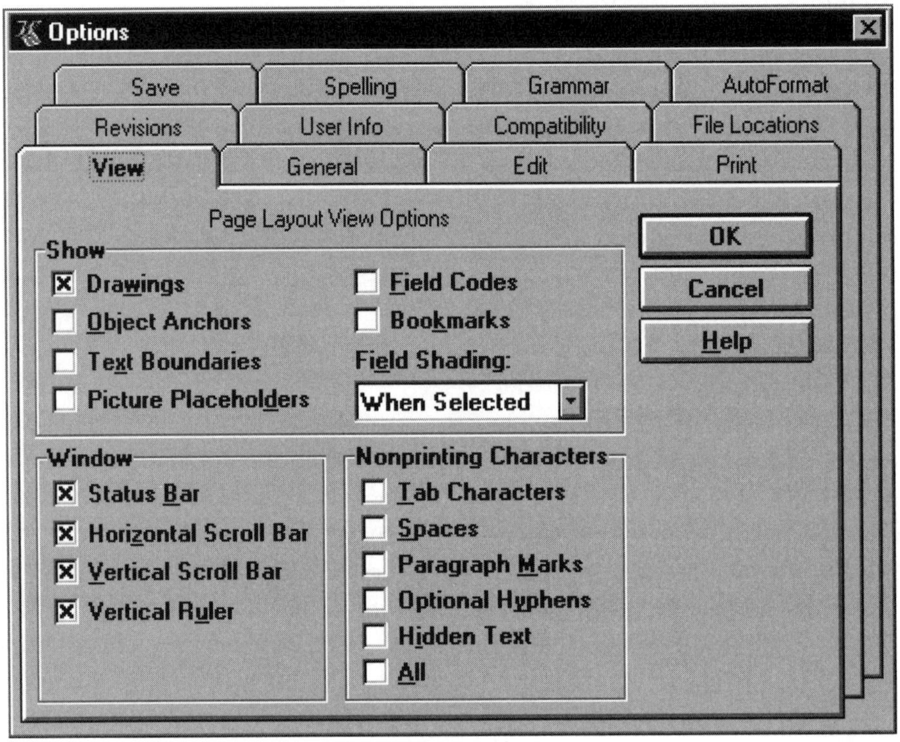

Figure 22-5

The Options dialog in Word is an extreme example of what can be done with tabs. There is certainly a lot of stuff crammed into this one dialog, which is good. The problem is that the tabs move around! The active tab must be on the bottom row, so if you clicked on "Grammar," for example, that row rolls down to the bottom and the other two rows bubble up one level. Everybody hates it when the tabs move underneath the cursor. It's better just to break this up into smaller dialogs.

are far too numerous to show in a single line, so they are stacked three deep. The problem with this implementation, which I call **stacked tabs**, is that, if you click on a tab in the back row, the entire row of tabs moves forward, shunting the other two rows to the back. Very few users seem to be happy with this because it is disconcerting to press on a tab and then have it move out from under the mouse. It works, true, but at what cost?

Stacked tabs illustrate an axiom of user interface design: That all idioms, regardless of their merits, have practical limits. A group of five radio buttons may be excellent, but a group of fifty of them is ridiculous. Five or six tabs in a row are fine, but adding enough tabs to require stacking destroys the usefulness of the idiom. Like overloading your Gremlin with 17 passengers, your performance edge decreases.

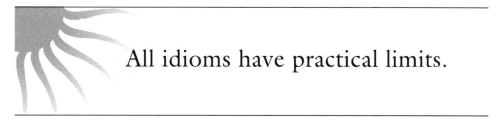

All idioms have practical limits.

So far, whenever I ask my colleagues for a viable alternative to the stacked tabs, they can't give me a good answer. They all see the advantage of twelve panes of options grouped in a common place, without incurring all of the other potential nasty problems with that many gizmos: There are no cascading dialogs; the dialog isn't too large; the gizmos are logically grouped; the implementation is simple. Although they accept its advantages, they all recognize its shortcomings, stemming almost completely from the dynamic rearranging of the tabs.

Design tip: Don't stack tabs.

A better alternative would be to just use three separate dialogs with four tabs each. There is little connection between the twelve panes, so there is little need to move between them. The solution lacks a certain programming elegance, but it is much easier for the user.

Expanding dialogs

Expanding dialog boxes were big around 1990 but have declined in popularity since then, largely due to the omnipresence of toolbars and tabbed dialogs. You can still find them in many mainstream applications, although Microsoft has been working hard to eliminate them from both Windows 95 and its applications.

Expanding dialogs "unfold" to expose more controls. The dialog shows a button marked "More" or "Expand," and when the user presses it, the dialog box grows to occupy more screen space. The newly added portion of the dialog box contains added functionality, usually for advanced users. The Color section ofthe Windows 3.x Control Panel is a familiar example of the expanding dialog box, as shown in Figure 22-6.

Usually, expanding dialog boxes allow infrequent or first-time users the luxury of not having to confront the complex facilities that more frequent users don't find upsetting. You can think of the dialog as being in either beginner or advanced mode, which is the cause of one of its more debilitating flaws. When a program has one dialog for beginners and one for experts, it both insults the beginners and hassles the experts.

As implemented, most expanding dialogs always come up in beginner mode. This forces the advanced user to always have to promote the dialog. Why can't the dialog come up in the *appropriate* mode instead? It is easy enough to know which mode is appropriate: it's usually the mode it was left in. If a user expands the dialog, then closes it, it should come up expanded next time it is summoned. If it was put away in its shrunken state last time, it should come up in its shrunken state next time. This simple trait could make the expanding dialog automatically choose the mode of the user, rather than forcing the user to select the mode of the dialog box.

For this to happen, of course, there has to be a "Shrink" button as well as an "Expand" button. The most common way this is done is to have only one button but to make its legend change between "Expand" and "Shrink" as it is pressed. Notice that the Color dialog in Figure 22-6 does not do this: Once the dialog has been expanded, it cannot be shrunk. Normally, changing the legend on a button is weak, because it gives no clue as to the current state, only indicating the opposite state. In the case of expanding dialogs, though, the visual

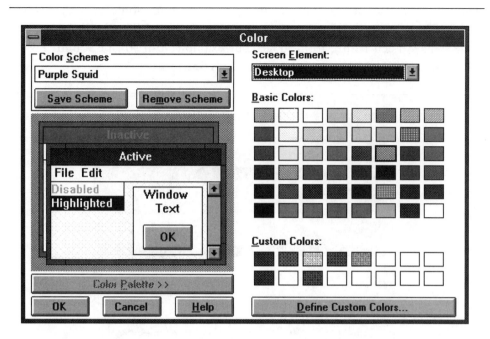

Figure 22-6

The Color tool in the Windows 3.x Control Panel is an expanding dialog box, shown here in its expanded state. When it first comes up, only the left half is visible. By pressing the "Color Palette>>" button, the right side of the dialog becomes visible. The left half is for normal users. Both halves are used by those fussy people who want to configure their own, private color schemes rather than selecting one from the standard palette. It sure would be nice if the dialog were smart enough to remember how I last left it!

nature of the expanded dialog itself is clear enough about the state the dialog is in.

A more mundane reason for its demise is the difficulty of coding an expanding dialog. The Windows API offers little help, whereas Windows 95 comes with the new tab control class pre-written.

Cascading dialogs

Cascading dialogs are a diabolically simple technique whereby gizmos, usually push-buttons, on one dialog box summon up another dialog box in a hierarchical nesting.

The second dialog box usually covers up the first one. Sometimes the second dialog can summon up yet a third one. What a mess! Thankfully, cascading dialogs have been falling from grace, but examples can still be found. Figure 22-7 shows an example taken from Windows 95.

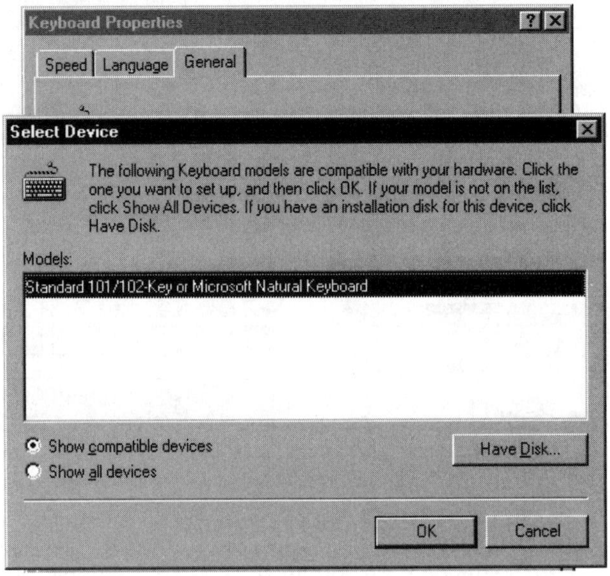

Figure 22-7

You can still find cascading dialogs in Windows 95. Double-click on the "Keyboard" icon in the Control Panel, then select the "General" pane of the dialog. You are greeted with a vast expanse of unused dialog pane space, yet if you press the "Change . . ." button, you get a second, cascading dialog that covers most of the first one. Why wasn't it part of the first dialog instead? The second dialog needlessly obscures the first one, and each dialog now offers up its own pair of terminating buttons resulting in a very unhelpful ambiguity.

It is simply hard to understand what is going on with cascading dialogs. Part of the problem is that the second dialog covers up the first. That isn't the big issue—after all, comboboxes and popup menus do that. The real confusion comes from the presence of a second set of terminating buttons. What is the scope of each CANCEL? What am I OKing?

The strength of tabbed dialogs is handling breadth of complexity, while cascading dialogs are better suited for depth. The problem is that excessive depth is a prime symptom of a too-complex interface. If you find your program requiring cascading dialogs for anything other than really obscure stuff that your users won't generally need, you should take another look at the overall complexity of your interface.

Examples of cascading are common. Most print dialogs allow print-setup dialogs to be called, and most print-setup dialogs allow print-driver-configuration dialogs to be called. Each layer of dialog box is another layer deeper into the process, and as the user terminates the uppermost dialog, the system returns control to the next lower dialog, and so on.

Cascading dialogs exist because they seem natural to programmers and because they mirror the physical processes underneath them. But this is about as backward a motivation as one can have—it ignores the user's goals and the user's mental model of the process. I'm not saying that cascading dialog boxes should be avoided entirely, but they represent a very weak idiom. Sometimes the situation demands them, as in the print dialog example described above. However, even in that case, I would combine them into one dialog with three tabs, or, at the least, I would combine the first two dialogs into a single one and only maintain the printer driver dialog separately from the main print dialog. Three dialog boxes in cascade is excessive for almost any purpose.

Directed dialogs

Most dialogs are pretty static, presenting a fixed array of gizmos. A variant that I call **directed dialogs** changes and adapts its suite of gizmos based on some user input.

A typical example of a directed dialog can be found in the "Customize" dialog of Windows Word, as shown in Figure 22-8. The gizmos on the face of the dialog change dynamically to adapt to the user's input to other gizmos on the same dialog. Depending on the selection the user makes in the "Categories:" gizmo, not only do the contents of the "Buttons" group control change, but sometimes the group gizmo itself is replaced by a different type of gizmo, usually a listbox. If the selection in the left-hand gizmo calls for buttons to be displayed, we see buttons in a groupbox, but if the selection in the left-hand gizmo calls for a list of fonts or macros, we see a listbox filled with text items. As the figure shows, the directed dialog technique can easily be combined with tabbing.

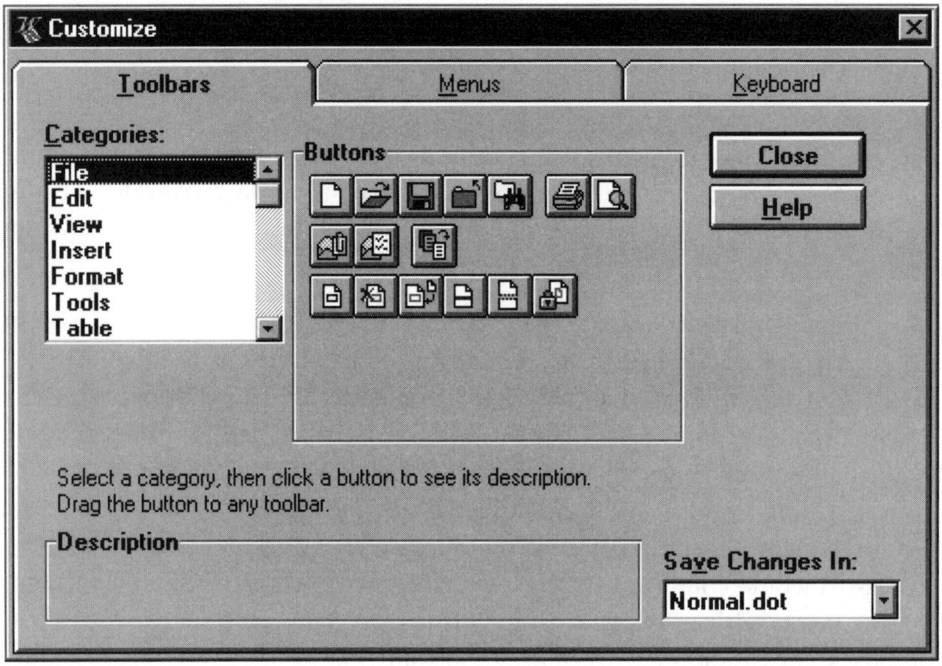

Figure 22-8

Word for Windows' Customize dialog box is an example of a directed dialog box.
Depending on what you select in the "Categories" listbox gizmo, the groupbox to its right
will either be a collection of buttons (as shown) or a listbox filled with macros, font names
or other items. The gizmos on the dialog box configure themselves in real-time to the
user's actions.

Programming a directed dialog can get complicated, so it is not done with great
frequency. The new nested dialog feature in Windows 95, however, may make
it easier to implement. It also may be confusing to the user, as he wonders
where certain gizmos went. But I think that it is particularly effective when the
user is entering settings in a clearly sequenced manner. For example, in a database access application where the user must select a server, then a database on
that server, then a table within that database, a directed dialog would be very
appropriate. The structure of the problem at hand calls for the server to be chosen first, so the user would select one from a list. As soon as the selection is
made, the dialog would configure itself to include a field for a password if the
server required it. If the server wasn't password-protected, the field would be

omitted. As soon as the user selects the database, one or more fields would appear as necessary to allow the user to select the table, its owner and other required information in sequence.

Toolbars

23

Toolbars are the new kid on the idiom block. Although not an exclusive feature of Windows, they were first popularized on this platform, not the Macintosh, like so many other GUI idioms. The toolbar has great strengths and weaknesses, but they are complementary to those of its partner, the menu. Where menus are complete toolsets with the main purpose of teaching, toolbars are only for frequently used commands and offer little help to the new user.

Visible and immediate

The typical toolbar is a collection of buttcons, usually with images instead of text captions, in a horizontal bar positioned adjacent to and below the menu bar. Essentially, the toolbar is a single, horizontal row of immediate, always visible menu items.

The toolbar really gave birth to the buttcon; a happy marriage between a button and an icon. As a visual mnemonic of

341

a function, buttcons are excellent. They can be hard for newcomers to interpret, but then, they're not *for* newcomers.

Great ideas in user interface design often seem to spring from many sources simultaneously. The toolbar is no exception. It appeared on many programs at about the same time, and nobody can say who invented it first (if *you* did, thanks!). What is clear, is that its advantages were immediately apparent to all. In a stroke, the invention of the toolbar solved the problems of the pulldown menu. Toolbar functions are always plainly visible, and the user can trigger them with a single mouse click. The user doesn't have to pull down a menu to get to a frequently used function.

Toolbars are not menus

Toolbars are often thought of as just a speedy version of the menu. The similarities are hard to avoid: They offer access to the program's functions, and they form a horizontal row across the top of the screen. Designers imagine that toolbars, beyond being a command vector in parallel to menus, are an *identical* command vector to those on menus. They think that the functions available on toolbars are supposed to be the same as those available on menus.

But the purpose of toolbars is actually quite different from the purpose of menus, and their composition shouldn't necessarily be the same. The purpose of toolbars and their controls is to provide fast access to functions used frequently by those who have already mastered the program's basics. Toolbars offer nothing to beginners and are not supposed to. The menu is where the beginner must turn for help.

> *Design tip:* Toolbars provide experienced users with fast access to frequently used functions.

The great strength of menus is their completeness. Everything the user needs can be found somewhere on the program's menus. Of course, this very richness means that they get big and cumbersome. To keep these big menus from consuming too many pixels, they have to be folded away most of the time and only "popped-up" on request. The act of popping up excludes menus from the ranks of visible and immediate commands. The tradeoff with menus is thoroughness and power in exchange for a small but uniform dose of clunkiness applied at every step.

The buttcons on toolbars, on the other hand, are incomplete and inscrutable, but they are undeniably visible and immediate. They are very space-efficient compared to menus. A simple, single click of the mouse on a toolbar buttcon generates instant action. The user doesn't have to search for the function a layer deep in menus—it's right there in plain sight, and one click is all it takes, unlike the mouse-dragging required by menus.

Why not text?

If the buttcons on a toolbar act the same as the items on a pulldown menu, why are the menu items almost always shown with text and the toolbar buttons almost always shown with little images? Why is the sky blue? No, wait, really, there *are* good reasons for the difference, although we almost certainly stumbled on them accidentally.

Text labels, like those on menus, can be very precise and clear—they aren't always, but precision and clarity are their basic purpose. To achieve this, they demand that the user take the time to focus on them and read them. As we discussed in Chapter 4, reading is slower and more difficult than recognizing images. In their pedagogic role, menus must offer precision and clarity—a teacher who isn't precise and clear is a bad teacher. Taking the extra time and effort is a reasonable tradeoff in order to teach.

On the other hand, pictorial symbols are easy for humans to recognize, but they often lack the precision and clarity of text. Pictographs can be ambiguous until you actually learn their meaning. However, once you've learned their meaning, you don't easily forget it, and your recognition remains lightning fast, whereas you still have to read the text every time. In their role of providing quick access to frequently used tools, familiar recognition by experienced users has the highest priority. The pictorial imagery of symbols suits that role better than text does.

Buttcons have all of the immediacy and visibility of buttons, along with the fast-recognition capability of images. They pack a lot of power into a very small space. As usual, their great strength is also their great weakness: the image part.

Relying on pictographs to communicate is all right as long as the parties have agreed in advance what the image means. They must do this because the meaning cannot be guaranteed to be unambiguous.

Many designers think that they must invent visual metaphors for buttons that adequately convey meaning to first-time users. This is a quixotic quest that not only reflects a misunderstanding of the purpose of toolbars, but reflects the futile hope for magical powers in metaphors, which we discussed in Chapter 5.

The image on the buttcon *doesn't* need to teach the user its purpose; it merely needs to have a bold and visual identity. He will have already learned its purpose through other means. This is not to say that the designer shouldn't strive to achieve both ends, but don't fool yourself: it can't be done very often. It's a lot easier to find images that represent *things* than it is to find images that represent actions or relationships. A picture of a trash can, printer or chart is pretty easy to interpret, but what icon do you draw to represent *apply style* or *cancel* or *connect* or *merge* or *convert* or *measurement* or *adjust*? Then again, perhaps the user will find himself wondering what a picture of a printer means. It could mean find a printer, change the printer's settings or report on the status of the printer. Of course, once he learns that the little printer means "print one copy of the current document on the active printer now," he won't have trouble with it again.

Modern programs like Microsoft Word offer a small library of predesigned icons to select from when customizing the toolbars. I wanted a buttcon that would insert today's date into a document and none of the predesigned ones particularly communicated "date" to me, so I just used a big, yellow smiley face. Its sole virtue is that once you know what it does, you don't forget it or confuse it with anything else.

The problem with both

It might seem like a good idea to label buttons with both text and images. There is not only logic to this argument, but precedent, too. I've seen many programs that do this. The original icons on the Macintosh desktop had text subtitles. Icons are really useful for allowing quick classification, but beyond that, we need text to tell us *exactly* what the object is for.

The problem is that using both text and images is very expensive in terms of pixels. Besides, toolbar functions are often dangerous or dislocating, and offering too easy access to them can be like leaving a loaded pistol on the coffee table. The toolbar is for users who know what they are doing. The menu is for the rest.

Some user interface designers have gone ahead and added text to buttons, either right on them or just below them, and left the images in place. This strikes me as a worst-of-both-worlds solution. After all, the space is far too valuable to waste this way. They are trying to satisfy two groups of users with two different goals: one wants to learn in a gentle, forgiving environment. The other knows where the sharp edges are but sometimes needs a brief reminder. Certainly, there must be a way to bridge the gap between these two classes of users. Later in this chapter, we'll discuss some methods that don't dedicate lots of precious video real estate to solving the problem.

Immediate behavior

Unlike menus, we don't depend on toolbar buttons to teach us how they are used. Although we depend on buttons primarily for speed and convenience, their behavior should not mislead us. Toolbar buttons should become disabled if they are no longer applicable due to the current selection. They may or may not gray out—this is up to you—but if a buttcon becomes moot, it must not offer the pliant response: The buttcon must not depress.

I've seen programs that make moot buttons disappear altogether, and the effect of this is ghastly. The supposedly Rock-of-Gibraltar-like toolbar becomes this skittish, tentative idiom that scares the daylights out of new users and disorients even those more experienced (me!). The path to modeless operation does not lie in becoming more ephemeral but rather in becoming more solid, permanent and dependable.

The toolbar freed the menu to teach

It was the toolbar's invention that finally allowed the pedagogical purpose of the menu to emerge. Once the frequently used functions were put into toolbar buttons, the pulldown menus immediately ceased to be the primary function idiom. For users with even slight experience, if a button existed, it was much faster and easier to use than pulling down a menu and selecting an item—a task requiring significantly more dexterity and time than merely pointing-and-clicking in one stationary spot. Before the advent of the toolbar, the pulldown menu was home to both pedagogy and daily-use functionality. Although the two purposes were intermixed, software designers didn't segregate them into different idioms until the toolbar demonstrated its potency. However, once the toolbar became widespread, the menu fell into the background as a supporting character.

The only programs where the menu is still used for daily-use functions are programs with poorly designed or non-existent toolbars.

ToolTips

The big problem with toolbar buttcons is that although they are fast and memorable, they are not decipherable. How is the new user supposed to learn what buttcons do?

Macintosh was the first to attempt a solution by inventing a facility called balloon help.

Balloon help is one of those frustrating things that everyone can clearly see is good, yet nobody actually uses, like no-fat cheese. Balloon help is a flyover facility (sometimes called rollover). This means that it appears as the mouse cursor passes over something without the user pressing a mouse button, similar to active visual hinting.

When balloon help is active, little speech bubbles like those in comic strips appear next to the object that the mouse points to. Inside the speech bubble is a brief sentence or two explaining that object's function.

Balloon help doesn't work for a couple of good reasons. Primarily, it is founded on the misconception that it is acceptable to discomfit daily users for the benefit of first-timers. The balloons are too big, too long, too obtrusive and too condescending. They are very much in the way. Most users find them so annoyingly in-your-face that they keep them turned off. Then, when they have forgotten what some object is, they have to go up to the menu, pull it down, turn balloon help on, point to the unknown object, read the balloon, go back to the menu, and turn balloon help off. Whew, what a pain!

Microsoft, on the other hand, is never one to make things easy for the beginner at the expense of the more frequent user. They have invented a variant of balloon help called ToolTips that is one of the cleverest and most-effective user interface idioms I've ever seen.

From a distance, ToolTips seem the same as balloon help, but on closer inspection you can see the minor physical differences that have a huge effect from the user's point of view. Unlike balloon help, ToolTips only explain the purpose of gizmos on the toolbar. They don't try to explain other stuff on the screen like scroll-bars, menus and status bars. Microsoft obviously understands that the user isn't a complete idiot and doesn't need to have the most basic stuff explained to him. It also shows an understanding that, although we are all beginners once, we all evolve into more-experienced daily users.

ToolTips contain a single word or a very short phrase. They don't attempt to explain in prose how the object is used; they assume that you will get the rest from context. This is probably the single most-important advance that ToolTips have over balloon help, illustrating the difference in design intent of Microsoft versus Apple. Apple wanted their bubbles to *teach* things to first-time users. Microsoft figured that first-timers would just have to learn the hard way how things work, and ToolTips would merely act as a memory jogger for frequent users.

By making the gizmos on the toolbar so much more accessible for normal users, they have allowed the toolbar to evolve from simply supporting menus. ToolTips have freed the toolbar to take the lead as the main idiom for issuing commands to sovereign applications. This also allows the menu to quietly recede into the background as a command vector for beginners and for invoking occasionally used functions. The natural order of buttons as the primary idiom, with menus as a backup, makes sovereign applications much easier to use. For transient programs, though, most users qualify as first-time or infrequent users, so the need for buttcons—shortcuts—is much less.

ToolTip windows are very small, and they have the presence of mind to not obscure important parts of the screen. As you can see in Figure 23-1, they appear underneath the button they are explaining and label it without consuming the space needed for dedicated labels. There is a critical time delay, about a half a second between placing the cursor on a button and having the ToolTip appear. This is just enough time to point to and select the function without getting the ToolTip. This means that in normal use, when you know full well what function you want and which buttcon to use to get it, you can request it without ever seeing a ToolTip window. It also means that if you forget what a rarely used buttcon is for, you only need to invest a half-second to find out.

That little picture of a printer may be ambiguous until I see the word "Print" next to it. There is now no confusion in my mind. If the buttcon were used to configure the printer, it would say "Configure Printer" or even just "Printer," referring to the peripheral rather than to its function. The context tells me the rest. The economy of pixels is superb.

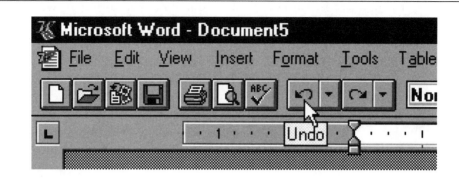

Figure 23-1

Microsoft's ToolTips were the solution to the toolbar problem. Although toolbars are for experienced users, sometimes these users forget the purpose of a less-frequently used command. The little text box that pops up as the cursor rests for a second is all that is needed to remind the user of the buttcon's function. The ToolTip succeeds because it respects the user by not being pedantic and by having a very strongly developed respect for the value of pixels. The idiom was the gate that allowed the toolbar to develop as the primary control mechanism in sovereign applications, while letting the menu fall quietly into the background as a purely pedagogic and occasional-use command vector.

I'm a very experienced user, and I leave ToolTips on all of the time. Balloon help on my Mac is never on except in rare cases in which I turn it on for just one balloon's worth of help. Microsoft's solution is a quantum leap beyond balloon help, and yet it is exactly the same. It just goes to prove that the devil is in the details.

> ***Design tip:*** ToolTips are indispensable to toolbars.

ToolTips have completely spoiled me for anything else. I now get upset with any program that doesn't offer them. Toolbars without ToolTips force me to read the documentation or, worse, to learn their function by experimentation. And because toolbars contain immediate versions of commands that should be used by moderately experienced users, they inevitably contain some that are dislocating or dangerous. Explaining the purpose of buttons with a line of text on the status line at the bottom of the screen just isn't as good as ToolTips that appear right there where I'm looking. That cheerful little yellow box with a terse word or two tells me all I need, where I need it, when I need it.

Do not create toolbars without ToolTips. In fact, ToolTips should be used on all pictographic buttons, even those on dialog boxes.

Beyond the buttcon

Once people started to regard the toolbar as something more than just an accelerator for the menu, its growth potential became more apparent. Designers began to see that there was no reason other than habit to restrict the gizmos on toolbars to buttons.

Opening the door to other popular gizmos was just the beginning. Soon designers began to invent new idioms expressly for the toolbar. With the advent of these new constructions, the toolbar truly came into its own as a primary control device, separate from—and in many cases superior to—pulldown menus.

After the buttcon, the next gizmo to find a home on the toolbar was the combobox, as in Word's style, font and fontsize controls. It is perfectly natural that these selectors be on the toolbar. They offer the same functionality as those on the pulldown menu, but they also offer a more object-oriented presentation by showing the current style, font and font size as a property of the current selection. The idiom delivers more information in return for less effort by the user.

Once comboboxes were admitted onto the toolbar, the precedent was set, the dam was broken, and all kinds of idioms appeared and were quite effective. The original buttcon was a **momentary buttcon**—one that stays pressed only while the mouse button is pressed. This is fine for invoking functions but poor for indicating a setting. In order to indicate the state of selected data, new varieties of buttons had to evolve from the original.

The first variant was a **latching buttcon**—one that stays depressed after the mouse button is released.

For example, the four alignment buttons shown in Figure 23-2 "latch" down to reflect the current status of the selected text. We'll talk more about these gizmos in Part VI.

Indicating state

This variety of gizmos contributed to a broadening in the use of the toolbar. When it first appeared, it was merely a place for fast access to frequently used *functions*. As it developed, gizmos on it began to reflect the *state* of the program's data. Instead of a button that simply changed a word from plain to italic text, the button now began to indicate—by its state—whether the

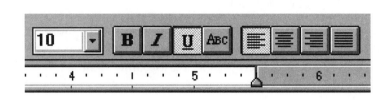

Figure 23-2

The development of the toolbar soon led to an extension of its purpose. It evolved from a mere repository of imperative command buttons to a place where gizmos could indicate the state of the currently selected item. This is a more object-oriented concept, and it makes our software more powerful. The toolbar has become the place for gizmo innovation, far beyond what we have come to expect from dialog boxes. This image shows the alignment buttons from Microsoft Word. They are latching buttons, staying down long after the user releases the mouse button. The buttcons indicate state in addition to allowing control of it. Good user interface idioms characteristically offer such richness.

currently selected text was already italicized. The buttcon not only controlled the application of the style, but it represented the status of the selection with respect to the style. This is a significant move towards a more object-oriented presentation of data, where the system tunes itself to the object that you have selected.

As the variety of gizmos on the toolbar grows, we find ourselves in the ironic position of adding pop-ups to it. The Word toolbar shown in Figure 23-3 shows the UNDO pop-up. It is ironic that such a very menu-like idiom should migrate onto the toolbar. Immediate UNDO certainly belongs on the toolbar, but does the associated pop-up that shows the history of past actions belong there, too? There isn't a clear answer. It is good that the historical list is positioned next to the UNDO buttcon because it makes it easy to find, but the toolbar is the place for frequently used functions. How frequently would one need to access the list? Ultimately, it comes down to pixels. As Microsoft implemented it, the pixel consumption is small enough to justify the idiom. What should be evident, though, is that the modern toolbar is increasingly pushing the old-fashioned menu bar into the background as a secondary command vector.

Toolbar morphing

Microsoft has done more to develop the toolbar as a user interface idiom than any other software publisher. This is reflected in the quality of their products.

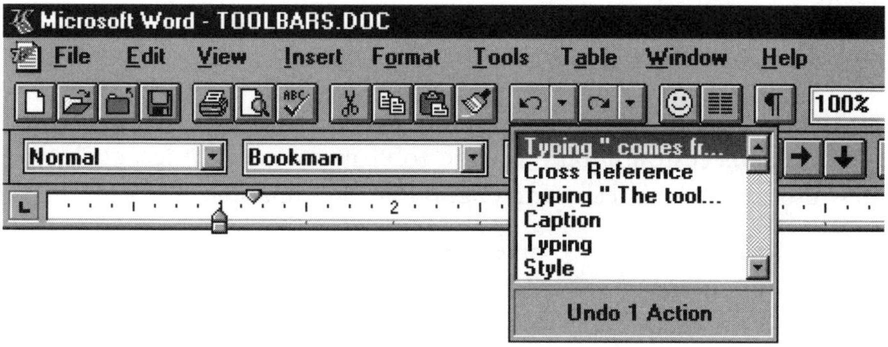

Figure 23-3

A typical Microsoft toolbar showing the half-button, half-icon gizmo I call a buttcon. Notice the evolution of the buttcon in the undo and redo functions on the right. They now have drop-down lists associated with them. Irony of ironies, the pulldown menu is migrating onto the toolbar, which began as a refutation of the old-fashioned pulldown!

In their Office suite, all of the toolbars are very customizable. Each program has a standard battery of toolbars that the user can choose to be visible or invisible. If they are visible, they can be dynamically positioned in one of five locations. They can be attached—referred to as "docked"—to any of the four sides of the program's main window. You click the mouse anywhere in the interstices between buttcons on the toolbar and drag it to any point near an edge and release. The toolbar attaches itself permanently to that side, top or bottom. If you drag the toolbar away from the edge, it configures itself as a floating toolbar, complete with mini-caption bar. Very clever, but not as clever as the customizability of the individual toolbars.

Customizing toolbars

Microsoft has clearly seen the dilemma that toolbars represent the frequently used functions for all users, but that those functions are different for each user. This conundrum is solved by shipping the program with their best guess of what an average person's daily-use gizmos will be and letting others customize things. This solution has been diluted somewhat, however, by the addition of non-daily-use functions. Clearly, amateurs (probably from marketing) got their hands on the Word toolbar. Its default buttcon suite contains functions that certainly are not frequently used. Things like "Insert Autotext" or "Insert Excel Spreadsheet" sound to me more like marketing features than practical daily options for a majority of users. While they may be useful at times, they are not used *frequently* by throngs of users.

The program gives the more advanced user the ability to customize and configure the toolbars to his heart's content. There is a certain danger in providing this level of customizability to the toolbars, as it is quite possible for a reckless user to create a really unrecognizable and unusable toolbar.

Mitigating this is that it takes some effort to totally wreck things. People generally won't invest "some effort" into creating something that is ugly and hard to use. More likely, they will do what I have done: make just a few custom changes and enter them one at a time over the course of months or years. The toolbars on my personalized copy of Word look just about the same as the toolbars on anyone else's, except for a couple of exceptions. I've added a smiley face buttcon that inserts the date in my favorite format. I've added a buttcon from the format library that specifies SMALL CAPS, a format I seem to use a lot more than most people. If you were to use my word processor, you might be thrown by the smiley face and the small caps, but the overall aspect would remain familiar and workable.

Of course, Microsoft has extended the idiom so that you can create your own completely new, completely custom toolbars. The feature is certainly overkill for normal users, but corporate MIS managers might like it a lot for creating that "corporate" look (see Chapter 32 for a discussion of such configuration needs).

My favorite part of the Microsoft toolbar facility is the attention to detail. You have the ability to drag buttons sideways a fraction of an inch to create a small gap between them. This allows you to create "groups" of buttons with nice visual separations. Some buttons are mutually exclusive, so grouping them is very appropriate. You can also select whether the buttons are large or small in size. This is a nice compensation for the disparity between common screen resolutions, ranging from 640×480 to 1280×1024. Fixed-size buttons can be either unreadably small or obnoxiously large if their size is not adjustable. You have the option to force buttons to be rendered in monochrome instead of color, though I don't really understand why you would want to. Finally, you can turn ToolTips off, though, again, I can't imagine why anyone would do this, and I don't know anyone who does.

One of the criticisms I have of the Microsoft toolbar facility is its scattered presence on the menus. There is a "Toolbars..." item on the "View" menu that brings up a small dialog box for selecting which toolbars are visible, creating new toolbars, turning ToolTips on or off, turning color on or off, and selecting large or small buttcons. However, if you want to change the selection of buttcons on a toolbar, you have to go to the "Customize..." item on the "Tools" menu, which brings up a dialog box that allows you to configure the toolbars, the keyboard and the menu (yes, there is a button on the Toolbars dialog that takes you directly to the Customize dialog, but that is a hack compared to a simple, unified view). I have the distinct impression that this design is the result of either accident or user testing rather than from the judgment of a skilled designer. Splitting the toolbar stuff into these two separate dialogs seems irrational to me. It is not at all clear how to find the various toolbar settings, nor do I think that the neophyte is effectively protected from self-defeating actions this way.

I'd much prefer a single dialog box, like the one in Figure 23-4, that enables the user to configure all aspects of the toolbars. A two-paned dialog would do the job well—one pane for the basic selections and a second pane for advanced stuff. This would be a classic rendition of increasing depth on additional panes.

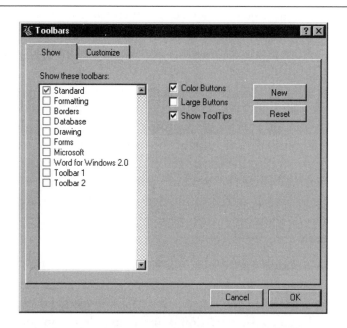

Figure 23-4

Here is a proposed solution to Microsoft's scattered toolbar dialogs. Instead of two dialogs available from two different menus, all toolbar operations are combined on a single dialog box with two panes. The "Show" pane contains the basics that most users may occasionally need to use. The "Customize" pane contains the more-sophisticated stuff that the experienced users might want.

Roll the Credits, Please

The modern desktop computer is getting quite crowded. A typical user has a half-dozen programs running concurrently, and each program must assert its identity. The user needs to recognize your application when he has relevant work to be done, and you should get the credit you deserve for the program you have created. There are several conventions for asserting your identity in software.

Your program's name

The most fundamental element of any program's identity is its name. By convention, this name is spelled out in the caption bar of the program's main window. I call this text value the program's **title string** because it is a single text value within the program that is usually owned by the main window.

The title string is used in several other places, too. In Windows 3.x, it is displayed beneath the program's icon. In

Windows 3.x, it is acceptable to have a very long title string because most programs have main windows that are at least eight to ten centimeters wide. Their correspondingly wide caption bars can easily render long program names.

Windows 95, though, introduces some complications. In Windows' latest version, the title string plays a greater role in the operating system's shell interface. Particularly, the title string is displayed on the program's **launch button** on the Startbar.

The launch buttons on the Startbar automatically reduce their size as more buttons are added, which happens each time the user launches more programs. As the buttons get shorter, their title strings are truncated to fit. If you add your company's name to your program's name, like, say "Microsoft Word," you will find that it only takes seven or eight running programs or open folders to truncate your program's launch-button string to "Microsoft...." If you are also running "Microsoft Excel," you will find two adjacent buttons with identical, useless title strings. The discriminating portion of their names—"Word" and "Excel"—are hidden. Yes, the launch buttons also contain your program's icon in the always-visible left end, but it sure would be nice if the programs were named "Word by Microsoft" and "Excel by Microsoft" instead.

You can rightfully say that this is a design fault of the Startbar and not your problem. You'd be right, of course, but this doesn't help the poor user. In the past, your program's title string was the place to show off your company or brand. It is now becoming a more-functional part of the interface.

The title string has, over the years, acquired another purpose. Many programs use it to display the name of the currently active document. Microsoft's Office suite of programs does this. They append the name of the active document to the right end of the title string using a hyphen to separate it from the program name. The File Manager shows the current pathname instead of a document name. The technique isn't a standard, but because Microsoft does it, it is often copied. It makes the title string extremely long—far too long to fit onto a launch button.

What Microsoft should have done with Windows 95 is add a new title string to the program's internal data structure. This string would be used only on the launch button, leaving the original title string for the window's caption bar. This would enable the programmer to tailor the launch-button string for its restricted space, while letting the title string languish full-length on the always-roomier caption bar.

Your program's icon

The second biggest component of your program's identity is its icon. A standard program icon is 32 pixels square. In Windows 3.x, the icon is usually shown—by convention—in the program's "About..." box. It is also displayed in the Program Manager and on the desktop when the program is minimized. The icon didn't do a lot in Windows 3.x.

In Windows 95, each program's icon is used much more widely than it is in Windows 3.x. First, there are now two icons: the standard one at 32 pixels square and a new, miniature one that is 16 pixels square.

The regular size is used on the desktop, but the miniature one is used on the caption bar, the Startbar, the Explorer and other locations in the Windows 95 interface. Because of this increased importance, you must pay greater attention to the quality of your program icon. In particular, you want your program's icon to be readily identifiable from a distance—especially the miniature version. The user doesn't necessarily have to be able to recognize it outright—although that would be nice—but he should be able to readily see that it is different from other icons. Bold color is especially helpful in accomplishing this, unlike Microsoft's white and pale-blue icons that are very hard to distinguish.

Dependencies

A nineteenth-century farm was a complex facility supporting many functions and, often, multiple families. The architecture reflected this, and the main house was always supported by a gathering of small outbuildings such as the stable, servants' quarters, the hen house, the stone house, the privy, the kitchen and the blacksmith's shop. These supporting structures were called "dependencies." Because modern software frequently consists of a single main screen supported by a family of smaller windows, I have adopted the old term. I call the many smaller, supporting windows dependencies.

I include in this category those windows that are not strictly needed to perform the main function of the program, particularly splash screens, About boxes and Easter eggs.

Dependencies are either available only on request or are offered up by the program only once. Those that are offered unilaterally by the program are erected when the program is used for the *very* first time or each time the program is initiated.

About boxes

The **About box** is a single dialog box that—by convention—identifies the program to the user.

The About box is also used as the program's credit screen, identifying the people who created it. Ironically, the About box rarely tells the user much "about" the program.

On the Macintosh, the About box can be summoned from the top of the "Apple" popup menu. In early versions of Windows, it could be called from the bottom of the "File" menu, but in modern Windows (3.x and 95), it is almost always found at the bottom of the "Help" menu.

Microsoft has been consistent with About boxes in their programs, and they have taken a simple approach to its design, as you can see in Figure 24-1. Microsoft sets the pace by using the About box almost exclusively as a place for identification; a sort of driver's license of software. I find this unfortunate, as it is a good place to give the curious user an overview of the program in a way that doesn't intrude on those users who don't need it. Programmers everywhere are following Microsoft's lead and making identity-only About boxes. It is often, but not always, a good thing to follow in Microsoft's design footsteps. This is one place where diverging from Microsoft can be a big advantage for you.

The main problem with Microsoft's approach is that the About box doesn't "tell me about" the program. In reality it is an "identification box." It identifies the program by name and version number. It identifies various copyrights in the program. It identifies the user and the user's company. These are certainly useful functions, but are more useful for Microsoft than for the user.

Because this facility just presents the program's fine print instead of telling the user *about* the program, I think it should be called an **identity box** instead of an About box.

The identity box identifies the program to the user, and the dialog in Figure 24-1 fulfills this definition admirably. It tells us all the stuff the lawyers require and the tech support people need to know. Clearly, Microsoft has made the decision that an identity box is important while an About box is expendable. Personally, I'd like to see the two combined into one, really helpful, dialog.

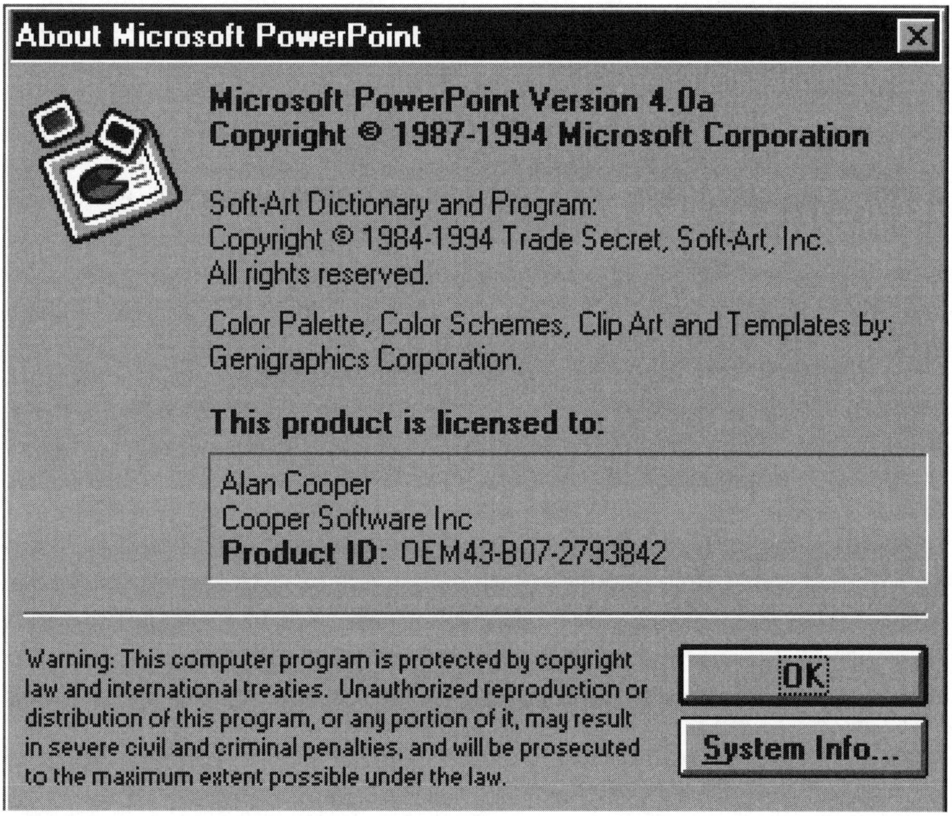

Figure 24-1

This About box from PowerPoint is a typical example of Microsoft's approach. It tells you the exact name and version of the program, states relevant copyrights, issues legal warnings (ugh!) and displays the user's name and company. The program's icon is traditionally shown in the upper left corner. The problem is, if I asked you to "tell me about PowerPoint," you probably would not bother to recite the relevant copyrights to me but would instead say something to me regarding what the program is about. What is wrong with this picture?

As we've seen, the About box must offer the basics of identification, including the publisher's name, the program's icons, the program's version number and the names of its authors. Another item that could profitably belong here is the publisher's technical support telephone number.

Many software publishers don't identify their programs with sufficient discrimination to tie them to a specific software build. Some vendors even go so far as to issue the same version number to significantly different programs for marketing reasons. Get a clue! The version number in the identity—or about—box is mainly used for technical support. A misleading version number will cost the publisher a significant amount of phone-support time just figuring out precisely which version of the program the user has. It doesn't matter what scheme you use, as long as this number is very specific.

An important part of reporting the version number is telling the user which previous version it replaces. Knowing that this is Version 3.2 isn't tremendously meaningful. Knowing that Version 3.2 fixes bugs in Version 3.1 and supersedes all Versions 2.x, however, *is* useful. Vendors work hard to improve their software, and each version is usually intended to replace some previous version. Smaller, incremental revisions are released to fix bugs but may not entirely replace a predecessor. Similarly, a special version may be shipped that allows compatibility with certain new hardware or software. This should be stated, as well.

If you are going to display an informative version number, it wouldn't hurt to explain the details of the numbering scheme on this box. Most users will ignore it, but it will be appreciated by many curious users, not to mention thousands of professional users and installers.

Many programs are uniquely identified by their serial number. This, of course, is the place to display that number. The user may need to use that number in correspondence with the publisher, or for his own company records, so the program should let the user view it and select it for copying.

The About box is absolutely the right place to state the authors' names. Most modern programs are built by teams of technical experts that can range from three or four to thirty or forty individuals. As a former software author, I'm very bullish on the idea of giving credit where credit is due in the design and development of software. Programmers, designers, managers and testers all like to see their names in lights. Like the credits in a movie, the people who labored over the product deserve their day in the sun. The documentation writers often get to put their names in the manual, but the others only have the program itself. The About box is one of the few dialogs that has no functional overlap with the main program, so there is no reason why it can't be oversized. Take the space to mention everyone who contributed. Although some programmers are indifferent to seeing their names on the screen, many programmers are powerfully motivated by it and really appreciate managers who make it happen.

What possible reason could there be for *not* naming the smart, hard-working people who built the program?

That last question was directed at Bill Gates, who has a corporate-wide policy that individual programmers *never* get to put their names in the About boxes of programs. Having sold him some software, I can tell you that it is his personal belief that no programmers should ever be identified, although I was able to convince him to bend sufficiently to include the name of my company in the Visual Basic About box. He feels that it would be difficult to know where to draw the line with individuals. I understand his plight, but as I watch the credits for modern movies scroll for ten minutes or so, I'm not terribly sympathetic.

Microsoft's policy in this area bothers me because their conventions are so widely copied across the industry. As a result, their no-programmer-names policy is also widely copied by companies who have no real reason for it other than wanting to be like Microsoft.

System information

Some vendors put system information on the About box, particularly information about the amount of memory used and available in the system. Why do they do this? I know that some Microsoft programs did it, so maybe vendors are just copying Microsoft. (An undocumented function in Windows 3.x enables this for all of the utilities in that version.) If you put a memory-meter in the About box, the only effect it can have is to bother new users by implying that they need to know about memory consumption. What possible connection could be made between asking "about" the program and learning how much memory is left in the system? It might make sense if the dialog told how much memory were used by the particular program, especially if it were expressed in terms of the percentage of memory available. At least then the user could see that the program in question is using up, say, 20% of the memory available to applications.

The About box in Figure 24-1 has a push-button that launches the Microsoft system utility that reports on the capabilities of the entire system. This is a nice feature, but it would make more sense as part of the online help facility rather than as part of the About box facility.

The desire to make About boxes more useful is clearly a strong one. Otherwise, we wouldn't see memory usage and system-information buttons on them. This is admirable, but, by taking a more goal-directed approach, we can add information to the About box that can really help the user. The single most important thing that the About box can convey to the user is the scope of the program. It should tell, in the broadest terms, what the program can and can't do. It should also state succinctly what the program's purpose is. Most program authors forget that many users don't know what the InfoMeister 2000 Version 3.0 program actually does. This is the place to gently clue them in.

The About box is also a great place to give the one lesson that might launch a new user successfully. For example, if there is one new idiom—like a direct-manipulation method—that is critical to the user interaction, this is a good place to briefly tell him about it. Additionally, the About box can direct the new user to other sources of information that will help him get his bearings in the program. Pointing him to online help or to other informational facilities built in to the interface can give a nascent user a real boost.

Splash screens

A **splash screen** is an identity dialog box displayed when a program first loads into memory.

Sometimes, it is just the About box that is displayed unilaterally, but often a publisher creates a separate splash screen that is more engaging and visually exciting than a boring, old About box. Not every program will have a splash screen, whereas almost every Windows application will have an About box.

The splash screen must be placed on the screen immediately when the user begins loading the program so that he can read it while the bulk of the program loads and prepares itself for running. It isn't really fair for the program to finish loading and prepping before it erects the splash screen. The user is then penalized for loading it, and will sense this and be irked by it. The program must show the utmost respect for the user's time, even if it is measured in milliseconds.

Shareware splash screens

If your program is shareware, the splash screen can be your most important dialog. It is the mechanism whereby you inform the user of the terms for using the product and the appropriate way for him to pay for the product. I've heard the shareware splash screen referred to as the **guilt screen**. Of course, this information will also be embedded in the program where the user can request it, but by forcing it in the user's face every time the program loads, you can reinforce the concept that the program *should* be paid for. Some shareware splash screens go so far as to include the text of a license agreement and buttons labeled "I Agree" and "I Don't Agree." The program only runs if the user presses the "Agree" button.

The splash screen should appear as soon as possible after the program is invoked. As soon as a decent interval has passed, it should disappear and the program should go about its business. If, during the splash screen's tenure, the user presses any key or mouse button, it also should disappear. If the program is still loading or deploying, it will then have to use some other idiom to indicate this to the user.

The splash screen is an excellent opportunity to create a good impression in the user's mind about your program. It can be used to reinforce the idea in the user's mind that he made a good choice by purchasing your product. It also helps to establish a visual brand by displaying the company logo, the product logo, the product icon and other appropriate visual symbols.

Help the first-time user

Splash screens are also excellent tools for directing first-time users to training resources that are not used in the normal course of daily usage. If the program has built-in tutorials or wizards, the splash screen can provide push-buttons that move the user directly to these facilities.

Microsoft has begun including a variant of the splash screen in their Office suite of programs. These little dialogs offer up a handy "Tip of the Day," shown in Figure 24-2, that helps the beginner become a more sophisticated user.

Because splash screens are going to be seen by every user, it means that even first-timers will see it, so if you have something to say to them, this is a good place to do it. On the other hand, the message you offer to those first-timers will probably get pretty boring for more-experienced users who must see it over and over. So whatever you say, say it clearly and tersely and without ornamentation or cuteness. An irritating message on the splash screen is like a pebble in your shoe, rapidly creating a sore spot if it isn't removed promptly. Although the Tip of the Day dialog is well-liked by many beginners, experienced computerphiles tend to hate them. The "Show Tips at Startup" checkbox gizmo allows the latter group to make the annoying idiom go away (but it might be a good idea to mention how to get it back next to the checkbox).

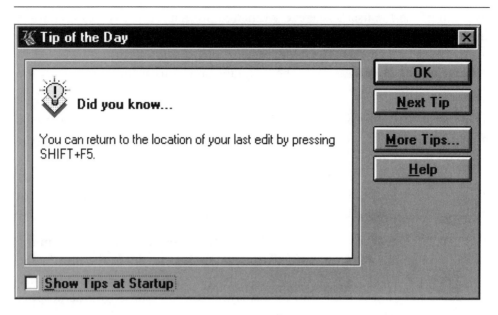

Figure 24-2

The Tip of the Day dialog from Microsoft Word is a variant of the splash screen. It appears once every time the program is invoked and offers the user a handy hint on how to use the program. Its intention is to make the user a better, more sophisticated user of the program. Don't overlook the potential of such artifacts; users like this kind of doting.

Easter eggs

If you call up the PowerPoint About box shown in Figure 24-1 and then click on it with the mouse *outside* either of the push-buttons, the box quickly flashes to black, and the names of all of the programmers who built it scroll smoothly upwards like the credits after a motion picture. Remember, this is a Microsoft program, and Bill doesn't allow the programmers to put their names in the program. But the philosophy in Redmond is "What Bill doesn't know, won't hurt him," and programmers have gotten their names into just about every program Microsoft ships. They do it by sneaking them into the interface with clever—but hidden—command idioms like this one.

Hidden surprises in a program are called easter eggs, and they are wonderful, engaging bonuses that contribute to the likableness of their host products.

Easter eggs don't have to be useful; in fact, practicality detracts from their appeal. The wonder of easter eggs is that they show off the astonishing power of the computer by doing something for pure entertainment. Like their name implies, the user gets the thrill of stumbling upon a secret: a flower in the forest; a pearl in the oyster; a prize in the Cracker Jack box; a winner in the Lotto. Users will cherish the knowledge and share it eagerly with their colleagues the way a good joke makes the rounds at the office. Whatever they say, they are talking about *your* program, and that is good for sales.

Easter eggs should be visually attractive. They are worth some time and effort in animating them or adding eye-catching artwork. I know one product whose About box, when you press the appropriately obscure key combination, changes to display a photograph of the company president in his cups at the office Christmas party. Nobody except employees know about this easter egg (maybe it should be called a Christmas egg?), but it has become part of the company lore. Good customers are shown this treat when they buy lots of copies, and then they feel like part of the inner circle. Just like any interface idiom, easter eggs are very memorable. It's harmless fun, and harmless fun is something that binds people tightly together.

In Windows 3.1, go into the Program Manager and hold the CTRL and SHIFT keys down and don't let go. Now pull down the Help menu and select About. When the about box appears, double-click on the Windows flag icon. Close the box with the OK button. Repeat, then repeat once again. On the second repetition, you see a waving flag. On the third repetition, you get a caricature of Bill Gates, Steve Ballmer, Brad Silverberg or a bear hosting a scrolling list of credits, naming every individual person who worked on the product. Stuff like this unites the team, creates legends and builds the corporate culture.

The About box is a common location for easter eggs, and whenever I get a new program, I try clicking in unlikely spots on the About box looking for them.

Easter eggs can be big or small, active or static. There are even a few of them in this book. Check out the fine print in Figure 7-1, for example.

Probably the most frequent use for easter eggs is the hidden credit box like the one described above, but they have other manifestations, too. The Tip of the Day issues random, helpful tips about the host program. In Word, though, you occasionally stumble on a real non sequitur of a tip as shown in Figure 24-3.

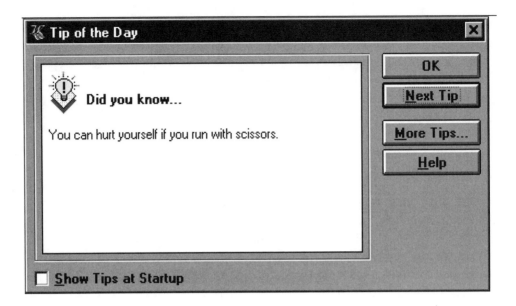

Figure 24-3

The Tip of the Day dialog from Microsoft Word also contains easter eggs. This one is pretty tame, but it is still worth calling over your buddy at the office and showing it to her. This curious message can't be argued with, but its placement is incongruous. Users really like easter eggs, and I think every program should have a few. The fuddy-duddies in your company probably disagree, as they do in most companies, which is why easter eggs are usually so well hidden.

Part VI: The Gizmos
Canned Visual Design

Gizmos are concentrations of interface design as much as they are modules of code. They offer the great advantage of shortening the development cycle while simultaneously presenting familiar affordances to the user. They also offer the great disadvantage of locking designers into old ways of thinking, instead of leaving them free to create methods of interaction that are more appropriate for the situation. They also give designers a false sense of security: using gizmos doesn't automatically make interfaces good. We need to look critically at these creations, understanding that they are as much a result of accident as they are of conscious design.

Imperative and Selection Gizmos

25

Gizmos are directly manipulable, self-contained, visual screen idioms. Gizmos, controls, widgets or gadgets—whatever you choose to call them, they are a primary building block for creating graphical user interfaces. They are closely identified with GUI programming, being as fundamental to GUI construction as windows, menus and dialog boxes.

This use of the word gizmo was coined by Mike Geary, a Windows programmer of legendary skill who worked with me to create the visual programming front-end for Visual Basic.

Microsoft calls gizmos "controls," but I avoid this term because it has so many other meanings in the same context: "How much control do I have over the code that controls that control that is busy controlling the modem controller?"

Gizmo-laden dialog boxes

Dialog boxes are the easiest things to build in Windows. The dialog box facility offers automatic tools for specifying how and where gizmos will be placed. The de facto definition of a dialog box is a modal window covered with gizmos. The ease with which programmers can create user interfaces based on one gizmo-laden dialog box after another is significant. Equally significant is the difficulty involved in creating Windows interfaces using any other visual, directly manipulable idioms. Essentially, Windows divides the universe of interaction into two worlds: the extremely easy to implement world of canned gizmos and the extremely difficult to implement world of direct visual interaction. Consistent with this, most existing literature—from Microsoft and elsewhere—covers the canned-gizmo world reasonably well, while utterly ignoring any other approach. Just for the record, let me say that canned-gizmo-laden dialog boxes are *not* the key to successful user interface design.

A multitude of gizmo-laden dialog boxes doth not a good user interface make

I'm not saying that we should toss out gizmos. I just want to make clear that while their inclusion may guarantee ease of implementation, it doesn't guarantee ease of use.

Most of the gizmos we are familiar with are those that come standard with the Windows system. This set of canned gizmos has always been very limited in scope and power.

Gizmo liberation

Using gizmos has always been pretty easy, but writing them is a lot tougher. Any journeyman C programmer can create a new gizmo, although it takes a considerable amount of attention to detail to code it fully. To comply with the de facto standards of gizmohood, it must offer many niceties, such as recognizing all keyboard commands, showing a dynamic gray rectangle to indicate it has the focus and having the ability to gray out when inactive. The difference in effort between writing and merely employing gizmos, though, has histori-cally kept most programmers out of the business of creating gizmos.

Microsoft Windows has always come with a standard suite of gizmos, and these form the basis of most interaction with applications. These standard gizmos are an integral part of the operating system. Technically, they are in USER.EXE, the portion of Windows that defines the GUI, or most of what we see on the screen. Although the programming interfaces to these gizmos bear a vague family resemblance, each one is quite different. There has never been a com-mon application programming interface (API) for them, and Microsoft has failed to define an acceptable standard for third-party vendors. This missing interface has really restricted the development of new gizmos.

Brave Windows developers have always invented new gizmos, but almost all of them remained proprietary. The lack of either a market or standards simply made it too difficult to distribute them, although a few aggressive companies developed one or two trademark gizmos to use in their own products. In the past, several companies tried to sell their gizmos but never seemed to make much headway. The only gizmos that had any universality were those that came as part of Windows itself.

The advent of Visual Basic in 1992 changed all that. VB has an interface that allows third-party gizmos to be installed dynamically. The gizmos are coded into dynamic link libraries (DLLs) with a commonly defined interface called VBX. The VBX interface isn't particularly pretty or powerful (I should know, I invented it), but it *is* standard, and it defines a method whereby a program can use a gizmo that isn't an integral part of Windows. Putting it another way, a programmer now has an easy way to use gizmos not made by Microsoft. Since the VBX interface gained popularity along with VB, there has been a veritable explosion in the gizmo market.

The VBX interface is giving way to OCX, and thence to OLE Custom con-trols—superior APIs all—but it was VBX that broke the dam and showed the way to decoupling gizmos from the operating system.

As the software market shook out in the last few years, many second- and third-tier software publishers saw the VBX phenomenon as an escape route from a one-way trip to Chapter 11. They took their powerful-but-money-losing spreadsheets, graphing programs and word processors and made them VBX-compliant. These products found a new lease on life in the thriving third-party gizmo marketplace, and programmers can now, for nominal fees, include in their software gizmos that provide functionality comparable to more main-stream products. This market shift has greatly expanded our old notions about gizmos and their capabilities.

The gizmos that Mother gives you

In USER.EXE of Windows 3.x, there were only six classes of gizmos: buttons, edit fields, static fields, listboxes, scrollbars and comboboxes. All of the other famil-iar, traditional gizmos like labels, group boxes, radio buttons, checkboxes, frames, rectangles and icons were derived from one or the other of these classes.

With Windows 95, the set of available gizmos has grown considerably, but even better, Microsoft is delivering these new gizmos to the developer by way of DLLs rather than as part of USER.EXE. This decoupling of user code from oper-ating system code is a very progressive step that will further encourage the development of third-party gizmos.

In spite of this, a huge amount of software already exists that was built with the notion that a gizmo can only be one of those six original ones that came with Windows 3.x. Much of what passes for interface design is really an artifact of the limited palette of gizmos available to the Windows programmers in their formative years. We are only slowly breaking out of that trap.

Although gizmos can be categorized by many factors, when you examine them in light of the user's goals, we find that they come in four basic flavors. They can be used to initiate a function, which I call an *imperative gizmo*. They can be used to select some option or data, which I call a *selection gizmo*. They can be used to enter some data, which I call an *entry gizmo*. And they can be used to directly manipulate the program visually, which I call a *display gizmo*. Of course, some gizmos combine one or more of these flavors. We'll now look at each type in more detail.

Imperative gizmos

In the interaction between humans and computers, there is a language of nouns (sometimes called objects), verbs, adjectives and adverbs. When we issue a com-mand, we are specifying the verb—the action of the statement. When we describe what the action will affect, we are specifying the noun of the sentence. Sometimes we choose a noun from an existing list and sometimes we enter a new one. We can modify both the noun and the verb with adjectives and adverbs, respectively.

I call the gizmo type that corresponds to a verb the imperative gizmo because it commands immediate action. Imperative gizmos take action, and they take it immediately. Menu items, which I discussed in Part V, are also immediate idioms. In the world of gizmos, the quintessential imperative idiom is the push-button; in fact, it is the only one, although it comes in numerous guises. Press the button and the associated action—the verb—executes immediately.

Push-buttons used to be identified by their unique outline, but since Windows went 3D (with Windows 3.0), buttons are now identified by their raised aspect. If the gizmo is rectangular and appears raised (due to its shadow on the right and bottom and highlight on the top and left), then it has the visual affordance of an imperative. It will execute as soon as the user presses and releases it with the mouse cursor.

The push-button is arguably the most visually compelling gizmo in the designers bag 'o gizmos. It isn't surprising that it has evolved with such diversity across the user interface. The manipulation affordances of contemporary faux-three-dimensional push-buttons have prompted their widespread use. It's a good thing—so why *not* use it a lot?

Part of the affordance of a push-button is its "pressability," which indicates its pliancy. When the user points to it and presses the mouse button, the push-button on screen visually changes from raised to sunken, indicating that it is pressed. This is an example of dynamic visual hinting, like I discussed in Part IV. I've seen programs where buttons are painted on the screen but don't actually move when pressed. This is cheap and easy for the programmer to do, but it is very disconcerting for the user, because it generates a mental question: "Did that actually do something?" The user expects to see the button move— the pliant response—and you must satisfy his expectations.

This is increasingly important in multimedia applications, many of which draw beautiful pictures on the screen and set aside portions of them as hotspots that are sensitive to clicking.

Cursor hinting isn't enough, though it's a desirable supplement. Even if the entire screen is consumed by a collage of, say, baseball collectibles, when the user clicks on a Louisville Slugger, the bat should move to visually confirm to the user that it is an imperative push-button—or, in this case, a push-bat!

The development of the push-button

In the early versions of Windows, push-buttons were stodgy beasts, largely used for terminating dialog boxes, which did the bulk of the heavy work of interaction.

On modal dialog boxes, the push-button is usually used only for terminating commands. This means that it is really an excise control; managing the window rather than directly affecting the user's information.

Concurrent with the release of Windows 3.0 came a surge of activity in user interface innovation across the industry. The toolbar was one of the great advances of that period, and it has quickly grown into a de facto standard as familiar as the menu bar. To populate the toolbar, the push-button was adapted from its traditional home on the dialog box. On its way, it changed significantly in function, role and visual aspect.

On dialog boxes, the push-button was rectangular and exclusively labeled with text, but when it moved to the toolbar, it became square, lost its text and acquired a pictograph, an iconic legend. Thus was born the buttcon: half button, half icon.

The invention of the toolbar qualitatively changed the role of the push-button. Actually, its role expanded rather than changed, as it is still a fixture of dialog box management.

Buttcons

Buttcons are easy: they are always visible and don't demand as much time or dexterity as a pulldown menu does. Because they are constantly visible, they are easy to memorize, particularly in sovereign applications. The advantages of the buttcon are hard to separate from the advantages of the toolbar—the two are inextricably linked. The consistently annoying problem with the buttcon derives not from its button part, but from its icon part. We instantly decipher the visual affordance—it screams "press me." The problem is that the image on the face of the buttcon never gets that clear.

Icons in general are hard to decipher with certainty, and icons of verbs are much harder to decipher than icons of nouns. Because buttcons are imperative, they are verbs, and thus remain problematic. It isn't really a matter of coming up with better visual metaphors or finding a better graphic artist. The problem is that visual symbols that convey actions and relationships are difficult, if not impossible, to find. If you do find an appropriate image, it may have good mnemonic qualities but will usually be inadequate to teach newcomers its purpose.

The dilemma arises because images do have such good mnemonic qualities. These qualities are good enough that the visual image is more than enough to remind the daily user of the command represented by the buttcon. The image buttcon is very space-efficient compared to the older, text-legend button. As long as there is a way to learn it initially, and it is part of the user's working set of commands, he will remember the image idiomatically and have no problem with the lack of innate learnability. The distinguishing quality of the buttcon's image is that it is visually distinct and memorable.

Without a mechanism for explaining their purpose, however, buttcons and toolbars are badly afflicted and significantly less useful than they could be. The rapid spread of buttons on toolbars caused a widespread grumbling about incomprehensible icons. In response, some companies pumped up their buttcons until they were big enough to hold text legends in addition to icons. Yet others made it the user's choice, adding another annoying layer of excise to the interface. Then, as I discussed in Chapter 23, Microsoft's ToolTips neatly solved the inscrutable buttcon problem once and for all. ToolTips provide initial learning without intruding on the view of the frequent user. They have spoiled me. I now find myself getting impatient and frustrated with programs whose buttcons lack them. The groundswell of grumbling over inscrutable buttons has subsided to inaudibility due to ToolTips. I am in constant wonder over the efficacy of the idiom. They seem so clunky, so much like a quick-fix solution, and yet they solve the problem very adroitly.

Selection gizmos

Since the imperative gizmo is a verb, it needs a noun upon which to operate. Selection and entry gizmos are the two types used to select nouns. A **selection gizmo** allows the user to choose an operand from a group of valid choices.

No action is associated with selection gizmos. Selection gizmos can either present a single choice (to which the user can only say "yes" or "no"), or it can present a group of choices (from which the user can select one or more choices, depending on how the gizmo is configured). The listbox and the checkbox are good examples of selection gizmos.

Checkbox

The checkbox was one of the earliest visual gizmo idioms invented, and it remains the favorite for presenting a single, binary choice. The checkbox has a strong visual affordance for clicking; it appears as a pliant area, either because of its little square or, in Windows 95, because of its 3D recessing. Once the user clicks on it and sees the checkmark appear, he has learned all he needs to know to make it work at will: click to check, click again to uncheck. The checkbox is simple, visual and elegant.

The checkbox is, however, primarily a text-based gizmo. The checkable box acts as a visually recognizable icon next to its discriminating text. This works in just the way that icons to the left of text items in a listbox help the user visually discriminate their type. Like those listbox entries, however, the graphic supports the text, rather than the other way around. The checkbox is a familiar, effective idiom, but it has the same strengths and weaknesses as menus. The exacting text makes checkboxes unambiguous. The exacting text forces the user to slow down to read it, and takes a considerable amount of real estate.

Traditionally, checkboxes are square. Users recognize visual objects by their shape, and the square checkbox is an important standard. There is nothing inherently good or bad about squareness; it just happens to have been the shape originally chosen, and many users have already learned to recognize this shape. There is no good reason to deviate from this pattern. Don't make them diamond shaped or round, regardless of what the marketing or graphic arts people say.

Perhaps we could do to the checkbox what the buttcon did to the menu. Perhaps we could develop a checkbox gizmo that dispensed with text and used an icon instead. Well, sort of. We won't get far trying to iconize the checkbox, but we can replace the checkbox function with another evolving idiom: the buttcon.

The push-button evolved into the buttcon by replacing its text with an icon, then migrating onto the toolbar. Once there, the metamorphosis of the button continued by the simple expedient of allowing it to stay in the recessed—or pushed-in—state when clicked, then returning to the raised aspect when it is clicked again. The character of the gizmo changed sufficiently to move it into an entirely different category, from imperative to selection gizmo! The state of the buttcon is no longer momentary, but rather locks in place until it is clicked again. I call this idiom, shown in Figure 25–1, a latching buttcon.

Figure 25-1

The latching buttcon was invented by applying the simple expedient of not letting the button pop back out after it has been clicked. What is remarkable about this idiom is that it moves the buttcon idiom from the imperative category—a verb—into the selection category—a noun. It has all of the idiomatic and space-saving advantages of the buttcon, except that it doesn't issue an immediate command.

The default toolbar configuration on Microsoft's Office suite of programs seems tacitly to separate the momentary, imperative buttcons from the latching, selection buttcons. Generally, they only put imperative buttcons on the top bar and put mostly selection buttcons on the others. Other than that, there are no visible differences between the two. There are no differences in their respective ToolTips, either. I don't believe that this sleight of hand has been noticed by anyone—Microsoft included—and it certainly doesn't bother me, though it is really a gross inconsistency. It is another example demonstrating how consistency is not a user interface design principle and is something that can often be flouted with impunity if the situation calls for it.

Consistency is not necessarily a virtue

The latching buttcon is widely superseding the checkbox as a single-selection idiom. Latching buttcons devote a smaller portion of their pixels to excise than checkboxes do, as you can see in Figure 25–2. They are smaller because they can rely on pattern recognition instead of text reading to indicate their purpose. Of course, this means that they exhibit the same problem as imperative buttcons: the inscrutability of the icon. We are saved once again by ToolTips.

Those tiny, yellow popup windows give us just enough text to disambiguate the buttcon, without permanently consuming too many pixels.

Figure 25-2

The venerable checkbox is an idiom that has been around since the beginning of GUIs. The buttcon is only a few years old. The latching variant of the buttcon is widely displacing the checkbox, and here is one reason why. If you compare the amount of video real estate devoted to excise (unproductive overhead) to the amount of real estate doing useful work as an operating gizmo, you see that buttcons are significantly more efficient. Not only are they more conservative of pixels overall, but the percentage of pixels devoted to useful work is much higher for latching buttons than for checkboxes. The disadvantage of the latching button is that it lacks the discriminating text of the checkbox. Ta da! Our old friend Mr. ToolTips to the rescue.

Menu items and momentary buttons often do the **flip-flop** thing.

If a flip-flop gizmo controls print resolution, for example, it will say "draft mode" until you click it then it will say "presentation mode." The control affords that you can click it, so when it says "presentation mode," it intends to mean that by pressing it you will get into presentation mode. Of course, then the gizmo changes to say "draft mode," to indicate that pressing it will get you there. This technique means that the control serves double-duty as an indicator of which state you are in. Unfortunately, it always shows "draft mode" when you are in presentation mode and vice versa. The gizmo can either serve as a state indicator or as a working control, but not both (see Figure 25–3).

The solution to this one is to either spell it out—"Change to presentation mode"—or to use some other technique entirely. Replacing it with two radio buttons is a popular choice. See Word's standard page setup dialog, which has mutually exclusive radio buttons for portrait and landscape orientation. They allow control and indicate current state. The downside is that they consume a lot of real estate.

Another approach is pictorial. Draw a picture of the page in portrait. When the user clicks on it, it rolls over onto its side to show that you are in landscape orientation. This is very memorable and engaging, but it is not necessarily very discoverable. That depends on how well the rest of your program has influenced the user to expect that a small picture is pliant and will have some effect. Cursor hinting will help. However, it's important not to put the image on top of a button. If you do, you will have just created a pictographic flip-flop with the same conflicting messages as those with a text label.

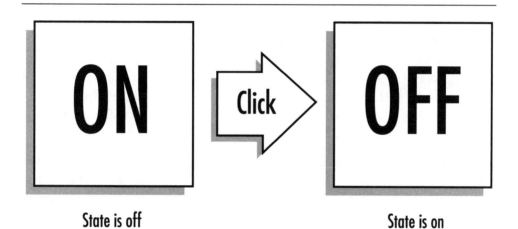

State is off   **State is on**

Figure 25-3

Flip-flop controls are very efficient. They save space by controlling two mutually exclusive options with a single gizmo. The problem with flip-flop controls is that they fail to fulfill the second duty of every gizmo—to inform the user of their current state. If the button says "ON" when the state is off, it is clear as mud what the setting is. If it says "OFF" when the state is off, though, where is the "ON" button? Don't use 'em. Not on buttons, and not on menus!

Radio buttons

A hoary variant of the checkbox is the **radio button**. The name says it all: When radios were first put in automobiles, it was discovered that manually tuning an analog radio with a rotating knob while driving was dangerous to your health, so automotive radios were offered with a newfangled panel consisting of a half-dozen chrome-plated push-buttons, each of which would twist the tuner to a pre-set station. Now you could tune to your favorite station, without taking your eyes off the road, just by pushing a button. The idiom is a powerful one, and it still has many practical uses in interaction design, but I get a spooky feeling when we use interface idioms in our programs that are copied from a tube-based, AM radio from a 1963 Studebaker.

The behavior of radio buttons is mutually exclusive, which means that when one option is selected, the previously selected option automatically deselects. Only one button can be selected at a time. We techno-geeks frequently use the word mux as a convenient contraction of the phrase "mutually exclusive," and we often use it in reference to these gizmos (some geeks use a slightly different contraction: mutex).

In consequence of mux, radio buttons always come in groups of two or more, and one radio button in each group is always selected. (Technically speaking, there is no enforcement of this mutual exclusion, nor is there enforcement of the always-one-selected rule. The individual programmer is quite free to break the rules.) A single radio button is undefined—it must act like a checkbox instead.

Radio buttons are even more wasteful of video space than checkboxes. They waste the same amount of space as checkboxes, and for the same reasons, but radio buttons are only meaningful in groups, so their waste is always multiplied. In some cases the waste is justified, particularly where it is important to show the user the full set of available choices at all times. This should sound vaguely pedagogic, and it is. Radio buttons are well suited to a teaching role, which means they can be justified on infrequently used dialog boxes but should not be visible on the surface of a sovereign application where we must cater to daily users.

For the same reason that checkboxes are traditionally square—that's how we've always done it—radio buttons are round. There are no reasons to change this shape other than aesthetic or marketing ones, and these reasons take back seat to the established tradition. Motif's radio buttons are diamonds so, I assume, this isn't hard-and-fast. Even Microsoft is susceptible to this silly and counterproductive thinking: One of the beta versions of Windows 95 was shipped with diamond-shaped radio buttons. Cooler heads prevailed, though, and the final version shipped with good 'ol round ones.

Radio buttons are one of the oldest GUI idioms, and consequently many designers see them as somehow better than other, newer idioms, but this isn't so. In some cases, radio buttons are being supplanted by more modern idioms.

As you might imagine, the buttcon has also done to the radio button what it did to the checkbox: replaced it on the surface of an application. If two or more latching buttons are grouped together and mux linked—so that only one of them at a time can be latched—they behave in exactly the same way as radio buttons. They form what I call a **radio buttcon**.

They work just like radio buttons: One is always selected—latched down—and whenever another one is pressed, the first one returns to its normal—raised—position. The alignment gizmos on Word's toolbar are an excellent example of a radio buttcon, as shown in Figure 25–4.

Figure 25-4

Word's alignment gizmos are a mux buttcon group, acting like radio buttons. One is always selected, and when another is clicked, the first one returns to its normal, raised position. This variant is a very space-conservative idiom that is well-suited for frequently used options.

Just as in all of the buttcon idioms, these are very efficient consumers of space, letting experienced users rely on pattern recognition to identify them and letting infrequent users rely on ToolTips to remind them of their purpose. First-time users will either be clever enough to learn from the ToolTips or will learn more slowly, but just as reliably, from other, parallel, pedagogic command vectors.

The combuttcon

A variant of the radio buttcon is a dropdown version. Because of its similarity to the combobox gizmo, I call this a **combuttcon**. It is shown in Figure 25–5.

Normally, it looks like a single latched buttcon, but if you click and hold on it, it drops down a menu of several latching buttcons. You slide the cursor down the same way you do on a pull-down menu to select one of the buttcon items. When you release the mouse button, the selection is made and the one you select now appears as the single buttcon on the toolbar. (Like menus, the menu of buttcons should also deploy if the user clicks once and releases. A second click makes the selection.)

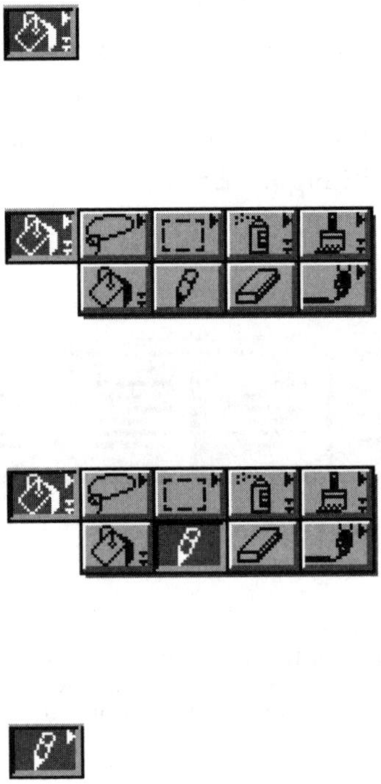

Figure 25-5

This is what I call a "combuttcon." It is a mux-linked group of latching buttcons that behave like a dropdown combobox. Pressing the mouse button while over the combuttcon drops down a menu of buttcons. Slide the cursor down to the desired one and release. The newly selected buttcon shows on the toolbar as the selected option. Think of this idiom as a way to cram several related buttcons into the space of a single one. It is less powerful than just putting up four latching buttcons, but useful when space is at a real premium.

Drawing a small, inverted triangle in the lower right corner of the combuttcon can serve as a visual hint that this buttcon is different. You can vary this idiom quite a bit, and creative software designers are doing just that in the never-ending bid to cram more functions onto screens that are always too small.

You can see a Microsoft variant in PowerPoint, where the buttcons for specifying the colors of fills, lines, text and shadows show combuttcon menus that look more like little palettes than stacks of buttcons. As you can see from Figure 25–6, these menus pack a lot of power and information into a very compact package. This facility is definitely for frequent users, particularly minnies, and not at all for first-timers. However, for the user who has at least a basic familiarity with the available tools, the idiom is instantly clear once it is discovered or demonstrated. This is an excellent gizmo idiom for sovereign-posture programs, with which users can be expected to spend long hours interacting. It demands sufficient manual dexterity to work a menu with relatively small targets but is much faster than going to the menu bar, pulling down a menu, selecting an item, waiting for the dialog box to deploy, selecting a color on the dialog box and then pressing the OK button.

Figure 25-6

This combuttcon is taken from PowerPoint. The buttcon in the upper left corner controls the "fill color" of the selected object. Clicking or pressing the buttcon causes the drop-down menu to appear. Colors are selected from the eight swatches at the top, or from one of the text items, most of which bring up selection dialogs. This dense packing of information, both input and output, is indicative of the direction in which good user interfaces are moving.

Listbox

Selection gizmos that present lists of text strings are often called picklists because they offer lists of items from which the user can pick a selection.

The picklist is a powerful tool for simplifying interaction because it eliminates the possibility of making an incorrect selection. Essentially, a picklist is a gizmo for selecting from a finite set of text strings. The first picklist was the listbox gizmo. In Windows 95, it has been made largely obsolete by the listview gizmo.

Listboxes were one of the original six gizmo classes that came with Windows
1.0. They are little text windows with a vertical scrollbar on the right-hand
edge. You can add lines of text to the box, and the scrollbar will move them up
or down. The user cannot select text as in a word processor—on a character-
by-character basis—but he can select a single line of text at a time. A listbox
variant allows multiple selection, where the user can have more than one line
selected at one time.

The original listbox gizmo was for text only—it wasn't until Windows 3.0 that
non-text items could be inserted—and that strong influence permeates its
operation to this day. A listbox filled with line after line of text unrelieved by
visual symbols is a dry desert indeed. Some adventurous programmers have
adapted them for graphics, but let's face it, most programmers aren't that
masochistic.

In Chapter 15, I talked about the problems with scrollbars, and later in this
chapter I'll talk about them some more. For now, suffice it to say that the problems with scrollbars are numerous. The traditional listbox gizmo joins a brain-
dead, text-only box with a clumsy, annoying scrollbar in a particularly fetid
combination of idioms.

I've often felt that the listbox control is the one whose potential was exploited
the least by Microsoft. In the early days of Windows, I, like many other developers, was forced to write my own listbox gizmo class. Succeeding versions of
Windows obsoleted my work, but my aspirations grew, too. Now that more
robust gizmo interfaces are here, I hope some ambitious gizmo builder creates
a really great listbox.

Actually, Microsoft seems to have done a pretty decent job in Windows 95 with
the new listview gizmo. Among other features, it allows each line of text to
automatically be preceded with an icon.

This is excellent news, because I believe that every item in every list should
show an identifying visual icon next to each text entry. Because of this, I will
now forget that listboxes ever existed and deal only with the listview gizmo for
all future design. I suggest you do the same. Too bad they didn't improve the
scrollbar while they were at it.

Design tip: Every text item in a list should have an
identifying graphic icon next to it.

What listboxes, er, I mean, listviews are good for is displaying lists of items and allowing the user to select one or more of them. They are also good idioms for providing a source of draggable items. If the items are draggable within the listview itself, it makes a fine tool for enabling the user to put items in a specific order. For example, you might want to rearrange a list of the people in your department in descending order by how frequently you work with them. There is no automatic function that will do this; you just have to drag them until it's right.

Many lists are not static but are modified by users adding, deleting and changing the text of entries. Supporting this requires the ability to key, directly into the listview, a new text item or a modification to an existing one.

Much to my surprise and pleasure, Microsoft did a pretty good job with the listview gizmo. In addition to icons, it supports drag-and-drop and edit-in-place. Both of these necessities were lacking from the older, Windows 3.x list-box gizmo. Until Windows 95, Microsoft handed rank and file programmers some pretty dull tools. It should come as no surprise that much of what they built with them is coarse and difficult to use.

The weight of history and habit still put the listbox gizmo onto a lot of dialog boxes. Thankfully, most of those dialogs appear quickly, allow the user to select a single item, and then go away. To provide better interaction, the programmer must use the listview gizmo exclusively (although I'll use the terms "listview" and "listbox" interchangeably).

Earmarking

Generally, the user selects an item in a listview as input to some function, like selecting the name of a desired font from a list of several available fonts. Selection in a listbox is discrete rather than concrete, and it is entirely conventional, with keyboard equivalents, focus rectangles and items shown with COLOR_HIGHLIGHT.

Occasionally, the listbox is used to select multiple items, and this can introduce complications. There is nothing conceptually wrong about using multiple selection in listboxes, but in practice it can be problematic. The selection idiom is very well suited for single selection but much weaker for multiple selection. In concrete data, multiple selection is contiguous, so it is, above all, visible. In discrete data, multiple selection works adequately if the entire playing field is visible at once, like the icons on a desktop. If two or more icons are selected at the same time, you can clearly see this because all of the icons are visible.

If the pool of available discrete items is too large to fit in a single view and some of it must be scrolled off screen, the selection idiom immediately becomes unwieldy. This is the normal state for listboxes and listviews. Their normal state of selection is mux; that is, when you select one thing, the previous selected thing deselects. If you are expecting different behavior, it is far too easy to select an item, then scroll it into invisibility and select a second item, forgetting that you have now *deselected* the first item because you can't see it anymore.

The alternative is equally unpalatable: the multiple selection option in the standard listbox merely disables the mux linking in the selection algorithm. Things now work absolutely perfectly: the user selects one item after another and each one stays selected. The fly in the ointment is that there is no visual indication that things are behaving differently from the norm. It is just as likely that a user will select an item, scroll it into invisibility, then spot a more desirable second item and select it *expecting the first—unseen—item to automatically deselect* by way of the mux standard. You get to choose between offending the first half of your users or the second half. Bad news.

The correct action, of course, is to use a completely different idiom from selection, one that is visually distinct. You only need to do this in the case where you have multiple selection within a list that may scroll off screen, but that case arises frequently. Please understand that what we are doing is nothing more or less than multiple selection; we are just doing it with a more appropriate visual idiom. The selection idiom is heavily used in GUIs and, in this case, it is overused. When things can scroll off the screen, multiple selection requires a better, more distinct idiom.

It just so happens we already have a well-established idiom to indicate that something is, well, let's say "chosen" instead of selected. Of course, that idiom is the checkbox. Checkboxes communicate their purpose and their settings quite clearly and, like all good idioms, are extremely easy to learn. Checkboxes are also very clearly *dis*associated from any hint of mutual exclusion. If we were to add a checkbox to every item in our problematic listbox, the user would not only clearly see which items were selected and which were not, he would also clearly see that the items were not mux linked, solving both of our problems in one stroke. I call this checkbox alternative to multiple selection **earmarking**.

An example of earmarking is shown in Figure 25–7.

Figure 25-7

Selection is normally a mutually exclusive (mux) operation. When the need arises to discard mux in order to provide multiple selection, things can become confusing if some of the items can be scrolled out of sight. Earmarking is a solution to this. Put checkboxes next to each text item and use them instead of selection to indicate the user's choices. Checkboxes are a clearly non-mux idiom and a very familiar GUI idiom. Users grasp the workings of this idiom right away.

Earmarking also solves another niggling problem with multiple selection. Multiple selection list gizmos, when they are created, have no selected items. However, in some variants, once the user selects an item, there is no way to return to a state where nothing is selected. In other words, there is no idiom for selecting nothing. If the listbox is used in the sense of an operand selector for a function dialog box, the CANCEL button provides the escape route if the user changes his mind; but if the listbox isn't on a dialog box, he may be stuck. Earmarking doesn't operate under the same rules as selection, and each item in the list is independent. One click checks the box; a second click unchecks the box.

The inability to deselect all items in a listbox has given rise to a kludge that can be seen on Word's Modify Style dialog box, among many others. There is an entry in the listbox for "(none)" or "(no selection)." What a hack! Don't stoop to this level of programming. If you need a way to turn off all of the selections, use an earmarking idiom to make choosing items different from selecting items.

Dragging-and-dropping

Listboxes can be imagined as little palettes of goodies to use in a direct-manipulation idiom. If the list in Figure 25–7 were on an email program, for example, you could click on an entry and drag it to a message to select a device for output. It's not really selection, because it is a completely captive operation. Without a doubt, many programs would benefit if their listboxes and listviews supported dragging-and-dropping.

Such listviews with draggable items are commonly used to gather items in a desired set for the user. Having two adjacent listboxes, one showing available items and the other showing chosen items, is a common GUI idiom. A pair of push-buttons placed between them allow items to be selected and transferred from one box to the other. It is so much more pleasant when the idiom is buttressed with the ability to just click-and-drag the desired item from one box to another without having to go through the intermediate steps of selection and function invocation.

Ordering listboxes

Sometimes, the need arises to drag an item from one position to another position in the same listbox. Actually, this need arises far more often than most designers seem to think. At least, I find myself frequently wishing that I could. I want to order the items in a list according to how often I use them or how important they are, for example, instead of just alphabetically. Many programs offer automatic sort facilities for important lists. The Explorer, for example, lets me sort my files by name, by type, by modification date and by size. That's nice, but what I really want is to order them by importance. Algorithmically, the program could order them by frequency of access, but that won't always get the results I want. For example, I may have to access Word's system files a lot, but they are important to Word, not to me. I'd like to press a sort button to get a good head start, then click-and-drag the Word files down to the bottom of the list. (Of course, this is the kind of thing that an experienced user wants to do after long hours of familiarization. It takes a lot of effort to fine-tune a directory like this, and the program *must* remember my exact settings from run-to-run—otherwise, the ability to reorder things is worthless.)

Being able to drag items from one place to another in a listbox is powerful, but it demands that autoscrolling be implemented. I discussed autoscrolling in Chapter 18. If you pick up an item in the list but the place you need to drop it is currently scrolled out of view, you must be able to scroll the listbox without putting down the dragged object.

Horizontal scrolling

Listboxes normally have a vertical scrollbar for moving up and down through the list, the way Santa scans his long strip of paper with the names of good boys and girls. Listboxes can also be made to scroll horizontally. This feature allows the programmer to put extra long text into the listbox with a minimum of effort. It offers nothing to the user.

Scrolling a list of text horizontally is a terrible thing, and it should never, ever need to be done. When a listbox scrolls up and down, entire lines come and go from view, but the text inside the box remains completely readable. However, when a text list is scrolled horizontally, it hides from view one or more of the first letters of every single line of text showing. This makes *none* of the lines readable and utterly destroys the continuity of the text. To see what I mean, take your bookmark and cover up just the first two characters of each line in this paragraph. See how hard it becomes to read? Yes, it is decipherable, but you have to strain at it. The purpose of computers is to eliminate strain from the lives of humans.

Design tip: Never scroll text horizontally.

The horizontal scrollbar provided for this action is the exact same gizmo as the vertical one (aside from its orientation, of course), and it was designed for a relatively permanent setting—not a temporary one. The whole action of horizontally scrolling a listbox is inappropriate: the user clicks on the scrollbar to read the right half of the entry in question, then must move the cursor back to the left and click again to restore the listbox to its normal, left-justified position. If the scroll took more than one click on the scrollbar, or worse yet, mixed an arrow click with a bar click, getting back to square one is extremely difficult and far more complex than the operation justifies.

If you find a situation that seems to call for the horizontal scrolling of text, search for alternative solutions. Begin by asking yourself why the text in the list-box is so long. Can you shorten the entries? Can you use more than one line per entry to avoid that horizontal length? Can you wrap the text onto the next line? Can you allow the user to enter aliases for the longer entries? Can you use graphical entries instead? Can you use a smaller typeface? You should alternatively be asking yourself if there is some way to widen the listbox. Can you rearrange things on the window or dialog to expand horizontally?

The best answer will usually be to wrap the text onto the next line, indenting it so it is visually different from other entries. This, of course, means that you now have a listbox with entries of variable height. The listbox gizmo from Microsoft lets you handle this with the ownerdraw option, but it demands lots of work by the programmer. Rats! The listbox gizmo just keeps giving us fits when we try to do the right thing. What a market opportunity for some clever entrepreneur.

Microsoft provides a multi-column option for their listbox gizmo, but I would still never use it. This option lets you organize listbox items like a newspaper, with snaking columns. This works for newspapers, because everything is laid out for us to read at once. However, once some of it is hidden off screen, the user must simultaneously scroll vertically with his eyes while scrolling horizontally with a mouse and scrollbar. The mental management is far too difficult. Multi-column display may help programmers, but it offers nothing to users.

Remember, I'm just talking about lists of text. For graphics, there is nothing wrong with horizontal scrollbars or horizontally scrollable windows in general. I am just saying that providing a text-based listbox with a required horizontal scrollbar is like providing a computer with a required pedal-powered electrical generator—bad news.

Entering data to a listbox

An enormous area where little work has historically been done is in enabling the user to make direct text entry into an item in a listbox. The old listbox gizmo merely punted on this, and it takes some pretty nifty coding to implement it by yourself. Of course, the need to enter text where text is output is widespread, and much of the hacky-kludgy nature of dialog box design can be directly attributed to its programmer trying to dodge the bullet of having to write edit-in-place code.

Finally, the listview and treeview gizmos in Windows 95 offer an edit-in-place facility. The Explorer in Windows 95 uses both of these gizmos, and you can see how they work by renaming a file or directory. Excellent! To rename a file, you just click twice on the desired name and enter whatever changes are desired. (I don't want to look a gift horse in the mouth, so I won't whine about the clunky way Microsoft implemented this idiom, except to say that you have to carefully delay that second click to shift into edit-in-place mode; otherwise, it will be interpreted as a double-click and launch the file. I think Microsoft could have done better, but, like I said, this is a tradeoff I'm happy to make to get free edit-in-place.) Many—no, most—of the items displayed in listboxes could benefit by being able to be edited by the user.

The edge case that makes edit-in-place a real problem is adding a new entry to the list. Most designers use other idioms to add list items: Press a button or select a menu item and a new, blank entry is added to the list, and the user can then edit-in-place its name. It would be more sensible if you could, say, double-click in the space between existing entries to create a new, blank one right there. Ahhh, wishful thinking...

The real-world solution to this problem that has actually emerged over the past few years is the combobox, which we'll talk about next.

Combobox

Windows 3.0 introduced a new gizmo called the combobox. It is—as its name suggests—a combination of a listbox and an edit field. It provides an unambiguous method of data entry into a listbox. This solution is something of a scatter-gun approach, but it is effective. The other attribute of the combobox that makes it a winner is its popup variant that is extremely conservative of video real estate.

With the combobox gizmo, there is a clear separation between the text-entry part and the list-selection part. The user's confusion is minimized, and you can bet that the programming was significantly easier. For single selection, the combobox is a superb gizmo. The edit field can be used to enter new items, and it also shows the current selection in the list. When the current selection is showing in the edit field, the user can edit it there—sort of a poor man's edit-in-place.

Because the edit field of the combobox shows the current selection, the combobox is by nature a single-selection gizmo. There is no such thing as a multiple-selection combobox. Single selection implies mux, which is one of the reasons why the combobox is fast replacing groups of radio buttons for mux-linked options. The other reasons include its space efficiency and its ability to add items dynamically, something that radio buttons cannot do.

When the dropdown variants of the combobox are used, the gizmo shows the current selection without consuming space to show the list of choices.

392 PART VI: THE GIZMOS

Essentially, it becomes a list-on-demand, sort of like a menu provides a list of immediate commands on demand. A combobox is a popup listbox.

The video efficiency of the combobox allows it to do something remarkable for a gizmo of such depth and complexity: it can reasonably reside permanently on a program's main screen. No listbox in a supporting role could ever do that. It can even fit comfortably on a toolbar. It is a very effective gizmo for deployment on a sovereign-posture application. There are currently four comboboxes visible on my word processor's toolbars, for example. This effectively crams a huge amount of information and usefulness into a very small space. Using comboboxes on the toolbar is more effective than putting the equivalent functions on menus, because the comboboxes show me their current selection without requiring any action on my part, such as pulling down a menu to see the current status. Once again, the gizmo that delivers the goods with the smallest permanent video footprint wins the Darwinian battle for pixels.

If drag-and-drop is implemented in listboxes, it should also be implemented in comboboxes. For example, being able to open a combobox, scroll to a choice and then drag the choice onto a document under construction is a very powerful idiom. Because comboboxes fit so well on toolbars, the idiom has real appeal for adding direct manipulation to sovereign applications. Drag-and-drop functionality should be a standard part of comboboxes.

The utility of the combobox collapses if the situation calls for multiple selection; the idiom just can't handle it, and you must return to the plain listbox. The listbox consumes significant space on-screen—enough so that it should probably never be considered practical for permanent deployment. Instead, it should be relegated to transient dialog boxes.

Treeview gizmo

Windows 95 brings us this new gizmo. It is a listview that can present hierarchical data. It shows a sideways tree, with icons for each entry. The entries can be expanded or compressed the way many outline processors work. As a programmer, I like this presentation. It is used for the left half of the Explorer, and I find the format of the display to be effective—certainly more effective than scattering icons around on my desktop. Unfortunately, it is problematic for users because of the trouble many people have with hierarchical data structures. If the treeview contents are restricted to no more than two levels, however, it can nicely show a monocline grouping of data.

Entry and Display Gizmos

26

In the last chapter, I discussed imperative and selection gizmos. In this chapter, I will examine the remaining two types of gizmos, those for entry and display. Display gizmos enable the user to configure the form and appearance of their windows. The job of entry gizmos is to accept the user's unstructured data, which puts them squarely in between error-prone, fallible humans and rigid, deterministic data management software.

Entry gizmos

Entry gizmos enable the user to enter new information into the program, rather than merely selecting information from an existing list.

The most basic entry gizmo is a text-edit field. Like selection gizmos, entry gizmos represent nouns to the program. Because one half of a combobox is an edit field, some combobox variants qualify as entry gizmos, too. Also, any gizmo

393

that lets the user enter a numeric value is an entry gizmo. Many of the new gizmos from third-party developers—like spinners, gauges, sliders and knobs—fit in this segment. Microsoft has not shipped any other standard entry gizmos, so there isn't a single dominant form, but in a vacuum standards form from the bottom up, so stay tuned.

Bounding

I call any gizmo that restricts the available set of values that the user can enter a **bounded-entry gizmo**. A slider that moves from 1 to 100, for example, is bounded (but don't confuse this with a "bound" gizmo used for database access).

Regardless of the user's actions, no number outside those specified by the program can be entered with a bounded gizmo. The essential fact about bounded gizmos is that it is impossible to enter an invalid value with one.

Conversely, an edit field can accept any data the user keys into it. I call an open-ended entry idiom like this an **unbounded-entry gizmo**.

With an unbounded-entry gizmo, it is easy to enter an invalid value. The program may subsequently reject it, of course, but the user can still enter it.

Simply put, bounded gizmos should be used wherever bounded values are needed. If the program needs a number between 7 and 35, presenting the user with a gizmo that will accept any numeric value from −1,000,000 to +1,000,000 is not doing him any favors. He would much rather be presented with a gizmo that embodies 7 as its bottom limit and 35 as its upper limit. Users are smart, and they will immediately comprehend and respect the limits of their sandbox.

Design tip: Offer bounded gizmos for bounded input.

It is important to understand that I am talking here about a quality of the entry gizmo and not of the data. To be a bounded gizmo, it needs to clearly communicate, preferably visually, the acceptable data boundaries to the user. An edit field that rejects the user's input *after* he has entered it is *not* a bounded control. Edit fields are never bounded entry fields.

Most quantitative values needed by software are bounded, yet many programs allow unbounded entry with edit fields. When the user inadvertently enters a value that the program cannot accept, the program issues an error message box. This is cruelly teasing the user with possibilities that aren't. "What would you like for dessert? We've got everything," we say. "Ice cream," you respond. "Sorry, we don't have any," we say. "How about pie?" you innocently ask. "Nope," we say. "Cookies?" "Nope." "Candy?" "Nope." "Chocolate?" "Nope." "What, then?" you scream in anger and frustration. "Don't get mad," we say indignantly, "we have plenty of fruit compote." This is how the user feels when we put up a dialog box with an unbounded edit field and ask for the number of desired veeblefetzers. He enters "17" and we reward this innocent entry with an error message box that says "You can only have between 4 and 8 veeblefetzers." This is extremely bad user interface design, and don't ever let me catch you doing it. You should use a bounded gizmo that automatically limits the input to 4, 5, 6, 7 or 8.

If the bounded set of choices is composed of text rather than numbers, you can still use a slider of some type, or a combobox or listbox. Figure 26-1 shows a bounded slider used by Microsoft in the Display Settings dialog box of Windows 95. It works like a slider or scrollbar but has four discrete positions that represent distinct resolution settings. They could easily have used a combobox in its place, but isn't the slider nicer to look at and friendlier? Part of its appeal comes from the innate visibility of the gizmo: you can see the scope of the control just by looking. A combobox isn't much smaller, but it keeps its cards hidden—a less friendly stance.

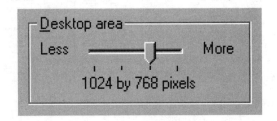

Figure 26-1

A bounded gizmo only lets you enter valid values. It does not let you enter invalid values, only to reject them when you try to move on. This figure shows a bounded slider gizmo from the Display Settings dialog in Windows 95. The little slider has four discrete positions. As you drag the slider from left to right, the legend underneath it changes from "640 by 480 pixels" to "800 by 600 pixels" to "1024 by 768 pixels" to "1280 by 1024 pixels." Why didn't they use a combobox? Which would you prefer? I rest my case.

If the program requires a numeric value that must remain within specific boundaries, give the user a control that intrinsically communicates those limits and prevents him from entering a value outside of the boundaries. The scrollbar control class does this; it is a bounded gizmo—the only one that comes with Windows. Although scrollbars have significant drawbacks, they are exemplary in one area: they allow the user to enter quantitative information by analogy. Scrollbars allow the user to specify numeric values in relative terms, rather than by directly keying in a number. That is, the user moves the sliding thumb to indicate, by its relative position, a proportional value for use inside the program. They are less useful for entering precise numbers, though many programs use them for that purpose. Newer gizmos, like spinners, are better for entering exact numbers.

Spinners

A new gizmo type, commonly called a **spinner**, is rapidly gaining currency, especially in Microsoft's Office suite.

It grays the difference between bounded and unbounded gizmos to a certain extent. The spinner gizmo is a small edit field with two half-height buttons attached, as shown in Figure 26-2.

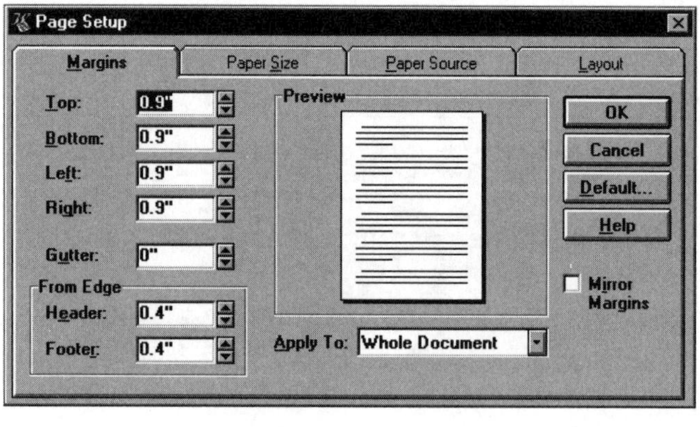

Figure 26-2

The Page Setup dialog from Word for Windows makes heavy use of the spinner gizmo. On the left side of the dialog, you see a stack of seven of these new controls, whose popularity is growing fast. By clicking on either of the small, arrowed buttons, the specific numeric value is made to increase or decrease in small, discrete steps. If the user wants to make a large change in one action, or to enter a precise setting, he can use the edit field portion for direct text entry. The arrow button portion of the gizmo embodies bounding, while the edit field portion does not. Does that make this a bounded gizmo?

Using either of the two small arrow buttons enables the user to change the value in the edit window in small, discrete steps. These steps are bounded—the value won't go above the upper limit set by the program or below the lower limit. If the user wants to make a large change in one action, or to enter a specific number, he can do so by clicking in the edit window portion and directly entering keystrokes into it, just like entering text into any other edit field. Unfortunately, the edit window portion of this gizmo is unbounded, leaving the user free to enter values that are out of bounds, or even unintelligible garbage. In the Page Setup dialog box in the figure, if the user enters a bad value, the program behaves like most other rude programs, issuing an error message box explaining the upper and lower boundaries and requiring the user to press the OK button to continue.

Overall, the spinner is an excellent idiom and can be used in place of plain edit fields for most bounded entry. In Part VII, we will discuss ways to improve gizmo error handling.

Unbounded-entry fields

The primary unbounded-entry gizmo is the text-edit gizmo. This simple box allows the user to key in any text value.

Edit fields are usually very simple boxes where a word or two of data can be entered by the user, but they can also be moderately sophisticated text editors in their own right. The user can edit text within them using the standard tools of concrete selection (as discussed in Chapter 16) with either the mouse or the keyboard.

Text-edit gizmos are generally used either as data-entry fields in database applications, as option-entry fields in dialog boxes, or as the entry field in a combobox. In all of these roles they are frequently called upon to do the work of a bounded-entry gizmo. However, if the desired values are finite, the text-edit gizmo should not be used. If the acceptable values are numeric, use a bounded numeric-entry gizmo, such as a slider or knob, instead. If the list of acceptable values is composed of text strings, then a picklist should be used so the user is not forced to type.

Sometimes the set of acceptable values is finite but too big to be practical for a picklist. For example, a program may require a string of any 30 alphabetic characters excluding spaces, tabs and punctuation marks. In this case, a text-edit gizmo is probably unavoidable even though its use is bounded. If these are the only restrictions, however, the edit gizmo can be designed to reject non-alphabetic characters and characters after 30, thus making it bounded.

Validation

From the gizmo's point of view, there is really no such thing as invalid data. Data can only be adjudged invalid in the context of the program. For example, "1995" is valid in a text-entry gizmo that gathers the year but not in one that gathers the month. Physically, an unbounded-entry gizmo cannot recognize invalid data—only the program can make the actual determination of validity. From the program's point of view, a *bounded*-entry gizmo will only hand it valid input. Thus, by definition, an *unbounded* gizmo *can* return invalid input to the program.

An unbounded gizmo that is used to gather bounded data is in a moral bind. It must serve two bosses: The gizmo must blithely accept whatever data the user keys in; then, if the program judges that input to be invalid, the gizmo is forced to be the bearer of someone else's bad news. I believe that this moral bind of putting unbounded gizmos in the role of accepting bounded input is one of the most important contributors to user dissatisfaction with computers.

Accepting bounded data into unbounded gizmos causes user dissatisfaction

If the data is bounded—but not too bounded—the program must let the user enter the data, only to reject it afterwards. Although there are some mitigating steps, there really is no good way to solve this problem. Unless...

There *is* one way to solve this problem: the program should just go ahead and accept whatever the user enters. In other words, eliminate semi-bounded data. Either coerce the correct data with a bounded gizmo, or accept whatever the user gives you in an unbounded gizmo. Most programmers reject this solution. They do not feel that their programs can accept, for example, "asdf;lkj" as input to a social security number field. I'll wait until Chapter 29, "Managing Exceptions," to argue the point.

The way most programmers have historically dealt with this dilemma is by creating what I call a **validation gizmo**, or an unbounded text-entry gizmo with built-in editing.

Many edits are commonplace, covering such things as dates, phone numbers, zip codes and social security numbers, and are packaged with text-edit gizmos as a unit, particularly for database data-entry applications. You can purchase variants of the text-entry gizmo that will only allow numbers or letters or phone numbers, or that will reject spaces and tabs, for example.

Although the validation gizmo is a widespread idiom, it is a very poor one. Tactically, though, it is often necessary, so we'll ignore the bigger issues for now and look at practical ways to make it better. The key to successfully designing a validation gizmo is to give the user generous feedback. An entry gizmo that merely refuses to accept input is just plain rude, not helpful, and will guarantee an angry, resentful and upset user.

A fundamental improvement, based on the axiom that things that behave differently should look different (Chapter 21), is to make validation gizmos visually distinct from unvalidated gizmos. I recommend using a different color and line style for the gizmo's border. A dashed line in blue instead of solid black would alert the user that something was up. He would then observe it more closely than usual when he used it for the first time, and would be poised to learn about its unique behavior.

Design tip: Show validated-entry gizmos with a different border.

The main tool for validation gizmos is to provide rich status feedback to the user. Unfortunately, the edit gizmo as we know it today provides virtually no built-in support for feedback of any kind. The designer must specify such feedback mechanisms in detail, or none will be provided.

Some gizmos reject the user's keystrokes as he enters them. When a gizmo actively rejects keystrokes during the entry process, I call it a **hot validation gizmo**. A text-only entry gizmo, for example, may accept only alphabetic characters and refuse to allow numbers to be entered. Some gizmos work the opposite way, rejecting any keystrokes other than the numeric digits 0 through 9. Other gizmos reject spaces, tabs, dashes and other punctuation in real-time. Some variants can get pretty intelligent and reject some numbers based on live calculations, for example, unless they pass a checksum algorithm.

When a hot validation gizmo rejects a keystroke, it must make it clear to the user that it has done so. It should also clue the user into why it made the rejection, though that is more difficult. If an explanation is proffered, the user will be less inclined to assume the rejection is arbitrary. He will also be in a better position to give the program what it wants.

The user is expecting to be able to enter keystrokes at will; this is the nature of the keyboard. If the gizmo is going to reject some keystrokes based on their value, it must clearly communicate this to the user.

Sometimes the range of possible data is such that the program cannot validate it until the user has completed his entry, rather than at each individual keystroke. The editing step then takes place only when the gizmo loses focus, that is, when the user is done with the field and moves on to the next one. The editing step must also take place if the user closes the dialog—or invokes another function if the gizmo is not on a dialog box. If the gizmo waits until the user finishes entering data before it edits the value, I call it a **cold validation gizmo**.

The gizmo may wait until a name is fully entered, for instance, before it interrogates a database to see if it is an existing entry. Each character is valid by itself, yet the whole may not pass muster. The program could attempt to verify the name as each character is entered, but that would probably bring the network and server to their knees with the extra workload. Besides, although the program would know at any given instant whether the name was valid, the user could still move on while the name was in an invalid state.

Another way to address this is by maintaining a countdown timer in parallel with the input and reset it on each keystroke. If the countdown timer ever hits zero, do your validation processing. The timer should be set to around 400 milliseconds, although you may wish to user test this for a more precise number. The effect of this is that as long as the user is entering a keystroke faster than once every 400 ms, the system is extremely responsive. If the user pauses for more than 400 ms, the program reasonably assumes that the user has paused to think (something that takes months in CPU terms) and goes ahead and performs its analysis of the input so far.

To provide rich visual feedback, the entry field could change colors to reflect its estimate of the validity of the entered data. The field could show in shades of pink until the program judged the data valid, where it would change to white or green.

Another good solution to the validation gizmo problem is what I call a **clue box**.

This little popup window looks and behaves just like a ToolTip. By convention, ToolTips are yellow, so the clue box would be pink or some other color, and it explains the range of acceptable data for a validation gizmo, either hot or cold. Whereas a ToolTip appears when the cursor sits for a moment on a gizmo, a clue box would appear as soon as the gizmo detects an invalid character (it can also display unilaterally just like a ToolTip if the cursor sits unmoving on the field for a second or so). If the user enters, for example, a non-numeric character in a numeric-only field, the program would put up a clue box near the point of the offending entry, yet without obscuring it. It would say, for example, "0–9." Short, terse but very effective. Yes, the user is rejected, but he is not also ignored. The clue box would work for cold validation, too, as shown in Figure 26-3.

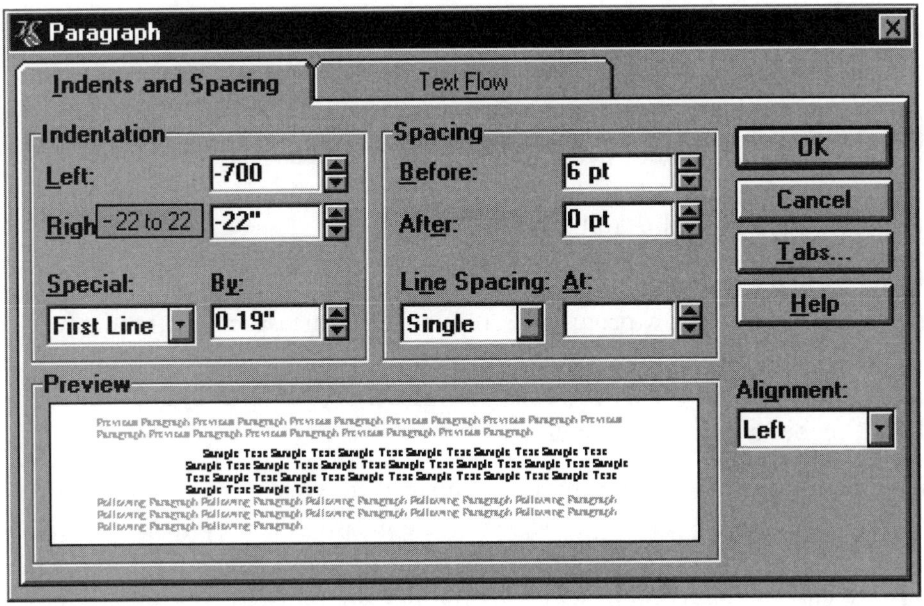

Figure 26-3

The ToolTip idiom is so effective I'm surprised that it hasn't been extended into other uses. Instead of yellow ToolTips offering flyover labels for buttons, we could have pink ones offering flyover limits for unbounded edit fields. These could easily double as error-message-box-eliminating hint windows that I call clue boxes. In the example shown here, when the user enters some value lower than the lowest allowable value, instead of stopping the proceedings with an idiotic error message box, the program could replace the value in the edit field with the lowest allowable value (–22 in this case) and display the pink clue box that modelessly explains the reason for the substitution. The user can enter some new value or accept the minimum but in either case he can proceed without getting an error message.

Typically, an edit field is used to enter a numeric value needed by the program, like the point size of a font. The user can enter anything he wants, from "5" to "500," and the field will accept it and return the value to the owning program. If the user enters garbage, the gizmo must make some kind of decision. In Microsoft Word, for example, if I enter "asdf" as a font point size, the program issues an error message box informing me that "This is not a valid number" and then reverts the size to its previous value. I think the error message box is rather silly, but the summary rejection of my meaningless input is perfectly appropriate. But what if I had keyed in the value "nine"? The program rejects it with the same curt error message box. I believe that if the gizmo were programmed to think of itself as a numeric-entry gizmo, it might take a different approach. It doesn't bother me if the program converts the "nine" into a "9," but it certainly is incorrect when it says that "nine" is "not a valid number." Without a doubt, it is valid and the program has put its foot in its mouth.

Barring other tools, a simple rejection of input data is better than a rejection coupled with an error message box. For example, if a cold validation gizmo can only accept a number between 5 and 25, and the user enters "50," the gizmo should change to 25 and proceed. If the user enters "2," the gizmo should change to 5 and proceed. If the user enters "asdf," the gizmo should revert to the previously valid value and proceed.

It's nice when a text-edit gizmo is smart enough to recognize appropriate qualifiers. For example, if a program is requesting a measurement, and the user enters "5i" or "5in" or "5 inches," the gizmo should not only report the result as *five*, but it should report *inches* as well. If the user enters "5mm," the gizmo should report it as five *millimeters*.

Say that the field is requesting a column width. The user can enter either a number or a number and an indicator of the measurement system as described above. The user could also be allowed to enter the word "default," and the program would set the column width to the default value for the program. The user could alternately enter "best fit," and the program would measure all of the entries in the column and choose the most appropriate width for the circumstances. There is a problem with this scenario, however, because the words "default" and "best fit" must be in the user's head rather than in the program somewhere. This is easy to solve, though. All we need to do is provide the same functionality through a combobox. The user can drop down the box and find a few standard widths and the words "default" and "best fit." The dropdown would look like the one in Figure 26-4.

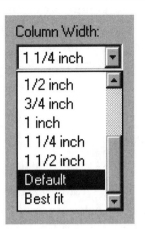

Figure 26-4

The dropdown combobox makes an excellent tool for bounded entry fields, because it can accommodate entry values other than numbers. The user doesn't have to remember or type words like "default" or "best fit" because they are there to be chosen from the drop-down list. The program interprets the words as the appropriate number, and everyone is satisfied.

The user can pull down the combobox, see the words "Default" and "Best fit" and choose the appropriate one. With this idiom, the information has migrated from the user's head into the program where it visible and choosable. This is good.

In Chapter 29, "Managing Exceptions," I'll talk about using audible feedback with validation gizmos.

Using an edit field for output

The text-edit gizmo, with its familiar system font and visually articulated white box, strongly affords data entry as well as data output. Yet software developers frequently use the text-edit gizmo for output only. The edit gizmo certainly works as an output field, but to use this gizmo for output only is to bait-and-switch your user, and he will not be amused. If you have text data to output, use a text gizmo and not a text-edit gizmo. If you want to show the amount of free space on disk, for example, don't use a text-edit field, because the user is likely to think that he can get more free space by entering a bigger number. At least that is what the gizmo is telling him with its equivalent of body language. There's a good example of this in Chapter 11 (see Figure 11-6).

On the other hand, if you are going to output changeable information, go ahead and output it in a fully editable text gizmo and wire it up internally so that it works as it appears to. For example, output the volume name in a text-edit gizmo so that the user can directly edit the visible name to change it on the disk.

Rich text gizmos

With the advent of the rich text gizmo in Windows 95, it will be very possible for simple text-edit gizmos to take on the excise overhead of word processors.

It is important for designers to be clear about the scope of options that should be exposed to the user when edit fields are implemented with rich text gizmos. Activating entire paragraph formatting subsystems is not appropriate for simple entry fields that are expecting a single word or number as input.

The rich text gizmo isn't really useful as a tool for entering structured data for fitting into rigidly structured databases. It is, however, handy for such tasks as composing email messages or taking notes.

Insert and overtype

The handling of insert and overtype is another example where good judgment is called for. In most text editors there is a user-settable option toggling between insert and overtype mode. These two modes are omnipresent in the world of word processors and, like FORTRAN, never seem to die. Insert and overtype are modes that would make Larry Tesler scream: they are significant changes in the behavior of an interface, with no visible indication until after the user has interacted, and there is no clear way into or out of these modes except by means of a rather obscure key.

Fifteen years ago when I regularly used a primitive, character-based text editor, I used both modes. Although I was a power user, I needed all the help I could get with that program, and overtype mode let me shave away many keystrokes. Today, with my modern GUI word processor, I can't imagine using overtype mode, and I can't imagine anyone else actually wanting to use anything other than insert mode, but I know they are out there—I had a long exchange on the Net with one of them just recently. For edit fields of one line, adding controls beyond simple unimodal entry and editing is foolish—the potential for trouble is far greater than the advantages delivered to users. Of course, if you are writing a word processor, the story is different.

Display gizmos

I call the fourth category display gizmos. These are the adjectives of the gizmo grammar, modifying how our screens look.

These gizmos are used to display and manage the visual presentation of information on the screen rather than the information itself. Typical examples include scrollbars and screen splitters. Gizmos that control the way things are displayed visually on the screen fall into this category, as do those that merely display static information for output only. These include paginators, rulers, guidelines, grids, groupboxes, and those 3D lines called dips and bumps. Although many of these gizmos are familiar to Windows users under various names, only groups and scrollbars actually come with Windows.

Probably the simplest display gizmo is the text gizmo. This variant of the STATIC control class merely displays a written message at some location on the screen. The management job that it performs is pretty prosaic, serving only to label other gizmos and to output data that cannot or should not be changed by the user.

Text gizmos instead of edit gizmos

The only significant problem with text gizmos is that they are often used where edit gizmos should be. Most information in a computer can be changed by the user. Why not allow the user to change it at the same point the software displays it? Why should the mechanism to input a value be different from the mechanism to output that value? The answer is that the program should not separate these related functions. In almost all cases where the program displays a value, it should do so in an editable field so the user can click on it and change it.

For example, the Windows 3.1 File Manager program shown in Figure 26-5 displays the name of the disk drive currently displayed but, in order to change its value, the user must go to the menus and request a dialog box. The user should be able to enter the new value directly where the program displays it. Of course, this is a low-frequency operation, so putting a permanent edit gizmo there may not be necessary (it would then have to be in the tab-navigation sequence and need a keyboard accelerator). Instead, if the user clicks the mouse anywhere over the name, an edit gizmo could appear, filled with the current value as a fully selected default and allow the user to enter a new name or modify the old one.

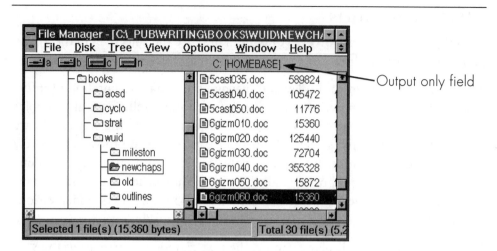

Figure 26-5

The Windows 3.1 File Manager program displays the name of the current disk volume. The user should be able to change the name by keying it in right here where the program outputs it, instead of having to go through a menu item and dialog box. Because the frequency of update is low, it doesn't need a permanent edit field, but rather, when the user clicks directly on the volume name, an edit field should appear to allow entry. Once the name has been entered, a click outside of the field, or a keypress of ENTER closes the field and records the new name.

Those darned scrollbars

Scrollbars are a very frustrating gizmo, fraught with problems, hard to manipulate and wasteful of pixels. The idiom is another of those originals that came from Xerox PARC, so it has a certain cachet that is difficult to overcome. The scrollbar is, without a doubt, both overused and under-examined. In its role as a window scroller—a display gizmo—its application is appropriate, at least. In many cases, though, it is used where it shouldn't be only because designers don't seem to have any better ideas. That's a bad rationale for any aspect of software design.

The singular advantage of the scrollbar—aside from its availability—is its proportional rendering of value. The scrollbar's **thumb** is the central, draggable box that indicates the current position.

If a scrollbar represents percentage, for example, the user can see that a scrollbar whose thumb is about equidistant between the ends represents a quantity of 50%. The fact that the scrollbar conveys no information about its terminal values detracts considerably from its usefulness as a sliding value selector. The scrollbar's proportional rendering, flawed in implementation though it may be, is an excellent type of visual feedback. The lessons of the scrollbar should not be ignored by gizmo designers.

A big shortcoming of the scrollbar is its parsimonious doling out of information to the user. It should instead generously inform us with information about the information it is managing. The new Windows 95 scrollbar uses thumbs that are proportionally sized to show the percentage of the document that is currently visible. It could also tell us

○ What page we are on

○ How many pages there are in total

○ The first sentence (or item) of each page as we scroll with the thumb

○ The page number (record number, graphic) as we scroll with the thumb

Additionally, the scrollbar is parsimonious with functions. It manages the bulk of our navigation within documents; it should give us powerful tools for going where we want to go quickly and easily. It could

○ Offer us buttons for skipping ahead by pages/chapters/sections

○ Offer us buttons for jumping to the beginning and end of the document

○ Give us tools for setting bookmarks that we can quickly return to

The scrollbar also demands a high degree of precision with the mouse. Scrolling down or up in a document is generally much easier than scrolling down *and* up in document. You must position the mouse cursor with great care, taking your attention away from the data you are scrolling.

The scrollbar consumes a relatively large amount of video real estate. For what it takes, it doesn't give much back to us. I'd really like to see some better scrolling idioms come into popular use.

New Gizmos

27

Gizmos are valuable tools for interacting with users because they encapsulate lots of complex behavior in a ready-to-use package. The ready availability of gizmos causes us to rely on them for designing user interfaces. We use them because they are available. Unfortunately, the set of gizmos that come with Windows is pallid and thin. Those available through the emerging APIs like VBX, OCX and OLE show promise but are still incomplete and not yet available to all tool platforms. Gizmos remain a significant arena for invention and entrepreneurship. Here are some ideas for future gizmo innovation.

Directly manipulable tools

The most striking area for invention is in bounded-entry gizmos. So many programs offer us dialog boxes with edit fields or spinners to gather data that could more easily be entered through direct manipulation. Using click-and-drag idioms in place of entry gizmos not only makes input clearer and easier, but it can also automatically change a previously unbounded gizmo to a bounded one.

One of my clients had a program with some rudimentary drawing tools, including a drop shadow and a drawing grid. The drop shadow put a black shape behind and slightly offset from any graphical object to make it visually distinct. The drawing grid forced all drawing-related direct manipulations to normalize to an invisible grid, allowing drawn objects to neatly line up automatically.

Both of these facilities were adjustable by way of simple, nearly identical dialog boxes. The drop shadow offset (or grid span) was controlled by two edit gizmos, one specifying the horizontal offset, the other specifying the vertical offset. I replaced both of these with what I call a **sun gizmo**, as shown in Figure 27-1.

Because drop shadows usually appear at the bottom and to the right of an object, the sun gizmo showed a small, round sun above and to the left of a sample graphical object. The user could click and drag the sun around and, as he did so, the drop shadow under the sample object would move in response, growing or shrinking in the vertical and horizontal axes. The physical limitations of where the sun could be dragged automatically bounded the gizmo, so the user could not "enter" an invalid offset. The drop shadow could easily be turned off by dragging the sun to the center of the object, where the shadow would, according to the laws of physics, disappear.

When the user moved his cursor over the sun, cursor hinting indicated that the sun was directly manipulable.

The grid in this program was similarly controlled through a small dialog box with two edit gizmos for specifying the horizontal and vertical interval of the grid. I replaced these gizmos with a swatch of grid whose spacing the user could adjust by direct manipulation. When the cursor moved over the swatch, the cursor changed to indicate that the sample grid was pliant. The user could then just click-and-drag anywhere in the swatch to adjust the spacing. Dragging up closed the vertical interval. Dragging down opened it. Dragging right or left worked the same for the horizontal axis. In order to adjust one axis without inadvertently affecting the other, we used a drag threshold like the one described in Chapter 18.

If the resolution—the drag distance required to increment by one—is high enough, no supporting edit fields are needed to set the values at exactly some

Figure 27-1

The small image of a sun in the upper left corner is a directly manipulable idiom for telling the program how to place a drop shadow on the selected object. Not only is the direct manipulation easier and less obscure than entering a numeric value, but the very nature of the sun also incorporates protective borders: the user cannot physically drag it to an invalid location; therefore, he cannot inadvertently enter an invalid value. This means that the sun gizmo is a bounded gizmo.

desired number. Of course, that number would have to be displayed either on (or alongside) the sun or swatch for this to work well. The principle of "enter where you output" demands that those numbers be editable anyway, for those who would rather keyboard than directly manipulate.

Both the sun gizmo and the grid swatch gizmo replaced ugly, inappropriate text gizmos with the direct manipulation of graphical objects that were visually appropriate to the desired result. The user could stay in context, even though the tools were used rarely enough to justify them residing on dialog boxes. Both gizmos finessed away the need for text entry and provided visual, bounded, direct manipulation of the settings.

Rubberweeks

Another client needed a calendar gizmo for a scheduling application, so we designed a new gizmo that we called **rubberweeks**. The requirements for this gizmo included the ability to adapt to any time scale from several hours to several weeks. In addition, the user needed to be able to place small icons on the calendar to indicate deadlines and other events that need to be firmly anchored in time.

The key feature of rubberweeks was its ability to stretch. When the user dragged along it with the mouse, the calendar scrolled, but when the user dragged with the ALT-shifted mouse, the calendar's scale changed. If the user dragged right, the scale stretched longer. If the user dragged left, the scale stretched shorter. If the user needed to schedule a series of events that would occur within the next three days, for example, he could ALT-stretch the rubberweeks to display a total of just three days. This allowed him to take maximum advantage of the space available on the screen.

By double-clicking on the rubberweeks, a small, triangular icon could be physically placed on the calendar to indicate a deadline. Once placed, the icon could be freely dragged to adjust its place in time.

The advantages of gizmos like the sun, the grid swatch and rubberweeks are their proportional representations of the information they represent and manage. To duplicate their functionality with existing gizmos would require descending into a world of text, where abstract symbols need interpretation. In the graphic world, the sun gizmo shows the current setting visually and immediately, and the control of it is direct and proportional. Dragging a sun gizmo to set the extent of a drop shadow much more closely approaches the ideal of a directly manipulable interface. Like the carpenter swinging his hammer, the user can place the sun just so, and clearly and immediately receive direct feedback regarding his input. He doesn't have to wonder whether three pixels are too few or four pixels are too many. He can *see* when it's just right.

Extraction gizmos

One of the most noticeable attributes of text, edit gizmos is how stupid they generally are. If the application at hand calls for entering an address, for example, there are no "address" gizmos, yet that is just what we need. Validation gizmos exist, true, but their ability to adapt to variable input, like a whole address, is nil. In fact, they are designed purposely to reject variable input. A simple zip code validation gizmo, for example, will reject anything that doesn't fit the archetype of a zip code: five (or nine) contiguous digits.

An address gizmo is an example of what I call an extraction gizmo.

This is a completely different approach to the problem of data entry. An extraction gizmo parses the contents of a free-form text-entry gizmo according to some rules about the general class of input. For example, instead of having one field for street address, one for apartment, suite or mail stop, one for city, one for state, and one for zip code, there is a single text-entry gizmo, several lines tall. The user keys in the entire desired address in the single field, and the gizmo makes sense of the various parts of that address.

A normal text-edit gizmo has a method (or entry point, or value, depending on your language/coding model) to examine its "contents." The contents of a normal zip code entry field would be whatever the user entered. An extraction gizmo would have several other "content" examination methods in addition to the traditional one. They would include

- Street address line
- Street
- Number
- Geographical designation
- Second address line
- Suite number
- Building
- Apartment
- Mail stop
- Floor
- City line
- City
- State
- Province
- District
- Zip code
- Postal code
- Country

Not all of these values would be filled, only those that are relevant, depending on what the user entered. The gizmo would do its best to determine which parts of the entered text belonged in each category. There are basically three levels of discrimination in this process. The gizmo would return the text verbatim as the user entered it. Each line of the address would be separated: Street address line, Second address line, City line. Then each separate element of the address would be parsed into its appropriate category.

A gizmo like this enables users to enter addresses the same way they manually prepare an envelope: by typing the address as a block. The computer does the work of separating the fields out for efficient categorizing in a database program. A program would then be able to, for example, sort the addresses by street name or by zip code even though the address was entered as just a human-readable block.

Useful types of extraction gizmos include those for proper names, email addresses, physical descriptions and telephone numbers. An extraction gizmo could easily pull a person's first name, last name, middle name, honorific, rank and title from a single field so the user isn't forced to manually separate them out at entry time.

Yes, there will be an error rate, but it won't be high and it won't be significant. An address-parsing algorithm can easily pull apart the vast majority of addresses. If someone tried deliberately to enter garbage, the extraction gizmo would probably fail to discriminate accurately, but then again, how many of your employees deliberately enter garbage? An end user with a shrink-wrapped application who deliberately enters garbage into his own system certainly won't blame *you* for the problem.

When coded into a dialog box, a telephone-number extraction gizmo, for example, would recognize phone numbers by applying a series of simple lexical and semantic rules. The outputs of the field would consist of the raw text as entered by the user, along with an array of possible phone, fax, cellular and pager numbers. If the gizmo is unable to discern these numbers from the contents, well, it can't, but in most cases where these numbers are discernible by humans they are also discernible by software. Let's take an example: Say that I key this text into a phone number extraction gizmo:

```
415-366-2300w, Home:367-9824 (415) 367-9976 fax 508 2031 pager
```

I entered some pretty torturous stuff here: inconsistent and missing symbols and varying labels. Can you figure out what I've typed? Sure you can. I bet a computer program could, too! The first number is a well-formed number with area code, prefix and body. It has a "w" appended to it that can reasonably be interpreted as being my work phone. The comma is just a separator. The next number is prefixed by the word "Home:" so it's nature is clear. The absence of an area code is not much of a crisis. The program could easily assume it is a 415 number—the same as all of the others. If it were different, it is likely that I would have entered it. If not, it's not a hanging offense. The third number is trickier. Certainly, it a well-formed number, but what is it? The word "fax" is ambiguous. It could be referring to the third number or the fourth number. The last word in the entry, "pager," disambiguates the two because it must be referring to the fourth number, so "fax" must refer to the third. The lack of a hyphen in the fourth number should be no problem because the number is still a recognizable, well-formed phone number.

If I wanted to really tax the gizmo, I could enter something more problematic, like this:

```
4558, 1-800-555-1212 25433 976-PORN
```

Well, this would certainly put a strain on things, but it wouldn't be impossible. The first number, 4558, is not a recognizable phone number, but it is a recognizable fragment of a phone number. When you want to call someone within your company through a private PBX, you often just enter a four-digit number. If the PBX's prefix is 488—which the program is likely to already know—the number from the outside would be 488-4558. The second number is still a well-formed number; it is just more complete than many others. It includes the long distance prefix "1" and adds a five-digit extension. We guess that it is an extension because it is not delimited from the 800 number. If it were four digits, we might have trouble discriminating between its being an extension or another in-house number. The last number is, well, recognizable even though it doesn't use all-numeric digits because its form is recognizable. Software might otherwise have difficulty determining that "976-PORN" is a phone number, except that we are talking about a field that is designed to process phone numbers—that's a big hint.

If experience is any guide, many of you are probably having trouble swallowing the idea of extraction gizmos. They seem to fly in the face of our tradition of guaranteed data integrity. Well, yes and no. We will discuss this aspect of extraction gizmos in Part VII, "The Guardian."

Visual gizmos

Most of the traditional gizmos are merely encapsulations of text. Checkboxes, radio buttons, menus, text edits, listboxes and comboboxes are mostly text with a thin veneer of graphics added. They don't exploit the full potential of the GUI medium.

Most programs, when they have options to offer to the user, describe those options with text and offer that text to the user in a text-based selection gizmo like a combobox. If the options can be rendered visually, however, we should discard the combobox and let the user point-and-click on a picture of what he wants instead of just a text description.

Figure 27-2 shows a dialog box from Word with a couple of very visual gizmos. The gizmo in the lower left corner lets the user request complex bordering options by clicking on little images of borders, instead of asking for them by name. In this situation, this gizmo rescued Microsoft from a difficult dilemma because the number of bordering options is large. Rules can be independently specified for the top, bottom, left, right and in-betweens of a paragraph, and each border can have its own weight and style. Offering a combobox filled with hundreds of options like "thin left, really thin right, thick top, dashed thin bottom" would be pathologically bad. Alternatively, a dialog box with an array of individual comboboxes for each of the five possible borders would still be a nasty morass for the user. Microsoft's solution makes a feature out of a bug.

We don't have to save visual, directly manipulable gizmos for the tough stuff, though. In the upper left corner of the dialog in Figure 27-2 is another visual gizmo that offers an extremely simple mux-linked choice of one of three options: an outline, a drop-shaded outline or no border at all. These could easily have been radio buttons, but clicking on the little pictures is soooo much better. The user can click on the image of what he wants, instead of having to click on the words that describe what he wants. It is less ambiguous, faster and more direct.

Most publishers of software use radio buttons instead of visual gizmos like these because radio buttons come free with Windows and the visual gizmos don't. If publishers want a visual gizmo, they must pay designers and programmers to create them. This is not an expensive thing to do, relative to other

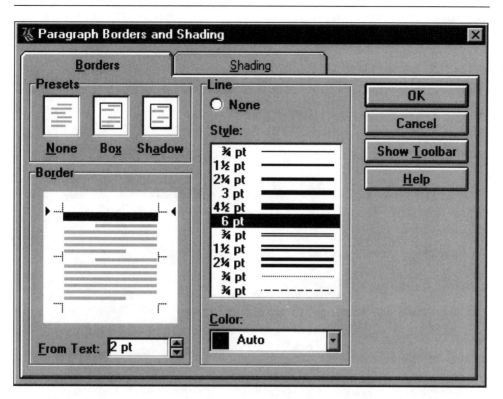

Figure 27-2

The Borders dialog box from Word shows the admirable trend toward visual, directly manipulable gizmos. On the left side of the dialog, there are two non-traditional gizmos labeled "Presets" and "Border." Preset lets the user click once on a miniature image of his desired result to quickly and easily achieve a frequently used result: a box, a drop shadow, or no border at all. Below it, the border gizmo not only acts as a preview of the current settings, but by clicking on any of the five places where lines can be specified, the user can create highly customized borders, one line at a time. Although I have some significant reservations about how Microsoft implemented borders and shading in the larger sense, this dialog box is exemplary in its use of non-text gizmos.

custom coding, but compared to a free text-based gizmo, it is very costly. Microsoft didn't put such visual gizmos into their word processor until the eighth or ninth revision, and it had generated many millions of dollars of revenue before then.

Figure 27-3 shows a beautifully crafted visual gizmo in the control panel of Windows 95. Instead of picking a time zone from a text list (although such a list exists on the dialog), you choose your time zone by clicking on a blue and green map of the world. When you select a zone, the map sensuously slides so that your selection is centered in the window. *There was no need for Microsoft to do this,* just as there is no reason for a downtown law firm to have marble floors instead of linoleum. But as you run your hand along the teak and cherrywood trim of the lobby furnishings and slide gently into a soft, supple leather wing chair, you know true comfort and luxury. Sure, you'll pay for it; those lawyers are going to be a lot more expensive than their competitors with plywood, Formica and naugahyde. It all depends on what image you wish to convey.

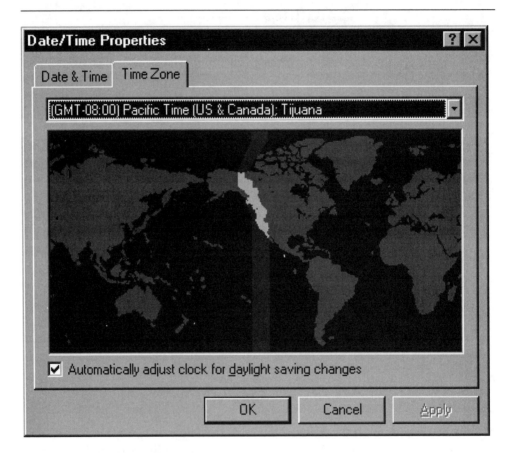

Figure 27-3

The new time zone dialog box in Windows 95 is an excellent visual gizmo. It clearly shows the selections available to the user attractively and graphically. If you live on the East Coast of the US, for example, all you need to do is click somewhere along the eastern seaboard and the map smoothly scrolls until the Eastern US is centered and highlighted. The animation speeds up and slows down so nicely that the effect is almost sensual. I've seen people spend many minutes playing with the dialog box for the sheer, tactile pleasure of it. Wow! It's like walking into the lobby of someone's office and finding marble, walnut and leather instead of stucco and plywood. If you want to add a sense of aesthetics to your program, make them tactile aesthetics.

Paradoxically, gizmos are distinct objects on the surface of an application, but the path to improving them is to integrate them more intimately into the visual fabric of the program. All of the examples I've shown so far are undoubtedly hand-coded one-offs. This is an area of significant opportunity for a vendor: creating a generic visual-gizmo development kit that allows average programmers on average budgets to create visual, animated, directly manipulable gizmos for their products.

Adding visual richness

Adding visual richness to traditional gizmos, like adding icons to buttons, is an area whose potential has barely been scratched. Most gizmos can be enhanced with the addition of graphics, animation and sound.

We designed a progress meter that was functionally identical to run-of-the-mill implementations but was a lot more engaging because of its visual richness. The program downloaded a newspaper from an online service, and the progress meter reflected the status of that operation. Instead of a simple horizontal row of little rectangles that appear one at a time, we showed a dog walking from the left end of the gizmo to the right end of the gizmo, where a folded newspaper waited. When Rover got to the newspaper, the download was complete, and he gave a friendly bark before returning to sit attentively on the left again, waiting for the next download. Good doggie!

In a well-written novel, the protagonist usually doesn't come right out and state her views and opinions. Instead, she demonstrates her point of view by her actions. The novelist is showing us, instead of telling us, and this is a fundamental technique of good fiction. It is also a fundamental technique of good user interface design.

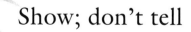

Show; don't tell

Instead of using words to tell your story, use pictures to show the user. I'm not talking about metaphoric icons here; rather, I'm saying that instead of using text to communicate some setting, draw a picture. Even though the picture probably consumes more space, its ability to clearly communicate is well worth the pixels. In recent years Microsoft has discovered this fact, and the dialog boxes in Windows Word, for example, have begun to fairly bristle with little visualizations of their purpose instead of mere textual controls.

The Page Setup dialog box, shown in Figure 26-2, offers an image labeled "preview." This is an output-only gizmo, showing a miniature view of what the page will look like with the current margin settings on the dialog. Most users have trouble visualizing what a 1.2" left margin *looks* like. The preview gizmo shows them. You could go Microsoft one better by allowing input on the preview gizmo in addition to output. Drag the left margin of the picture and watch the numeric value in the corresponding spinner ratchet up and down.

The associated text field is still important—you can't just replace it with the visual one. The text shows the result with precision, while the visual gizmo shows the result with accuracy.

Part VII: The Guardian
Protecting the User

Human beings make mistakes all of the time. They are constantly making minor slip-ups and false starts, putting their feet in their mouth and stepping on each other's toes. This state of ambient errors is so normal that most people don't consider such actions to really be "errors." Computers, on the other hand, are inherently perfect and never make mistakes. So the question arises: How should a perfect program react to the inappropriate, inadvertent and incorrect actions of the human user? The answer to this question dictates much of the quality of a program's user interface.

The End of Errors

28

In Part V, I discussed in detail all of the variants of the dialog box except one: the bulletin. The bulletin dialog box is issued unilaterally by the program when it is having some sort of problem or is confronting a decision that it doesn't feel capable of answering on its own. In other words, bulletin dialog boxes are used for error messages and confirmations, two of the nastiest components of modern software design. I believe that, with proper design, all error message and confirmation dialogs can be eliminated. Further, I believe that most of them *should* be. In this chapter, I'll tell you how.

Eliminating the error message box

There is probably no more-abused idiom in the GUI world than the error message box. When I lecture to groups of programmers, I make many bold assertions, but when I assert that all error message boxes can be eliminated from all programs, it provokes them more than any other statement. Some of my listeners have come so unglued by this claim that they became apoplectic and couldn't consider any of my other thoughts or ideas. The proposal that a program doesn't have the right—no, the duty—to reject the user's input is so heretical that many practitioners dismiss it summarily. Yet, if we examine this assertion rationally and from the user's—rather than the programmer's—point of view, it is not only possible, but quite reasonable.

When I say to eliminate error messages, I don't mean to just discard the code that shows the actual error message dialog box, while still letting the program crash if a problem arises (although many programmers assume that is what I mean). Instead, I mean that we should alter our programs so they are no longer susceptible to the problem. You cannot just yank the error messages out of a program. You must replace the error-message-method of software protection with a kinder, gentler, more robust type of software that prevents error conditions from arising, rather than having the program merely complain when things aren't going precisely the way it wants. Like vaccinating it against a disease, we make the program immune to the problem, and then we can toss the message reporting it. To eliminate the error message, we must first eliminate the possibility of the user making the error.

I don't want you to crusade to eliminate all existing error messages. Instead, I want you to change your mental assumptions about all *future* error messages. Instead of assuming that error messages are normal, I want you to think of them as abnormal solutions to rare problems—as surgery instead of aspirin. Treat them as an idiom of last resort.

Users never want error messages. Believing that your users are satisfied with error messages confuses what they don't want with what they do. Users want to avoid the *consequences* of making errors, which is very different from saying that they want error messages. It's like saying people want to abstain from skiing when what they really want to do is avoid breaking their legs. Don Norman points out that people frequently blame themselves for errors in product design. Just because you aren't getting complaints from your users doesn't mean that they are happy getting error messages.

Bulletin Dialog Boxes

The familiar error message box is normally an application modal dialog that stops all further progress of the program until the user issues a terminating command—like pressing the OK button. I call this a <mark>blocking bulletin</mark> because the program cannot continue until the user responds.

It is also possible for a program that has put up a dialog box to unilaterally take it down again. I call this a <mark>sustaining bulletin</mark> because the dialog disappears and the program continues without user intervention.

Sustaining bulletins are most frequently used as progress dialog boxes, reporting on the status of a time-consuming procedure. During the process, the dialog offers a CANCEL button so the user can terminate it if he changes his mind or grows impatient with the delay. In any case, when the program has completed the procedure, it pulls down the dialog.

Sustaining bulletins are sometimes used for error reporting. A program that erects an error message to report a problem may correct the problem itself or may detect that the problem has disappeared via some other agency. Some programmers issue an error message box merely as a warning—"Your disk is getting full"—and take it down again after it has been up for, say, 10 seconds.

An error message *must* stop the program. If it doesn't, the user may not be able to read it fully, or if he is looking away, he either won't see it or worse yet, see only a fleeting glimpse out of the corner of his eye. He will be justifiably suspicious that he has missed something important; something that will come back to haunt him later. He will now begin to worry: What did I miss? Was that an important bit of intelligence that I will regret not knowing? Is my disk full? Am I about to crash? This is true even if the problem has gone away by itself.

If a thing is worth saying with a dialog box, it's worth assuring that the user definitely gets the message. A sustaining bulletin can't make that guarantee. For this reason, the only justification for a sustaining bulletin dialog box is to report a process. It should never be used in the role of error reporting or confirmation gathering.

> **Design tip:** Never use sustaining dialogs as error messages or confirmations.

Stopping the proceedings

We have established that error messages must stop the proceedings with a modal dialog box. Most user interface designers—being programmers—imagine that their error message boxes are alerting the user to serious problems.

This is a widespread misconception. Most error message boxes are informing the user of the inability of the program to work flexibly. You can see an example of this back in Chapter 13 in Figure 13-1. Most error message boxes seem to the user like an admission of real stupidity on the program's part. In other words, to most users, error message boxes are seen not just as the program stopping the proceedings but, in clear violation of the axiom presented in Chapter 13, as *stopping the proceedings with idiocy*. We can significantly improve the quality of our interfaces by eliminating error message boxes.

> ***Design tip:*** Error message boxes stop the proceedings with idiocy.

Why we have so many error messages

The first computers were undersized, underpowered, expensive, and didn't lend themselves easily to software sensitivity. The operators of these machines were white-lab-coated scientists who were sympathetic to the needs of the CPU and weren't offended when handed an error message. They knew how hard the computer was working. They didn't mind getting a core dump, a bomb, an "Abort, Retry, Fail?" or the infamous "FU"* message. This is how the tradition of software treating people like CPUs began. Ever since the early days of computing, programmers have accepted that the proper way for software to interact with humans was to demand input and to barf when the human failed to achieve the same perfection level as the CPU.

I call this attitude silicon sanctimony. Examples of silicon sanctimony exist wherever software demands that the user do things its way instead of adapting to the needs of the human. Nowhere is it more prevalent, though, than in the omnipresence of error messages. Silicon sanctimony is a negative feedback loop, ignoring users when they do what the software wants, but squawking at the slightest deviation from what they expect.

Silicon sanctimony is a requirement for actions *within* software. Every good programmer knows that if module A hands invalid data to module B, module B should clearly and immediately reject the input with a suitable error indicator. Not doing this would be a great failure in the design of the interface between the modules. But human users are not modules of code. Not only should software not reject the input with an error message, but the software designer must reevaluate the entire concept of what "invalid data" is. When it

---

*File Unavailable.

comes from a human, the software must assume that the input is correct, simply because the human is more important than the code. Instead of software rejecting input, it must work harder to understand and reconcile confusing input. The program may know what the state of things is inside the computer, but only the user knows what the state of things is outside in the real world. Ultimately, the real world is more relevant and important than what the computer thinks.

Humans have emotions and feelings: computers don't. When one chunk of code rejects the input of another, the sending code doesn't care; it doesn't scowl, get hurt or seek counseling. The processor doesn't even care if you flip the Big Red Switch.

On the other hand, humans—even phlegmatic programmers—have emotions, and they are raging out of control compared to anything happening in silicon. When you offer some information to a colleague and she says "Shut up, that's stupid," your feelings get hurt, your ego crushed. You search for mistaken meanings in what you said. You look in the mirror, checking your teeth for bits of spinach. You cancel your afternoon appointments so you can sulk in private and wonder what is wrong with your personality. All of these actions are part of human nature.

People hate error messages

When users see an error message box, it is like another person telling them "Fatal error, buddy. That input really sucked!" in a loud and condescending voice. Users hate this! Putting interaction like this in your program is extremely bad human interface design. (See Figure 28-1.) Despite this, most programmers just shrug their shoulders and put error message boxes in anyway. They don't know how else to create reliable software.

Many programmers and user interface designers labor under the misconception that people either like or need to be told when they are wrong. This assumption is false in several ways. The assumption that people like to know when they are wrong ignores human nature. Many people become very upset when they are informed of their mistakes and would rather not know that they did something wrong. They would be happier if the issue were never raised and the problem just got lost in the detritus of the everyday. Many people don't like to hear that they are wrong from anybody but themselves. Others are only willing to hear it from a spouse or close friend. Very few wish to hear about it from a

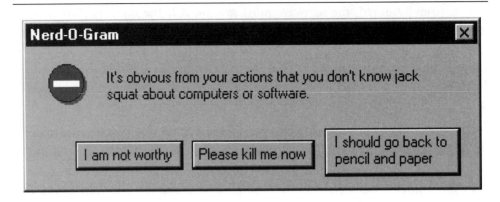

Figure 28-1

This is what all error messages feel like to users. They are not particularly sympathetic to the idiosyncrasies of the central processing unit, so it just feels like a rude rejection and personal condemnation. No matter how nicely your error messages are worded, this is how they will be interpreted.

machine. You may call it denial, but it is true, and users will blame the messenger before they blame themselves.

The assumption that users *need* to know when they are wrong is similarly false. How important is it for me to know that I requested an invalid typesize? Most programs can make a reasonable substitution. It may or may not be important, but why should the program assume that it is? We think that the program must be dependable because most programs don't offer sufficient visual cues for the user to supervise its actions. If we push our power lawnmower off the grass onto the gravel, we can *see* our error, not to mention hear the rattle of rocks and feel the sting of flung pebbles. If we choose a bad typesize, does the program show us what we have done? If it does, the user can see the results of his choice if he cares to see. If the program communicates clearly with the user, he can make up his own mind about his "need to know" when something isn't as he expected.

The assumption that it is good to tell users of their transgressions is one of the silliest canards to permeate the world of software design. It is indicative of just how socially inept most programmers are that they find such an assumption easy to swallow. No marketing person would ever fall for it. Nobody likes to be told when he makes a mistake. We consider it very impolite to tell people when they have committed some social faux pas. Telling someone he has a bit of lettuce sticking to his teeth or that his fly is open is equally embarrassing for both parties. Sensitive people look for ways to bring the problem to the attention of the victim without letting others notice. Yet programmers assume that a big, bold box in the middle of the screen that stops all of the action and emits a bold "beep" is the appropriate way to behave.

Whose mistake is it anyway?

Another method of eliminating error messages is for the program to assume, when it receives bad input, that maybe it doesn't understand it because the program, not the user, is ill-informed. Conventional wisdom says that error messages tell the user when he has made some mistake. Actually, most error bulletins report to the user when the *program* gets confused. Most programmers, in the grip of silicon sanctimony, perpetually think about users "making mistakes," and conceive of error messages as tools for correcting the user's actions. Users make far fewer substantive mistakes than imagined. Typical "errors" consist of the user inadvertently entering an out-of-bounds number, or entering a space where the computer doesn't allow it. When the user enters something unintelligible by the computer's standards, whose fault is it? Is it the user's fault for not knowing how to use the program properly, or is it the fault of the program for not making the choices and effects clearer?

Information that is entered in an unfamiliar sequence usually is considered an error by software, but people don't have difficulty with this concept. Humans know how to wait, to bide their time until the story is complete. Software usually jumps to the erroneous conclusion that out-of-sequence input means wrong input, and issues the evil error message box.

When, for example, the user creates an invoice for an invalid customer number, most programs reject the entry. They stop the proceedings with the idiocy that the user must make the customer number valid *right now*. Alternatively, the program could accept the transaction with the expectation that a valid customer number would eventually be entered. It could, for example, make a special notation to itself indicating what it lacks. The program would then watch to make sure the user entered the necessary information to make that customer number valid before the end of the month book-closing. In fact, this is the way most humans actually work. They don't usually enter "bad" codes. Usually, they just enter codes in a sequence that the software isn't prepared to accept.

Our programs make the assumption that a customer account must be established before an invoice debited to that account can be valid, but nowhere is this carved in stone. Why can't software accept invoices independently of account information and merely assume that things will be explained to it in due course? If the human forgets to fully explain things to the computer by month's end, the program can dump irreconcilable transactions into a suspense account. The program doesn't have to bring the proceedings to a halt with an error message. After all, the transactions in the suspense account will almost certainly amount to only a tiny fraction of the total sales, so they will not be a significant factor in the business reporting cycle. If they are significant, though, the program will remember the transactions so they can be tracked down and fixed. This is the way it worked in manual systems, so why can't computerized systems do at least this much? Why stop the entire process just because something inconsequential is missing? Why ground the airplane because the bar is short one little bottle of Scotch?

If the program were a human assistant and it staged a sit-down strike in the middle of the accounting department because we handed it an incomplete form, we'd be pretty upset. If we were the boss, we'd consider finding a replacement for this anal-retentive, petty, sanctimonious clerk. Just take the form, we'd say, and figure out the missing information yourself.

I have a name and address program that demands I enter an area code with a phone number even though I have already entered the person's address. It doesn't take a lot of intelligence to make a reasonable guess at the area code. Most of the people in my address book live nearby. If I enter a new name with an address in Menlo Park, the program can reliably assume that the area code is 415 by looking at the other 25 people in my database who also live in Menlo Park and have 415 as their area code. Sure, if I entered a new address for, say, Boise, Idaho, the program might be stumped. But how tough is it to keep a list of the 1,000 biggest cities in America along with their area codes? I can hear the protest already: "The program might be wrong. It can't be sure. Some cities have more than one area code. It can't make that assumption without approval of the user." Bullpucky!

If I asked my human assistant, Chris, to enter Joe's information, and I neglected to mention his area code, Chris would accept it anyway, expecting that the area code would arrive before its absence was critical. Alternatively, Chris could look the address up in a directory. Let's say that Joe lives in Los Angeles, so the directory is ambiguous: his area code could be either 213 or 310. If Chris rushed into my office in a panic shouting, "Stop what you're doing, Mr. Cooper! Joe's area code is ambiguous!" I'd be sorely tempted to fire poor Chris and hire somebody with a greater-than-room-temperature IQ. Why should my software assistant be any different? Kim, Chris's replacement, just wrote "213/310?" into the area code field. The next time I need to call Joe, I'll have to determine which area code is correct, but in the meantime, life can go on.

Again, I can hear the squeals of protest: "But, but, but the area code field is only big enough for three digits! I can't fit '213/310?' into it!" Gee, that's too bad. You mean that rendering the user interface of your program in terms of the underlying implementation model—a rigidly fixed field width—forces you to reject natural human behavior in favor of obnoxious, computer-like, inflexibility supplemented with demeaning error messages? Not to put too fine a point on this, but error message boxes come from a failure of the program to behave reasonably, not from any failure of the user.

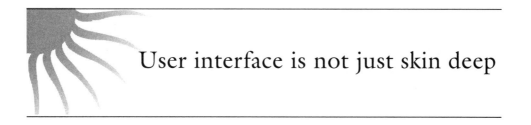

User interface is not just skin deep

The previous example illustrates another important observation about user interface design. It is *not* only skin deep. The user just happens to be the last person in a long chain of hard-working, deadline-facing professionals. Problems that aren't solved in the code are pushed through the system until they fall into the lap of the user. There are a variety of ways to handle the exceptional situations that arise in interaction with software—and a creative programmer can probably think of a half-dozen or so off the top of her head—but most programmers just don't do it. They are compromised by their schedule and their preferences, so they tend to envision the world in the terms of perfect CPU behavior rather than in the terms of imperfect human behavior.

Make errors impossible

Making it impossible for the user to make errors is the best way to eliminate error messages. By using bounded gizmos for all data entry, users are prevented from ever being able to enter bad numbers. Instead of forcing a user to key in his selection, present him with a list of possible selections from which to choose. Instead of making the user type in a state code, for example, let him choose from a list of valid state codes or even from a picture of a map. In other words, make it impossible for the user to enter a bad state.

Make errors impossible

Another excellent way to eliminate error messages is to make the program smart enough that it eliminates the need to ask the user questions. Many error messages say things like "Invalid input. User must type xxxx." Why can't the program, if it knows what the user must type, just enter xxxx by itself and save the user the tongue lashing? Instead of demanding that the user find a file on disk, introducing the chance that the user will select the wrong file, have the program remember which files it has accessed in the past and allow a selection from that list. Another example is designing a system that gets the date from the internal clock instead of asking for input from the user.

Undoubtedly, all of these solutions will cause more work for programmers. This doesn't bother me a bit. I don't want programmers to have to work harder just for the sake of working harder, but given the choice between programmers working harder and users working harder, I'll put the programmers to work in an instant. It is the programmer's job to satisfy the user and not vice versa. If the programmer thinks of the user as just another input device, it is easy to forget the proper pecking order in the world of software design.

Users of computers aren't sympathetic to the difficulties faced by programmers. They don't see the technical rationale behind the rejection in an error message box. All they see is the unwillingness of the program to deal with things in a human way. They see all error messages as some variant of the one shown in Figure 28-2. This is how most users perceive error message dialog boxes. They see them as Kafka-esque interrogations with each successive choice leading to a yet blacker pit of retribution and regret.

One of the big problems with error messages is that they are usually post facto reports of failure. They say "Bad things just happened and all you can do is acknowledge the catastrophe." Such reports are not helpful. And these dialog boxes always come with an OK button, requiring the user to collaborate in the mayhem. These error message boxes remind me of the scene in old war movies

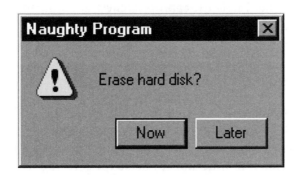

Figure 28-2

This is how most users perceive error message dialog boxes. They see them as Kafka-esque interrogations with each successive choice leading to a yet blacker pit of retribution and regret.

where an ill-fated soldier steps on a landmine while advancing across the rice paddy. He and his buddies clearly hear the click of the mine's triggering mechanism and the realization comes over the soldier that although he's safe now, as soon as he removes his foot from the mine, it will explode, taking some large and useful part of his body with it. Users get this feeling when they see most error message boxes, and they wish they were thousands of miles away, back in the real world.

Positive feedback

Humans respond more favorably to positive feedback than to the negative feedback of error messages. Instead of issuing a corrective message when things are wrong, your program could issue support messages when things are right, so the absence of a message would indicate a problem. Whenever the software can adapt to the input and accept it, the software replies with some indication of success. If the software cannot make sense of the input, it makes no reply at all—silence indicates failure. Just like Mom taught you when you were a tot: "If you can't say anything nice, don't say anything at all." Good advice, Mom, for software interaction with users.

The interaction I have with a hammer is illustrative of healthy interaction between a human user and a tool. When I use a hammer incorrectly, it doesn't give me an error message. It doesn't attempt to correct my behavior. It doesn't point out my failings as a carpenter. It just doesn't put nails in very well. The hammer rewards good use with good results and rewards poor use with bad results. The simplicity, appropriateness and human scale of the interaction between human and hammer are proven by the lack of professional societies devoted to hammer design and by the lack of Opinion columns in carpentry magazines on how toolmakers can create more harmonious relations with hammer users.

One of the big reasons why software is so hard to learn is that it so rarely gives positive feedback. People learn better from positive feedback than they do from negative feedback. People want to use their software correctly and effectively, and they are motivated to learn how to make the software work for them. They don't need to be slapped on the wrist when they fail. They do need to be rewarded, or at least acknowledged, when they succeed. They will feel better about themselves if they get approval, and that good feeling will be reflected back on the product.

Advocates of negative feedback can cite numerous examples of its effectiveness in guiding people's behavior. This evidence is true, but almost universally, the context of effective punitive feedback is getting people to refrain from doing things they want to do but shouldn't—things like not driving over 55 mph, not cheating on their spouses and not chiseling on their income taxes. But when it comes to doing what people *want* to do, positive feedback is best. Imagine a hired ski instructor who yells at you or a restaurant host who loudly announces to other patrons that your credit card was rejected.

Keep in mind that we are talking about the drawbacks of negative feedback from a computer. Negative feedback by another person, although unpleasant, can be justified in certain circumstances. One can say that the drill sergeant is at least training you how to save your life in combat, and the imperious professor is at least preparing you for the vicissitudes of the real world. But to be given negative feedback by software—any software—is an insult. The drill sergeant and professor are at least human and have bona fide experience and merit. The program is doo-doo, pond scum. It is less than zero. To be told by software that you have failed is humiliating and degrading. Users, quite justifiably, hate to be humiliated and degraded.

Users get humiliated when software tells them they failed

There is nothing that takes place inside a computer that is so important that it can justify humiliating or degrading a human user. Nothing. I don't care how important you think your precious database integrity is, it isn't worth insulting a person if you have effectiveness as your goal. If data integrity is a big deal for you, you need to work on methods of maintaining it without pissing off the user. There are plenty of good ways to do this. We only resort to the negative feedback ways of silicon sanctimony out of habit.

No crisis inside a computer is worth humiliating a human

So much effort is put into protecting the poor, fragile computer from mishandling. It's all right to protect the computer but not at the cost of bothering the user. Instead, we should put more effort into protecting the poor, fragile user from mishandling by the software.

Treat error messages like GOTOs

When I make the statement to groups of *users* that error message boxes should be eliminated, they generally agree, some with enthusiasm and some with mild reluctance. When I make that same statement to groups of programmers, they almost always protest vehemently. This reinforces my belief that the continued presence of error message boxes is due to programmers and not to users.

The debate reminds me of a similar one that began almost thirty years ago with the work of mathematician Edsgar Dijkstra, the inventor of structured programming. Dijkstra proved mathematically that the GOTO instruction could be eliminated from high-level programming languages and the result would be code whose correctness could be proven. His assertion sparked a firestorm of controversy in the industry that raged for a decade. Programmers of the '60s and '70s matured in their craft in the days of assembler language where the ability to jump randomly and without trace to anywhere in the program was considered a fundamental right and a necessary tool to achieve adequate performance. The structured programming revolution eventually proved these Luddites to be wrong, and few contemporary programmers working in languages like C, Pascal and BASIC resort to GOTOs.

It is well known that programs filled with GOTOs are nightmarishly difficult to understand and maintain although it is generally acknowledged that an occasional, well-commented GOTO harms no one. So, although programmers still use GOTOs occasionally, they treat them as a last resort. They only code GOTOs when the equivalent, structured, GOTOless code would be significantly more complex and wasteful to write. They know GOTOs are wrong, and using them is only rarely justified by extreme circumstance. They double-check their decision with their peers. They carefully add comments to the code describing the circumstances that justified the failure. They feel guilty.

I want programmers to feel the same way about error message boxes as they do about GOTOs. I want them to feel guilty when they code an error message box. I want them to know that they have better methods at their disposal for handling the situation. I want them to realize that error messages are not a fundamental right or a necessary tool to achieve adequate performance.

All error message boxes can be eliminated. If you examine the situation from the point of view that the error message box must be eliminated and that everything else is subject to change in search of this objective, you will see the truth of this assertion. You will also be surprised by how little else needs to be changed in order to achieve it. In those rare cases where the rest of program must be altered too much, that is the time to compromise with the real world, and go ahead and use an error message box. But I want the community of programmers to understand that this compromise is an admission of failure on the programmer's part. That they resorted to a low blow, a cheap shot, a GOTO in their code.

Exceptions?

I used to make a single exception to my dictum about no error message boxes. I believed that failed or missing hardware was adequate justification for an error message. I have since reconsidered this exception and decided that it doesn't hold water. As our technological powers grow, the portability and flexibility of our computer hardware grows, too. Windows 95 establishes a new standard called Plug-and-Play that allows networks and peripherals to be connected to and disconnected from your computer without having to first power it down. This means that, with Windows 95, it is now normal for hardware to appear and disappear ad hoc. Printers, modems and file servers can come and go like the tides. With the development of wireless network connectors, our computers will be attaching and detaching from networks frequently, easily, and all in the normal course of walking from meeting to meeting with your sub-notebook. Is it an error if you print a document, only to find that no printers are connected? Is it an error if the file you are editing normally resides on a drive that is no longer reachable? Is it an error if your communications modem is no longer plugged into the computer?

The deeper we wade into the Internet ocean, the more this conundrum of here-today-gone-tomorrow becomes commonplace. The Internet can easily be thought of as an infinite hard disk—one that is out of the control of any one person, company or system administrator. A valid pointer today can be meaningless tomorrow. Is this an error?

I think that none of these occurrences should be considered as errors. If I try to print something and there is no printer available, my program should just spool the print image to disk. The print manager program should quietly indicate when it reconnects to a printer while it has unprinted documents in its queue. This should be an aspect of normal, everyday computing. It is not an error. The same is true for files. If I open a file on the server and begin editing it, then wander out to a restaurant for lunch, taking my notebook with me, the program should see that the normal home of the file is no longer available and do something intelligent. It could use the built-in digital cellular phone to log onto the server remotely, or it could just save any changes I make locally, synchronizing with the version on the server when I return to the office from lunch. In any case, it is normal. It is not an error.

The most frequent cause of error messages is in responding to the user asking for some resource that is not available. This error can be eliminated by assuring that the program doesn't offer to the user things that might not be present. If the program offers picklists instead of text-edit fields, the user will not be able to enter the name of an unavailable file.

Yes, I'd like to see an error message on my screen if the printer catches on fire, but I'd also like to see one if my colleague down the hall has a heart attack. Error messages should be reserved for emergencies, real emergencies.

Do they work?

There is a final irony to error messages: *They don't prevent the user from making errors.* We imagine that the user is staying out of trouble because our trusty error messages keep them straight, but this is a delusion. What error messages really do is prevent the program from getting into trouble. In most software, the error messages stand like sentries where the program is most sensitive, not where the user is most vulnerable, setting into concrete the idea that the program is more important than the user. Users get into plenty of trouble with our software, regardless of the quantity or quality of the error messages in it. All an error message can do is keep me from entering letters in a numeric field—it does nothing to protect me from entering the wrong numbers—which is a much more difficult design task.

What error message dialog boxes should look like

Now we will discuss some methods of improving the quality of error message boxes. In light of my attitude towards them, you can understand the reluctance I feel about doing this. Remember, use these only as a last resort. It is better just to take care of the problem behind the scenes and only bother the user with it if he asks.

A well-formed error message box should be

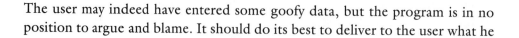

- Polite

- Illuminating

- Helpful

Never forget that an error message box is the program reporting on *its* failure to do its job, and it is interrupting the user to do this. The error message box must be unfailingly polite. It must never even hint that the user caused this problem, because that is simply not true. The customer is always right.

The customer is always right

The user may indeed have entered some goofy data, but the program is in no position to argue and blame. It should do its best to deliver to the user what he asked for, no matter how silly. Above all, the program must not, when the user finally discovers his silliness, say, in effect, "well, you did something really stupid and now you can't recover. Too bad." It is the program's responsibility to protect the user even when he takes inappropriate action. This may seem draconian, but it certainly isn't the user's responsibility to protect the computer from taking inappropriate action.

The error message box must illuminate the problem for the user. This means that it must give him the kind of information he needs to make an appropriate determination to solve the program's problem. It needs to make clear the scope of the problem; What the alternatives are; What the program will do as a default; What information was lost, if any. The program should treat this as a confession, telling the user everything.

It is wrong, though, for the program to just dump the problem on the user's lap and wipe its hands of the matter. It should directly offer to implement at least one suggested solution right there on the error message box. It should offer buttons that will take care of the problem in various ways. If a printer is missing, the message box should offer options for deferring the printout or selecting another printer. If the database is hopelessly trashed and useless, it should offer to rebuild it to a working state, including telling the user how long that process will take and what side effects it will cause.

Figure 28-3 shows an example of a reasonable error message. Notice that it is polite, illuminating and helpful. It doesn't even hint that the user's behavior is anything but impeccable.

The end of errors

Error message boxes validate the idea that the computer is the final arbiter of correctness and the user is there just to serve its digital majesty. This attitude influences both programmers and users. It tempts programmers to make bad judgments in design and to take shortcuts in implementation. These compromises necessitate the use of yet more error messages. Also, users are anesthetized by error messages so they cannot visualize the benefits of error-free computing.

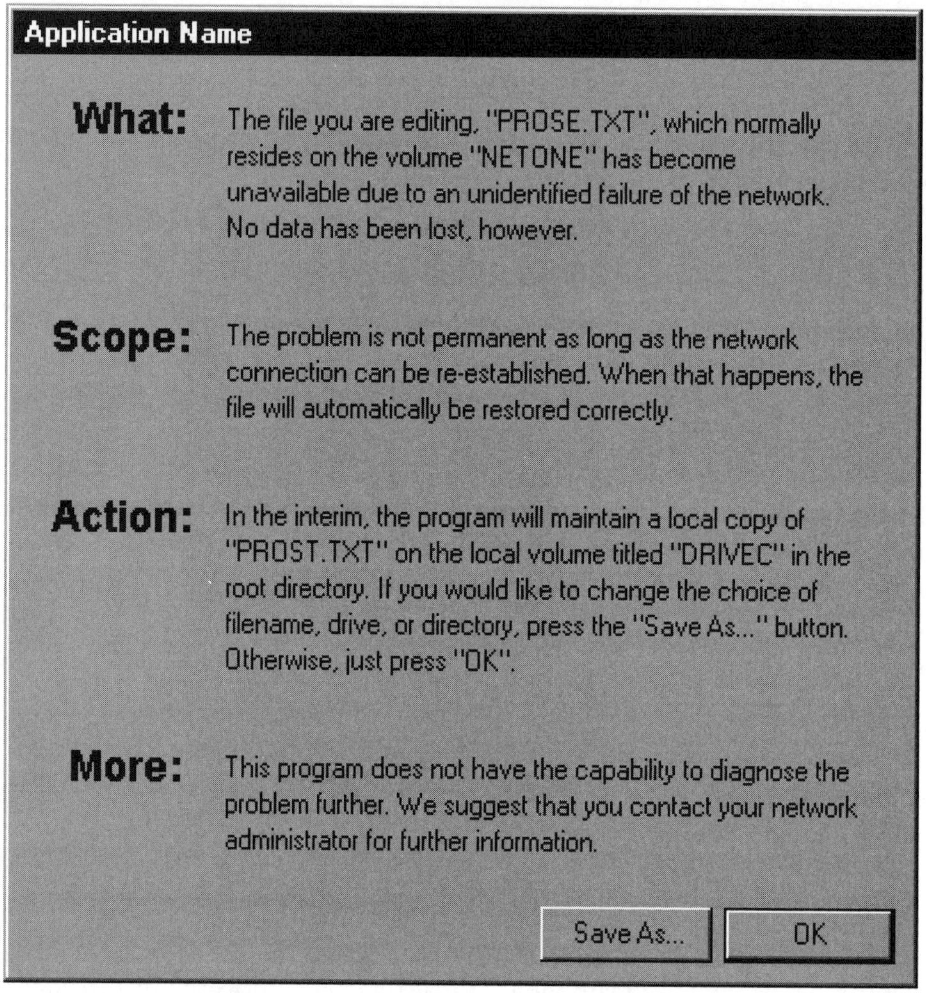

Application Name

What: The file you are editing, "PROSE.TXT", which normally resides on the volume "NETONE" has become unavailable due to an unidentified failure of the network. No data has been lost, however.

Scope: The problem is not permanent as long as the network connection can be re-established. When that happens, the file will automatically be restored correctly.

Action: In the interim, the program will maintain a local copy of "PROST.TXT" on the local volume titled "DRIVEC" in the root directory. If you would like to change the choice of filename, drive, or directory, press the "Save As..." button. Otherwise, just press "OK".

More: This program does not have the capability to diagnose the problem further. We suggest that you contact your network administrator for further information.

[Save As...]   [OK]

Figure 28-3

Just like there is rarely a good reason to ever use a GOTO in your code, there is rarely a good reason to issue an error message box. However, just as programmers occasionally compromise with one or two convenient GOTOs, they might occasionally issue an error message. In that case, your error message should look something like this one. It politely illuminates the problem for the user, offering him help in extricating the program from its dilemma. This error bulletin has four sections, labeled What, Scope, Action and More, that clearly help the user understand the options available and why he might choose each. The program is intelligent enough not to lose the file just because the volume became unavailable. The dialog offers an alternative action to the user by way of the Save As... button.

Managing Exceptions

29

Aside from errors, which we dealt with in the last chapter, there is a potpourri of exceptional user interface artifacts that we must examine. These include message and confirmation dialog boxes as well as the structure of many interactions and the underlying assumptions about them. To begin with, we will look at more ways in which poorly designed programs stop the proceedings with idiocy.

Alerts

There is another category of conditions that I call **exceptions**. Like errors, they stop the proceedings with idiocy, but they are not reporting malfunctions. Exceptions pop up like weeds in most programs, and I would like to give them the same treatment I give to errors: the old heave ho. Exceptions come in two basic varieties, *alerts* and *confirmations*. An alert notifies the user of the program's action, while a confirmation also gives the user the authority to override that action.

441

When the program exercises authority that it feels uncomfortable with, it often takes steps to inform the user of its actions. This is called an **alert**. Alerts violate the axiom that a dialog box is another room and you should have a good reason to go there (see Chapter 7). Even if an alert is justified (ha!), why go into another room to do it? If the program took some indefensible action, it should confess to it in the same place where the action occurred and not in a separate dialog box.

Conceptually, a program should either have the courage of its convictions or it should not take action without the user's direct guidance. If the program, for example, saves the user's file to disk automatically, it should have the confidence to know that it is doing the right thing. It should provide a means for the user to find out what the program did, but it doesn't have to stop the proceedings with idiocy to do so. If the program really isn't sure that it should save the file, then it shouldn't save the file, but should leave that operation up to the user.

Conversely, if the user directs the program to do something—dragging a file to the trash can, for example—it doesn't need to stop the proceedings with idiocy to announce that the user just dragged a file to the trash can. The program should assure that there is adequate visual feedback of the action, and if the user has actually made the gesture in error, the program should silently offer him a robust undo facility so he can backtrack.

The rationale for alerts is that they inform the user. I'm a real fan of informing the user, but not at the expense of a smooth and flowing interaction. I get a lot of high-quality information from my watch, but it doesn't need to tap me on the shoulder and interrupt me every hour to keep me informed of the time.

The alert shown in Figure 29-1 is a classic example of how alerts throw rocks at the user's feet. The Find dialog (the one at the bottom) already forces the user to press CANCEL when the search is completed, but the superimposed alert box makes it a brace of flow-breaking buttons: First the OK to the alert, then the CANCEL to the Find. If the information aspect of the alert were built into the main Find dialog, the user's burden would be reduced by half at no expense. That is good economy for user interface designers.

Alerts are so numerous because they are so easy to create. Most languages offer some form of message box facility in a single line of code. Conversely, building an animated status display into the face of a program might require a thousand or more lines of code. Programmers cannot be expected to make the right

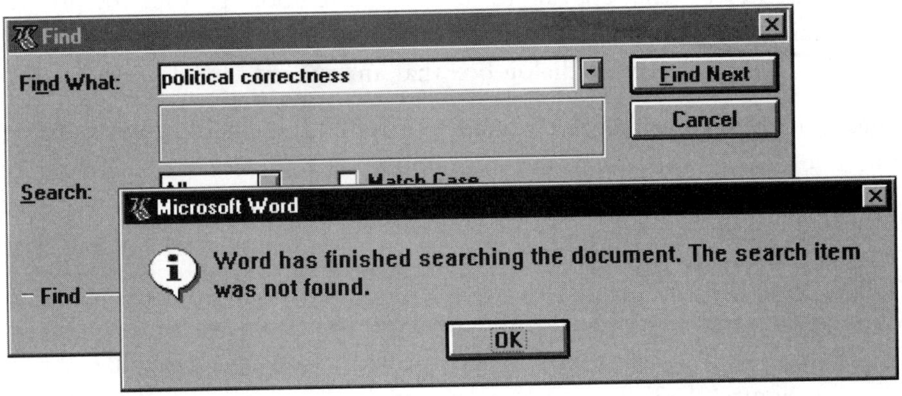

Figure 29-1

Here is a typical alert dialog box. Unnecessary, inappropriate, and it stops the proceedings with idiocy. The Find dialog in Word has finished searching the document. Is reporting that fact a different facility of Word? If not, why does it use a different dialog? It's like having to go into one dining room to use a fork and other one to use a spoon. The little "I" icon is a sure tip-off to smarmy, sanctimonious, clumsy interface design. Yes, software must constantly and effusively report its status to the user. But doing so with proceedings-stopping alert dialogs is wrong.

choice in this situation. They are too tied by conflict of interest, so designers must be sure to specify precisely where information is reported on the surface of an application, and they must follow up to be sure that the design wasn't compromised for the sake of code. Imagine if the contractor on a building site decided unilaterally not to add a bathroom because it was just too much trouble. There would be repercussions.

Announcing the obvious

Software needs to keep the user informed of its actions. It must have lights, meters or other gizmos built into its interface to make such status information available to the user, should he desire it. Putting up an alert to announce an unrequested action is bad. Putting up an alert to announce a *requested* action is pathological.

Software needs to be flexible and forgiving. It doesn't need to be fawning and obsequious. The dialog box shown back in Chapter 3 (Figure 3-2) is a classic example of an alert that should be put out of our misery. It announces that it added the entry to our phone book, immediately after we told it to add the entry to our phone book, which was mere milliseconds after we physically added the entry to what appears to be our phone book. It stops the proceedings to announce the obvious. It wouldn't surprise me if they first popped up a dialog box to announce the dialog box that announced the addition.

It's as though the programmer wanted approval for how hard he worked: "See, dear, I've cleaned your room for you. Don't you love me?" If a person interacted with us like this, we'd suggest that he seek counseling.

Confirmations

When a program does not feel confident about its actions, it often asks the user for approval with a dialog box. This is called a **confirmation**, like the one shown in Figure 29-2. Sometimes the confirmation is offered so the user has the opportunity to second-guess one of his own actions. Sometimes the program feels that it is not competent to make a decision it faces and uses a confirmation to give the user the choice instead.

Confirmations always come from the program, and never from the user. This means that exceptions are a reflection of the implementation model, and are not representative of the user's goals. All confirmation dialog boxes can be eliminated just by changing the program's attitude. Look, for example, at the dialog in Figure 29-2.

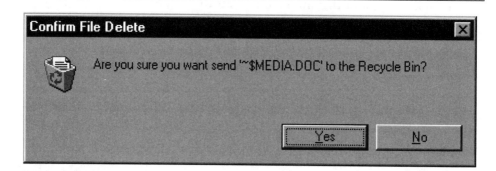

Figure 29-2

Every time I delete a file in Windows 95, I get this confirmation dialog box asking me if I'm sure. Yes, I'm sure. I'm always sure. And if I'm wrong, I expect you to be able to recover the file for me. Miracle of miracles, this version of Windows can finally live up to that expectation with its "Recycle Bin." So why does it still issue the confirmation message? When a confirmation box is issued routinely, users get used to approving it routinely. So when it eventually reports an impending disaster to the user, he goes ahead and approves it anyway, because it is routine. Confirmation boxes only work if they are unexpected. When users are performing new tasks, their senses will be alert to danger, so the only time they need unexpected confirmation boxes is when they are doing routine tasks. Deterministic algorithms can't do that. Do yourself and your users a favor, and never code another confirmation dialog box.

As I discussed in Part I, rendering the implementation model is a sure fire way to create a bad user interface. This means that the confirmation method of dealing with exceptions is wrong. Confirmations get written into software when the programmer arrives at an impasse in her coding. Typically, she realizes that she is about to take some bold action and feels that the user would want full control over this action. Sometimes the bold action is based on some condition the program detects, but more often it is based on a command the user issued. Typically, the confirmation will be erected after the user issues a command that is either irrecoverable or whose results might cause undue alarm.

In both of these circumstances, the programmer is passing the buck to the user, which is wrong. The user trusts the program to do its job, and the program should both do it and assure that it does it right. If it can't be absolutely sure it is doing it right, the program should at least be sure that it is able to backtrack on request. In other words, the program should assure that startling gizmos are clearly identified, and no actions should be irrecoverable.

Passing the buck to the user is also known as stopping the proceedings with idiocy. Yes, even if the program has found some exceptional condition, it is still idiocy from the user's point of view.

As a program's code grows during development, programmers detect numerous situations where they don't feel that they can resolve issues adequately. Programmers will unilaterally insert buck-passing code in these places, almost without noticing it. This tendency needs to be closely watched, because programmers have been known to insert dialog boxes into the code even after the user interface specification has been agreed upon. Programmers often don't consider confirmation dialogs to be part of the user interface, but they are.

Confirmations don't work

Here is a fact about confirmation messages: They only work when they are unexpected. That doesn't sound so remarkable until you examine it in context. If confirmations are offered in routine places, the user quickly becomes inured to them and routinely dismisses them without a glance. The dismissing of confirmations thus becomes as routine as the issuing of them. If—someday—a really unexpected and dangerous situation arises—one that should be brought to the user's attention, he will go ahead and dismiss the confirmation just because it has become routine. Like the fable of the boy who cried wolf, when there is finally real danger, the confirmation box won't work because it cried too many times when there was no danger.

For confirmation dialog boxes to work, they must only appear when they are unexpected. Another way of saying this is that confirmations should only bother to appear when the user will almost definitely press the "NO" button, and they should never appear when the user is likely to press the "YES" button. Seen from this vantage, they look pretty pointless, don't they?

The confirmation dialog box shown in Figure 29-3 is a classic. It appears whenever I press the DELETE button. This means that it appears every time I want to say "YES," so I *always* push the "YES" button. If I ever want to say "NO," I probably won't even notice that there was a confirming dialog box at all. The irony of the confirmation dialog box in the figure is that I often have trouble with this dialog determining which styles I want to delete and which I want to keep. If the confirmation box appeared whenever I deleted a style that was currently in use, say, it would at least be a help because it would be less routine. But why not just put an icon next to the names of styles that are in use instead and dispense with the confirmation? It gives me a better view of what is happening so I can make a more informed decision about what to delete. Also, if the DELETE button were separated from the OK and CANCEL buttons, the chance of an inadvertent button press would be dramatically reduced.

How to eliminate confirmations

There are three axioms that tell us how to eliminate confirmation dialog boxes. The best way is to obey the simple dictum: do, don't ask. When you design your software, go ahead and give it the force of its convictions. Make sure that if it is going to do something, that it has the guts to go ahead and do it without whining and mewling about it. Users will respect its brevity and its confidence.

Do, don't ask

Of course, if the program confidently does something that the user doesn't like, it must have the ability to reverse the operation. Every aspect of the program's

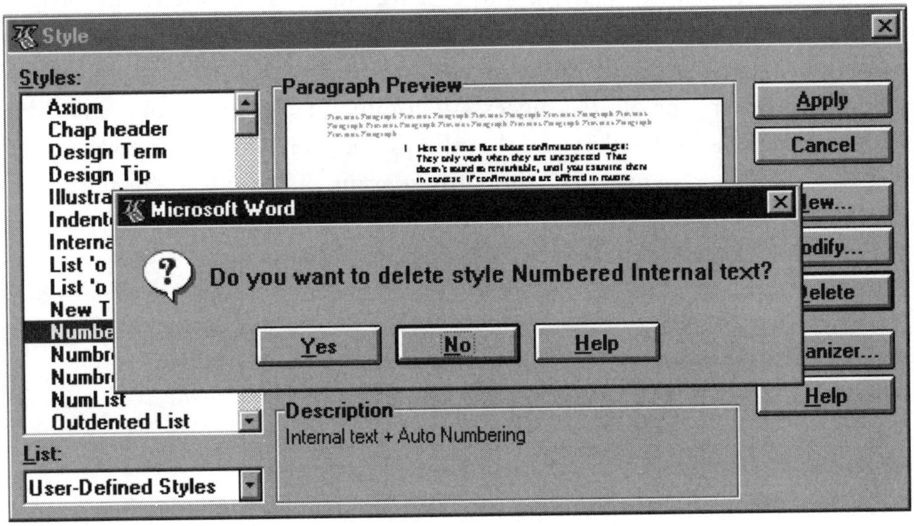

Figure 29-3

If you press the DELETE button in the Style dialog box in Word, you get this typical confirmation box. I always press YES. I never press NO. I wish, oh, how I wish that I could make this dialog go away forever. In the Style dialog, I occasionally inadvertently delete a style I really wanted to keep. This confirmation, however, doesn't help me prevent that. If its appearance were based on some criteria other than merely asking for a deletion, there is some faint chance that it would be useful. As it is, it merely irritates me. Tell me you won't ever create one of these, please?

action must be undoable. Instead of asking in advance with a confirmation dialog box though, let the user issue the stop-and-undo command on those rare occasions when the program's actions were out of turn.

Most situations that we currently consider unprotectable by undo can actually be protected fairly well. Deleting or overwriting a file is a good example. The file can be moved to a suspense directory where it is kept for a month or so before it is physically deleted. Actually, the Recycle Bin in Windows 95 uses this strategy, except for the part about automatically erasing them after a month: the user has to manually take out the garbage.

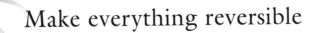

Make everything reversible

Even better than acting in haste and forcing the user to rescue the program with undo, you can make sure that the program offers the user adequate information so that the user will never issue a command that leads to an inappropriate action (or never omits a necessary command). The program should use sufficiently rich visual feedback so that the user is constantly kept informed, the same way the instruments on dashboards keep us informed of the state of our cars.

Directly offer enough information for the user to avoid mistakes

Occasionally, there arises a situation that really can't be protected by undo. I can't think of any right now, and you probably can't either, but we all know programmers who can. Is this a legitimate case for a confirmation dialog box? No. The program can't offer sufficient protection to the user, so it demands that the user waive his right to protection instead. A better approach is to provide him with protection the way we give him protection on the freeway: with consistent and clear markings. We can build really good quality, but modeless, warnings right into the interface. Isolated, brightly colored gizmos next to listboxes that offer full disclosure about the data to be messed with are a good start.

Much more common than honestly irreversible actions are those actions that are easily reversible but still uselessly protected by routine confirmation boxes. The confirmation in Figure 29-2 is an excellent specimen of this species. There is no reason whatsoever to ask for confirmation of a move to the Recycle Bin. The sole reason that the Recycle Bin exists is to implement an undo facility for deleted files. This goes beyond belt and suspenders. This confirmation box stops the proceedings with idiocy. It is more like belt, suspenders and handcuffs.

Who are we protecting, anyway?

Let's face it, most programs don't work all that hard to protect the user. However, they do work hard to protect themselves. Programs are tender, brittle souls, and a single bit in the wrong place can crash a big program.

Programmers—quite understandably—are protective of their creations. Error messages are the outward symptoms of this protection, but it is the software design imperative that shapes the program in such a way that it generates these symptoms.

This design imperative is characterized by the goal of never letting tainted, unclean data get into the software. The programmer erects barriers in the user interface so that bad data can never enter the system. This pure internal state is commonly called **data integrity**.

Data integrity posits that there is a world of chaotic information out there, and before any of it gets inside the computer it must be filtered and cleaned up. The software must have an outer barrier, a thin crust of protection, like sentries posted on the perimeter of a military base (see Figure 29-4). All data is made valid at its point of entry. Anything on the outside is assumed to be bad, or at least suspect, but anything that has penetrated the crust can be assumed to have satisfied the rigorous vetting of the barrier's best efforts. Once it has been allowed inside, it is assumed to be valid. The advantage is that once inside the database, the code doesn't have to bother with successive, repetitive checks on the validity or appropriateness of the data.

There is a completely different approach possible to protect sensitive software. Instead of keeping bad data out of the system, the programmer must make the system immune to inconsistencies and gaps in the information. This method involves writing much smarter, more sophisticated code that can robustly handle all permutations of data. I call this **data immunity**.

Programmers have traditionally used data integrity and have spurned the idea of data immunity, generally because it takes more complex code. Programmers are reluctant to accept the need to write more complex code. After all, they have deadlines, too.

Now, before you get too steamed and complain that we can't just let garbage into our systems, let me make it clear that that is not my intention.

Data integrity is a good concept on paper, but it has some severe failings in the real world. Mainly, it dumps the burden of entering correct data in the user's lap, and it demands that he do this at entry time, rather than when—and if—the correct data is actually needed. Data immunity doesn't tolerate bad data when correct data is needed. It does, though, tolerate bad data in the system when its "badness" doesn't really matter.

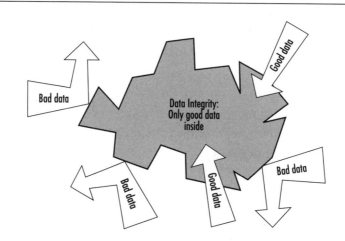

Figure 29-4

Underneath the rhetoric of data integrity—that there is an objective imperative of protecting the user and computer with sanctified data—there is a disturbing subtext. That subtext says that humans are ill-intentioned screwups; that users will, given the chance, enter the most bizarre garbage possible in a deliberate attempt to bring the system to its knees. This is not true. I'm certainly aware that users can, given the chance, enter garbage, but that is a far cry from saying that they do it intentionally. Users are very sensitive to subtext, though, and they will know that the program doesn't trust them. Data integrity not only hampers the system from serving the user for the dubious benefit of easing the programmer's burden, but it also offends the user with its accompanying attitude. It's another case of the user having to adapt to the needs of the computer, instead of vice versa. The philosophy of data integrity is based on scarcity thinking; there aren't enough precious computing resources to go around, so we must protect them from chaotic, bad data. That just isn't true anymore. It's time we start devoting some of our excess capacity to helping protect the user from chaotic, bad user interfaces.

Data integrity helps programmers, not users

Data integrity is a straitjacket placed on software design by programmers and computers and not by users. The user doesn't know or care about how much work the programmer must do to make things work correctly. The user is not concerned with the difficulties the programmer might have keeping the program from blowing up if it finds an alphabetic character in a numeric field. Yes, the user cares about having the program function reliably and about having it yield good results, but that doesn't mean he necessarily wants to have to do the scut work of correcting the details. He also wants his lawn trimmed, but it doesn't follow that he must be the one to personally wield the lawnmower.

Data integrity demands that all data be vetted at the door, and that all outliers are detected and bounced back. Once in, the data is good. This is nothing more than a performance hack. The only reason suspect information is bounced on entry is to make things easy for the programmer and for the computer. The user doesn't count.

An invoice database, for example, may be used to generate statistical sales reports for management in addition to printing invoices to mail to customers. The absence of valid postal codes in the customer records might well hamper the invoice mailing, but it won't have any effect on the sales report. Data integrity, however, demands that the product manager can't get her report until those postal codes are perfect. From a systems point of view, getting postal codes perfect once and for all is the most efficient method. From the product manager's point of view, though, the silly program is demanding irrelevancies with an obnoxious rigidity.

The database programmer will counter that it is too difficult for the program to have to deal with possible bad data at each step of the way—that it is more efficient for the program to eliminate the bad data at entry time and assume goodness from then on. This is true, but not relevant. Efficiency is a concept that applies to machinery and central processing units. It has little or no applicability to human beings, and our task as programmers and designers is to improve the user's lot. The efficiency demanded by the database programmer is a vestige of the scarcity thinking that infects our entire generation of programmers. Today, we have plenty of computing power available to protect against bad data. But programmers drag their heels, not wanting to do the hard work. It is easier for programmers to invoke data integrity than it is for them to take the necessary effort to implement data immunity.

In particular, programmers who work with databases generally consider the integrity of their databases to be the primary, overriding concern of their work. The user's concerns rarely penetrate this deeply into the system end of the program code. Programmers may never admit it, but their decisions all seem to go in favor of data integrity at the expense of user considerations. Their sympathies are with the database rather than with the user. Users and user interface designers are told flatly "we *must* maintain the integrity of the database" with the same intensity as if the database were sustaining the life-support system on a spacecraft.

Data integrity is so widely accepted as good software design that its hegemony is rarely even questioned. Pretty much all of the art and science of database administration, management and programming is based on the assumption that data integrity is reliably maintained. Programmers who write user-centered software that happens to rely on databases also unconsciously inculcate the data integrity principle into their work.

The database, whether residing on an aging mainframe or on an au courant client/server platform, makes louder, more immediate and more strident demands than users can, and so most applications are more sensitive to the needs of the server program than they are to the user. As a pragmatic developer of software, I know it is vital to address the needs of the platform, but I also know that someday a vendor will figure out how to keep the software happy while simultaneously giving users new and higher levels of interactive satisfaction. This vendor will cut through the marketplace like a scythe. It can be you, or it can be your competitor, but it is only a matter of time. As a designer, my allegiance is to the future, not to the database.

Data immunity

To implement data immunity, our programs must be trained to look before they leap, and they must be trained to ask for help.

Most software blindly performs arithmetic on numbers without actually examining them first. The program assumes that a number field must contain a number—data integrity tells it so. If the user entered the word "nine" instead of the number "9," the program would croak, but a human reading the form wouldn't even blink. If the program simply looked at the data before it acted, it would see that a simple math function won't do the trick.

Here's where looking for help comes in. Wait! I know what you are thinking: put up a message box asking the user. That is precisely the wrong thing to do. We must train our programs to believe that the user will enter what he means to enter, and if the user wants to correct things, he will without our paranoid insistence. But the program can look elsewhere in the computer for assistance. Is there a module that knows how to make numeric sense of alphabetic text? Is there a history of corrections that might shed some light on the user's intent?

If all else fails, the program must add annotations to the data so that when—and if—the user comes to examine the problem, he finds accurate and complete notes that describe what happened and what steps the program took.

Yes, if users enter "asdf" instead of "9.38," the program won't be able to arrive at satisfactory results. But stopping the program to resolve this *right now* is not "satisfactory" process, either; the entry process is just as important as the end report. If the user interface is designed correctly, the program issues some visual feedback when the user enters "asdf," so the likelihood of the user entering hundreds of bad records is very low. Generally, users only act stupidly when programs treat them stupidly.

Most often, the incorrect data that the user enters is still reasonable for the situation. If the program expects a two-letter state code, the user may enter a "TY" by accident. However, that same user enters the city as "Louisville" and it doesn't take a lot of intelligence to figure out the problem. Missing postal codes can be solved by a relatively simple and small program that won't tax our modern, powerful computers. In the rare cases where the postal code locator program fails, most humans would have failed, too.

Data integrity is a privilege, not a right

From a computer's point of view, it doesn't make any difference whether garbage got into the system intentionally or not. This has been used as a justification for the autocracy of data integrity. However, from the human user's point of view, the difference between intentionally entering a bad postal code and unintentionally entering it is very great indeed. Back when computers cost millions and were slow and temperamental, the user's feelings could be justifiably snubbed for practical considerations. Those days are gone forever, hustled to the door and booted into the street by the information revolution.

This is how I justify demoting data integrity from its position as a guiding principle of software design. When our software shakes down data at the point of entry, when it strip-searches the user to assure that he isn't carrying any contraband into the high-security depths of the computer, it makes a very clear statement: that the user is insignificant and that the program is god-like; that the user works for the good of the program and not vice versa. This is not the impression that we want to give. We want the user to feel in charge; to feel that the program works for him; that the program is doing the work, while the user makes the decisions.

Data integrity helps reduce the burden on the programmer, while saying nothing about what it does for the user. Programmers who cut their teeth on mainframes with batch-processed COBOL applications (I did) learn the concept of data integrity early. Today, the gospel of data integrity is being taught to a new generation of programmers using Visual Basic to access department-level SQL

PART VII: THE GUARDIAN

databases. The computational landscape is completely different than it was twenty years ago. While the power of the host computers has increased ten-thousand-fold, not much else has. The quantities of data typically handled haven't changed more than an order of magnitude, and the humans who use them are the same. Yet we still put data integrity at the top of our priority list, even though the demand for it is vestigial.

Audible feedback

In mass-production data-entry environments, professional data-entry clerks—touch-typists all—sit for hours in front of video screens and enter data. These users may well be examining source documents and typing by touch instead of looking at the screen. If they enter something erroneous, they need to be informed of it both audibly and visually. The clerk can then use his sense of hearing to monitor the success of his inputs while he keeps his eyes on the document.

Here, I'm absolutely *not* talking about the beep that accompanies an error message box. In fact, I'm not talking about a beep at all. When I talk about audible feedback as a problem indicator, I'm talking about silence.

With the exception of computer software, almost every object and system offers sound to indicate success rather than failure. When we close the door, we know that it is latched when we hear the click, but silence tells us that it is not yet secure. When we are talking with a group of people and they say "Yes" or "Uh-huh," we know that we have gotten through to them. When they are silent, we know our arguments have slipped off the track somehow. When we turn the key in the ignition and get silence, we know we've got a problem. When we flip the switch on the copier and it stays coldly silent instead of humming loudly, we know that there is trouble. Even things we consider silent make noise: Turning on the stovetop returns a sibilant hiss of gas and a quietly gratifying "whoomp" as the pilot ignites the burner. Electric ranges are inherently less friendly and harder to use because they lack that sound—they have to have indicator lights to tell us of their status.

When success with our tools yields a sound, that is called **positive audible feedback**.

Our software tools are mostly silent; all we hear is the quiet click of the keyboard. Hey! That's positive audible feedback. Every time you press a key, you hear a faint but positive sound. Keyboard manufacturers could easily make perfectly silent keyboards, but they don't because we depend on audible feed-back to tell us how we are doing. The feedback doesn't have to be sophisti-cated—those clicks don't tell us much—but they must be consistent, because if we ever detect silence, we know that we have failed to press the key. The true value of positive audible feedback is that its absence is an extremely effective problem indicator.

The effectiveness of positive audible feedback comes from its human sensitiv-ity. Nobody—no human, that is—likes to be told that they have failed. Error message boxes are negative feedback, telling the user that he has done some-thing wrong. Ah, but silence assures that the user knows this without actually being told of the failure. It is remarkably effective, because the software does-n't have to insult the user to accomplish its ends.

Our software should give us constant small audible cues just like our keyboards. Our programs would be much friendlier and easier to use if they issued barely audible but easily identifiable sounds when user actions were correct. The pro-gram could issue a soft "coo" every time the user entered valid input to a field. If the program didn't understand the input, it would remain silent and the user would be immediately informed of the problem and be able to correct his input without embarrassment or ego-bruising. Whenever the user starts to drag an icon, the computer would issue a short "toot-toot," then an effervescent hiss as the object was dragged. When it was dragged over pliant areas, the hiss would rise a note in pitch. When the user finally released the mouse button, he would be rewarded with a nearly silent "Yeah!" from the speakers for a success, or frigid silence if the drop wasn't meaningful.

People frequently counter this argument by telling me how users don't like audible feedback, how they are offended by the sounds that computers make and how they don't like to have their computer beeping and booping at them. To this I say "Bunk!" People are conditioned by two things about computer sound:

○ Computers have always accompanied error messages with noises.

○ Computer noises have always been loud, monotonous and unpleasant alarms.

Emitting noise when something bad happens is called negative audible feedback.

On most systems, error message boxes are normally accompanied by loud, shrill, tinny little "beeps," and audible feedback has become strongly associated them. That beep is a public stigmata of the user's failure. It coldly announces to all within earshot that you have done something execrably stupid. It is such hateful silicon sanctimony that most software developers now have an unquestioned belief that sound is bad and should never again be considered as a part of interface design. Nothing could be further from the truth. It is just the negative feedback aspect that is bad, not the audible aspect.

Negative audible feedback has several things working against it. Because the negative feedback is issued at a time when a problem is discovered, it naturally takes on the characteristics of an alarm. Alarms are designed to be purposefully loud, discordant and disturbing. They are supposed to wake sound sleepers from their slumbers when their house is on fire and their lives are at stake. They are like insurance, because we all hope that they will never be heard. Unfortunately, users are constantly doing things that programs can't handle, so these actions have become part of the normal course of interaction. Alarms have no place in this normal relationship, the same way we don't expect our car alarms to go off whenever we accidentally change lanes without using our turn indicators. Perhaps the most damning aspect of negative audible feedback is the implication that success must be greeted with silence. Humans like to know when they are doing well. They *need* to know when they are doing poorly, but that doesn't mean that they like to hear about it. Negative feedback systems are guaranteed to be appreciated less than positive feedback systems.

Given the choice of no noise versus noise for negative feedback, people will choose the former. Given the choice of no noise versus unpleasant noises for positive feedback, people will choose either based on their personal situation and taste. Given the choice of no noise versus soft and pleasant noises for positive feedback, however, my experience tells me that people will almost universally choose the audio. We have never given our users a chance by putting high-quality, positive audible feedback in our programs, so it's no wonder that people associate sound with bad interfaces.

The audible feedback must be at the right volume for the situation. Most computers don't offer volume controls, so sound is usually either too loud or too soft. Windows 95 finally offers a standard volume control, so one obstacle to beneficial audible feedback has been overcome.

Using your powers for good

Many programmers believe that it is their duty to inform the user when he has made an error. It is certainly the program's duty to inform *other programs* when they make an error, but I don't believe that this rule should extend to users. The customer is always right, so the program must accept whatever the user tells it, regardless of what the program does or doesn't know. This is similar to the concept of data immunity because whatever the user enters is acceptable, regardless of how incorrect the program believes it to be.

This doesn't mean that the program can wipe its hands and say "all right, he doesn't want to be protected, so I'll just let him crash." Just because the program must act as though the user is always right, this doesn't mean that the user actually *is* always right. Humans are always making mistakes, and your users are no exception. I can guarantee you that they will screw up. It may not be your fault, but it's your responsibility. How are you going to fix it?

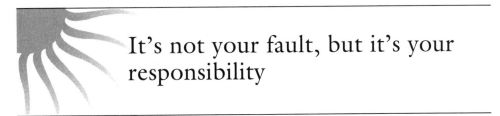

It's not your fault, but it's your responsibility

The program can erect warning signs—as long as they don't stop the proceedings with idiocy—but if the user chooses to do something suspect, the program can do nothing but accept the fact and work to protect the user from harm. Like a faithful guide, it must follow its master into the jungle, making sure to bring along an elephant gun and plenty of ammo.

The warning signs must use modeless techniques on the surface of the active window to inform the user of what he has done, much like the way the speedometer silently reports our speed violations. It is not reasonable, however, for the program to stop the proceedings with modal idiocy, just like it is not right for the speedometer to cut the gas when we edge above 65 miles per hour. Instead of an error message box, for example, edit fields can have little, graphic, simulated LEDs attached to them that change from green to red depending on how the program evaluates the current input.

Once the user has gone ahead and done something that the program is sure is wrong, there is only one way to protect him. If we edit his work without telling him, he will be proceeding into the jungle on false pretenses, so we cannot do that. If we edit his work and assure that he knows about it, we will have had to use an error message or a confirmation dialog box. This is also not acceptable. The only choice we have is to run along behind our brave user, making sure that he doesn't come to harm. We keep track of his path into the jungle; we remember each of his actions; we assure that each action can be cleanly reversed; we assure that no collateral information is lost. Essentially, we maintain a clear audit trail of his actions. This is why I formed the axiom: Audit, don't edit.

Audit, don't edit

If you can't bound input data with gizmos, just go ahead and accept whatever the user gives you. Then keep track of what you did and didn't get, and if anybody demands that things get straightened out, you will have full records that will enable you to do so. You could, for example, make an internal note that the data wasn't quite right yet, and make that information available to the user. The user can then judge whether the absence of the data will cause the planets to halt in their orbits. This means that the software should keep track of who, what, where, how and when the user is doing things, so the situation can be modified, rectified or just plain understood at some later date. This is much more human than merely forcing the data into some arbitrary format whose correctness is judged mostly on its compliance to a file schema rather than to a human need.

Now calm down! In the real world, we accept partially and incorrectly filled-in documents all of the time. We make a mental (or otherwise) note to fix it later, and we usually do. If we forget, we fix it when we eventually discover the omission. Even if we never fix it, we somehow muddle through. Who said that values are different for computer software than it is for humans? Well, programmers, that's who. They say they are rejecting incomplete or inaccurate data for our own good, but actually they are doing it for *their* own good—so they don't have to write the more difficult code that deals with the unexpected. Humans don't die if they try to divide by zero, but stupid computer programs do. We have a choice: We can either demand that humans *also* die or we can make our programs smarter. I know which method I choose: the one that makes the most money.

What about the—gasp!—lost data?

Yes, I realize that it is counter to everyone's wishes if information is lost. The data-entry clerk who fails to key in the invoice amount and then discards the invoice is creating a real problem. But is it really the righteous duty of the program to stop the user and point out this failure? No, it isn't. You have to consider the situation. If the application is a desktop productivity one, the user will be interacting with the program, and the results of his error will likely become apparent. In any case, the user will be driving the program like a car, and won't take kindly to having the steering wheel lock up because the stupid Chevy discovered it was low on windshield-washer fluid.

On the other hand, let's say the user is a full-time data-entry clerk keying forms into a corporate data-entry program. Our clerk does this one job for a living, and he will have spent hundreds—maybe thousands—of hours using the program. He will have a sixth sense for what is happening on the screen, and will know with a glance whether he has entered bad data, particularly if the program is using subtle, modeless visual and audible cues to keep him informed of the status of the data.

Remember, the program will be helping out: It won't demand that the user enter bounded information into unbounded gizmos. Things like part numbers that must be valid aren't going to be typed in anyway, but will be entered through a picklist of some sort. Things like addresses and phone numbers will be entered into extraction gizmos so that he can enter information more naturally. And the program will constantly give the user positive audible feedback, so the program begins to act as a partner, helping him stay aware of the status of his work.

So, how serious is the loss of data?

In a data-entry situation, a missing field can be serious, but the field will usually be entered incorrectly rather than just omitted. The program can easily help the clerk detect the problem and change it to a valid entry without stopping the proceedings. If the clerk is determined to omit necessary fields, the problem is the clerk and not the program. The percentage of clerks who fail because of either lack of ability or sociopathic tendencies is likely quite low. It isn't the job of the data-entry program to treat all data-entry clerks as though they can't be trusted to do a simple job just because one out of a hundred can't.

Windows 95 actually offers a reasonable example of "audit, don't edit" in its installation procedure. The program is not only smart enough to adapt to unexpected situations, but it also keeps copious internal notes on its progress. If it ever crashes, it leaves behind a record of its progress up until the problem, the way a bomb-disposal expert telephones her every move to the team so that if the bomb goes off they will know what not to do next time. When the user runs the install program again, the program reads those notes and uses them to succeed. The notes tell it what it has already done successfully, so it doesn't have to do those items over. The last entry in the notes also tells it the thing that didn't work. The install program will either omit the offending task this time around or take a different tack at solving it.

Most of our information processing systems are really very tolerant of missing information. A missing name, code, number or price can almost always be reconstructed from other data in the record. If not, the data can always be reconstructed by asking the various parties involved in the transaction. Businesses do this all the time and its cost is high, but not as high as the cost of Novell's technical help lines, for example. Actually, our information processing systems can work just fine with missing data. The programmers who write these systems just don't like all of the extra work involved in dealing with missing data, so they invoke data integrity as an unbreakable, deified law, and thousands of clerks must interact with rigid fascistware to keep databases from crashing—not to prevent their business from failing.

This book isn't about worker productivity or job psychology, but it is counter-productive to treat all of your workers like idiots to protect against those few who are. It lowers everyone's productivity, encourages rapid, expensive and error-causing turnover, and decreases morale, which increases the unintentional error rate of the clerks who want to do well. It is a self-fulfilling prophecy to assume that your information workers are untrustworthy.

The moguls of the industrial age know that what I just said is true, but marginal. Oppression clearly worked well enough for them to grow and prosper, so a counter-argument can be made. However, the stereotypical role of the data-entry clerk mindlessly keypunching from stacks of paper forms while sitting in a boiler room among hundreds of identical clerks doing identical jobs is dying out very rapidly. The task of data entry is becoming less a mass-production job and more a productivity, desktop job performed by intelligent, capable professionals and even directly by the customers. In other words, the population interacting with data-entry software is increasingly less tolerant of being treated like an unambitious, uneducated, unintelligent clerk. The imperatives of the industrial age are giving way to the imperatives of the information age, and users won't tolerate stupid software that insults them; not when they can just push a button and net surf for another few milliseconds until they find a vendor of similar goods or services that offers a software interface that treats them with respect.

Fudging

In the real world, missing information, and extra information that doesn't fit into a standard field, is an important tool for success. Information processing systems rarely handle this real-world data. They only model the rigid, repeatable data portion of transactions; a sort of skeleton of the actual transaction, which may involve dozens of meetings, travel and entertainment, names of spouses and kids, golf games and favorite sports figures. Maybe a transaction could only be completed if the termination date was extended two weeks beyond the "official" limit. Most companies would rather fudge on the termination date than see a million-dollar deal go up in smoke. In the real world, limits are fudged all of the time.

While entry systems are working to keep bad data out of the system, they almost never allow the user to fudge. There is no way to make marginal comments or to add an annotation next to a field. For example, maybe a vitally necessary item of data is missing, an interest rate, say. If the system won't allow the transaction to be entered without a valid interest rate, it stops the company from doing business. What if the interest rate field on the loan application had a penciled note next to it, initialed by the bank president, that said: "prime plus three the day the cash is delivered"? The system, working hard to maintain perfection, fails the reality test.

If the automated data-processing system is too rigid, it doesn't allow fudging. In other words, it won't model the real world. A system that rejects reality is not a good thing, even if it doesn't have any "invalid" fields. You must ask yourself the question "what is more important: Your database or your business?" The propeller-heads who manage the database and create the data-entry programs that feed it serve the CPU as master, and neither the needs of the user nor the needs of your business can overcome that. There is a significant conflict of interest that only software design, knowledgeable in, but detached from, the development process, can resolve.

If the program is used in a professional setting and information is actually lost, this is a bad thing, but not a *big* bad thing, because it only happens very occasionally. If, however, the interface protects against losing data, it will be obnoxious to *every* entry clerk, *all* of the time, and this *is* a big bad thing. It's kind of Zen-like: if you trust your data-entry clerks, they will perform better with the increased responsibility.

Besides, the amount of lost data will be insignificant and probably recoverable. More importantly, all of the software that I have seen that had rigid validation to guarantee data integrity was as full of holes as Swiss cheese. The bottom line is that all of that data integrity stuff doesn't work against a determined invader anyway, so you might as well try a different approach.

Imagine how nice it would be if, when a user finished editing, he could request a dialog box that listed the details of suspected errors he had made, along with some suggestions as to why, and possibly some hints on fixing them. There is usually plenty of information that an auditing program can gather when it suspects problems, and most of our computers have space for it. It's a good investment.

Failing gracefully

I've already said what I think about error messages, but I'm under no illusions about the impact it will have on an industry that is chock-full of error messages. Facing reality, I accept that programs are going to issue error messages, so now I'd like to talk about how to fail with grace.

Digital computers are absolute in their behavior. They either work or they don't. Good programmers are sensitive to this nature, and tend to create programs that reflect it. When programs detect errors—really nasty internal errors—they tend to crash absolutely. Let's say a program is merrily computing along, say, downloading your email from a server, when it runs out of memory at some procedure buried deep in the internals of the program. Most of the software I know and use issues a message that says, in effect, "You are completely hosed," and then shuts down the entire program. You restart the computer only to find that the program lost your email and, when you interrogate the server, find that it has also erased your mail because it had already handed it to your program.

This is not good.

When a program discovers a fatal problem, it knows it will die. Before it goes, however, it can follow one of two strategies. It can just go ahead and crash, or it can take the time and effort to prepare for its death without hurting the user. In other words, it can go out like a disgruntled, psychotic ex-employee, taking a dozen coworkers with him in a blaze of automatic machine pistol fire, or it can tidy up its affairs, assuring that its will is complete and all of its insurance policies, bank accounts and safe deposit boxes are identified and recorded for its heirs before it peacefully goes to meet its silicon god.

Most programs are filled with data and settings. When they crash, that information is normally just discarded. The user is left holding the bag. In our email example, the program accepted email from the server—which then erased its copy—but didn't assure that the email was properly recorded locally. The email program surely didn't crash because of its own incompetence—nawwww—it was brought down by the foolishness of some irresponsible screen saver program running in the background; but the email program was the victim. No, you are the victim. If the email program had made sure that those messages were promptly written to the local disk, even before it informed the server that the messages were successfully downloaded, the problem would never have arisen, even if the stupid screen saver then crashed things.

I constantly see the unwillingness of software to dismantle itself benignly before it crashes. Even if it doesn't crash, the attitude is still there, particularly in dialog boxes. A dialog will come up and the user will enter several complex inputs and settings. On the tenth or eleventh field, the dialog rejects the user's input and shuts down the dialog. The user then calls the dialog back up, and lo, the first ten valid entries were inconsiderately discarded. Remember Mr. Jones, that incredibly mean geography teacher in high school who ripped up your entire report on South America and threw it away because you handed it in in pencil instead of ink? Why couldn't he have just asked you to transcribe it instead of forcing you to do it over? Don't you hate South America to this day? Mr. Jones could easily have been a programmer.

Undo

30

Undo is that remarkable facility that lets us reverse a previous action. Simple and elegant, the feature is of obvious value. Yet, when we examine undo from a goal-directed point of view, there appears a considerable variation in purpose and method. Undo remains important, but it's not as simple as you might think.

Assisting the exploration

Undo is the facility traditionally thought of as the rescuer of users in distress; the knight in shining armor; the cavalry galloping over the ridge; the superhero swooping in at the last second.

As a computational facility, undo has no merit. It contributes nothing to the world of computer software. Mistake-free as they are, computers have no need for undo. Human beings, on the other hand, make mistakes all of the time, and undo is a facility that exists for their exclusive use. This singular observation should immediately tell us that of all the facilities in a program, undo should be modeled the least like its construction methods—its implementation model—and the most like the user's mental model.

Not only do humans make mistakes, they make mistakes as part of their everyday behavior. From the standpoint of a computer, a false start, a misdirected glance, a pause, a hiccup, a sneeze, a cough, a blink, a laugh, an "uh," a "you know" are all errors. But from the standpoint of the human user, they are perfectly normal. Human mistakes are so quotidian that if you think of them as "errors" or even as abnormal behavior, you will screw up the design of your software.

The user's mental model of mistakes

Saying that the user doesn't imagine himself as making mistakes is another way of saying that his mental model doesn't include an error on his part. Following the user's mental model means absolving the user of blame. The implementation model, of course, is based on the error-free CPU. Following the implementation model means acknowledging that all culpability has to be the user's. The typical programmer normally blames the user before he blames the software. Wooop! Wooop! Wooop! Model conflict! Most software assumes that it is blameless, and any problems are purely the fault of the user.

The solution is for the user interface designer to completely abandon any shred of thought that the user could make a mistake. Users don't make mistakes in their own minds, so the program shouldn't contradict them in its user interface.

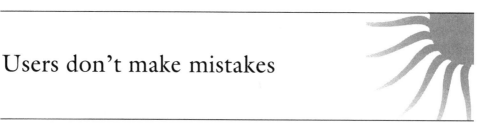

Users don't make mistakes

If we design software from the point of view that users never make mistakes, we immediately begin to see things differently. We cease to imagine the user as a module of code or a peripheral that drives the computer, and we begin to imagine him as an explorer, probing the unknown. We understand that exploration involves inevitable forays into blind alleys and box canyons, down dead ends and into dry holes. It is natural for humans to experiment, to vary their actions, to probe gently against the veil of the unknown to see where their boundaries lie. How can he know what he can do with a tool unless he experiments with it? Of course the degree of willingness to experiment varies widely from person to person, but most people experiment at least a little bit.

From the implementation model, the programmer's point of view, such gentle, innocent probing is just a continuous series of "mistakes." From our more-enlightened, mental model point of view, his actions are natural and normal. The program has the choice of either rebuffing those perceived mistakes or assisting him in his explorations.

Undo is for exploration, not mistakes

Undo is the primary tool for supporting exploration in software user interfaces. It allows the user to reverse one or more previous actions if he decides to change his mind.

The secret to designing a successful undo system is to create it from the assumption that it supports a normal part of the everyday working set of the program's tools, avoiding any hint that undo is a tacit acknowledgment of failure by the user. The key to this is to design it so that it is less a tool for reversing errors and more one for supporting exploration. Primarily, errors are single, incorrect and unintentional actions. Exploration, by contrast, is a long series of probes and steps, some of which may be keepers and others of which need to be abandoned. Most existing undo systems treat things as single, incorrect actions, but this model is less helpful.

Undo is distastefully human

Undo is one of the more difficult exercises in practical software development. It isn't very tough algorithmically—you won't find much discussion of it in computer science textbooks—but it necessitates adding a non-trivial facility to the program and putting a lot of convoluted code into virtually every other part of it. This difficulty of construction is a big reason why undo is often omitted or implemented poorly.

Probably an equally significant barrier to the adequate implementation of undo is a psychological one: Undo is not very computer-like. Computers never make mistakes, and this is one of the programmer's main career attractions. Programmers, as a group, really appreciate the deterministic behavior of computers. A large part of what makes programming so appealing to them is the ability to create a self-contained, self-consistent world of logical, rational behavior—a world of squared-off corners and clean-room streets. Undo, on the other hand, is all about rough edges and discards, inconsistencies and miscon-strued artifacts. Undo is a human thing, not a computer thing, and because it deals with human fallibility, it represents an unpleasant and vaguely distasteful part of the programmer's job.

Undo reassures

A significant contribution that undo makes to the user is purely psychological: it reassures him. It is much easier to enter a cave if you are confident that you can get back out of it at any time. The undo function is that comforting rope ladder to the surface, supporting the user's willingness to explore further by assuring him that he can back out of any dead-end caverns.

Curiously, users often don't think about undo until they need it, in much the same way that homeowners don't think about their insurance policies until some disaster strikes. Users will frequently charge half-prepared into the cave and only start looking for the rope ladder—for undo—after they have encoun-tered trouble.

User's mental model of undo

The user's mental model of undo is predictably variable for the simple reason that, although users need undo, it doesn't directly support a goal they bring to the task. Rather, it supports a necessary condition—trustworthiness—on the way to a real goal. It doesn't contribute positively to attaining the user's goal, but keeps some negative occurrence from spoiling the effort.

The user will visualize the undo facility in many different ways depending on the situation and his expectations. If the user is very computer-naive, he might see it as an unconditional "get-me-out-of-here" button—an escape valve or ejector-seat lever for extricating himself from a hopelessly tangled misadven-ture. A more experienced computer user might visualize undo as a storage facil-ity for deleted data. A really computer-sympathetic user with a logical mind might see it as a last-in-first-out, or LIFO, stack of procedures that can be undone one at a time.

In order to create an effective undo facility, we must satisfy as many of these mental models as we expect our users will bring to bear.

The undo language gap

As is so common in the software industry, there is no adequate terminology to describe the types of undo that exist—they are uniformly called "undo" and left at that. This language gap contributes to the lack of innovation in new and better variants of undo. I have created a taxonomy for undo, and I show the specific names for undo variants and define them as each one is discussed.

Let's first talk about what undo operates on: the user's actions. A typical user action in a typical application has a procedure component—what the user did—and an optional data component—what information was affected. When the user requests an undo function, the procedure component of the action is reversed, and if the action had an optional data component—the user added or deleted data—that data will be deleted or added back, respectively. Cutting, pasting, drawing, typing and deleting are all actions that have a data component, so undoing them involves removing or replacing the affected text or image parts. I call functions with both a procedure and a data component **incremental actions** or **incrementals**.

Many undoable functions are dataless transformations such as a paragraph reformatting operation in a word processor or a rotation in a drawing program. Both of these operations act on data, but neither of them adds or deletes data. I call functions like these that have just a procedure component **procedure actions** or **procedurals**. Most existing undo functions don't discriminate between procedurals and incrementals but simply reverse the most recent action.

The two most-familiar types of undo in common use today are single undo and multiple undo. **Single undo** is the most basic variant, non-repeatably reversing out the effects of the most recent user action, whether procedural or incremental.

This facility is very effective because it is so simple to operate. The user interface is simple and clear, easy to describe and remember. The user gets precisely one free lunch. This is by far the most frequently implemented undo, and it is certainly adequate, if not optimal, for many programs. For some users, the absence of this simple undo is sufficient grounds to abandon a product entirely.

The user generally notices most of his command mistakes right away: something about what he did doesn't feel or look right, so he pauses to evaluate the situation. If the representation is clear, he sees his mistake and selects the undo function to set things back to the previously correct state, then proceeds from there.

Multiple undo is repeatable—it can revert more than one previous operation, in reverse temporal order.

Normally, undo is invoked by a menu item or buttcon with an unchanging label. The user knows that triggering the idiom will undo the last operation, but there is no indication of what that operation is. I call this **blind undo**.

On the other hand, if the idiom includes a textual or visual description of the particular operation that will be undone, I call it **explanatory undo**.

If, for example, the user's last operation was to type in the word "design," an explanatory undo function on the menu would say "undo typing 'design.'" Explanatory undo is generally a much more pleasant feature than blind undo. It is fairly easy to put on a menu item, but more difficult to put on a buttcon, although putting the explanation in a ToolTip is a good compromise.

The trouble with single undo

The biggest limitation of single-level, incremental undo is when the user accidentally short-circuits the ability of the undo facility to rescue him. This problem crops up when the user doesn't notice his mistake immediately. For example, assume he deletes six paragraphs of text, then deletes one word, then decides that the six paragraphs were erroneously deleted and should be replaced. Unfortunately, performing undo now merely brings back the one word, and the six paragraphs are lost forever. The undo function has failed him by behaving literally rather than practically. Anybody can clearly see that the six paragraphs are more important than the single word, yet the program freely discarded those paragraphs in favor of the one word. The program's blindness caused it to keep a quarter and throw away a fifty-dollar bill, simply because the quarter was offered last.

In some programs any click of the mouse, however innocent of function it might be, causes the single undo function to forget the last meaningful thing the user did. This can be really frustrating if you expect undo help from the program. Although multiple undo solves these problems, it introduces some significant problems of its own.

Multiple undo

The response to the weaknesses of single-level undo has been to create a multiple-level implementation of the same, incremental undo. The program saves each action the user takes. By selecting undo repeatedly, each action can be undone in reverse order of its original invocation. In the above scenario, the user can restore the deleted word with the first invocation of undo, and can restore the precious six paragraphs with a second invocation. Having to redundantly re-delete the single word is a small price to pay for being able to recover those six valuable paragraphs. The excise of the word re-deletion tends to not be noticed the way we don't notice the cost of ambulance trips: we don't quibble over the little stuff when lives are at stake. But this doesn't change the fact that the undo mechanism is built on a faulty model, and in other circumstances, undoing functions in a strict LIFO order can make the cure as painful as the disease.

Imagine again our user deleting six paragraphs of text, then calling up another document and performing a global find-and-replace function. In order to retrieve the missing six paragraphs, the user must first unnecessarily undo the rather complex global find-and-replace operation. This time, the intervening operation was not the insignificant single-word deletion of the earlier example. The intervening operation was complex and difficult and having to undo it is clearly an unpleasant, excise effort. It would sure be nice to be able to choose which operation in the queue to undo and to be able to leave intervening—but valid—operations untouched.

Any program with undo must remember the user's last operation and, if applicable, cache any changed data. If the program implements multiple undo, it must maintain a stack of operations, the depth of which may be settable by the user as an advanced preference. Each time undo is invoked, it performs an incremental undo; reversing the most recent operation, replacing or removing data as necessary, and discarding the restored operation from the stack.

The model problems of multiple undo

The problems with multiple undo are not due to its behavior as much as to its manifest model. Most undo facilities are constructed in an unrelentingly function-centric manner. They remember what the user does function-by-function and separate the user's actions by individual function. In the time-honored way of creating manifest models that follow implementation models, undo systems tend to model code and data structures instead of user goals. Each press of the undo button reverses precisely one function-sized bite of behavior. Reversing on a function-by-function basis is a very appropriate mental model for solving most simple problems caused by the user making an erroneous entry. Users sense it right away and fix it right away, usually within a two- or three-function limit. The new Paint program in Windows 95, for example, has a fixed, three-action undo limit. However, when the problem grows more convoluted, the incremental, multiple undo model doesn't scale up very well.

You bet your LIFO

When the user goes down a logical dead end, rather than merely mis-keying data, he can often proceed several complex steps into the unknown before realizing that he is lost and that he needs to get a bearing on known territory. At this point, however, he may have performed several interlaced functions that are not all bad. He may well want to keep some actions and nullify others, not necessarily in strict reverse order. What if the user entered some text, then edited it, then decided to undo the entry of that text but not undo the editing of it? Sort of like dividing by zero, such an operation is undefined and problematic to implement and explain. Neil Rubenking offered me this pernicious example: suppose the user did a global replace changing "tragedy" to "catastrophe," then another changing "cat" to "dog." To undo the first without the second, can the program reliably fix all of the "dogastrophes"?

In this more complex situation, the simplistic representation of the undo as a single, straight-line, LIFO stack of incrementals doesn't satisfy the way it does in simpler situations. The user may be interested in studying his actions as a menu and choosing a discontiguous subset of them for reversion, while keeping some others. This demands an explanatory undo with a more robust presentation than might otherwise be necessary for a normal, blind multiple undo. Additionally, the means for selecting from that presentation must be more sophisticated. Representing the operation in the queue to clearly show the user what he is actually undoing is a problem of some difficulty.

Redo

If you don't believe that programmers are designing our software, the redo function should convince you beyond a shadow of a doubt. By adhering rigorously to the implementation model for undo, whereby functions are literally undone in reverse sequence, the inability to select the particular operation to undo without first undoing all of the valid intervening operations has caused the redo function to come into being. Redo essentially undoes the undo.

Redo mostly exists because it is easy to implement if the programmer has already gone to the effort to implement undo. Many programs that implement single undo treat the last undone action as an undoable action. In effect, this makes a second invocation of the undo function a redo function.

The real purpose of redo ends up being to avoid a diabolical situation in multiple undo. If the user wants to back out of a half-dozen or so operations, he presses the undo buttcon a few times, waiting to see things return to the desired state. It is very easy in this situation to press undo one time too many. He immediately sees that he has undone something desirable. Redo solves this problem by allowing him to undo the undo, putting back the last good action. Redo is really nothing more than a substitute for better visualization tools in an explanatory undo.

Special undo functions

Incremental undo

The backspace key is really an undo function, albeit a special one. When the user mis-types, the backspace key "undoes" the erroneous characters. If the user mis-types something, then enters an unrelated function such as paragraph reformatting, then presses the backspace key repeatedly, the mis-typed characters are erased and the reformatting operation is ignored. Depending on how you look at it, this can be a great flexible advantage giving the user the ability to "undo" discontiguously at any selected location, or this can be a trap for the user, as he can move the cursor and then inadvertently backspace away characters that were not the last ones keyed in.

Logic says that this latter case is a problem. Empirical observation says that it never bothered anybody. Such discontiguous incremental undo—so hard to explain in words—is so natural and easy to actually use, because everything is visible: The user can clearly see what will be "backspaced" away. Backspace is a classic example of an incremental undo, reversing only data while ignoring other, intervening actions. Yet if I described to you an undo facility that had a "pointer" that could be moved, and that undid the last function that occurred where the pointer points, you'd probably tell me that such a feature would be patently unmanageable and would confuse the bejabbers out of a typical user. Experience tells us that backspace does nothing of the sort. It works as well as it does because its behavior is consistent with the user's mental model of the cursor: because it is the source of added characters, it can also reasonably be the locus of deleted characters.

Using this same knowledge, we could create different categories of incremental undos, like a format-undo function that would only undo preceding format commands. I call this **category-specific undo**. If the user entered some text, changed it to italic, entered some more text, increased the paragraph indentation, entered some more text, then pressed the format-undo key, only the indentation increase would be undone. A second press of the format-undo key would reverse the italicize operation. But neither invocation of the format-undo would affect the content of what the user typed in.

What are the implications of category-specific undo in a non-text program? In a graphics drawing program, for example, we could have separate undo commands for pigment application tools, transformations, and cut-and-paste. There is really no reason why we couldn't have independent undo functions for each particular class of operation in a program.

Pigment application tools include all drawing implements—pencils, pens, fills, sprayers, brushes—and all shape tools—rectangles, lines, ellipses, arrows. Transformations include all image-manipulation tools—shear, sharpness, hue, rotate, contrast, line weight. Cut-and-paste tools include all lassos, marquees, clones, drags and other repositioning tools. Unlike the backspace function in the word processor, undoing a pigment application in a draw program would be temporal and would work independent of selection. That is, the pigment that is removed first would be the last pigment applied, regardless of the current selection. In text, there is an implied order from the upper left to the lower right. Deleting from the lower right to the upper left maps to a strong, intrinsic mental model, so it seems natural. In a drawing, no such conventional order exists, so any deletion order other than one based on entry sequence would be disconcerting to the user.

A better alternative would be to undo within the current selection only. The user selects a graphic object, for example, and requests a transformation-undo. The last transformation to have been applied to that *selected object* would be reversed.

Most software users are familiar with the incremental undo and would find a category-specific undo novel and possibly disturbing. However, the ubiquitousness of the backspace key shows that incremental undo is not intrinsic to the idiom, but is, rather, a learned behavior. If more programs had modal undo tools, users would soon adapt to them. They would even come to expect them the way we expect to find the backspace key on our word processors.

Deleted data buffer

As the user works on a document for an extended time, the desire for a repository of deleted text grows. It is not that he finds the ability to incrementally undo commands useless, but, rather, that reversing actions can cease to be so function-specific. Take for example, our six missing paragraphs. If separated from us by a dozen complex formatting commands, they can be as difficult to reclaim by undoing as they are to re-key. The user is thinking "if the program would just remember the stuff I deleted and keep it in a special place, I could go get what I want directly."

What the user is imagining is a repository of the data components of his actions, rather than merely a LIFO stack of incrementals. I call this a deleted data buffer.

His mental model wants the missing text without regard to which function elided it. The usual manifest model forces him to not only be aware of every intermediate step but to reverse each of them in turn. To create a facility more amenable to the user, we can create, in addition to the normal undo stack, an independent buffer that collects all deleted text or data. The user can open this buffer at any time as a document and use standard cut-and-paste or click-and-drag idioms to examine and recover the desired text. If the entries in this deletion buffer were headed with simple date stamps and document names, navigation would be very simple and visual.

The user could browse the buffer of deleted data at will, randomly, rather than sequentially. Finding those six missing paragraphs would be a simple, visual procedure, regardless of the number or type of complex, intervening steps he had taken. A deleted data buffer should be offered in addition to the regular, incremental multiple undo because it complements it, and besides, the data must be saved in a buffer anyway. This feature would be quite useful in all programs, too, whether spreadsheet, drawing program, or invoice generator.

Other manifest models

The manifest model of undo in its simplest form—single—conforms to the user's mental model: *I just did something I now wish I didn't do. I want to press a button and undo that last thing I did.* Unfortunately, this manifest model rapidly diverges from the user's mental model as the complexity of the situation grows. The need for an incremental undo remains, but discerning the individual components of more than the last few operations is overkill in most cases. The user wants to back up long distances occasionally, but when he does, the granular actions will not be terrifically important to him.

Milestoning

There are yet other ways to implement undo. One of the most powerful is what I call milestoning, discussed in Chapter 8. Milestoning simply makes a copy of the entire document the way a camera taking a snapshot makes an image frozen in time. Because milestoning involves the entire document, it is always implemented by directly using the file system. The biggest difference between milestoning and other undo systems is that the user must explicitly request the milestone—the saving of the document. Once he has done this, he can proceed to safely modify the original. If he later decides that his changes were undesired, he can return to the saved copy; to a previous version.

The milestoning concept is an excellent one, and many tools exist to support it for source code. Unfortunately, no program (that I know of) supports it directly to the user. Instead, they all rely on the file system's interface, which, as we have seen, is difficult for many users to understand. If milestoning were rendered in a non-file-system user model, implementation would be quite easy, and its management would be equally simple. A single buttcon would save off the entire document in its current state. The user could save as many versions at any interval that he desires.

The step for returning to a previously milestoned version is what I call a reversion.

The reversion facility shown in Chapter 8 is extremely simple—too simple, actually. Its menu item merely says "Revert to Milestone," and this was sufficient for a discussion of the file system, but when considered as part of undo, it should really offer more information. Typically, it should show a list of the available saved versions of that document, along with some information about each one, like the time and day it was recorded, the name of the person who recorded it, the length, and some optional user-entered notes. The user could choose one of these versions and the program would back down to it, discarding any intervening changes.

A relative of milestoning and reversion is a variant that I call freezing.

Sort of the opposite of milestoning, freezing involves locking the data in a document so that it cannot be changed. Anything that has been entered becomes unmodifiable, although new data can be added. Existing paragraphs are untouchable, but new ones can be added between older ones.

This method is much more useful on a graphic than on a text document. It is much like an artist spraying a drawing with fixative. All marks made up to that point are now permanent, yet new marks can be made at will. Images already placed on the screen are locked down and cannot be changed, but new images can be freely superimposed on the older ones. Fractal Design Painter offers a similar feature with its "wet" and "dry" paint commands.

Comparison: What would this look like?

The redo function isn't useful without the undo function, so the two have to be evaluated together to be meaningful. Besides providing robust support for the terminally indecisive, the undo-redo function is a convenient comparison tool. Say you'd like to compare the visual effect of ragged-right margins against justified right margins. Beginning with ragged-right, you invoke JUSTIFICATION. Now you press UNDO to see ragged-right and now you press REDO to see justified margins again. In effect, pressing UNDO and then REDO implements a "comparison" function; it just happens to be rendered in its implementation model. If this same function were to be added to the interface following the user's mental model, it might be manifested as a COMPARISON buttcon. This function would let you repeatedly take one step forward or backward to visually compare two states.

On my television remote control is a function labeled "Jump" (my television is a Sony; the function is present on other manufacturer's controls as well, where it has other names), which switches between the current channel and the previous channel—very convenient for viewing two programs concurrently. The jump function provides the same usefulness as the undo-redo function pair with a single command—a 50% reduction in excise for the same functionality.

When used as comparison functions, undo and redo are really one function, not two. One says "apply this change" and the other says "don't apply this change."

A single COMPARE button might more accurately represent the action to the user. Although we have been describing this tool in the context of a text-oriented word processing program, a compare function might be most useful in a graphic manipulation or drawing program, where the user is applying successive visual transformations on images. The ability to see the image *with* the transformation quickly and easily, compared to the image *without* the transformation would be a great help to the digital artist.

Doubtlessly, the compare function would remain a moderately advanced function. Just as the jump function like the one on my TV remote is probably not used by a majority of TV users, the compare button would remain one of those niceties for frequent users. This shouldn't detract from its usefulness, however, because drawing programs tend to be used very frequently by those who use them at all. For programs like this, catering to the frequent user is a reasonable design choice.

Undo is a global facility and should not be managed by local controls

We don't have individual undo functions on dialog boxes. Instead, the undo is a global, program-wide function that undoes the last action, regardless of whether it was done by direct manipulation or through a dialog box.

This makes undo problematic for embedded objects that use the OLE model. If the user makes changes to a spreadsheet embedded in a Word document, then clicks on the Word document, then invokes undo, the most recent Word action will be undone instead of the most recent spreadsheet action. I believe that users will have a difficult time with this. It fails to render the juncture between the spreadsheet and the word processing document seamlessly: the undo function ceases to be global and becomes modal. This is not an undo problem, however, but an OLE problem.

Undo-proof operations

Some operations simply cannot be undone because they involve some action that triggers a device that is not under the direct control of the program. Once an email message has been sent, for example, there is no undoing it. Once a computer has been turned off without saving data, there is no undoing it. Many operations, however, masquerade as undo-proof but are easily reversible. For example, when you save a document for the first time in most programs, it lets you choose the name for the file. But almost no programs let you rename that file. Sure, you can "Save As..." under another name, but that just makes *another* file under the new name, leaving the old file untouched under the old name. Why? Changing the name of a file is a frequently desired "undo" feature. Because it doesn't fall into the traditional view of undo as reversing procedures one at a time, we generally don't provide an undo function for setting a file-name.

Explanatory undo

Microsoft Word for Windows Version 6.0 has an unusual undo. I call it **group multiple undo**.

It is multiple-level, showing a textual description of each operation in the undo stack in a toolbar combobox. You can examine the list of past operations and select some point down in the list to undo; however, you are not undoing that one operation, but rather all operations back to that point, inclusive.

Essentially, you cannot recover the six missing paragraphs without first reversing all of the intervening operations. Once you select one or more operations to undo, the list of undone operations is now available in reverse order in the redo combobox. Redo works exactly the same way as undo works. You can select as many operations to redo as desired and all operations up to that specific one will be redone.

The program offers two visual cues to this fact. If the user selects the fifth item in the list, that item and all four items previous to it in the list are highlighted. Also, the text legend says "Undo 5 actions." The fact that they had to add that text legend tells me that, regardless of how the programmers constructed it, the users were applying a different mental model. The users imagined that they could go down the list and select a single action from the past to undo. The program didn't offer that option, so the signs were posted. This is like that door with the very pullable handle pasted with "Push" signs, and everybody still pulls on it anyway.

Part VIII: The Teacher
Education on Demand

*Learning to use software should be as easy as learning the way
around a new office. A little benign exploration, a couple of
interesting side trips, a fortuitous meeting in the hallway; this
is how we get oriented in real life. We should expect
nothing less from our software. The user should be reassured
at every step and generously rewarded for his curiosity. In
today's information age, creativity, excitement and a sense of
adventure are more important, ultimately, than correctness.
There are no mistakes, only opportunities to learn.*

Good at What You Do

So much emphasis has been placed on making it easy for new users to get acquainted with software that an essential point is often missed: Users spend more time as average users than they do as beginners. Software shouldn't be purposefully difficult for new users, of course, but it is even more important that the software makes everyday users powerful and satisfied. If software is part of your life or your job, it has to make you good at whatever you do.

The time users spend

Most computer users know all too well that opening the shrink-wrap on a new software product usually augurs several days of frustration and disappointment in learning the new interface. On the other hand, many experienced users of a program may find themselves continually frustrated because the program always treats them like a rank beginner. It seems impossible to find the right balance between catering to the needs of the first-timer and the needs of the expert.

Most developers are—naturally—expert users of their programs, and they tend to create interfaces that are best suited for other experts. Unfortunately, for any program, no matter how popular, there aren't going to be too many expert users out there. Prodded by complaints from customers or the marketing department, the developers add pedantic aids to the interface to lend beginners a helping hand. Unfortunately, these aids often condescend to the first-time user's ignorance. Besides, most users don't spend much time as raw beginners, so the training aids quickly turn offensive. It seems that the well-intentioned developer is cursed either way. The solution to this predicament lies in understanding the time users spend with software.

Intermediate users

Most users remain in a perpetual state of adequacy striving for fluency, with their skills ebbing and flowing like the tides, depending on how frequently they use the program. I call this a state of perpetual intermediacy, and such users are perpetual intermediates.

Imagine software users as skiers. All skiers spend time as beginners, but those who find they don't rapidly progress beyond more-falling-than-skiing quickly abandon the sport. The rest soon move off the bunny slopes onto the regular runs. Only a few ever make it onto the "double-black diamond" runs for experts. Most skiers live in the cities and only come up to the mountains a few times a year. The first trip of the season, they are very rusty, slowly and consciously recalling the little tips that they learned last year to keep themselves moving smoothly. By the last trip of the year, they have integrated all of those consciously recalled tips into their technique, so they no longer need to think about them. They are getting pretty good, boldly pushing into new territory and trying new moves. They don't have the time, money or inclination to quit their day jobs and spend all season on the slopes becoming real hot dogs, but they aren't beginners either. They are perpetual intermediates.

A well-rounded ski resort has a gentle slope for learning, and a few expert runs to really challenge the serious skier. But that resort also has an order of magnitude more runs for average skiers than any other. If the resort wants to stay in business, it will cater to the perpetual intermediate skier, without scaring off the beginner or insulting the expert. The beginner must find it easy to matriculate into the world of intermediacy, and the expert must not find his vertical runs obstructed by aids for bewildered perpetual intermediates.

Every software user passes through the beginner phase. Some users eventually become experts, too, but they will always be a small minority. Most users rapidly pass the beginner state but will never become experts with a particular program. Just like recreational skiers, they will spend the majority of their time as intermediate users.

A well-balanced software user interface takes the same approach as the successful ski resort. It doesn't cater to the beginner or to the expert, but rather devotes the bulk of its efforts to satisfying the perpetual intermediate. At the same time, it avoids offending either of its smaller constituencies, recognizing that they are both vital.

Most users in this middle state would like to learn more about the program, but they usually don't have the time. Occasionally, the opportunity to do so will surface. Sometimes these intermediates will use the product extensively for weeks at a time to complete a big project. During this time, they learn new things about the program. Their knowledge grows beyond its previous boundaries.

Sometimes, however, they do not use the program for months at a time and forget significant portions of what they knew. When they return to the program, they are not beginners again, but they will need reminders to jog their memory back to its former state.

Nobody wants to remain a beginner

As a percentage of hours spent with a program, beginning hours are very few, possibly less than one percent. If a user finds himself not satisfactorily progressing beyond the beginner stage after only a few hours, he will often abandon the program altogether and find another to take its place. No one is willing to remain incompetent at his job.

One of the most frequent mistakes committed by the design community is striving to make beginners happy. Beginnings are undeniably sensitive times, and it is easy to demoralize a first-timer, but keep in mind that the state of beginner-hood is *never* an objective. Nobody wants to remain a beginner. It is merely a rite of passage everyone must pass through. Good software shortens that passage without bringing attention to it.

Those who can't move beyond the beginner stage soon tire of the game because there isn't much reward in it for them. The person who never gets off the bunny slope will quickly tire of skiing, so trying to make him happy there will be a waste of effort. Instead, we should determine ways to quickly hustle him out of beginner-dom into the intermediate state. Our goal should be to get him and keep him with the pack: as a perpetual intermediate.

Experts are also a vital group because they have a disproportionate influence on less-experienced users. When a prospective buyer considers your product, he will trust the expert's opinion more than an intermediate's. If the expert says "it's not very good," she may mean "it's not very good for experts," but the beginner doesn't know that and will take the expert's advice, even though it may not apply.

Perpetual intermediates usually know that advanced features exist, even though they may not need them or know how to use them. But the knowledge that they are there is reassuring to the perpetual intermediate, convincing him that he made the right choice investing in this program. The average skier may find it reassuring to know that there is a really hairy black diamond expert run just beyond those trees, even if she never intends to use it. It gives her something to aspire to and dream about.

Optimize for intermediates

Our goal is neither to pander to beginners nor to rush intermediates into expertise. Our goal is threefold: to rapidly and painlessly get beginners into intermediacy, to avoid putting obstacles in the way of those intermediates who want to become experts, and most of all, to keep perpetual intermediates happy as they stay firmly in the middle of the skill spectrum.

Command vectors

In Chapter 19, I introduced the design term "command vector" to describe different classes of control idioms. For example, menus are one command vector, while keyboard mnemonics are another. Buttons and direct-manipulation idioms are two other command vectors. Some command vectors offer a lot of support to new users; typically, menus and dialog boxes offer the most, which is why I call them the "pedagogic vector." Beginners will avail themselves of the pedagogy of menus as they get oriented in a new program, but perpetual intermediates often want to leave them behind to find slimmer, quicker vectors.

Head and world vectors

I describe pedagogic vectors using Don Norman's phrase "information in the world." By this, Norman means that there is a sufficiency of information available just by looking. A kiosk showing a printed map of the campus, for example, is information in the world. We don't have to bother remembering where Norman Hall is, but can find it just by reading. Opposing this is Norman's phrase "information in your head," which refers to knowledge that you have learned or memorized, like the shortcut through Alexander Hall that isn't printed on any map. Information in your head is much faster and easier to use than information in the world, but you are responsible for assuring that you learn it, that you don't forget it and that it stays up-to-date. Information in the world is slower and more cumbersome, but very dependable. A pedagogic vector is necessarily filled with information in the world, which is why I call it a world vector.

Conversely, keyboard commands constitute a head vector, because using them requires the user to have filled his head with information about the functions and their commands.

It is a mistake to impute values for these two types of command vectors. World vectors are neither better nor worse than head vectors. Either one's usefulness depends entirely on the situation. When you first moved into your neighborhood, you probably had to use a map—a world vector. After living there a couple of days, you abandoned the map because you had learned how to get home—a head vector. On the other hand, even though you know your house intimately, when you had to adjust the temperature setting on the water heater, you needed to read the instructions—a world vector—because you didn't bother to memorize them when you moved in.

Our relationship to our software works the same way. We find ourselves easily memorizing facilities and commands that we use frequently and ignoring the details of commands that we use only rarely. This means that any operation that is used frequently will automatically become a candidate for a head vector. After daily use, for example, we no longer really read the menus but find what we need by recognizing patterns: pull down the second menu and select the bottom-most item in the next-to-last section. We read only to verify our choice.

Because each user unintentionally memorizes commands that are used frequently, perpetual intermediates memorize a moderate subset of commands and features. This subset is called a working set, and the mix of commands in it is unique to each individual.

In any particular program, the working set for all perpetual intermediates will include many commands in common. In Excel, for example, most every user will enter formulas and labels, specify fonts, and print. But Sally's working set might include goal-seeking, while Elliot's working set includes linked spreadsheets. From a designer's point of view, there is no such thing as a standard working set. Although a program's mainstream functions will certainly be part of each user's working set, his individual preferences and job requirements will dictate which additional features will be included. Even custom software written for corporate operations offer a range of features from which each user will pick and choose.

Any command is a working set candidate

The commands in any person's working set will be those used frequently. The user wants those commands to be especially quick and easy to invoke. This means that the designer must provide multiple command vectors for *all* commands, because there is no way to know in advance which ones might get used over and over.

Programs that decide for the user which functions are going to be frequently used and which aren't will almost always be incorrect for a plurality of their users. The program must allow the user himself to choose his own working set.

Having said that, I'll now backpedal to say that really dangerous commands (like erase all, clear undo, abandon changes, and so on) should not have easy, parallel command vectors. Instead, they need to be protected with menus and dialog boxes. However, if you have more than one or two dangerous commands in your program, you have way too many of them.

New users are happy with world vectors, but as they progress to become perpetual intermediates, they begin to develop their own working set and the world vectors begin to seem tedious. Each user wants to find head vectors for the contents of their working set. This is a natural and appropriate user desire and, if our software is to be judged easy-to-use, we must satisfy it. The solution consists of two components. First, we must provide a head vector in parallel to the world vector, and second, we must provide a path from the world vector to the head vector. This path, of course, is a vector itself, and I call it the **graduation vector**.

There are several ways to provide a graduation vector. The worst way is by writing it up in the program's documentation. The second worst is through the program's main online help system. These methods not only put the onus of finding the graduation vector on the user, but they leave it up to the user to realize that he needs to find it. Superior graduation vectors are either subliminally built into the interface or are at least offered in the program's interface by way of their own world vector. The latter can be implemented very easily just by adding a menu item to the standard HELP menu called SHORTCUTS. This item takes the user directly to a section of help that describes available shortcuts. This method has the benefit of being explicit and therefore pedagogic. New users can see that multiple command vectors exist and that there is an easy-to-find resource for learning them. All programs should have this shortcut item.

Design tip: Offer shortcuts from the HELP menu.

Adding subliminal graduation vectors is less problematic than it sounds. There are already two on the menus of most programs. As defined by Microsoft, a typical Windows application has two keyboard head vectors: Mnemonics and accelerators. For example, in Word, the mnemonic for SAVE is ALT-F S and the visual graduation vector for it is the underlining of the F and S in the menu name and the menu item, respectively. The accelerator for SAVE is CTRL-S. CTRL-S is noted explicitly on the right side of the menu on the same line as the SAVE item, which acts as a graduation vector.

Neither of these vectors intrudes on the new user. He may not even notice their existence until he has had the opportunity to use the program at some length—that is, until he becomes an intermediate user. Eventually, he will notice these visual hints and will wonder about their meaning. Most reasonably intelligent people—most users—will get the accelerator connection without any help. The mnemonic vector is slightly tougher, but once the user is clued into the use of the ALT meta-key, either by direction or accident, the idiom is extremely easy to remember and use wherever it occurs.

If you turn back to Figure 20-4, you can see another excellent technique where small icons are used to form a graduation vector from menus to buttcons. This repetitive use of visual images helps build the "visual fugue" I mentioned in Chapter 4. The icon identifying each function or facility should be shown on every artifact of the user interface that deals with it: each menu, each buttcon, each dialog box, every mention in the help text, every mention in the printed documentation. This graduation vector formed of visual symbols is the strongest and best technique, yet it is tragically unexploited.

ToolTips are another place where visual symbols can be used to good effect in indicating parallel command vectors. A tiny symbol—just a dot or triangle, for example—could be shown on every ToolTip that accompanied buttons with synonymous direct-manipulation idioms.

What beginners need

Let's get one thing straight: Beginners are not stupid. As a software designer, I find it best to imagine that users are simultaneously very intelligent and very busy. They need some instruction, but not very much, and the process has to be very rapid. It can't get bogged down in training or explanation. If the ski instructor begins lecturing on meteorology and alpine ecology, he will lose his students, regardless of their aptitude for skiing. Just because a user needs to learn how to operate a program doesn't mean that he needs or wants to learn how it works inside.

Imagine users as very intelligent but very busy

On the other hand, intelligent people always learn better when they understand cause and effect, so you must give them an understanding of why things are working the way they are. It may seem like a contradiction to say they don't have the patience for explanations but that they must understand why, and I suppose it is, but most of real life is a minestrone of contradictions. Get over it. We use mental models to bridge the contradiction. The mental model provides all the explanation the user needs without forcing him to plumb the depths of the implementation model. The user can ignore the physical functions but will need to know the scope, the benefits and the risks.

Getting beginners on board

To get beginners into a state of intermediacy requires extra help from the program, but this extra help will quickly get in their way as they become intermediates. This means that the extra help you provide must not be fixed into the interface. It must know how to go away. Generally, beginner-level assistance is designed as add-ons to the product.

This beginner information should not be permanently built into the program's interface. Our new user will either grasp the concepts and scope of the program right away or he will abandon it. He may not recall from use to use exactly which command was needed to fratz the veeblefetzer, but he will definitely remember that the veeblefetzer needs fratzing if it is consistent with his mental model.

Online help is a really bad tool for providing such add-ons. We'll talk more about help later in this chapter, but its main purpose is as a reference, and beginners don't need reference information; they need understanding. What they really need is a guided tour.

And that is precisely the way beginners should be indoctrinated: with a guide. A separate facility—a dialog box springs to mind—is a fine tool for communicating overview, scope and purpose. It doesn't necessarily have to be tightly connected to the actual controls that invoke functions because those controls already have ToolTips (they have to, to satisfy perpetual intermediates). As the user begins the program, a dialog box can appear that states the basic goals and tools of the program, naming the main features. This dialog can be quite sophisticated or simple; it doesn't really matter, as long as it stays focused on beginner issues like scope and goals and avoids perpetual intermediate and expert issues.

Beginners rely heavily on the menu to give commands. Menus may be slow and clunky, but they are thorough and wordy, so they offer reassurances. Also, the dialog boxes they usually bring up are expository and explanatory and come with a convenient CANCEL button. The toolbar is a bit too drastic for newcomers.

What perpetual intermediates need

Perpetual intermediates need access to tools. They don't need scope and purpose explained to them because they already know these things. ToolTips are the perfect perpetual intermediate idiom. ToolTips say nothing about scope and purpose and meaning, they only state function in the briefest of idioms, consuming the least amount of video space in the process.

Perpetual intermediates know how to use reference materials. They are motivated to dig deeper and learn, as long as they don't have to tackle too much at once. This means that online help is a perpetual intermediate tool. They will use it by way of the index, so that part of help must be very comprehensive.

Perpetual intermediates will be establishing the functions that they use with regularity and those that are only used rarely. The user may experiment with obscure features, but he will soon identify—probably subconsciously—his frequently used working set. The user will demand that the tools in his working set are placed front-and-center in the user interface, easy to find and to remember.

What experts need

Experts will occasionally look for esoteric features, and they might make heavy use of a few of them. However, they primarily demand faster access to their working set of tools, which may be quite large. In other words, they want shortcuts to everything.

Any person who uses a program for hours a day will very quickly internalize the nuances of its interface. It isn't so much that users *want* to cram frequently used commands into their heads, as much as it is unavoidable. Their frequency of use both justifies and requires the memorization. If they were perpetual intermediates, they would be remembering only to forget again by the next time.

The expert is constantly, aggressively seeking to learn more and to see more connections between his actions and the program's behavior and representation. Experts appreciate new features. Their mastery of the program insulates them against becoming disturbed by the added complexity.

Beginning User	Perpetual Intermediate User	Expert User
What does the program do?	What new features are in the upgrade?	How do I automate this?
What is the program's scope?	I forgot how to import	What are the shortcuts for this command?
Where do I start?	What is this gizmo for?	Can this be changed?
How do I print?	Oops! Can I undo?	What is dangerous?
	How do I find facility X?	Is there a keyboard equivalent?
	What was the command for X?	How can I customize this?
	Remind me what *this* does	

Figure 31-1

The demands users place on software varies considerably with their experience. The tools presented to the user need to reflect this disparity. It won't be appreciated much if your program is very easy for first-timers to learn if most users are going to be perpetual intermediates. Similarly, if only professional, full-time experts will use the product, the interface needs to cater to their unique needs.

Idiosyncratically modal behavior

Many times a user population divides rather cleanly on the effectiveness of an idiom. Half of the users like one idiom while the other half strongly prefer another. I've seen development shops emotionally split on issues like this. One group becomes the "menu item" camp while the rest of the developers are the "buttcon" camp. They wrangle and argue over the relative merits of the two methods while the real answer is staring them in the face: Use both!

When a population splits like this on preferred idioms, the software designers must offer *both* idioms. Both groups must be satisfied. It is no good to satisfy one half of the population while angering the other half, regardless of which particular group you align yourself with.

I'm not saying that every individual preference needs to be accommodated. Many individuals have amusing design suggestions that should be adamantly ignored. I've heard developers state unequivocally that "dialog boxes are bad" and that "sticky menus are hateful things." These fringe voices reflect only personal taste and must be ignored. But if, in development or user testing, you find that a significant group of users has a similar preference, you must satisfy it, even if there are three or four conflicting groups. When I see this clear division of a population's preferences into two or more large groups, I say that the user's preferences are **idiosyncratically modal**.

Windows offers an excellent example of how to cater to idiosyncratically modal desires in its menu implementation. Some people like menus that work the way they do on the Macintosh: you press the mouse button on a menu bar item to make the menu appear; then—while still holding down the button—drag down the menu and release the mouse button on your choice. Other people find this procedure difficult and prefer a way to accomplish it without having to awkwardly hold the mouse button down while they drag. Windows neatly satisfies this by letting the user click-and-release on the menu bar item to make the menu appear. Then the user can move the mouse—button released—to the menu item of his choice. Another click-and-release selects the item and closes the menu. Just as on the Macintosh interface, the user can still click-and-drag to select a menu item. The brilliance of these idioms is that they coexist quite peacefully with each other. Any user can freely intermix the two idioms, or stick consistently with one or the other and the program requires no change. There are no preferences or options to be set; it just works.

In Windows 95, Microsoft has added a third idiosyncratically modal idiom to the menu behavior with their new "menu mode." The user clicks-and-releases as before, but now he can drag the mouse along the menu bar and the other menus are triggered in turn. Amazingly, now all three idioms are accommodated seamlessly and integrally. It's as though the lion lay down with the lamb *and* the hyena.

If you are writing a transient posture application that won't be used frequently, go ahead and provide just one command vector. If you are creating a sovereign application that will be used frequently by a broad spectrum of users, however, you must expect idiosyncratically modal behavior, along with very individual working sets. The only solution is multiple command vectors for all functions.

Commensurate effort

There is a principle that grants some measure of relief to overburdened interface designers. I call it the principle of **commensurate effort** and although it applies to all users, it is particularly pertinent to perpetual intermediates and experts.

The principle merely states that people will willingly work harder for something that is more valuable to get. If I really want something, I will work hard to get it. The catch, of course, is that value is in the eye of the beholder. It has nothing to do with how technically difficult a feature was to implement. If a person wants to become a good tennis player, for example, he will get out on the court and play very hard. To someone who doesn't like tennis, any amount of the sport is tedious effort. If a user really wants to format beautiful documents with multiple columns, several fonts and fancy headings, he will be highly motivated to explore the recesses of the program to learn how. He will be putting commensurate effort into the project. If some other user just wants to print plain old documents in one column and one font, no amount of inducement will get him to learn those more-advanced formatting features.

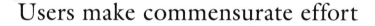

Users make commensurate effort

This means that if you add features to your program that are necessarily complex to manage, users will be willing to tolerate that complexity only if the rewards are worth it. This is why a program's user interface can't be complex if it's being used to achieve simple results. Of course, as users get more experienced with the feature, they search for shortcuts, and you must provide them. When software follows commensurate effort, the learning curve doesn't go away, but it disappears from the user's mind, which is just as good.

The typers versus the pointers

Beginners like to point gingerly with the mouse the way they might dip their toe in the surf. Frequent users like to remember and use keyboard idioms that speed up their work. Everybody uses both and, surprisingly, many people tend to use an unorthodox combination of keyboard and mouse idioms to select and manipulate information in Windows. The truth is that we use both interchangeably; and often within a single object-verb operation. This situation was not well understood by the GUI inventors, and it was summarily rejected by the original Macintosh, though they eventually added arrow keys in deference to it.

IBM's PC was very influential in the '80s, dictating many of our still-extant standards. IBM made the indefensible argument that the mouse wasn't necessary; an argument equivalent to saying that the rear view mirrors on your car aren't necessary for driving. Strictly true, but counterproductive. I can't prove it, but I suspect that IBM thought this whole GUI thing was just a passing fad and were unwilling to commit to it. Even after events proved them wrong, IBM remained ambivalent about the mouse, refusing to adopt it wholeheartedly in both their hardware and their software.

CUA

IBM's ambivalence affected the development of their user interface standard for all IBM software, which was called Common User Access, or CUA. Notably, CUA included both the mouse and the keyboard as co-equal command vectors. Back when Microsoft was pals with IBM, Windows was mandated to be CUA compliant (about the time of Windows 3.0). The CUA requirement was obnoxious because IBM was unable to define it precisely or completely, yet their world-class bureaucracy was very skilled at assuring that it wasn't ignored. As soon as Bill Gates and IBM ceased their intimate relationship, most talk of CUA was abandoned at Microsoft. However, the seeds had been sown, the advantages made visible, and Windows today wisely supports the notion that users may wish to use the keyboard or the mouse in any mix and that well-behaved Windows applications will support them.

Apple was the opposite of IBM, very sympathetic to the beginning computer user. They envisioned touch-typists as corporate-drones and thumbed their noses at them. Apple treated the keyboard as a significantly less important and less useful command vector, adamantly refusing to put special function keys and arrow keys on it for several years. This choice was as silly in its way as IBM's insistence that software work totally without mice.

The argument between the Macintosh "pointers" and the PC "typers" has raged loudly and inconclusively for many years. The truth, as might be expected, eluded both camps and involves compromise.

The big problem with CUA is its demand that the keyboard must be capable of doing *everything;* that computers will normally not be equipped with a mouse. This demand and the expectation it is based on have been proven incorrect. Today, the mouse is omnipresent, as is the keyboard. Many tasks are very easy and natural with a mouse and very difficult and unnatural with the keyboard. For example, moving a pluralized window from one position on the desktop to another is trivial with the mouse but demands a tortuous evolution when done with the keyboard. I don't know of anybody who moves windows around with the keyboard, do you?

CUA's all-or-nothing attitude is wrong and the omnipresence of mice can now be taken for granted. Operations that are simple and direct with a mouse and complex and indirect with the keyboard can safely be supported only by the mouse idiom. It is a waste of time to implement them with the keyboard.

Having said that, I should emphasize that such idioms are not common, and this shouldn't be used as an excuse for dropping keyboard support of actions that are not clearly better in every respect with the mouse.

The diamond

In the '70s and early '80s, computer users mastered either CP/M or DOS, both command-line operating systems. The programs that ran on these operating systems were also structured with command-line interfaces, and the learning curve for these programs was steep indeed. However, the rewards were great for undergoing the initial torture of learning. Now, I'm not advocating a return to WordStar or VisiCalc, but there was much of value in those old programs that shouldn't be tossed out indiscriminately.

Without a mouse, those old programs could only provide head vectors—the user had to memorize all commands—on the only input device commonly available at the time: the keyboard. Even though beginners couldn't be accommodated with world vectors, the perpetual intermediates and experts were happy with the high-productivity keyboard command vectors and they were willing—commensurate effort, remember—to memorize them if they had to. Software designers took full advantage of the ten (later twelve) special function keys that IBM made a standard. They also made extensive and effective use of the two meta-keys, CTRL and ALT.

WordStar, in particular, had a powerful influence over microcomputer users who were touch-typists. By holding down the CTRL key with your left pinkie and simultaneously pressing a letter key with your left fore- or middle-finger you could navigate your document with incredible speed and ease. That is, *if* you were a touch-typist and *after* you memorized the idiom. WordStar called it "the diamond" because the salient keys were arranged in the slightly mnemonic diamond shape, shown in Figure 31-2. Beginners and hunt-and-peck typists *hated* WordStar. I used WordStar (and its predecessor, WordMaster) for at least a dozen years. My fingers still remember that diamond even though I couldn't consciously tell you any of the commands. I still find myself fruitlessly typing a CTRL-SOMETHING to move up and down in Word and Excel.

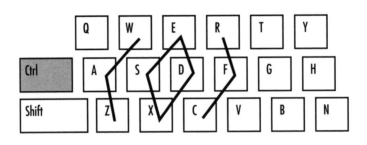

Figure 31-2

The basic diamond in WordStar was the E, S, D and X. You held the Ctrl key down with your pinkie, then pressed the E to move the cursor up one line, the X to move down one line, the S to move left one character, the D to move right one character. Ctrl-A moved the cursor left one word, and Ctrl-F moved right one word. Ctrl-W scrolled the screen up one line, and Ctrl-Z scrolled the screen down one line. Ctrl-R scrolled the screen up one page, and Ctrl-C scrolled it down one page. The diamond could be mastered in a few hours of practice; it was and still is the fastest way to move around in a document if you are a touch-typist. I blame IBM for destroying this wonderful idiom. They moved the Ctrl key away from the pinkie position, and forced all navigation functions onto the ten-key pad to the right of the regular keyboard. Now you have a Hobson's choice between two typist-hostile navigation methods: IBM's ten-key or Apple's mouse.

WordStar owned some ninety percent of the word processor market in the late-seventies and early-eighties, but in the late-eighties lost virtually all of its clientele to the GUI-based word processors like Microsoft Word, WordPerfect and Lotus's Ami Pro. These new products made it easy for beginners, but unfortunately, the baby got tossed out with the bath water. You can point-and-click in Word, and there are parallel keyboard commands for navigating, but they are all based on the numeric keypad and require you to move your right hand away from the home row to use them. This doesn't sit well with touch-typists, nor with me. I'm a reasonably skilled touch-typist (thanks, Dad, for insisting I learn when I was 13 years old!) and I would still like to use that old WordStar diamond in all of my contemporary programs. I don't want to return to the days when the diamond was forcibly inflicted on users, but perpetual intermediates and experts can still benefit from such high-speed, high-productivity command vectors, despite their high demands.

Standards

It has been said that the great scientific disciplines are examples of giants standing on the shoulders of other giants. It has also been said that the software industry is an example of midgets standing on the toes of other midgets. This old joke seems particularly relevant with respect to standards.

Nothing is more paradoxical in the software industry than standards. Standards are easily the biggest aid to interface designers. Standards are also the biggest obstacle for user interface designers. The lack of standards is the biggest aid to interface designers. The lack of standards is also the biggest obstacle for user interface designers.

If this were the business of making soap or paper or drinking glasses, we would have well-established standards and they would be slowly, so slowly creeping forward decade by decade. The solidity of standards allows producers and consumers alike to depend on quality, features and price. There are no great technological changes in the world of soap or paper or drinking glasses, so their respective apple-carts remain upright. In software, though, new technologies and techniques appear monthly. In the world of user interface design, we desperately need all the advances we can get. Naturally—it seems—we should immediately discard the old for the new, except that users and vendors hate moving targets.

Standards allow us to consolidate our technological gains and exploit our collective accomplishments. Standards are a plateau in the steep climb of invention. They may hinder innovation, but they allow commercial products to build a base of customers. This commercial success in turn funds more invention.

The big standards, like interface paradigms and platforms, are set de facto—by the market. Only now, after twenty years, is Microsoft powerful enough to establish standards de jure—by declaration. And even there, Microsoft is only effective on the fringe standards like MAPI and TAPI, while standards on center stage like ODBC and OLE are fiercely contended by others.

IBM's foolish CUA was a last-gasp attempt by the fading giant to set a standard de jure in an area where none was wanted; plus, they had virtually no expertise.

CUA failed because it was too much, too soon and too much of a lowest common denominator. Calculated to offend no one, it offended all.

On the other hand, designers and inventors hate standards because they cramp their style and obstruct their pushing out of the boundaries of the envelope.

I hear amateur user interface designers and programmers speak of user interface standards all the time as though they are codicils recorded in a big book somewhere. It's though Apple or Microsoft had figured out the right methods for all time and it is our duty to perpetuate them. Sure, both companies actually have published user interface guidelines, but both companies freely break them and then update the guidelines.

In the Windows world, we really don't have standards as much as we have big examples. Our standards are "what Excel does" or "what Word does." Every time Microsoft proposes something as standard, they willfully go ahead and change it for something better in the next version. And they should. Interface design is today in its infancy and it is silly to think that there is benefit in chiseling our baby steps in granite.

Windows 1.0 violated the standards set by MS-DOS. Windows 2.0 violated the standards of 1.0. Windows 3.0, 3.1 and Windows 95 each stepped on their predecessors in turn. The Macintosh was such a spectacular achievement because it absolutely abandoned all of Apple's previous platforms.

Conversely, much of the strength of the Mac came from the fact that vendors all followed Apple's lead and made their interfaces look, work and act alike. Similarly, many successful Windows programs have been unabashedly modeled after Word or Excel. You should be getting a sense for where I'm going by now, as I keep goring user interface design on the horns of the "standard" dilemma. When we find two otherwise true propositions in direct opposition, the answer is to rephrase the question. Instead of asking whether we should follow standards, the question must be articulated more like this: When should we *violate* standards? The answer to this question is simple, but difficult: We should violate standards whenever we have a darn good reason to.

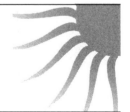

Obey standards unless you've got a darn good reason

Of course, this begs the question: What makes a darn good reason? Personal preference is out, including those of your client or user-test subjects. I'd like to answer "when a new idiom is measurably better," but I am deeply suspicious of the objectivity of contemporary "measurement" approaches. The real answer is the de facto answer: when the idiom can be seen to be manifestly better, go ahead and use it. This is how the toolbar came into existence, along with buttcons, outlines, tabbed dialogs and many other idioms. Scientists and academics may have been examining these artifacts in their labs, but it was their presence in real-world software that showed the way. Your reason may ultimately prove to *not* be darn good and your product will suffer—possibly die— but designers will learn from its lack of merit. This is what Christopher Alexander, in *Notes on the Synthesis of Form* (Harvard University Press, 1964), calls the "unselfconscious process," an indigenous and unexamined process of slow and tiny forward increments as individuals attempt to improve solutions. Like art.

Online help

Online help is not a part of good user interface design. Online help is really the same as, and not significantly better than, printed documentation, and in many ways it is a lot worse. Both forms of documentation are largely useless for anything other than a reference tool for perpetual intermediates. Ultimately, online help is not important, the way that the user manual of your car is not important. If you find yourself needing it, it means that your car is badly designed. The design is what is important.

A complex program with many features and functions should come with a reference document: a place where users who wish to expand their horizons with a product can find definitive answers. This document can be a printed manual or it can be online help. The printed manual is comfortable, browsable and friendly and can be carried around. The online help is searchable, semi-comfortable, very lightweight and cheap. Online help could be improved somewhat.

The index

Because you don't read a manual like a novel, the key to a successful and effective reference document is the quality of the tools for finding what you want in it. Essentially, this means its index. A printed manual has an index in the back that you use manually. Online help has an automatic index search facility. It is often said by the defenders of online help that the automatic search facility is more powerful than a manual, hardcopy version. This is theoretically true, but not relevant. The difference between a good index and a bad index is the quality of its entries and not of its search tools.

I suspect that few if any of the online help facilities I've seen were indexed by a professional indexer. Certainly, I can never find what I need in the help systems I've used, and I can find dozens of entries whose presence would seem totally reasonable and obvious that are missing from any help system. Even the help system in Word, for example, which has a really superb index, offered up these omissions in about five minutes of random probing: *lost, can't find, video, sound, report, backspace, escape, enter, page down, page up*. However many entries are in your program's index, you could probably benefit from doubling the number.

What's more, the index has to be generated by examining the program and all of its features, not by examining the help text. This is not easy, because it demands that a highly skilled indexer be intimately familiar with all of the features of the program. I suspect it's easier to rework the interface to improve it than to create a really good index.

The list of index entries is arguably more important than the text of the entries themselves. The user will forgive a poorly written entry with more alacrity than he will forgive a missing entry. The index must have as many synonyms as possible for topics. Prepare for it to be huge. The user who needs to solve a problem will be thinking "how do I turn this cell black," not "how can I set the *shading* of this cell to 100%." If the entry is listed under shading, the index fails the user. The more goal-directed your thinking is, the better the index will map to what might possibly pop into the user's head when he is looking something up. The index model that I like is the one in *The Joy of Cooking*, by Irma S. Rombaur & Marion Rombaur Becker (Bobbs-Merrill, 1962). That index is one of the most complete and robust of any I've used.

Shortcuts

One of the features missing from every help system I've seen is an option I call "Shortcuts." In my designs, I place this option prominently on the help menu. It is a graduation vector, showing in digest form all of the head vectors for the program's various features. It is a very necessary component on any online help system because it provides what perpetual intermediates need the most: access to features. They need the tools and commands more than they need detailed instructions.

The other missing ingredient from online help systems is overview. I want to know how the "Enter Macro" command works, and the help system explains uselessly that it is the facility that lets me enter macros into the system. What I need to know is scope, effect, power, up-side, down-side and why I might want to use this facility both in absolute terms and in comparison to similar products from other vendors.

Not for beginners

I see many help systems that assume that their role is to provide assistance to beginners. This is not true. Beginners stay away from the help system because it is generally just as complex as the program. Besides, any program whose basic functioning is too hard to figure out just by experimentation is unacceptably bad, and no amount of help text will resurrect it. Online help should ignore first-time users and concentrate on those people who are already successfully using the product, but who want to expand their horizons: the perpetual inter- mediates.

About boxes are an excellent idiom for offering basic assistance to users, though it is rarely done.

Better help

ToolTips are modeless online help, and they are incredibly effective. Why can't we have more idioms like these? Our "standard" help systems are implemented in a separate program that covers up most of the program for which it is offer- ing help. If I asked a human about some feature, chances are excellent that he would use his finger to point to something on the screen to augment his expla- nation. A separate help program that obscures the main program cannot do this. The basic form of current online help systems is weak. I'd rather see the help presented transparently over the program or built right into the face of it.

Wizards

Wizards are a new idiom unleashed on the world by Microsoft, and they are rapidly gaining popularity among programmers and erstwhile user interface designers. I have big reservations about their popularity among users.

Basically, a wizard is a series of dialogs that attempt to guarantee success in using a feature by stepping the user through a series of dialog boxes. These dialogs parallel a complex procedure that is "normally" used to manage a feature of the program. For example, a wizard helps the user create a presentation in PowerPoint 4.0.

Programmers really like wizards because they get to treat the user like a peripheral device. Each of the wizard's dialogs asks the user a question or two, and in the end the program performs whatever task was requested. They are a fine example of interrogation tactics on the program's part.

Wizards are written as step-by-step procedures, rather than as informed conversations between user and program. The user tends to feel like the conductor of a robot orchestra: swinging the baton to set the pace, but otherwise having no influence on the proceedings. In this way, wizards rapidly devolve into exercises in confirmation messaging. The user learns that he merely presses the NEXT button on each screen without critically analyzing why.

There is a place for wizards in actions that are very rarely used, like installation or deinstallation. They are too demeaning to the user to be used in daily services, though.

A better way to create a wizard is to make a simple, automatic function that asks no questions of the user but that just goes off and does the job. If it creates a presentation, for example, it should create it, and then let the user have the option, using standard tools, to later change the presentation. The interrogation tactics of the typical wizard are not friendly, reassuring or particularly helpful. The wizard often doesn't explain to the user what is going on.

I'd much rather see the effort that is going into wizards go into designing better user interfaces. Wizards are having the opposite effect, though. They are giving programmers license to put raw implementation model interfaces on complex features with the bland assurance that "we'll make it easy with a wizard." This is all too reminiscent of the "we'll be sure to document it well in the manual" cry of years past.

The inverted meta-question

In Chapter 13, I introduced the concept of the meta-question, where the user must ask the program for permission to ask a question. This is pure excise and should never be used, but its opposite can be useful in certain circumstances. I call this the **inverted meta-question**.

Instead of forcing the user to ask to ask, the inverted meta-question tells a dialog to go away and not ask again. In this way, a user can make an unhelpful dialog box stop badgering him, even though the program mistakenly thinks it is helping. For example, every time I ask my drawing program to insert clipart, it asks me what directory to search in. It would be great if I could check a box on that dialog telling it to never come back again. From now on, it would only look for clipart in the last directory, which is always correct. If I were to change the directory, I could get the dialog back by requesting the function in a special way, such as with a meta-key. If a beginner inadvertently dismisses a dialog box and can't figure out how to get it back, he may benefit from an easy-to-identify safety net idiom in some prominent place. A help menu item saying "Bring back all dismissed dialogs," for example, may be just the ticket.

We need to spend more time making our programs powerful and easy to use for perpetual intermediate users. We must accommodate beginners and experts, too, but not to the discomfort of the largest segment of users.

Installation, Configuration and Personalization

Most user interface designers find themselves facing a conundrum regarding whether to make their products user-customizable. It is easy to be torn between the user's need to have things done his way, and the clear problem this creates when the program becomes hard to navigate because familiar elements of it are either gone or moved. The solution is not to choose one or the other of these options but to cast the problem in a different light.

Navigation is by reference to permanent objects

The user must be able to **navigate** through the features and facilities of a complex and powerful program. He must be able to stay oriented in the program as he moves from screen to screen.

A user can navigate a program if he always understands what he has to do next, knows what state the program is in and knows how to find the tools he needs.

One of the most important aids to navigation is a simple interface without a lot of places to navigate to. By places, I mean modes, forms and major dialogs. If the number of modes is kept to a minimum (like one or two), the user's ability to stay oriented in them increases dramatically. Similarly, if the number of forms or views is never more than one or two, the user can make sense out of them. Programs with thirty, forty or more forms are not navigable under any circumstances.

Beyond reducing the number of navigable places, the only way to enhance the user's ability to find his way around in the program is by providing better points of reference. In the same way that sailors navigate by reference to shorelines or stars, users navigate by reference to **permanent objects** placed in the program's user interface.

These permanent objects, in a GUI world, always include the program's windows. Each program will most likely have a main, top-level window. Also considered permanent objects are the salient features of that window: things like menu-bars, toolbars, and other palettes or visual features like status bars and rulers. Generally, each window of the program has a distinctive look that will soon become instantly recognizable.

Depending on the application, the contents of the client area of the program's main window will also be easily and permanently recognizable. Some programs may offer a few different views of their data, so the overall aspect of their screen will change depending on the view chosen. Generally though, a program's distinctive look will come from its unique combination of menus, palettes and toolbars. This means that menus and toolbars must be considered permanent objects and aids to navigation. You don't need a lot of permanent objects to navigate successfully. They just need to be visible. Needless to say, permanent objects can't aid navigation if they are removed.

On the other hand, people like to change things around to suit themselves. Even beginners, not to mention perpetual intermediates, like to put their own personal stamp on a program, changing it so that it looks or acts uniquely their own. You can see this in any office, where, even though everyone has an identical little gray cubicle, you can tell them apart by the pictures of spouses and kids, plants, favorite paintings or quotes, and Dilbert cartoons.

Actually, those pictures and cartoons are serious aids to navigation because, although they may not be permanent objects themselves, they are decorations placed on permanent objects. Decorating the permanent objects—the walls—

gives them individuality without removing them. It allows you to recognize one hallway as being different from dozens of identical hallways because it is the one with the big poster of Christie Brinkley, Brad Pitt or Opus. I use the term **personalization** to describe the decoration of permanent objects.

Personalization makes the places in which we work more likable and familiar. It makes them more human and pleasant to be in. The same is true of software, and giving the user the ability to decorate his personal program is good, both for fun and for practical purpose.

On the other hand, actually moving a permanent object around can really hamper navigation. If the facilities people come into your office over the weekend and rearrange all of the cubicles, Dilbert cartoons notwithstanding, finding your office again on Monday morning will be tough.

Is this an apparent contradiction? Not really. Adding decoration to permanent objects helps navigation, while moving the permanent objects hinders navigation. I use the term **configuration** to describe adding, moving or deleting permanent objects.

Configuration is desirable for experienced users. Perpetual intermediates, when they have established a working set of functions, will want to configure the interface to make those functions easier to find and use. They will also want to tune the program itself for speed and ease. They won't do excessive configuration, but they will want to make a couple of changes, and the ability to do so can make the difference between liking the program and not liking it.

Configuration is a necessity for expert users. They are already well beyond the need for more traditional navigation aids because they are so familiar with the product. Experts may use the program for several hours every day; in fact, it is probably their main application for accomplishing the bulk of their job, the way Word is my constant companion as I write this book. I have gone ahead and configured the toolbar for my version of Word so that it fits my style of working. There are cryptic-looking tools present that only I know about, and I have removed some standard tools that other users might expect.

What are typical permanent objects

The most prominent permanent object in a program is the main window and its caption and menu bars. Part of the pedagogic benefit of the menu comes from its reliability and consistency. Unexpected changes to a program's menus can deeply reduce the user's trust in them. This is true for menu items as well as for individual menus. It is okay to add items to the bottom of a menu, but the standard suite of items in the main part of it should change only for a clearly demonstrable need.

If the program has a toolbar, it should also be considered a recognizable permanent object. Because toolbars are idioms for perpetual intermediates rather than for beginners, the strictures against changing menu items don't apply quite as strongly to individual buttcons. Removing the toolbar itself is certainly a significant motion of a permanent object, and, although the ability to do so should be there, it shouldn't be offered casually, and the user should be protected against accidentally triggering it. I've seen programs that had buttcons on the toolbar that made the toolbar disappear! This is completely inappropriate.

Status bars, tool palettes and fixed areas of the screen where data is displayed or edited should also be considered permanent objects that cannot be changed without penalty.

Pull at your own risk

Configuring software can be dangerous. It is a double-edged sword, offering power and flexibility, but demanding in turn that its user understand the potential danger of his actions. Command vectors that control configuration are what I call ejector seat levers.

In the cockpit of every jet fighter is a brightly painted lever that, when pulled, fires a small rocket engine underneath the pilot's seat, blowing the pilot, seat and all, out of the aircraft to parachute safely to earth. Ejector seat levers can only be used once, and their consequences are catastrophic. The jet will be destroyed, the pilot may be injured by the sudden and violent acceleration, and, depending on where and how she lands, she may not even survive. On the other hand, a damaged, out-of-control jet airplane headed for certain disaster is not a healthy place for pilots to remain either.

Just like a jet fighter needs an ejector seat lever, complex business programs need configuration facilities. The vagaries of business and the demands placed on the software force it to adapt to specific situations, and it had better be able to do so. Companies that pay millions of dollars for custom software or site licenses for thousands of copies of shrink-wrapped products will not take kindly to a program's inability to adapt to the way things are done in that particular company. The program must adapt, but such adaptation can be considered a one-time procedure, or something done only by the corporate IS staff on very rare occasions. In other words, ejector seat levers may need to be used, but they shouldn't be used very often. After all, the pilot's seat is normally considered a permanent object in the airplane.

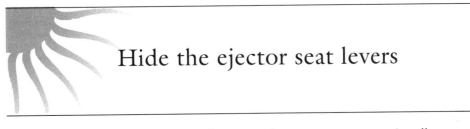

Hide the ejector seat levers

Programs must have ejector seat levers so that users can—occasionally—move permanent objects around. But the one thing that must never happen is accidental deployment of the ejector seat. See Figure 32-1. The interface design must assure that the user can never inadvertently fire the ejector seat when all he wants to do is make some minor adjustment to the program.

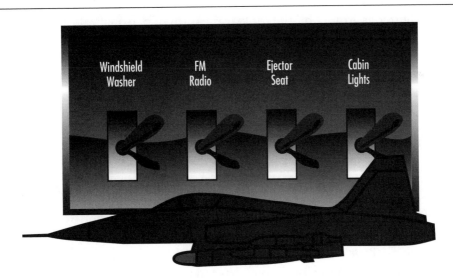

Figure 32-1

Ejector seat levers have catastrophic results. One minute, the pilot is safely ensconced in her jet, and the next she is tumbling end-over-end in the wild blue yonder while her jet goes on without her. The ejector seat is necessary for the pilot's safety, but a lot of design work has gone into assuring that it never gets fired inadvertently. Allowing an unsuspecting user to configure a program by changing permanent objects is comparable to firing the ejection seat by accident. Hide those ejector seat levers!

Ejector seat levers come in two basic varieties: those that cause a large visual dislocation in the program and those that perform some irreversible action. Both of these functions should be hidden from inexperienced users. In PowerPoint, for example, you can switch views between drawing, outline and slide sorter. Going between any of these, particularly from drawing to outline, can be shocking to a user who is unfamiliar with the feature. If the user is in draw mode and accidentally presses the outline button, for example, all of those nice graphic images that he has been working on immediately disappear to be replaced by a list of the slide text. Both views are excellent tools, and frequent switching between them is normal for perpetual intermediate users. We don't want to remove this function—actually we want to make it quite prominent and easy to reach; we do, however, want to assure that it doesn't get used inadvertently. Microsoft has solved this problem by putting buttons that control changes in the view at the bottom of the screen—on the left end of the horizontal scroll-bar—and kept them off of the main toolbar at the top of the screen, where new users are more likely to experiment. A first-timer may find the view buttons at the bottom of the screen, but their segregated presence clearly, and visually, indicates that they are special.

Moving buttons around on the toolbar is a form of personalization. However, the leftmost three buttons on many programs, which correspond to File New, File Open and File Save, are now so common that they can be considered permanent objects. A user who moves these around is configuring his program as much as he is personalizing it. Thus, you can see that there is a gray boundary between configuration and personalization.

Changing the color of objects on the screen is clearly a personalization chore, and one that is appreciated by many users. Windows has always been very accommodating in this respect, allowing users to independently change the color of each component of the windows interface, including the color and pattern of the desktop itself. Windows 95 finally gives users a *practical* ability to change the system font, too. Personalization is one of those idiosyncratically modal things. People either like it or don't. I have shown new users how to configure their screen's colors only to have them plead with me to "put it back" as though I were dangling them out the door of an airplane. I also know users who change every color on the screen as their first task when installing a new system. You must accommodate both of these categories of users.

Personalization isn't just a system-wide activity. You can add the ability to do it to your own program. It is easy to find opportunities for personalization, just ask around your company. People will say things like "I think this should be over here" or "I don't like this shade of yellow." These are good indicators of areas for allowing personalization in your application.

The tools for personalizing must be simple and easy to use, giving the user a visual preview of their selections. Above all, they must be easy to undo. A dialog box that lets users change colors should offer a function that returns everything to the factory settings.

Users really like personalization. It allows them to feel part of the computing process; to buy into the task being performed. If you want users to like your program, offer them little perquisites like personalization, and they will really appreciate it. A user that appreciates your program will tell his friends, and, as marketing people know, there is no more convincing form of advertising than word of mouth.

Conversely, most users won't squawk if they can't configure your program as long as it does its job well. Some really expert users may feel slighted, but they will still use and appreciate your program if it works the way they expect.

Corporate MIS managers really like configuration. It allows them to subtly coerce corporate users into using common methods. The MIS manager (or the equivalent person whose task it is to purchase and configure PC software for the entire corporation) will really appreciate the ability to add special macros and commands to menus and toolbars that make the off-the-shelf software work more intimately with established company products and standards. An MIS manager who appreciates your program will tell his friends, and, as marketing people know, there is no more convincing form of advertising than word of mouth.

Many companies base their buying decisions on the configurability of programs. They figure that they are buying ten or twenty thousand copies of a program and they should be able to adapt it to their particular style of work. It is not a whim of the programming staff that has made the programs in Microsoft Office among the most configurable shrink-wrapped applications available.

The corporate look

Following visual standards is great, but this doesn't mean that your program has to have the exact, pixel-for-pixel look of the big guys. There is a lot to be said for establishing your own identity, your own look.

The same way that an individual user improves navigation by personalizing his program, as a software publisher, you can personalize your entire application. By putting identifying marks on all of the components of the program, you help in creating a branded product, one that the user subconsciously recognizes and imputes value to.

If all of the windows in your program, particularly all of the dialog boxes, have a consistent family appearance, the user can navigate more easily among the welter of windows on the screen. I'm talking only about decoration here, not behavioral divergence. All of the dialog boxes in Microsoft's Office suite, for example, use the 3-D, conservative gray, corporate etched look. Borland uses the 3-D, mottled-steel, big-bright-bit-mapped button look. Many users can identify the publisher of a program from just a glance at a dialog box. Unfortunately, many application developers think this means that their dialogs should look exactly, pixel-for-pixel, like a Microsoft, Lotus or Borland dialog box.

I'm not sure why they believe this. Most companies want to establish a proprietary look in all other corporate artifacts, so why would the boss insist on such slavish similarity on the screen? If every envelope, sheet of paper and business card has the company logo printed prominently on it, why shouldn't it also be present on each dialog box? Admittedly, it seems that logos consume pixels only to serve the publisher, but there are some collateral benefits for the user in better navigation and trust.

Users *like* brands. They buy Kleenex, Nike and Ralph Lauren because it lets them feel they are part of an exclusive club. Brands indicate quality in the product and discrimination and taste in the user. Indicating your company brand on a product can reassure users. The visual recognition afforded by logos can also help users find their way around a crowded screen.

There are several easy ways to create standard, yet visually unique, dialog boxes. You can change the background color of all dialog boxes from the common gray to a gentle but different hue—say, light yellow or light blue. Or, instead of changing the background to a color, change it to an image. You must be subtle here, but try taking your company's logo, rendering it in a single hue screened back 80% on a background of the same color screened back 90%. Place the gizmos directly on that image. The gentle shading won't intrude on the work at hand, but the pattern will be easily recognizable.

If you are more adventurous, you can try using the "ownerdraw" capability of push-buttons and slightly alter their shape. For example, add a tiny tab on the top, snip off one corner or round off all of the corners. You must be very careful not to affect the basic shape and shading of the button so that it doesn't change its affordance as a button, but the uniquely modified shape also whispers your company's name.

There is no reason that your dialogs can't say "you" instead of "them" and still be just as usable and consistent as though you copied the big guys verbatim. It will help the user navigate visually and will contribute positively to the branded look of your product.

Installation

Whether you install software off a CD-ROM, several 3 ½" floppies, a file server or the Internet, the process you go through is basically the same, consisting of two steps. First, the software must be copied or loaded onto your local hard disk. Second, the software generally requires some initial configuration so that both you and it can work smoothly.

The installation process is a necessary evil. There is no constructive need for an installation process—it doesn't help the user to achieve his goals; it doesn't help the program to perform its functions. In fact, most software development teams don't really give the installation process much thought at all. The effect is that most installation programs are written as afterthoughts. They are rarely designed and almost never designed well. Some clever vendors have developed a market selling installation-program-making tools. These have tended to institutionalize the drawbacks of bad installation procedures. The dreary sameness of most installation programs somehow lends an unwarranted credibility to them. But installation should be treated as an opportunity to excel. Instead of the normal, demoralizing test of user patience, installation can be a chance for your program to show off its good manners and consideration for the user.

Most software development managers are fooled by the unproductive nature of installation programs, so that they fail to see this as an opportunity. Installation programs are the first part of the program that the user sees, and they give the user his first impression of your product. If your installation program is a showcase of effective user interface design, the user will be in a fine frame of mind as he begins to use your program in earnest. Conversely, if your installation program is given the same afterthought-design that most of them get, your user will be disinclined to tolerate anything less than instant perfection in the balance of your product.

Some modern installation programs have been given a visual once-over by a graphic artist, so they look pretty spiffy. But little consideration has been given to the interaction, and certainly not from a goal-directed point of view. The nature of installation programs remains one of blindly interrogating the user, forcing him to make uninformed decisions, and of the program making selfish assumptions about the way the computer is used.

What is wrong with installation

Possibly the biggest failure of most installation programs is their blind refusal to see that the user may wish to *un*install the program at some time. Very few installation programs also know how to uninstall themselves, so the option is rarely offered. The installation process often includes writing dozens or hundreds of command lines of code into various configuration files. It forces the Program Manager to create special windows and icons to accommodate it. It may add or modify files in the operating system's private directories, but it has no facilities for even remembering what it did, let alone a facility for reversing its actions. Complicating the problem is the difficulty—in many cases, the impossibility—of fully uninstalling a program.

The typical installation program is usually quite stupid in the way it does its job. For example, an installation program might create a new icon in the Program Manager, and then, when it is rerun after a failure, will create a new, redundant icon. The installation program assumes that it is flawless and that mistakes or misapprehensions will never happen. It assumes that it only needs to be run once, and no thought is ever given to the possibility that it might have to be run subsequently. The program doesn't even bother to look around and see its own spoor.

Klingon battle-cruiser mode

Installation programs usually behave in what I call **Klingon battle-cruiser mode**. Klingon battle-cruiser mode is characterized by the program behaving like a shoot-em-up arcade game. You grab the joystick and the program puts a diabolical Klingon battle-cruiser of a dialog box up on the screen. The dialog demands that you make an arbitrary (and usually irreversible) decision about something of which you are completely ignorant. If you answer correctly, the installation program gives you ten thousand points, and another Klingon battle-cruiser dialog box appears. This time it asks you which interrupt vector is not conflicted with your SCSI adapter and, if you choose right, the dialog box disintegrates into space dust and you can proceed to the next Klingon battle-cruiser dialog box in the sequence. You never know how many Klingon battle-cruiser dialog boxes you are going to get, and you don't get much chance to go back and ponder. You never know when you might answer one incorrectly and the pesky Klingons will format your hard disk, scramble all of your INI files or just unceremoniously dump you at the C> prompt. All you see is a seemingly endless sequence of cryptic dialog boxes asking you for information you don't have and don't want to know.

Edward Tufte, author of *The Visual Display of Quantitative Information* (Graphics Press, 1983), detests the Klingon battle-cruiser mode, calling it "one damn thing after another." The program metaphorically pushes you into the hard-backed chair, aims the bare light bulb right into your eyes, menacingly slaps its palm with a rubber hose, and then proceeds to demand answers to difficult questions. This hyperbole may seem a little thick to those of you who work with computers on a daily basis (particularly you programmers out there), but this is really what it feels like to most users. It isn't pleasant. It isn't nice. It doesn't generate customer loyalty, and customer loyalty is what generates word-of-mouth sales and repeat buys and upgrades. In other words, it costs you money. You can always sell your product once if it does the job, but you won't last in this business if your product and your company don't generate customer loyalty. The industry is littered with companies that owned the market but failed to claim their customer's loyalty. I've already mentioned WordStar, née MicroPro, whose WordStar word processor dominated the market in the early '80s. As soon as WordPerfect and Microsoft Word became available, WordStar hit the skids faster than you can say Lotus Symphony. Digital Research's CP/M operating system had well over 90% of the microcomputer market in 1981. Within four years, the company was on the ropes and CP/M was just a fading memory.

Most, but by no means all, big manufacturers of shrink-wrapped software have at least attacked these problems in the last few years. Notably, the installation of Windows 95 shows a quantum leap forward in installation design.

The most common problems exhibited by installation programs are a micro-cosm of some of the nastiest software interface design problems in general. Most installation programs exhibit at least several of these design errors:

- Demanding responses without informing you of the consequences of your actions

- Not informing you of the scope of your actions

- Asking you questions about things to which you are unlikely to know the answer

- Asking you for answers that the program can determine for itself

- Acting really stupidly

- Not failing gracefully

- Not providing for uninstallation

- Ignoring evidence of their previous activity

- Abusing system-wide INI files

- Putting files where they don't belong

- Overwriting shared files

- Not offering you any information about the program

- Confusing installation with configuration

- Demanding your active participation

I'll now discuss each of these transgressions in detail.

Demanding responses without informing you of the consequences of your actions

Without a doubt, this is the most common of all of the transgressions of installation programs. It is the essence of Klingon battle-cruiser mode. The installation program puts up a dialog box that looks something like the one in Figure 32-2.

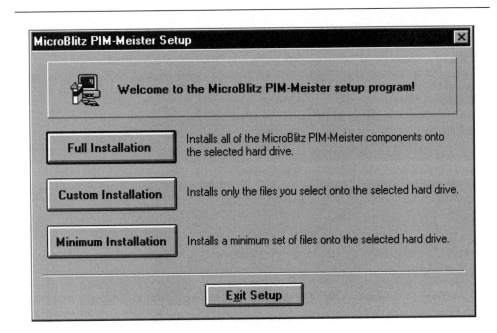

Figure 32-2

This is a typical installation program's first dialog box. Like playing a video game, you have only your wits to guide you. Is a full installation too much for me to handle? Am I smart enough to customize this program? Does it make me a wimp if I choose a minimum installation?

The program starts right off by asking you a question that will clearly have global consequences, is probably not reversible, and of which you have no understanding of the effects. Some more-advanced installation programs, notably those from Microsoft, make a pretty good disclosure of the effects of your choice on how much disk space will be consumed. However, you are still guessing about the meaning of the choice. What the user needs to know is exactly what functionality he will be sacrificing if he chooses a minimal installation. It isn't enough to merely know the disk space implications, he must know the usefulness implications of his choice, too.

Some versions of this question deal with system-level resources such as interrupts, communications ports, video drivers and the like. These are particularly vexing, because making the wrong choice can instantly lock up the computer system, crash other running programs, lose data, and sometimes even require rebooting the computer from a boot diskette and manually fixing the damage done by the installation program. Although the consequences for making a wrong choice are severe, the user is rarely made aware that this is not the time for a guess—not even an educated guess. To counter user interactions with this kind of problem, software should be imbued with a quality I call informed consent. The user should only be asked questions about which he understands the consequences. In particular, he must understand the consequences to *him*, not just to his computer. If the program offers configuration choices, the user must be well-informed about how the various configurations affect the program's ability to help him achieve his goals.

For example, an appropriate way to create an atmosphere of informed consent would be to offer an itemized list of the features, expressed in terms of what they do for the user, that are either included or excluded from the various choices. Additionally, a prose description of the big picture from the user's point of view would be necessary. Something like the following would be nice:

"A minimal configuration is designed for laptop and notebook computers with available disk space of less than 100 megabytes. The MicroBlitz PIM-Meister will consume about 40% less space on your hard disk without sacrificing any critical functions. What you will sacrifice includes: most, but not all, online help text; the tutorial program for beginners; four out of seven Wizards; and most of the more obscure import and export utilities. If you want the minimal configuration but feel that you must have one or more of the excluded facilities, you can easily request the minimal configuration with *special options* and add the desired facilities back in. Also, you can always easily change your existing configuration by running the installation program a second time."

First, this statement describes the main reason why the user might want to choose the "minimum installation" option. Second, it describes in some detail exactly what is sacrificed to get it. Third, it informs the user how and why he can override the setting if he wants to. Fourth, it reassures the user by informing him how he can change things if he later changes his mind. This is informed consent, and the user will be able to make intelligent choices and feel good about them. Can you write the corresponding paragraphs for the other two installation choices?

Not informing you of the scope of your actions

A typical installation program wastes no time on what a programmer considers idle chit-chat with the user, but that chit-chat is important to dispel the user's uneasiness. Imagine if an appliance repair person arrived at your house and, without a word to you, started wrenching apart your plumbing and dismantling your refrigerator. You would feel much better if the repair person gave you the big picture first:

"The compressor on your refrigerator is completely dead because the motor has seized. I will have to replace it completely. I have the replacement motor in my truck and it will take about an hour-and-a-half to make the repair, including recharging the system with coolant in an environmentally, friendly way. Your warranty will cover the cost of the parts but not my labor. I charge $45 per hour. The plumbing will need some minor work because the icemaker is directly connected to your pipes. Any time existing iron-pipe plumbing is disturbed, there is a slight risk of starting leaks elsewhere in the system. I will make every effort to keep the pipes from moving to reduce that chance."

You are now informed of how much time the operation will take; how much money it will cost; and what the risks of failure are. You are aware of the scope of the operation.

Wouldn't it be nice if our install program told us something like this:

"I am going to install MicroBlitz PIM-Meister on your system. This means copying the program from the distribution floppy diskettes onto your hard disk, decompressing the files and then configuring the program for your specific needs. I will need you to place the seven diskettes into the floppy drive one at a time as I read them. I will ask you for each one by the name shown on the diskette label. Judging from the speed of your processor, I estimate the entire process will take about 17 minutes for a full install and as little as 11 minutes for a minimal installation. The program will occupy between 8 and 14 megabytes on your hard disk, depending on which configuration you choose. In other words, it will take between 2.7 and 4.7 percent of your total capacity. Your disk is currently less than half full, so the available space will be reduced by 4.6 to 8 percent.

"I will place all parts of the program and all associated information in a special directory that I will create new. You will be given the choice of where that directory is located and what it will be called, but you can also just keep the default of PIMMEIST. By necessity, I must make at least one entry in your system files (in WIN.INI). This entry will be restricted to a single parameter line that will have absolutely no effect on the system or any other program, even if you later decide to uninstall PIM-Meister. If you select the checkbox, I will also create an icon for launching PIM-Meister in the "Main" group of the Program Manager.

"This installation program maintains an internal status log so that, in the unlikely event it crashes, it will know how to pick up the pieces intelligently if you merely re-run it.

"You can uninstall this entire program at any time simply by pushing the uninstall button. The program will be removed from your system, leaving as few traces as possible, but leaving any data files you created with PIM-Meister untouched. If desired, you may request the space-saver uninstall, where the program is removed but all of your personal settings are saved. A subsequent execution of the install program can put PIM-Meister back exactly the way it was."

This monologue is pretty prolix, and experienced users won't want to read it. But new users will find it very reassuring to hear from the horse's mouth what the implications of the installation process are. They will understand the scope of the process they are about to undergo.

Asking you questions about things to which you are unlikely to know the answer

A typical installation program question for a communications program asks the user to specify the desired serial port. Most users don't know what a serial port is or how many they have, let alone which one is best for this program. Game and sound-card installation programs frequently ask users about available interrupt vectors, a question that can't be adequately answered by most computer engineers, let alone a typical home user. Business software installations can be expected to ask about network support and the type of mouse in use. Most users are completely unaware of the answers to such questions.

Asking the user a question to which he is unlikely to know the answer is very bad practice. First, it doesn't get the program the answer it needs. Instead, it gets a guess. Second, it makes the user feel bad—after all, he just failed a test and proved himself inadequate in front of a machine. How embarrassing! Third, it shows the program to be pretty stupid. It's like seeing somebody wandering on the street asking strangers "how many ergs are there to a joule?" What a dufus! Nobody knows the answer and nobody cares and there are better ways to find out stuff like that.[*]

---

[*] 10^7

If the program needs to know about serial ports, it should test them and see which ones are occupied. It can search in various configuration files for clues as to how they are currently being used. It can even ask the user to move the mouse and look for activity on the various ports to eliminate that possibility.

If the program needs to know about interrupts, it can examine them or listen to them to determine whether they are in use or available. The installation program can make a very good guess (and probably a much more reliable guess than the user's) about what interrupts are available by deduction and by looking at system information files. By recording its findings and then telling the user it is about to do something that might lock up the system, the user can close all other running programs and be prepared for the program's error. If one occurs, he can then rerun the program, and it will find its earlier notes. It now knows what *didn't* work, which should be enough to enable it to deduce the correct choice. Don't force this choice onto a user who cannot be expected to know the answer.

Asking you for answers that the program can determine for itself

This is a common problem in all software, but the authors of installation programs are deservedly notorious for it. The program asks you what type of display device your computer has, when it can easily check inside Windows for the answer to that question. The program asks you how much disk space is available, when it can interrogate the file system to get the exact answer. The program asks you where another program or file is located, when it can easily search the disk to find it. The program asks you which hard disk you want to install on, when you only have one hard disk.

The computer's job is to remove unnecessary trivia from our lives. Questions like these only add more pointless trivia and are offensive. Most information needed by any program can and should be determined without asking the human user.

Acting really stupidly

I wish I didn't have to write this paragraph, but I do. There are many installation programs that begin the process of copying the program from the floppy to the hard disk without first checking for a sufficient amount of free disk space on the destination drive. The program then blows up on a disk-full error. This is tantamount to walking into a post.

There are other ways that installation programs can get really stupid, like installing a Windows application on a system that doesn't have Windows or blindly configuring a program for color on a monochrome system.

One of the most obnoxious ways an installation program can behave is by not being aware of its own existence. The installation program goes ahead blithely installing an identical copy of a program that already exists. The installation program doesn't know that it is being used just to change a configuration, so it goes ahead and copies files from floppy to hard disk that are already there. The installation program doesn't realize that it blew up previously and is being re-run, so it mindlessly retraces its steps until it blows up again in the same way.

The designer of an installation program should write a list of all of the environmental givens that the program needs, including such things as RAM, video, disks, microphones, joysticks, mice, modems or speakers. The installation program should then check that these assumptions are indeed true before proceeding. The program should perform a commonsense examination of the system before it starts working. It should look for previous copies of itself; it should look for other, required software; it should check for fatal or dangerous conditions like lack of memory or disk storage.

Just yesterday, I installed a program (from a major vendor) that offered me the opportunity to put the program in either a default directory or one of my choosing. I chose one different from the default. Unfortunately, after I had installed the system, I found that significant portions of the program wouldn't work because the program would only look in the "default" directory. I had a hard time figuring out which was more stupid: That they couldn't find files on a hard disk or that they offered me an option that would cause fatal problems if I should choose to use it.

It isn't that hard for a program to find files on disk. If there is a name collision, the program can easily open the file and look inside to see if it is in the expected format. For any program to not be able to find its own files is just plain stupid.

Not failing gracefully

Because installation programs are often built as afterthoughts, they don't get the polishing, testing and refining that the main program gets. In particular, installation programs have a penchant for crashing in very catastrophic ways. Where a regular application will report to the user that it is running out of memory before gently and safely divesting itself of unnecessary functions, features and data in order to continue, the average install program is very brittle. When it runs out of memory, it is not aware of the problem and merely dies, usually taking the rest of the system with it.

First, the memory requirements of an installation program are usually very static and predictable, so running out of memory is usually very avoidable. But if the program does run out, it should be sufficiently robust to detect the problem, make a permanent note of its current position so it can resume its task, then inform the user of the problem and give him the opportunity to adjust things and give the program another chance.

Most installation programs can only do an entire install process from scratch. If the installation consists of decompressing and copying the contents of ten floppies onto the hard disk and the program crashes on disk ten, it usually requires that the user pointlessly recopy the first nine floppies. The program should be smart enough to, before it begins copying, check to see if the copy process is really needed.

Not providing a means for uninstallation

Although many software vendors seem unaware of the fact, customers often want to remove software from their computers. A customer would remove software because it is needed on another computer; because it is not needed on this computer any longer; because it takes up space needed by other, more important, programs; and even because the user has decided that the program is not good enough to keep.

Every vendor should provide a tool for removing their program, just as they provide a tool for installing it. The uninstallation tool should be just as robust and full-featured as the installation tool. It should follow the principle of informed consent, telling the user what the scope and consequences of the program are.

The uninstallation program should remove all traces of the program where possible, including any entries made into system files such as WIN.INI and AUTOEXEC.BAT. If entries to these files are—or might be—shared with other programs, they must remain untouched. If the installation procedure created directories, and if no user-created files are in them, those directories and their contents should be deleted. Those directories should be deleted from the PATH variable, too. If the program put anything in any directories outside of its own (a very bad practice), those items should be hunted down and deleted. The uninstallation process should also remove all files and directories created by the application program and not just those created by the installation program. Of course I don't mean any files created by the program for the user, like documents. Those—and their directories—must stay around for whatever plans the user has.

If the installation program loaded any dynamic link libraries (DLL) that are shared resources, it shouldn't delete them, unless it can absolutely confirm that no other programs depend on them. The uninstallation program should alert the user if it leaves DLLs behind but can't confirm whether they are used by other applications. If the user knows, he can then do it manually. In the current state of the system, it is usually impossible to know whether it is safe to delete a DLL, so this must remain just a goal for now.

It is reasonable to assume that the user does not hate your program, but is removing it because he merely wishes to regain some disk space by removing a no-longer-needed tutorial or some subsystems that have proven unnecessary. The uninstallation program should give the user the ability to remove individual pieces of your program without affecting the main function of the application.

The user may wish to move the application to a different hard disk or to a different place on the same hard disk. The uninstallation program should know how to make the transfer so that all references are updated and the program works smoothly despite the transition. Such references include the WIN.INI file references, including the file association for that extension, the GRP file references used by the Program Manager and the Registration Database.

If a user needed to temporarily reclaim the space on disk occupied by the program (say he needed additional free space for a two-week business trip), the uninstallation program should make this easy to do. It should remove all of the big, space-consuming files but leave behind all of the directories, configuration files and entries in other system files. When he returns from his business trip, the installation program can be used to put the big files back on his disk without overwriting or forgetting about his personal settings. The program would be reinstalled just as before.

Some programs such as networks, peripheral drivers and printer-sharing software are not only installed on the hard disk, but are also activated by the AUTOEXEC.BAT or CONFIG.SYS files at boot time, thus becoming a permanent part of the operating system. Software like this makes a special demand on its uninstallation program. It must be able to disable the program without physically removing it. If the user wants to, for example, run a game program that demands absolutely all available memory, the user should be able to disable the network drivers for the duration without physically removing them from disk.

Ignoring evidence of their previous activity

Installation programs should keep a log of their activity on the user's hard disk. This log tells the program what it has done before and what it is doing now. If the program learns anything from a previous execution, either by testing the system or by asking the user, it should be recorded here so reprocessing can be speeded up and the user doesn't have to be bothered again. The new installation facility for Windows 95 has this feature that Microsoft calls "SmartRecovery" and it works well. I hope it sets a standard for the entire industry.

Abusing system-wide INI files

Application software programs should limit themselves to no more than two or three lines of information in system-wide files such as WIN.INI, AUTOEXEC.BAT and CONFIG.SYS. If the program needs more information, it should create its own INI file and store the information there. In almost all cases, there is no need whatsoever to put anything at all in the system files and, if this is the case in your situation, please refrain from doing so.

Putting files where they don't belong

The application should operate in its own directory. If it requires multiple directories, they should be made subordinate to the program's main directory. The program should never put files in any other directories, particularly the WINDOWS directory or any of its subdirectories, the DOS directory, and the root directory. If the user were to install a new version of Windows or DOS, for example, the application's files might very well be deleted in the process. The resultant malfunctioning and confusion would be very unpleasant and completely avoidable.

Application programs often ignore the possibility that the operating system will be reinstalled or upgraded. The program is often inextricably dependent on entries in system files that, when the OS is reinstalled, will disappear. Most programs then require a complete reinstallation, including redundantly re-copying the files, when all it really needed to do was rewrite a line or two in the WIN.INI file. Better yet, the program should work without any entry in that—or any equivalent—file.

Overwriting shared files

Many applications use run-time libraries of some sort. Visual Basic applications in particular use the VBRUN dynamic link library (DLL) and usually a few VBX or OCX DLLs for each of the installable controls used in the program. When a program installs the DLL or VBX, it may overwrite one with the same name already installed by another program. For example, if program A uses a commercially available VBX grid control named "GRID.VBX" and program B, from another vendor, uses a proprietary VBX grid control that is also named "GRID.VBX," the installation process will cause problems. Even though the names are the same, the functionality and interfaces may be quite different. When program B is installed, it must ensure that it doesn't just overwrite the GRID.VBX file by assuming that it is an earlier version of itself. If it makes this assumption, program A will crash violently and mysteriously. The ensuing confusion will leave the user perplexed and angry.

A similar problem arises if two different programs use different versions of the same DLL. Imagine that both programs A and B use Version 1.0 of a DLL called DATBASE.DLL. The user then purchases the newest release of program B which includes the newest release of DATBASE.DLL, Version 2.0. The installation program for B likely assumes that it can blithely replace Version 1.0 of DATBASE.DLL with Version 2.0. But program A won't know how to deal with the new version of the library and a tragic crash is unavoidable. Crashes like this are particularly insidious, because the user could install the new release of program B in January and not get around to running program A until June. He will have no clue as to what caused the problem. If anything, he will blame the completely innocent program A. Because this problem can affect any vendor, even though they are not strictly at fault, it means that you must take defensive action to keep the problem from happening to you.

The problem can be avoided by following two simple guidelines. First, use names that aren't likely to collide with those from other vendors. Instead of naming a library "GRID," try using "XGRID," "GRD" or even "G7QL." The user will likely never see these names, so they don't have to be mnemonic. Second, append a unique number indicating the version of the library. Name the first release "XGRD1," the second release "XGRD2," and so on.

Just yesterday, this problem happened to Alice, our seminar manager. She installed a brand new copy of Adobe PhotoShop on her plain, vanilla IBM Aptiva computer, the computer crashed, and now she cannot get Windows to run at all. The installation program diddled evilly with something in the system—none of us in the office can figure out what—but there is no recovery path.

Not offering you any information about the program

The installation program should keep the user informed at all times of what it is doing and what remains to be done. Many contemporary installation programs put a dialog box on the screen with a small completion meter showing the amount done expressed as a percentage. Most of these meters are frustrating and confusing, however, because they don't explain what it is they are saying. Does the meter show the progress for this file? This section? This floppy? The copy process, but not the configuration process? The entire installation? Is it expressed as time or as bytes copied? Users have become used to being burned by meaningless meters, and they know enough to ignore them. They know that the installation program is just being stupid.

Confusing installation with configuration

Because most programs need some rudimentary configuration before they can run well, the installation procedure usually includes a configuration step. This is reasonable, but the configuration process is one that may need to be performed more than once, whereas the copying of files from the floppy is usually just a one-time thing. Installation designers frequently forget this and intertwine the two processes so that a reconfiguration cannot be done without an unnecessary re-copy operation. The installation program should be smart enough to recognize that it is being rerun and offer the user the option of just reconfiguring the existing instance of the program, without incurring all of the unnecessary overhead of re-copying.

Demanding your active participation

Some installation programs make unreasonable demands on your time and attention. They require that you actively participate in the installation process, even though you would just as soon delegate the job to the software. The WordPerfect for Windows installation program, for example, intersperses questions for the user with the actual copying of the program onto the hard disk. In other words, it asks you a question, then installs a few files, then asks you another question, then installs a few more files. The effect of this is incredibly annoying, because you are forced to consciously baby-sit the entire process. It should just ask you all of the questions at the beginning, then let you get up and walk away while the installation proceeds. If the install is from floppies instead of from CD-ROM or a file server, you still must stick around and feed it disks every few minutes, but at least you can let your mind roam, read or think about something else. Of course, it should also issue an audible alert every time a new floppy disk needs to be inserted, releasing you from having to watch the screen.

Shouldering the Burden

Because every instruction in every program must pass single-file through the CPU, we tend to optimize our code for this needle's eye. Programmers work hard to keep the number of instructions to a minimum, assuring snappy performance for the user. What we often forget, though, is that as soon as the CPU has hurriedly finished all of its work, it just waits, idling, doing nothing, until the user issues another command. We invest enormous efforts in reducing the computer's reaction time, but we invest little or no effort in putting it to work proactively when it is not busy reacting to the user. Our software commands the CPU as though it were in the army, alternately telling it to hurry up and wait. The hurry up part is great, but the waiting has got to stop.

The division of labor in the computer age is very clear: The computer does the work and the user does the thinking. Computer scientists have focused our attention on artificial intelligence, tantalizing us with visions of computers that think for themselves. This pursuit is a rewarding intellectual exercise for computer scientists, but users don't really need much help in the thinking department. They do, however, need a lot of help with the work of information management, activities like finding and organizing information, but the actual decisions made from that information can best be made by the wetware—real people.

The computer does the work and the user does the thinking

There is some confusion about "smart" software. Some naive observers think that smart software is actually capable of behaving intelligently, but what the term really means is that these programs are capable of working hard even when conditions are difficult. Essentially, smart software is a lot less brittle than other software. When we create smart bombs, after all, we create bombs that will hit *our* targets with great precision under trying circumstances, not bombs that make their own decisions about which target to hit.

The opportunity is in work, not in thinking

Regardless of our dreams of thinking computers, there is a much greater and more immediate opportunity simply in getting our computers to work harder. I'd like to see us give our software the virtue of conscientiousness. A conscientious person has a larger idea of what it means to perform a task. Instead of just washing the dishes, for example, a conscientious person also wipes down the counters and empties the trash because those tasks are also related to the overall goal: cleaning up the kitchen. Instead of just drafting a report, a conscientious person puts a handsome cover page on it and makes enough photocopies for the entire department.

Most of our existing software, regardless of the power it can bring to bear on a given task, is not conscientious. It has a very narrow understanding of the scope of most problems. It may willingly perform difficult work, but only when given the precise command at precisely the correct time. If, for example, you ask the inventory query system to tell you how many widgets are in stock, it will dutifully ask the database and report the number as of the time you ask. But what if, twenty minutes later, someone in the Dallas office cleans out the entire stock of widgets. You are now operating under a potentially embarrassing misconception, while your computer sits there, smugly idling away billions of wasted instructions. It is not being conscientious. It doesn't have to be "intelligent," artificially or otherwise, to help you out here. If you want to know about widgets once, isn't that a good clue that you probably will want to know about widgets again? You may not want to hear widget status reports every day for the rest of forever, but maybe you'll want to get them for the rest of the week. It doesn't take a neural network to lend a helping hand.

In our current computing systems, the user has to remember the names he gives to files and where he puts them. If he wants to find that spreadsheet with the quarterly projections on it again, he must either remember its name or go browsing. Meanwhile, the processor is sitting there, wasting billions of cycles, without even bothering to lift a register to help. Software just doesn't seem to want to work very hard or help out. When the user is struggling with a particularly difficult spreadsheet on a tight deadline, for example, the program offers precisely as much help as it offers when he is just noodling with numbers in his spare time. All of the user's human colleagues know that the job is critical, so they help if they can or at least stay out of his way. But not the program. It just plods along, oblivious to the storm brewing over its head.

This model has to stop. There is a lot of work to be done, and the software can no longer in good conscience spend so much time twiddling its digits while the user works. It is time for our computers to begin to shoulder more of the burden of work in our day-to-day activities.

Let's put those idle cycles to work

Software is designed to perform sequentially, one action after another, and as each chunk of code talks to other chunks of code, they wait for the response. This is fine for code, because the wait is a few millionths of a second. If there's a peripheral involved, the wait might be a few thousandths of a second, but it's still quite fast. However, if the program tosses the ball into the user's court, things are dramatically different.

Most normal users in normal situations can't do diddlysquat in less than a few seconds. That is enough time for a typical computer to execute a few dozen *million* instructions. Almost without fail, those interim cycles are dedicated to idling. The processor does nothing except wait. The argument against putting those cycles to work has always gone something like this: "We can't make assumptions; those assumptions might be wrong." Our computers today are so powerful that, although the argument is still true, it is frequently irrelevant. Simply put, it doesn't matter if the program's assumptions are wrong, it has enough spare power to make several assumptions, and merely toss the results of the bad ones out as soon as the user makes his choice.

Now with Windows 95's preemptive, threaded multi-tasking, you can perform extra work in the background without affecting the performance the user sees. The program can launch a search for a file, and if the user begins typing, merely abandon it until the next hiatus. Eventually, the user stops to think and the program will have time to scan the whole disk. The user won't even notice.

Every time the program puts up a dialog box, it goes into an idle waiting state, doing no work while the user struggles with the dialog. This should never happen. It would not be hard for the dialog box to hunt around and find ways to help. What did the user do last time? Maybe the program could offer the previous choice as a suggestion for this time. Maybe the program could count and display the number of occurrences of widgets in the program. Maybe it could report on the history of the widget. Maybe it could find out if other users had accessed the widgets. If it stayed up for several seconds without activity, it could offer more assistance.

Memory

In Chapter 14, I talked at length about giving your program a memory. This is the primary tool for making your program shoulder more of the burden of work. Everything that happens should be remembered. There is plenty of storage on our big hard disk drives, and a memory for your program is a good investment of storage space. We tend to think that programs are wasteful of disk space, because a big horizontal application might consume 30 or 40 MB of space. That is typical usage for a program, but not for user data. If your word processor saved off 1 KB of execution notes every time you ran it, it still wouldn't amount to much. Let's say that you use your word processor ten times every business day. There are approximately 200 work days per year, so you run the program 2,000 times a year. The net consumption is still only 2 MB, and that gives an exhaustive recounting of the entire year! Most screen savers take ten times that much storage!

All file-open facilities should remember where the user gets his files. Most users only access files from a few directories for each given program. The program should remember these source directories and offer them on a combobox on the file-open dialog. The user should never have to step through the tree to a given directory more than once.

And don't just remember the explicit things, also remember what can be deduced from explicit things. If the program remembers the number of bytes changed in the file each time it is opened, it can help the user with some reasonableness checks. Imagine that the changed-byte-count for a file was 126, 94, 43, 74, 81, 70, 110, 92. If the user calls up the file and changes 100 bytes, nothing would be out of the ordinary. But imagine if the number of changed bytes suddenly shoots up to 5,000. The program might suspect that something was amiss. Although there is a significant chance that the user has inadvertently done something about which he will be sorry when compared to the other edits, the actual chance of a problem is low, so it isn't right to bother him with a confirmation dialog. It is, however, very reasonable for the program to make sure to keep a milestone copy of the file before the 5,000 bytes were changed, just in case. The program probably wouldn't need to keep it beyond the next time the user accessed that file, because the user would likely spot any mistake that glaring the next time he accessed the file and would demand an undo.

For that matter, most programs discard their stack of undo actions when the user closes the document or the program. This is short-sighted on the program's part. Instead, the program could write the undo stack to a file. When the user reopens the file, the program could reload its undo stack with the actions the user performed the last time the program was run—even if it were over a week ago. These actions are likely not needed, but in the rare case where they are, it's certainly better to have them than not to, and the processor was just idling anyway.

Stamp out foolish software behavior

I want to tell you about my imaginary secretary, Rodney. If I hand Rodney a manila folder and tell him to file it away, he checks the writing on the folder's tab—let's say it reads "MicroBlitz Contract"—and proceeds to find the correct place in the filing cabinet for it. Under M, he finds, to his surprise, that there is a manila folder already there with the identical "MicroBlitz Contract" legend. Rodney notices the discrepancy and investigates. He finds that the already-filed folder contains a contract for 17 Doppelgängers that were delivered to MicroBlitz four months ago. The new folder, on the other hand, is for 32 Relativity-Podensers slated for production and delivery in the next quarter. Conscientious Rodney changes the name on the old folder to read "MicroBlitz Doppelgänger Contract, 7/97" and then changes the name of the new folder to read "MicroBlitz Relativity-Podenser Contract, 11/97." This type of initiative is why I like the conscientious Rodney.

My former imaginary secretary, Elliot, was a complete idiot. He was not conscientious at all, and if he were placed in this same situation he would have just dumped the new "MicroBlitz Contract" folder into the cabinet next to the old "MicroBlitz Contract" without a second thought. Sure, he got it filed safely away, but things could have been done better. That's why Elliot isn't my imaginary secretary anymore.

If, on the other hand, I rely on software, my word processor, to draft the new Relativity-Podenser contract and then try to save it away in the MicroBlitz directory, the program offers me a Hobson's choice of overwriting and destroying the old Doppelgänger contract or just not saving it at all. The program not only isn't as capable as Rodney, it isn't even as capable as Elliot. It is stupider than a complete idiot. Even Elliot didn't come unglued when he found the old, identically named folder. Even Elliot figured out how to make do on his own initiative (small though it might have been) without having to bother me with silly demands and pointless details. Only the software is dumb enough to make the assumption that because they have the same name, I meant to throw the old one away. The choices the software offers are terrible! There is simply no excuse for behavior this dumb.

The program should have, at the very least, taken the same action that Elliot did, and merely marked the two files with different dates and saved them away. Even if the program refuses to take this "drastic" action unilaterally, it could at least show me the old file, letting me rename *that* one before saving the new one. There are numerous actions that the program can take that aren't as insultingly stupid as what it currently does. They are easy to think of, too. All you have to do is pretend the software is human.

Things your program can do in the background

Each application could leave a small thread of itself running between invocations. This little program could keep an eye on the files it worked on. It could track where they go and who reads and writes to them. This information might be helpful to the user when he next runs the application. When he tries to open a particular file, the program can help him find it, even if it was moved. The program could keep the user informed about what other functions were performed on his file, like whether or not it was printed or faxed to someone. Sure, this information might not be needed, but the computer can easily spare the time, and it's only bits that have to be thrown away, after all.

Microsoft's new Plug-and-Play standard is a move in this direction, because it demands that programs be cognizant of the changing world around them. If the user plugs in a sound card or a tape drive, programs should notice the difference immediately.

If the user resizes a pluralized application, the program can take the time to quickly rearrange gizmos on the toolbar and items on the menu so that they make better use of the new, more-restricted space. Even better, if the program keeps track of the frequency of each gizmo's use, the ones very rarely used can be omitted to make more space for the more needed ones.

Galleries

Many programs offer tools to users. That is fine as far as it goes, but why can't the program offer complete solutions, too? A program that lets you configure your own personalized newspaper from information on the Internet is nice. Some users will really appreciate being able to put sports at the top of page one. Most users, however, will probably want a more traditional view, with world news at the top and sports at the back. Even these more-traditional users will appreciate the configurability, though, so they can add their local news and news concerning topics of particular personal interest. Typically, though, a configurable program offers the user a blank slate and a suite of tools for filling it. Our sports enthusiast won't see this as a drawback, since she planned on making extensive changes anyway, but most other users will. If they want something standard but with a few differences, they shouldn't have to start from scratch to get it. They should be able to pick a pre-made newspaper and then make the few small changes to it needed to get their custom version. The user should be allowed to choose a starting design from a gallery of likely designs.

Design tip: Offer the user a gallery of good solutions.

Some programs already offer galleries of pre-designed work, but many more should do so. Most users are intimidated by blank slates, and they shouldn't have to deal with one if they don't want to. A gallery of good, basic designs is a fine solution.

Natural language output

There are some functions found in software that are really difficult for users to control. For example, querying a database is always tough, because it calls for Boolean algebra. I talked about the problems with Boolean notation in Chapter 3. Just because the program needs Boolean queries, users shouldn't have to use it, too.

An alternative is to use natural language processing, where the user can key in his request in English. The big problem with this method is that it is not possible for today's run-of-the-mill computers to effectively understand natural language queries. It might work in the laboratory under tightly controlled circumstances, but not in the real world, where it is subject to whim, dialect, colloquialism and misunderstanding.

One approach that I have used successfully is what I call natural language output. Using this technique, the program proffers to the user an array of bounded gizmos to choose from. The gizmos line up so that they can be read as an English sentence. Notice, in this case, the user is merely choosing from valid alternatives and only the output is "natural." Figure 33-1 shows how it works.

Remember, English isn't Boolean, so the English clauses aren't joined with AND and OR, but rather with English phrases like "all of the following apply" or "not all of the following apply." The user finds that making the choices is easy because they are very clear and bounded, and when he is done, he can read it like a sentence to check its validity.

Extraction gizmos

In Chapter 27 I introduced the concept of extraction gizmos—text gizmos that are smart enough to recognize their contents. They are very consistent with the idea of having computers shoulder the burden, because they are willing to do more than just pass ASCII characters between the user and the program. They are willing to put some effort into breaking those strings of characters into meaningful pieces.

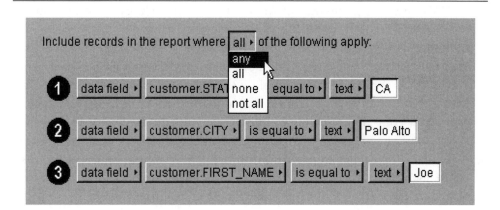

Figure 33-1

Here is a sketch of a dialog box that produces natural language as output, rather than attempting to accept natural language as input. Each button is actually a drop-down with a list of selectable options. Essentially, the user constructs a sentence from a dynamic series of choices that always guarantees a valid result. The user can enter text or numbers into the white fields.

There are dozens of types of extraction gizmos that could be written to handle dates, distances, currencies and similar things. There are probably several that would be uniquely beneficial just for your company's software; they could tackle input like employee numbers, job titles, part numbers or divisions.

See if you can design algorithms for processing input for other types of extraction fields. It seems daunting at first, but it is actually quite easy if you remember the simple fact that you don't have to decipher 100% of the information. It is okay to be 80 or 90% accurate. If the user enters information that is indecipherable, it means, by definition, that you can't decipher it. The user certainly cannot blame the software in this case. On the other hand, if the software doesn't even try, the user can, will and should blame the software.

Visual richness

Sid Meier is the genius designer at MicroProse who created the best-selling games *Railroad Tycoon* and *Civilization*, among others. I love his games; *Civilization*, in particular, is addictive. I strongly recommend that every software designer spend time learning from Meier's work.

Sid Meier's programs are instantly recognizable because of the visual richness he gives them. Visual richness in games is no big thing in these days of

CD-ROMs and lush graphics, but Meier creates this richness with dynamic— rather than static—output that represents changing values. In *Civilization*, for example, he uses little icons that resemble sheaves of wheat to represent the food output of your civilization; the more sheaves, the more food. There is no specific number shown, but you can always count the sheaves if you'd like. The sheaves are displayed in a horizontal line in a fixed-size box about two inches across. When your civilization is young, there may only be five or ten sheaves in a row, and they are easy to count. As time passes and your civilization matures, the sheaves may number 50 or more. There simply isn't room to display that many in the space allotted. Meier's solution is brilliantly simple: he merely overlaps one sheaf on another in the space available. Yes, they are harder to count when they overlap, but when they overlap, who needs to count? He puts a short gap in the line of sheaves between the amount of food that is necessary for survival and the amount of food that goes towards future growth. With a glance, the length and density of the line of sheaves tells you how well your civilization is doing, and the relative position of the gap (or its absence) tells you your rate of expansion.

The sheaves are just one of the measures. Next to them are arrows for trade, shields for productivity, light bulbs for intellectual achievement, and more. Meier crams an enormous amount of quantitative information into a very small space completely symbolically. Any beginner can intuit that more symbols are better, without needing to understand the details to successfully play the game. However, if you find that you like the game (and who wouldn't?), you will play it more and more, and will inevitably find yourself wondering about those little lines of symbols. A quick check of the manual points out the secret of the gap and how they are counted, and you will immediately become a much better player.

Another of Sid Meier's masterpieces is *Railroad Tycoon*. In this game, you create a commercial railroad empire—setting up routes and running trains to earn revenue. The game has pleasant sound effects, with locomotive whistles blowing and bells ringing. After playing the game for many hours, I discovered that the whistles and bells weren't random, but that one sounded every time a train passed through a station. After more hours, I became curious about why there would sometimes be a bell and sometimes be a whistle. A quick check of the documentation (commensurate effort made me very motivated to read the manual) explained that a bell rings if the train makes money at that station and the whistle blows if there is no revenue. Wow! Immediately, I could tell the financial health of my railroad just by listening. If the bell rang constantly with just a few toots, I was doing okay, but if there was a lot of whistle blowing with just a few dings, I could tell that I needed to reassign my trains and alter their cargoes.

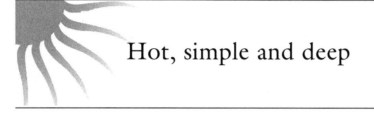

Hot, simple and deep

Game publisher Trip Hawkins used to say that good games are hot, simple and deep. They are hot if they are interactive and fun. They are simple if they are easy to understand and use right away. And they are deep if they offer continual learning and challenge to the persistent user. This is a fine axiom for all software, not just games. The same way that Sid Meier densely crams dynamic information into the interface of his games, you can cram useful information into yours. You're not going to have sheaves of wheat, but you will have lines of little symbols indicating the number of cells your spreadsheet refers to in other sheets, for example. Or the number of records in the database could be indicated with tiny little dots. The number of updates to the current record could be shown with a row of tiny icons. None of these values are critical for the user's success, but as the users become more experienced with the program, they will appreciate the depth of its feedback. Don't disappoint them.

Get our software talking to our hardware

Some process dialogs just tease the poor user with their CANCEL buttons. In a typical print operation, for example, the program begins sending the 20 pages of a report to the printer and simultaneously puts up a print process dialog box with a CANCEL button. If the user quickly realizes that he forgot to make an important change, he presses the CANCEL button just as the first page emerges from the printer. The program immediately cancels the print operation. But unbeknownst to the user, while the printer was beginning to work on page 1, the computer has already sent 15 pages into the printer's buffer. The program cancels the last five pages, but the printer doesn't know anything about the cancellation; it just knows that it was sent 15 pages, so it goes ahead and prints them. Meanwhile, the program smugly tells the user that the function was canceled. The program lies, as the user can plainly see.

The user isn't very sympathetic to the communication problems between the application and the printer. He doesn't care that the communications are one-way. All he knows is that he decided not to print the document before the first page appeared in the printer's output basket, pressed the CANCEL button, and then the stupid program continued printing for 15 pages even though he acted in plenty of time to stop it, and it even acknowledged his CANCEL command. As he throws the 15 wasted sheets of paper in the trash, he growls at the stupid program.

Imagine what his experience would be if the application could communicate with the print driver and the print driver could communicate with the printer. If the software were smart enough, the print job could easily have been abandoned before the second sheet of paper was wasted. The printer certainly has a cancel function—it's just that the software is too indolent to use it, because its programmers were too indolent to make the connection.

Too much software takes the attitude that "it isn't my responsibility." When it passes a job along to some hardware device, it washes its hands of the action, leaving the stupid hardware to finish up. Any user can see that the software isn't being conscientious, that the software isn't shouldering its part of the burden for helping the user become more effective.

Where Do We Go from Here?

Software marketing consultant Seymour Merrin says, "We found it easier to convince people that software was easy to use than it was to actually make it easy to use." There is sad wisdom in this observation. The power inherent in computers is forcing them into every industry and practice whether they are easy to use or not. It is up to us as users to demand better. The economics will force us to use them, but only acting on our conscience will make it pleasant and really effective.

Software sucks

In general, the software we use here in my office frustrates us intensely. We don't have a complex setup here, just a half-dozen relatively new computers running Windows 95 or Windows for Workgroups 3.11 on some vanilla network. Right now, Wayne is meandering the halls muttering to himself because the server is down again. Poor Wayne is really a Macintosh guy at heart, but he's reduced to specifying obscure text commands to the format program in trying to resurrect the server's hard disk. Geetha, down the hall, is trying to learn Canvas, a drawing program. She's a user interface designer, and finds Canvas personally and professionally insulting because its interface is so horrendously bad. She would rather use PhotoShop, except that it doesn't let her draw good screen images for several reasons, mostly because it's designed for photo manipulation and not for screens with buttons and gizmos. I've got a problem on my computer, too, where the neat new power-saving features of the software are in conflict with the neat new power-saving features of the hardware. The net effect is that every few minutes my computer goes completely stupid for a few seconds while the disk wakes up again. The other result is that I can't turn the screen saver off, but when the screen saver runs, it crashes the system completely. If I leave my computer for more than an hour, it will die. Just a few minutes ago, my seven-and-a-half-year-old son Marty telephoned me in tears from home. He is trying to make his new Kid Cad drawing program work, but he can't make all of the "windows go away." The File Manager and the Program Manager are making his life miserable with meaningless excise. I'm not making this up. It's just a typical day with computers.

Not all of these are user interface problems, but all of them are problems that users must grapple with and solve. Frankly, I don't understand how non-computer-professional people can make computers work. This situation is really not acceptable. It's certainly not acceptable in the long run for the computer industry. The vendor who can solve the problem will surely win customers. Until then, bad software is our own fault, because we buy it, even though it makes fools of us.

Saved by the Net. Not.

People who should know better are getting excited about the potential of the Internet, the World Wide Web and Interactive Television to change the user interface landscape. Why should things be any different just because there are some underlying hardware and bandwidth changes? I am very enthusiastic about the potential of the Web, but I don't see much progress on the user interface front reflected there. I see the same old problems of stupid, rude, inappropriate software that hardly lifts a finger for the user. It just happens to be wired and have a high cool-quotient.

Ultimately, we will make good software by examining and satisfying the user's goals. We will not make it by moving to new platforms or by improving the technology. Our technology is superb. What it lacks is some consideration of the human.

We know a lot about old technology

We now have more than a decade of refinements to the PARC paradigm. We know how to create good error messages, confirmation dialog boxes and buttcons. We don't have anywhere near as much experience in creating rich, visual, unified interfaces that work hard to support users. We have years of experience building systems with robust data integrity and sophisticated hierarchical file systems, but we don't yet have experience creating systems with data immunity and associative storage systems.

The problem is quite simple: Everything we know about computers is wrong! Forty years ago, there was less computing power on the entire planet than is in your wristwatch today. There is literally more computing power in your family car than there is in the space shuttle. Just twenty years ago, computers were precious commodities that were extremely expensive, limited and weak. In 1974, when I began working with computers, I cut my teeth on an IBM 370/135 mainframe that was absolutely brand new and state of the art. It had 144 KB of main memory. Yes, KB! It had two 100 MB hard disk drives, each the size of a big refrigerator. It had a card reader and a card punch and a chain printer. It resided in its own room, nestled deep inside its own building. The room had mostly glass walls, a raised floor, powerful air conditioning, three full-time operators and an IBM systems engineer who came around every two weeks to perform preventive maintenance. I learned the hard way that computing resources were always very scarce. In fact, all of the senior programmers and computer scientists in business or academia today learned this attitude, which I call scarcity thinking.

We all knew, deep in the fabric of our thinking, that there was never enough memory, never enough storage, never enough cycles and never enough bandwidth. We all wanted to be good at what we did, so we worked hard to maximize the scarcest resource: We made sure that the CPU got all of the breaks. We developed systems to maximize the use of disks, of RAM, even of punched cards. If you are too young today to be of this group, doubtlessly you were taught by this group, and the senior developers at your shop are probably members of this group, and most of the software you use was designed by this group. The men and women who know, deep down in their guts, that computer resources are scarce are running the show and setting the pace in the software industry today.

My mother and father grew up during the Great Depression. To them, a steady, well-paying job was a luxury, and they had learned this lesson the hard way. They could never understand my entrepreneurial tendencies and my disdain for traditional employment. It was as though I disdained oxygen. When you have lived with real scarcity, you can never unlearn the lessons; they bury you with their scars.

Today, by comparison, our computing power is an embarrassment of riches. My little, aging desktop computer has 16 megabytes of main memory, 1.7 giga-bytes of hard disk and a processor that can execute 66 million instructions per second. It has an order of magnitude more memory on its *video card* than that old 370 had in its main memory. Within a couple of years the state-of-the-mar-ket computer will have a processor ten times faster with ten times more mem-ory and storage than even today's fastest and biggest. It will be connected to every other computer in the world by digital phone lines that pass data at tens of thousands of bits per second. We have, within a short score of years, left behind a world of scarcity and entered a world of abundance, with even greater realms of abundance just beyond the horizon. Our computers are as powerful as we want them to be. We have all of the bits and bytes and cycles we need to design software that really serves humans.

The opposite of scarcity thinking is abundance thinking, and good software designers will have this sense in their minds instead. Abundance thinking frees designers from worrying about memory, storage or cycles. They must worry instead about users, and they have the design sense and training to provide those users with interfaces and features that make them more effective.

The trouble is that we have constructed the entire industry in the image of that old, obsolete scarcity thinking. At the top of the heap are programmers who can work close to the metal; who can create software that maximizes the per-formance of the scarce hardware. At the bottom of the pyramid are unskilled users who haven't become "computer-literate." We sweep these people under the rug because they aren't as important as smoothing the way for the precious, struggling CPU.

The very fabric of our thinking is strongly and powerfully colored by this scarcity thinking. All of the software technologies we prize so much are really tools for relaxing the demands on memory, on storage, on processor cycles. This includes databases, networks and even the way we write files. For example, most human beings who handle paper forms file away a filled-out form, yet almost every computer program that files away filled-out forms first eliminates the form. It just files away the answers. This storage technique—used by virtually every program ever written—makes it easier for the disk drive. The fact that it simultaneously reduces the software's capacity to adjust, to adapt, to conform to the idiosyncratic behavior of humans, is considered merely a necessary cost of doing business. In a world of computer scarcity, this is a reasonable compromise with users. We ask users to tolerate the compromise because they are strong and computers are weak. But we don't live in this world of scarcity any longer. We live in a world of abundant computing resources, and computers are strong and users are weak.

Don't ask programmers to design while they code

Programmers are squeezed into a conflict of interest between serving the CPU and serving the user. They cannot successfully be asked to design for users because good coding demands that the CPU be serviced with a single-minded commitment. Inevitably, they will make judgments based on the difficulty of coding and not on the user's real needs. This is not to say that any given programmer can't make the right choice, just that programmer's can't make the right choice while they are actively employed producing the code that results from their choice. These tasks must be separated for the user design part to have a chance. Some of the greatest design ideas have come from programmers, but this is a happy accident. If we want good design industry-wide, we will not get it by accident.

A great basketball player can either play or be a referee, but he cannot be both simultaneously. My doctor has a doctor; he doesn't self-diagnose. The NFL wisely doesn't let players bet on games. Venture capitalists can't invest their personal money in companies. Politicians must put their investments in blind trusts. Judges cannot adjudicate cases for their friends and neighbors. We recognize the ethical quandaries created by a conflict of interest in most of our other activities. We just seem to ignore them in software development.

Even when the designer creates a solution, the programmer might go away and edit it independently. Anyone who has worked for a while with programmers has had this experience: the team meets and everyone agrees on the course of action. Everyone acknowledges their tasks and what the program will look like. Two weeks later, when the group reconvenes, a programmer says—without any trace of irony—"yeah, I decided to do it this way instead. I thought it was better," while the rest of the team gnashes their collective teeth. Even if it *is* better, it is still wrong to change things unilaterally when a team is depending on you. If a marketing-communications junior executive, for example, came back after two weeks with the same outrageous claim about a brochure, he would likely be fired. Generally, technical managers are protective of their programmers and refuse to call them on their willful behavior.

Solving the problem

One area where the software industry, including Microsoft, is making headway is with usability. Usability is a science, consisting mostly of empirical testing and observation of users interacting with software or prototypes of software. Those observations illustrate problem areas, which can then be addressed. Usability testing has been adopted by many companies in the last few years.

The chief drawback of usability is that it sidesteps actual design. The process of testing is very different from the process of design. Design springs directly from the knowledge of goals. Usability derives from specific objects. Usability testers refine what programmers create, rather than fabricating solutions from first principles. There is merit to this refinement—if Microsoft's recent efforts are any evidence—but limited post facto influence cannot change software down to its roots. And good user interface begins way down deep, not on the surface.

The other drawback of usability testing is that it leaves the programmers in charge. If you want to create a beautifully cut diamond, you cannot begin with a lump of coal. No amount of chipping, chiseling and sanding will turn that coal into a diamond. At best, the gentle sanding and polishing that results from usability testing will only give you an attractively carved lump of coal. Programmers have had unchallenged say over the software for too long, and usability testing leaves untouched the assumption that programmers should devise the point of departure.

One of the central tenets of usability engineering is that design should be "user-centered." This certainly sounds good, but it has serious problems. The biggest problem is that it is widely interpreted to mean that your users can tell you how to design software. Saying "user-centered software design" is like saying "fish-centered aquarium design." You wouldn't ask the fish, would you? Although most usability professionals understand the distinction and don't let themselves get jerked back and forth by the results of focus groups and user tests, many others believe that what users say is gospel. What users say is generally goofy. They can only give faint indications of places where problems may exist. They do not have the training necessary to actually solve the problems.

Nathaniel Borenstein, in his book *Programming as if People Mattered* (Princeton University Press, 1991), says, "Listen to your users, but ignore what they say." This is a very accurate instruction for software designers. Users are filled with raw information. What they lack is wisdom, a sense of design, an understanding of the medium, a willingness to break out of the box of existing solutions, a language to express their desires and any experience in delivering software solutions. Borenstein goes on to say about those who ignore his advice, "The world is full, accordingly, of bad user interfaces that were essentially designed (or redesigned) by nontechnical people with no real idea of what they were doing, and implemented uncritically by programmers who were, like Adolf Eichmann scheduling deportations to the Nazi death camps, 'just following orders.'" I really admire his gutsy willingness to state this in such extreme terms. The key to good user interface design is not users, but user interface designers.

Anyone who has argued with a programmer knows how difficult it is. They are very intelligent and are only swayed by logic and reason. Unfortunately, you can't defend the user's needs very well with mere logic and reason. They aren't bad tools, just inappropriate ones for the problem at hand. Programmers will always design logically and rationally, and they will rarely produce good design. After all, those logical tools got us into this predicament.

More than a few of the usability professionals I have met resist the idea of software design because it is done without much user testing. I suspect that these people are too used to fighting with recalcitrant programmers. Programmers fight desperately against the insistence that their creations can't be valid until they are tested by users, and usability professionals seem to have retreated to the empirical as their only way to convince the logical, rational, engineering mind that there is another, better approach to designing the user interface.

They drag programmers into dark rooms, where they watch through one-way mirrors as hapless users struggle with their software. At first, the programmers suspect that the test subject has brain damage. They cannot believe that any user could be so stupid as to not understand their program. Finally, after much painful observation, the programmers are forced to bow to empirical evidence. They admit that their interface design needs work, and they vow to fix it.

But empiricism is not a method of design, it is a method of *verification* of design. It is one thing to use blind testing as an indicator of problems. It is quite another to use it as a source of solutions. Forcing programmers to watch users struggle is good therapy for the programmer, but it doesn't do a heckuva lot for the user, or for the software. The programmers go right back to their computers and apply a bit more logic and reason to the user interface. We will only get significant quantities of well-designed software when its design is in the hands of software designers and not programmers; not even programmers assisted by user testing.

I have seen usability professionals run rigorous user tests, tests that were conducted with superb methodology. Upon reviewing the results, they said things like "Well, I'd prefer to see those gizmos lined up better," or "I guess we could move this button over here." User interface design is not guesswork. When good user interface designers create a dialog box, they know why. When they populate it with gizmos, they understand the purpose that each of them serves. And just as important, they know when to *not* create a dialog box.

User interface design is not guesswork

Most programmers design in one of two ways: they make guesses based on their programming expertise, or they copy from existing programs. Either way, they usually end up rendering the implementation model and trapping the user in a prison of technology. Usability testing responds to this guesswork with empirical observation. This testing ends up being guesswork, too, because the insights tend to come from users and not from designers. User testing is to user interface design what market research is to sales. You can dispense with one but not the other, and market research can never substitute for sales. Likewise, user testing can never substitute for user interface design.

User testing can never substitute for user interface design

User testing can tell an observer when a program is too complex, too misleading or too confusing. Armed with this information, it is possible for a programmer to reduce its complexity and confusion, but it takes a designer to synthesize a proper solution from scratch. That solution will conform to the user's natural mental model, giving him what he needs in terms he understands. Designers have an understanding of how users think and also know how software is built. They bridge the two worlds with their natural design sense. In the same way that a programmer is born with a sense for how to imagine complex procedural systems, or an artist is born with a sense for creative expression, a designer is born with the vision to see what technology can offer in human terms.

This is a power struggle. Programmers have dominated all aspects of software development for decades, and for the first time they find themselves up against a problem—designing for users—that their trusty logical tools are failing to vanquish. Designers are stepping into the fray and succeeding in their place. This is certain to be seen as a threat to programmers, but it need not be. Programming takes great skill, talent and creativity. It is not diminished by design; it is exalted by it. Programming won't diminish in importance, any more than surgery is diminished by epidemiology. If the technical management in our industry understands this, they can make a place in the development process for design, and much of the rancor in the struggle can be avoided. In sequence, design comes first, then user testing, then programming, then more design and more user testing, then more programming. Design leads the parade. Programming brings up the rear. Programmers sense that they have a lot to lose, they don't like it, and they will fight it. I don't blame them, but they must relinquish a seat at the table in order to continue eating well.

User interface designers will not come from the ranks of programmers but will be very technically savvy people. Non-technical people cannot imagine the wonderful new things that computers can do for us. Non-technical people will not understand the delicate balance between a CPU with time on its hands and one rushing to complete ten million instructions before the user's next keystroke. The non-technical people will have our computers treating us in the same lousy way they already do but with prettier pictures. It is not obvious what computers can do for us. It takes natural talent, skill, training and experience.

Well, now that I've said that, you are probably asking "trained where?" and I must admit I don't have a ready answer. Academia has a hard time with processes that cannot be tested scientifically, so design doesn't compete well in ivy-covered halls against usability testing. This is why I believe that the majority of tomorrow's software design leaders will come from industry rather than from college.

Most universities that I am familiar with are teaching empirical user-centered usability testing more than they are creativity-based design. But things are bound to change, and more and more designers are appearing every day. Many of them come from the ranks of technical support people, quality assurance testers, technical writers and other professions that are often viewed as subordinate to programming. User interface design is not an art, like painting and sculpture, but its beating heart is creativity. Ironically, so is programming's.

"I'm mad as hell, and I'm not gonna take it anymore"

In the early '70s, Detroit said that they gave the American consumer just what they wanted: big, heavy, powerful, gas-guzzling, chrome-encrusted, fin-studded symbols of post-war largesse. Then Japanese and German cars built with very different sensibilities became available. The American public bought them by the millions, and Detroit was devastated by the foreign invasion. To their credit, American auto manufacturers cleaned up their act. But one thing you never hear from Detroit anymore is that old saw about "what the consumer wants." We've learned not to trust a statement like that.

The conundrum is that the American automobile consumer of the early '70s was perfectly happy with those gas-guzzling behemoths from Detroit. They didn't realize that they could do better until they had their noses rubbed in it by the availability of something better, cheaper and more environmentally kind.

The American software consumer today is just like the typical auto consumer of the '70s. The quality and usability of all of the software available is about the same: Big, monolithic, implementation model, only available from one or two sources who make design decisions based on what is good for the CPU instead of what is good for the consumer.

I want to show today's software consumer that things can be different. I want him to see the potential for software that is designed to help him reach his goals instead of programmed for the convenience of his computer. I don't want the domestic software industry to undergo the same painful upheaval that Detroit did in the '70s. I don't want to see the wind banging through the Microsoft campus like it does in abandoned Rust Belt steel mills. Before that happens, I want consumers to get angry and demand better. I would like to see the user community rise up in protest at the sorry state of software. I'd like to hear them protesting in the streets and picketing Oracle, Novell, Lotus, Apple and Microsoft, chanting—as viewers did in Paddy Chayevsky's classic screenplay *Network*—"I'm mad as hell, and I'm not gonna take it anymore."

Reference Section
Axioms

A dialog box is another room. Have a good reason to go there.

A gallon of oil won't make a bicycle pedal itself

A multitude of gizmo-laden dialog boxes doth not a good user interface make

A rich visual interaction is the key to successful direct manipulation

A visual interface is based on visual patterns

Accepting bounded data into unbounded gizmos is an important source of user dissatisfaction

All idioms must be learned. Good idioms only need to be learned once.

Allow input wherever you output

Any command is a working set candidate

Ask forgiveness, not permission

Audit, don't edit

Consistency is not necessarily a virtue

Directly offer enough information for the user to avoid mistakes

Disks and files make users crazy

Disks are a hack, not a design feature

Do, don't ask

Don't hamper primary markets by serving secondary markets

Don't make the user look stupid

Don't put might on will

Don't stop the proceedings with idiocy

Good user interfaces are invisible

Hide the ejector seat levers

Hot, simple and deep

If it's worth asking the user, it's worth the program remembering

Imagine users as very intelligent but very busy

It's not your fault, but it's your responsibility

Make errors impossible

Make everything reversible

Never bend your interface to fit a metaphor

Never make the user ask to ask

No crisis inside a computer is worth humiliating a human

No matter how cool your interface is, less of it would be better

Nobody wants to remain a beginner

Obey standards unless you've got a darn good reason

One user's excise task is another user's revenue task

Optimize for intermediates

Provide an escape from dragging, and inform the user

Purchase the right software then buy the computer that runs it

Put primary interaction on the primary window

Questions aren't choices

Show don't tell

Sovereign users are experienced users

The computer does the work and the user does the thinking

The customer is always right

The goal of all software users is to be more effective

Things that behave different should look different

Transliterated mechanical models are always worse on computers

User interface design is not guesswork

User interface is not just skin deep

User interfaces that conform to implementation models are bad

User testing can never substitute for user interface design

Users don't make mistakes

Users get humiliated when software tells them they failed

Users make commensurate effort

Users would rather be successful than knowledgeable

Visually hint at pliancy

Visually show what, textually show which

Design Tips

All dialog boxes should have caption bars

Any program that demands precise alignment must offer a vernier

Any scrollable drag-and-drop target must autoscroll

Build function controls into the window where they are used

Build the program to run on only one platform

Button-down means propose action, button-up means commit to action over gizmos

Button-down means select over data

Cancel drags on chord-click

Debounce all drags

Dialogs break flow

Dialogs should be as small as possible, but no smaller

Disable menu items when they are moot

Don't put close boxes on modal dialogs

Don't stack tabs

Don't use bang menu items

Don't use dialogs to report normalcy

Double-click means single-click plus action

Eliminating excise makes the user more effective

Error message boxes stop the proceedings with idiocy

Every text item in a list should have an identifying graphic icon next to it

Give modeless dialog boxes consistent terminating commands

Have a reason for each idiom

Indicating pliancy is the most important role of cursor hinting

Make selection visually bold and unambiguous

Menus and dialogs are the pedagogic vector

Never change terminating button captions

Never create a system modal dialog box

Never scroll text horizontally

Never use sustaining dialogs as error messages or confirmations

Never use terminating words in dialogs

Offer bounded gizmos for bounded input

Offer OK and CANCEL buttons on all modal dialog boxes

Offer shortcuts from the help menu

Offer the user a gallery of good solutions

Parallel visual symbols on parallel command vectors

Prepare for the probable case

Put terminating buttons on untabbed area

Show validated entry gizmos with a different border

Single-click selects data or changes the gizmo state

The drag cursor must visually indicate the master object

The drop candidate must visually indicate its dropability

The program must inform the user when it gets stupid

The program should be designed expressly for the target platform.

The program should perform optimally on hardware that doesn't exist yet

Toolbars provide experienced users with fast access to frequently used functions

Use COLOR_HIGHLIGHT and COLOR_HIGHLIGHTTEXT to show selection

Use cursor hinting to show meta-key meanings

Use object names in property dialog caption bars

Use verbs in function dialog caption bars

Users don't understand boolean

Visually differentiate modeless dialogs from modal dialogs

Index

/ (slash), 274-276

286 processor, 22, 169
386 processor, 22, 115
486 processor, 22

A

ABANDON button, 318
ABC Flowcharter, 231
"Abort, Retry, Fail?" error
   message, 426
About boxes, 357-362,
   364-365
abundance thinking, 546
accelerator keys, 87, 155,
   295-296, 297, 349
ACD (automatic call
   distribution). *See* call
   distribution programs
actions, performing,
   definition of, 257
additive selection, 222-223
address book software,
   39-40, 63, 430-431, 453
Adobe
   Illustrator, 7, 179-182,
      214, 257, 258
   PhotoShop, 31-32,
      227-228, 231, 528,
      544
affordances
   definition of, 64-65
   hinting and, 208-209
   manual, 65
   the mouse and, 196
   overview of, 53-65

tabbed dialog boxes and,
   332
After Dark screen savers, 161
aircraft, 18, 22
   cockpits of, 131, 155,
      510-513
   metaphor selection and,
      54
alarms, 456
alerts, 441-444
Alexander, Christopher, 501
algebra, Boolean, 34-35, 225,
   538
algorithms, 22, 34, 467
   cursor hinting and, 212
   dispatching, 212
   graphic input and,
      141-142
   listboxes and, 388
   saving changes and, 87
   the technology paradigm
      and, 55
alignment, offering precise,
   266
ALT key, 202, 214-215, 245,
   258-259, 267, 412, 497.
   See also ALT key
   combinations
   ALT+7, 296
   ALT+F, 489
   ALT+HYPHEN, 297
   ALT+SPACE, 297
   ALT+TAB, 164-166, 215
Alto, 67, 68, 204
Ami Pro, 498
AND operation, 34-35, 538
animation, 158, 419

anthropology, 4
anthropomorphism, 30
aphorisms, basic use of, 8
API (application program
   interface), 234, 305, 313,
   335, 370, 409
Apple Computer. *See also*
   Macintosh
   lawsuits and, 71
   PARC and, 67-69
   published guidelines, 230
   standards and, 500
APPLE key, 214
application modal, 303
Apply button, 306, 329
Aptiva, 528
archetypes, 38, 99, 230
architects. *See also*
   architecture
   design of houses by, vs. by
      structural engineers, 22
   regulation of, 23
   "software," 24
architecture. *See also*
   architects
   Metabolist, 55
   of modern desktop
      computers, 114-116
   of nineteenth-century
      farms, 357
archiving, 90-91
arithmetic, 452
arrowing, 244-245
arrow keys, 159, 267
artificial intelligence, 531
ASCII format, 94, 108-109,
   252, 256, 538

military software and, 18
reducing, implementation
models and, 29
use of the term intuitive
and, 57
easter eggs, 364-366
edge coherence, 186-187
edit-in-place mode, 390-391
Edit menu, 283-285, 304
accelerators and, 296
basic description of, 288
education. *See* learning
efficiency, 5, 451
Egyptian hieroglyphics, 139
Eichmann, Adolf, 549
Einstein, Albert, 48
"elephants," 200, 204-205,
234, 237
e-mail, 36, 77-79, 462-463
embedded systems, 6
empiricism, 550
engineering, software
mathematical thinking
and, 34-35
reasons for disks and, 97
software design and,
separation of, 3-4,
547-548
the technology paradigm
and, 55
English language, 47, 218,
219, 538
ENTER key, 224, 266
entrepreneurs, 546
envelopes, 39, 43, 514
epidemiology, 551
eraser mode, 257
ergonomics, 3, 25. *See also*
human body
error message boxes, 14,
177. *See also* errors
auditing vs. editing and,
458
as bulletin dialog boxes,
314
eliminating, 423-440
file systems and, 90, 92
flow-inducing interfaces
and, 129-130
GOTO instructions and,
435-436, 440

ineffectiveness of,
437-438
making them impossible,
431-433
people's reaction to,
427-429
vs. positive feedback,
433-435
protecting programs and,
449
as a result of the program
getting confused,
429-431
stopping the proceedings
and, 179-180,
235-233
validation gizmos and,
401, 402
what they should look
like, 438-439
why we have so many,
426-427
errors, 321, 326. *See also*
bugs; error message boxes;
undo action
extraction gizmos and,
414
installation and, 518, 524
modem, 116
ESC key, 233-234, 273
Ethernet, 67
etiquette, dialog box,
319-339
euphoria, 128
evolutional solution, to the
modeless dialog box
problem, 305-306
Excel, 7, 226, 251-252, 500
complexity of, from a
design standpoint, 22
cursor changes in, 246
cursor hinting and, 210,
211
deleting cells in, 137-138
MDI and, 168, 170
menus and, 284
mouse actions and, 214
Multiplan as the
forerunner of, 68
posture and, 151, 160
title strings and, 356

working sets in, 488
exceptions
announcing the obvious
and, 443-444
definition of, 441-442
managing, 441-464
excise, 172-178
definition of, 172
minimizing, in dialog box
design, 322-325
programs with good
memory and, 188
pure, 174-175
traps, list of, 177-178
visual metaphor, 175-177
experienced users. *See also*
intermediate users
commensurate effort and,
495
configuration and, 509
dialog boxes and, 301
excise tasks and, 173-174
frustration among,
because of programs
that treat
them like beginners,
483-484
intermediate users and,
484-486
needs of, 492-493
posture and, 152-153
providing sufficient depth
for, 20
toolbars and, 342, 347
experimentation, 66, 348,
467, 503
experts. *See* experienced users
exploration, 467
Explorer, 33, 84, 89-90,
140, 141, 144, 150, 157,
208
direct manipulation and,
246, 254
listboxes and, 388,
390-391
process dialog boxes and,
317-318, 320
program icons and, 357
treeview gizmos and, 390,
392

Dear Reader,

You have heard from me, now I would like to hear from you. Please write or e-mail me and tell me what you thought about this book, and about software design in general. Let me know your contact information by returning this form, and I will keep you informed about our products, services and activities.

My consulting company, Cooper Software Inc, designs state-of-the-art user interfaces for companies large and small. We help our clients to improve their existing products or to create new ones. Cooper Software also offers seminars and training in user interface and conceptual software design.

I look forward to hearing from you.

Sincerely,

Alan Cooper, *President*

- ❏ Put me on your mailing list.
    - ❏ I want to know more about your seminars and training.
    - ❏ Tell me about your consulting services.
    - ❏ Keep me posted about future publications.

Name	Title

Company

Address

City	State	Zip

Phone	Fax

e-mail

How can Cooper Software help you?

Cooper Software Inc
POB 4026
Menlo Park CA 94025

design@cooper.com
1-800-928-3374
Fax 1-415-322-8001

Visit Our Webpage At:
http://www.cooper.com

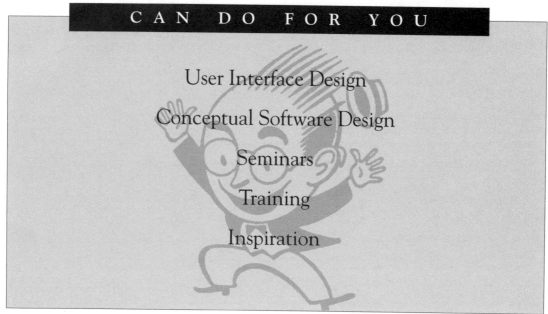

IDG BOOKS WORLDWIDE REGISTRATION CARD

RETURN THIS REGISTRATION CARD FOR FREE CATALOG

Title of this book: About Face: The Essentials of User Interface Design

My overall rating of this book: ❏ Very good [1]   ❏ Good [2]   ❏ Satisfactory [3]   ❏ Fair [4]   ❏ Poor [5]

How I first heard about this book:

❏ Found in bookstore; name: [6] _____   ❏ Book review: [7] _____

❏ Advertisement: [8] _____   ❏ Catalog: [9] _____

❏ Word of mouth; heard about book from friend, co-worker, etc.: [10] _____   ❏ Other: [11] _____

What I liked most about this book:

_____

_____

What I would change, add, delete, etc., in future editions of this book:

_____

_____

Other comments: _____

Number of computer books I purchase in a year: ❏ 1 [12]   ❏ 2-5 [13]   ❏ 6-10 [14]   ❏ More than 10 [15]

I would characterize my computer skills as: ❏ Beginner [16]   ❏ Intermediate [17]   ❏ Advanced [18]   ❏ Professional [19]

I use ❏ DOS [20]   ❏ Windows [21]   ❏ OS/2 [22]   ❏ Unix [23]   ❏ Macintosh [24]   ❏ Other: [25] _____

(please specify)

I would be interested in new books on the following subjects:

(please check all that apply, and use the spaces provided to identify specific software)

❏ Word processing: [26] _____   ❏ Spreadsheets: [27] _____

❏ Data bases: [28] _____   ❏ Desktop publishing: [29] _____

❏ File Utilities: [30] _____   ❏ Money management: [31] _____

❏ Networking: [32] _____   ❏ Programming languages: [33] _____

❏ Other: [34] _____

I use a PC at (please check all that apply): ❏ home [35]   ❏ work [36]   ❏ school [37]   ❏ other: [38] _____

The disks I prefer to use are ❏ 5.25 [39]   ❏ 3.5 [40]   ❏ other: [41] _____

I have a CD ROM: ❏ yes [42]   ❏ no [43]

I plan to buy or upgrade computer hardware this year: ❏ yes [44]   ❏ no [45]

I plan to buy or upgrade computer software this year: ❏ yes [46]   ❏ no [47]

Name: _____   Business title: [48] _____   Type of Business: [49] _____

Address (❏ home [50]   ❏ work [51] /Company name: _____)

Street/Suite# _____

City [52] /State [53] /Zipcode [54]: _____   Country [55] _____

❏ **I liked this book!** You may quote me by name in future IDG Books Worldwide promotional materials.

My daytime phone number is _____

IDG BOOKS

THE WORLD OF COMPUTER KNOWLEDGE

❏ YES!

Please keep me informed about IDG's World of Computer Knowledge.
Send me the latest IDG Books catalog.

BUSINESS REPLY MAIL
FIRST CLASS MAIL   PERMIT NO. 2605   FOSTER CITY, CALIFORNIA

IDG Books Worldwide
919 E Hillsdale Blvd, STE 400
Foster City, CA 94404-9691

NO POSTAGE
NECESSARY
IF MAILED
IN THE
UNITED STATES